20,00

D0802499

E

·49.5

A

A HISTORY OF
AFFIRMATIVE ACTION
—— 1619–2000 ——

GAYLORD FG

A HISTORY OF
AFFIRMATIVE ACTION
—— 1619–2000 ——

Philip F. Rubio

University Press of Mississippi
Jackson

www.upress.state.ms.us

Copyright © 2001 by University Press of Mississippi
All rights reserved
Manufactured in the United States of America

09   08   07   06   05   04   03   02   01   4   3   2   1
⊗

Library of Congress Cataloging-in-Publication Data
Rubio, Philip F.
   A history of affirmative action, 1619–2000 / Philip F. Rubio.
      p.   cm.
   Includes bibliographical references and index.
   ISBN 1-57806-354-X (cloth : alk. paper)—ISBN 1-57806-355-8 (pbk. : alk. paper)
   1. Affirmative action programs—United States—History.   I. Title.
HF5549.5.A34 R83   2001
331.13′3′0973—dc21   00-068559

British Library Cataloging-in-Publication Data available

They will have to pay us wages
The wages of their sins
They will have to bow their foreheads
To their colored kith and kin
They will have to give us house room
Or the roof will tumble in
As we go marching on.

—Sojourner Truth

For my parents and my family
and in memory of
Antonio Jesús Rubio, Ph.D.
Anna Peña Hass Morgan
Mark (Markos Kraniotakis) Kranos
Elizabeth (Elzbieta) Migda Kranos

CONTENTS

Contents

ACKNOWLEDGMENTS

I owe a great deal of gratitude to David Roediger, who encouraged me to write this book and offered valuable source ideas and suggestions for revising the book's original manuscript. Much appreciation goes out also to Mari J. Matsuda and Harvard Sitkoff for their very helpful comments on later drafts. I am indebted to my editors Craig Gill and Anne Stascavage and production coordinator Shane Gong at the University Press of Mississippi as well as copyeditor Robert Burchfield and indexer Beth Henson for their patience and hard work in producing this book.

I would especially like to thank my graduate professors at North Carolina Central University (NCCU): Freddie L. Parker (also my thesis adviser), Beverly Washington Jones, and Lydia Lindsey for their invaluable advice and guidance not only in enabling me to produce this work in its infancy in their classes but also in helping me acquire and employ the necessary research and critical thinking tools needed for serious historical study. For valuable suggestions and support in my research and writing I also thank other NCCU History Department faculty members: Sylvia Jacobs, Percy E. Murray, Oscar Williams, and Carlton Wilson. Kaye Rogers, department secretary, was always very helpful, as was my wife, Paula Rubio, in first setting this project up on the computer. Thanks also to William P. Jones; Spencie Love; Bruce E. Baker; Paula Rubio; my parents, Mary K. Rubio and Carlos M. Rubio (who first suggested that it be published); my grown children, Jessica Rubio and Carrol Pender; and my friends David Freeman and Olynda Spitzer for reading and offering comments on all or portions of the manuscript.

Special thanks is also owed to Noel Ignatiev for first posing the idea of abolishing "whiteness," along with his continuous flow of book suggestions, critical questions, and cogent observations over the years; John Garvey, who first suggested that I study the New Deal era for answers on the modern reconstruction of whiteness; Alice Eley Jones for her encouragement, materials, and fountain of knowledge and observations on African American history and culture; Marian L. Smith, senior historian at the U.S. Immigration and Naturalization Service, for providing me with information on the 1940 change in naturalization forms as well as general U.S. immigration policy and law; Herbert Hill, Herbert Aptheker, and Theodore W. Allen, for encouragement, advice, and materials; and the staff at Perkins Library and the Law Library at Duke University, Wilson Library at the University of North Carolina at Chapel Hill, Shepard Library at NCCU, the North Carolina Division of Archives and History in Raleigh, and the Durham County Library (Main and Stanford L. Warren branches) for their assistance and patience.

I would like to thank all my classmates at NCCU who both encouraged and challenged the arguments that I eventually developed in this pages, especially Dexter Blackman, Victor Blue, Shannon King, and Emily Dickens. The undergraduate Adult Degree Program (ADP) at Vermont College at Norwich University in Montpelier, especially my faculty advisers Richard Hathaway and Daniel Noel and staff adviser Sarah Jo Hooker, helped me to rekindle my passion for searching the past for truths we can use to understand our present and to present them in a disciplined as well as interdisciplinary form. The final revision of this book also benefited from the mentorship and instruction from my professors in the Duke University history doctoral program where I am currently enrolled: Raymond Gavins, Peter H. Wood, Edward J. Balleisen, Lawrence C. Goodwyn, Charles M. Payne, and David Barry Gaspar.

Finally, I thank my coworkers from all the blue-collar jobs that I've held for the last thirty years: without these people, insights, and experiences, I could not have understood much less written about American labor history the way I have.

INTRODUCTION

Just as the words "Freedmen's Bureau" once invoked anger and derision among many whites during Reconstruction according to the brilliant African American scholar, writer, and human rights leader W. E. B. Du Bois in his 1903 work *The Souls of Black Folk*, merely advocating for "affirmative action" today often provokes a similar response—despite the potential and actual benefits for all people contained in both programs. Why does just the mere mention of those modest compensatory civil rights enforcement programs known as affirmative action drive so many white people crazy? And why does the principal and most effective opposition come from white working people and not CEOs? Have white workers simply been manipulated, as some have suggested, or is their opposition autonomous and has this issue struck a nerve?

Is all the fuss really just over the issue of "fairness," as we often hear? Have we already achieved "equal opportunity," and does affirmative action actually compromise that ideal? Or does "opportunity" in the United States really mean getting some kind of personal connection, or "hook-up"—especially one based on the accident of white skin? And why are so many African Americans as well as other people of color so ambivalent on this issue? Doesn't affirmative action by definition represent a civil rights gain, or is there something about it that also evokes memories of white condescension?

These and other intriguing questions provoked me to start researching and writing this book in 1996, the year that a substantial majority of California voters (including a large number of blacks, Chicanos, and Asians) voted for the successful anti-affirmative action referendum known as Proposition 209. But there was also something else about this issue that I just didn't understand. Where were all the historians on a question that synthesizes so much of the American experience? I found it amazing that the overwhelming majority of scholarly works on this contentious issue were instead to be found in sociology, law, political science, and public policy. Only a handful of historians—for example, Herbert Hill, Manning Marable, Paul Moreno, Robert Weiss, and Alice Kessler-Harris—have published books or essays on this subject.

But in all the furious discussion of this issue, few scholars, policy makers, activists, or pundits have been willing to ask the toughest question, which is this: Given that the "white race" is a privileged entity that is historically and socially constructed ("race" being biological fiction but social fact), how would the majority of "white people" in America react to being told that from now on they would be judged solely on the basis of the "content of their character" and no longer judged on the basis of or given advantages based on the "color of their skin"? (Put another way: "white" would then only indicate a skin color but carry no currency value.) I would love for their collective response to be: "Free at last!" But the fact that most white people would probably react to both the suggestion and the question with either anger or incredulity is the reason why I wrote this book. I wanted to look at affirmative action another way: as a product of years of black-led protest against what might be called "white affirmative action" (or better put: "white-affirmative action").

What I set out to write, then, was a tracing of the historical roots of this question, combining social, cultural, labor, political, and intellectual history. The result became an examination of the development of an old legal term known as "affirmative action" (based on the old English common law principle of equity) that has today become part of American folklore and popular culture, as was the Black Power slogan of the late 1960s. I hope this explains why I took on such a daunting task, when it would have been easier to write a monograph devoted exclusively to jobs, education, or housing or a particular period or locale. But the fact is that this issue exists in a multifaceted social dynamic that I wanted to survey as broadly as I saw it and as Americans really experience it.

Affirmative action in reality represents a compromise fusion of disparate social and legal elements brought into being by the black protest tradition against white privilege. Those elements include Anglo-American common law tradition, liberal integrationism, black middle-class uplift ideology, and black nationalist reparations demands. At best, affirmative action provides some degree of challenge to white supremacy despite, at worst, its incorporation into a ruling-class agenda of social control. Affirmative action could never have become the demonized archetype that it is in so much public discourse today if the issue amounted to nothing more than differing interpretations of constitutional law. Affirmative action is not just public policy or political and legal history: it also represents a social and cultural struggle over whether there should exist a property value in whiteness and if equality should be really equal.

This book is not intended as some kind of history sampler or a general history of "race relations." The historical events and figures have not been chosen randomly to prove a point or simply to illustrate historical black oppression and thereby elicit sympathy for affirmative action. On the contrary, by dissecting the historical struggle against white privilege, it becomes easier to discover the source of the animosity over this issue. As Dr. Martin Luther King Jr. observed: "When the underprivileged demand freedom, the privileged at first react with bitterness and resistance."

For their part, political figures in this book are considered not so much in the way they shaped, opposed, or ignored human rights in the United States but rather in the way that they have responded to the power of both white supremacist and proequality movements. It is the history of those movements and the individuals who make them up that actually concerned me the most.

Chapter 1 discusses color-coded chattel slavery, indentured servitude, and resistance by slave rebels and abolitionists and considers Jacksonian democracy and the spoils system as an early form of white-affirmative action. Chapter 2 examines the debates over the Reconstruction amendments, the Port Royal Experiment, General William T. Sherman's Field Order Number 15, and the Freedmen's Bureau, and how they became affirmative action precedents in the face of the white supremacist resistance that ultimately overthrew Reconstruction before it could be completed. Chapter 3 discovers affirmative action struggle antecedents in the labor and social struggles of the period following Reconstruction. These include the black middle-class uplift ideology that emerged in the Progressive Era, the black community's fight for democracy, organized white labor's exclusion of black labor, white race riots and lynchings, the Homestead and Morrill Acts, and the early twentieth-century federal laws drastically limiting the entry of all immigrants except western and northern Europeans.

Chapter 4 looks at how the 1941 March on Washington Movement (among others) challenged the New Deal's offer of labor peace and union recognition to angry white workers at the expense of black workers—a challenge that created the Fair Employment Practices Committee as the forerunner to today's Equal Employment Opportunity Commission. Chapter 5 takes up the 1950s, in which pro-black political and labor activism survived during an era of antiblack, anti-Left, and antilabor political reaction—which happened at the same time that white privilege was being subsidized by government action at all levels. Chapter 6 surveys the autonomous civil rights and Black Power mass movements, the white mass movements that galvanized in opposition (both to desegregation and later to compensatory programs like affirmative action), and the political and legal struggles of this period that were critical to the formation of affirmative action. Chapter 7 considers recent United States Supreme Court decisions, popular movements, and issues related to affirmative action (like prison labor). It concludes that affirmative action constructed on the basis of "diversity" rather than reparations paradoxically ensures mainstream acceptance as a diluted compromise as well as its failure as an effective agent of social change.

The debate over affirmative action has deep roots in the historical battle in the United States over what could be called the white "hook-up." This book has attempted to reveal the connections between the affirmative action theme and working- class history in the United States of America. Its aim is to promote scholarly as well as activist debate on this revealingly contentious issue.

Philip F. Rubio
Durham, NC
December 2000

A History of
Affirmative Action
—— 1619–2000 ——

Chapter 1

"NO RIGHTS WHICH THE WHITE MAN IS BOUND TO RESPECT"

Bonded Labor, White Preferences and Quotas, and American Citizenship Debates, 1619–1861

I

"What is freedom?" cried abolitionist leader Frederick Douglass during a speech in Boston early in 1865, with the Civil War and the institution of slavery both coming to an end: "It is the right to choose one's own employment. Certainly it means that if it means anything; and when any individual or combination of individuals undertakes to decide for any man when he shall work, where he shall work, he or they practically reduce him to slavery."[1]

The roots of the 1990s' struggle over affirmative action in the United States go back to slavery and the invention (as historian Theodore Allen has called it) of the white race as an autonomous, privileged social caste and social control mechanism. Neither slavery nor the white race constituted fixed or "natural" categories or activity, but rather both were institutions devised over the course of the first century of settlement by Anglo-American colonial authorities in Virginia, Maryland, and the Carolinas in order to cut labor costs and blunt the threat of labor solidarity to their rule.[2] Central to the institution of slavery," points out labor historian Herbert Hill, "was the requirement that these less-

1

than-human chattels, or 'articles of commerce' (by legal definition), perform one of the most creative of human tasks: work."[3] It was work for no compensation, educational advancement, or wealth to bequeath to progeny—which the poorest white working person could do with their labor.

Critical to the affirmative action debate today is the legacy of the historic differential between black and white work, the differential in black and white compensation for that work, and the black challenge to what legal scholar Cheryl Harris calls "whiteness as property."[4] White opposition to those modest corrective compensatory programs known as affirmative action comes out of a long history of preservation of that property of whiteness that is also a kind of currency or collateral, but especially a dominant status. Similar to later Jim Crow segregation laws of the nineteenth and twentieth centuries, early American colonial and republican color-coded statutes were considered necessary by the early ruling class to discourage backsliding and potential challenges from both blacks and whites to this discriminatory system when mere "custom" was deemed insufficient.[5]

The concept of affirmative action originally "comes from the centuries-old English legal concept of equity, or the administration of justice according to what was fair in a particular situation, as opposed to rigidly following legal rules, which may have a harsh result."[6] (In the new American Republic, this was especially operative in the predominantly white veterans' benefits.)[7] Affirmative action, defined in a statement by the United States Civil Rights Commission in 1977, is "a term that in a broad sense encompasses any measure, beyond a simple termination of discriminatory practice, adopted to correct for past or present discrimination or to prevent discrimination recurring in the future."[8] Social scientists Nijole Benokraitis and Joe Feagin put it this way:

> Affirmative action means more than passive nondiscrimination. It means that various organizations must act positively, affirmatively and aggressively to remove all barriers, however informal or subtle, that prevent access by minorities and women to their rightful places in the employment and educational institutions of the United States.[9]

While the affirmative action debate often centers on nonemployment issues like electoral and public school redistricting, college admissions, and contracting awards, the struggle over affirmative action flows from the struggle over work and its compensation under capitalism. As Rep. Eleanor Holmes Norton (D-District of Columbia) points out: "Employment, more than other areas, has given definition to affirmative action. The term was first applied to employment and for years applied only to job discrimination. . . . [A]ffirmative action and jobs go together in the public mind."[10]

More than any other controversy in the late 1990s (with the possible exception of the one surrounding the criminal justice system), affirmative action sums up the story of the United States: the struggle for justice, equality, and self-determination and whether African Americans will or even should be able to enjoy chosen labor and increased life chances. It represents the history of white supremacy, privilege, and guilt versus black protest, militance, and demands for compensation and reparations; black reality against white denial; formal equality versus remedial "preferential" treatment; and the debate over integration, assimilation, segregation, and separation. The black-led struggle against discrimination has been the primary impetus for people of color, women, and other oppressed groups also to demand political and social equality.

But affirmative action is no longer just a set of voluntary and mandatory timetables, guidelines, quotas, and legal rulings that direct government, business, trade unions, and schools to hire, admit, and award contracts to more people of color, women, older people, and those with disabilities. It has become an amorphous category that also includes electoral redistricting that improves chances for African Americans and Latinos to hold elective office, as well as debates over quotas, statistics, and ideas of what constitutes merit. In fact, "affirmative action" has now become part of American folklore—and its main focus has been on what is called "race."

II

The United States of America was built on a racial inequality of wealth, work, and social benefits. The *Fundamental Constitutions of Carolina* drafted by English philosopher John Locke in 1690 (although never implemented) promised black subordination to white settlers: "Every Freeman of Carolina, shall have absolute power and authority over Negro Slaves, of what opinion or Religion soever."[11] The seizure of Native American lands "supported white privilege through a system of property rights in land," as Harris notes, citing among other things what Herman Melville referred to in the nineteenth century as "The Metaphysics of Indian-Hating."[12]

A consensus is emerging among historians which argues that, despite being kidnapped, bought, sold, and shipped as slaves from Africa, the actual status of the first Africans brought in chains to colonial America in 1619 was not yet fixed as being significantly different from that of European indentured servants. As historian John Hope Franklin states: "The twenty Africans who were put ashore at Jamestown in 1619 by the captain of a Dutch frigate were not slaves in a legal sense."[13] The 1661 Virginia statutory recognition of slavery exempted Africans who had already served their indenture—the average for all servants being four to seven years. Yet a differential was already being established: whites had never been enslaved, and only Africans and Indians could be; and servants freed of indenture were on their own, while slaves represented free labor for life.[14]

During this time, by first reckoning freedom or bondage by the condition of the father and then later changing it to that of the mother, Virginia and Maryland can both be seen taking further steps "in the act of inventing race," as historian Barbara Jeanne Fields has put it in her groundbreaking article.[15] In other words, slavery predated race prejudice because first *race* had to be invented as a social division with its own rules. "Race is not an idea but an ideology," explains Fields, one that forms

a coherent ideology [that] did not spring into being simultaneously with slavery, but took even more time than slavery did to become systematic. A commonplace that few stop to examine holds that people are more readily oppressed when they are already perceived as inferior by nature. The reverse is more to the point. People are more readily perceived as inferior when they are already seen as oppressed.[16]

The cementing of the American white racial caste system, arising from labor conflicts in late seventeenth-century Virginia, can be seen in the 1682 Virginia slave and indentured servant codes that became the first to make legal racial distinctions between *all* black and Indian "slaves" on the one hand and "Christian" (implicitly white) "servants" on the other.[17]

By analyzing court cases involving the disputes in the colonial-era population, historian Helen T. Catterall suggested the emergence of the following status hierarchy, starting from the top: "white indentured servants, white servants without indenture, Christian Negro servants, Indian servants, mulatto servants, Indian slaves, and Negro slaves."[18] (North Carolina followed form in 1715 and 1741. Its early statutes established a clear delineation between white *servants* and black *slaves*: a white servant enjoyed some rights of due process including redress for abuse by masters, and the promise of eventual freedom with some compensation—called "freedom dues.")[19]

"White-affirmative action" (but one based on privilege and not equity) could be said to have begun with the case of John Punch in 1640 in the Virginia colony. That was fifty-one years before "white" as a social status first appeared as a legal description of European Americans in that colony and thirty-one years before the earliest recording of its popular usage.[20] This incident represents the first recorded case of lifetime bondage in this country and emerged in the form of differential racial punishment. Three runaway indentured servants were involved: two of European and one of African descent. The Europeans received time added on to their servitude but eventually became free, while the African, John Punch, was sentenced to lifetime bondage.[21]

How was white bond-servant resistance and solidarity with blacks and American Indians affected by this kind of preferential treatment? "Significantly," writes historian Winthrop Jordan, "the only rebellions of white servants in the continental colonies came before the entrenchment of slavery."[22] He is referring here to Bacon's Rebellion in the Virginia colony in 1676, the last recorded united revolt of black and white bond servants against their masters. But in discussing this rebellion, Theodore Allen has noted the subsequent deliberate enactment by colonial authorities of laws to privilege white people of humble means in any of the plantation colonies and to make them the primary instrument for enforcing lifetime chattel slavery for Africans, and for a period of time, Native Americans, both of whose rights were rapidly eroding.[23]

First, says Allen, the Virginia General Assembly in 1691 forbade any owner of black bond-laborers to set them free, and in fact the Virginia Colony Council objected when a 1712 will of a slaveholder declared his African slaves free.[24] By 1723, blacks had lost the right to vote and were forbidden to strike or threaten whites or to mate with them.[25] By contrast, the 1705 Virginia Act concerning Servants and Slaves (similar to one passed in Maryland the same year) specified freedom dues for "christian white servants" and forbade their beating by masters without an order from the justice of the peace.[26] Beginning in late seventeenth and early eighteenth-century Virginia, Maryland, and South Carolina and extending throughout the South, many freed white indentured servants became obliged along with their former masters and most other white males to serve in special slave control militia units known as "the patrol" that could violate slaves' human rights with impunity.[27] As Frederick Douglass later observed: "There are seventy-two crimes in the state of Virginia which, if committed by a black man . . . subject him to the punishment of death; while only two of the same crimes will subject a white man to the like punishment."[28]

These status differences were part of the invention and cementing of the white race, concludes Allen in two groundbreaking works entitled *The Invention of the White Race.* The first volume chronicles the roots of that racial formation in England with the English treatment of the native Irish as an indentured "inferior race," in the six northern counties of Ulster, while the second volume details the colonial formation of white settlers as a "superior race" of social control in Anglo-America.[29] In England loyal Scots settlers were established as a social-control landlord class under the Penal Laws of the Protestant Ascendancy. These were codified in many ways like the colonial American slave codes of white supremacy. In the latter, most Europeans who emigrated to the colonies went as indentured servants for an average of five years in exchange for the privilege of not being slaves after that system was developed in the late 1600s.[30]

Of course, we are speaking in relative terms when we speak of "privilege" for European American bond servants. These were, after all, men, women, and children who were often kidnapped from England by men known as "spirits"—from the expression "to spirit them away."[31] They were compelled to work for the profit of the master, *not* just to pay the relatively cheap transportation cost as the popular myth still holds today.[32] And they were forced to work under abysmal conditions of long hours, backbreaking labor, and meager food and clothing rations. These were conditions that led John Lawson, a settler and traveler in colonial North Carolina, to make this declaration in 1700:

> In my opinion, it's better for Christians of a mean Fortune to marry with the Civiliz'd *Indians*, than to suffer the Hardships of four or five years Servitude, in which they meet with Sickness and Seasonings amidst a Crowd of other Afflictions, which the Tyranny of a bad Master lays upon such poor Souls, all which those acquainted with our Tobacco Plantations are not Strangers to.[33]

In fact, many European American servants fought back against this harsh regime, took their masters to court, ran away to the native peoples, or even committed suicide rather than live and work under such conditions.[34] But the prospect of a lifetime of freedom once the required period of bondage was served was clearly something to look forward to by the European servants, which made them feel more of a bond with their masters than with other laborers, the African and American Indian slaves. Of the latter, historian Edmund S. Morgan has observed: "Both were slaves and only they were slaves. It would have been natural not only for their owners but also for their fellow servants to lump them together in a lowest common denominator of racist hatred and contempt."[35]

Both the colonial assembly as well as Nathaniel Bacon, the leader of the unsuccessful 1676 rebellion that carries his name, understood the uses of that contempt. Bacon, a young wealthy planter who united black and white bonded labor against their masters and colonial authorities, himself had explicit designs on Indian land.[36] This would not be the last time that white labor would exchange the degradation of all labor for a minimum amount of exclusive aggrandizement.

III

What brought early white settler-laborers together as whites besides simply the prestige of a higher skin caste? If, according to Theodore Allen, the middle-class "yeoman farmer" made up 40 percent of eighteenth-century Virginia white males, (with most of this group owning the labor of bond servants), then the remaining 60 percent of white males

> were to be asked to be satisfied simply with the presumption of liberty . . . and with the right of adult males who owned sufficient property to vote for candidates for office. . . . The prospects for stability of a system of capitalist agriculture based on lifetime hereditary bond-servitude depended on the ability of the ruling elite to induce the non-"yeoman" European-Americans to settle for this counterfeit of social mobility.[37]

However, contrary to what Allen maintains, there seems to have been a structure in place providing for more than just the mere appearance of social mobility. It is true that there may have been "little opportunity" for poor white settler mobility into the "yeoman" class initially, as Allen says. But Allen neglects to mention two strong inducements to white racial solidarity in early America: the prospect of land ownership and tax reduction.

As Morgan relates: "In addition, at the insistence of the English government, servants on becoming free were entitled to fifty acres of land, even though they had not paid for their own transportation. . . . For free men already free the assembly made what was probably its most welcome gesture by drastically reducing the poll tax."[38] Morgan acknowledges that poor homeless whites continued to circulate, but also

the number of losers [among the ranks of the free] declined; and in the eighteenth century as the rich grew richer, so did the poor. The most concrete evidence comes from the tithable records. . . . If we compare surviving seventeenth-century records . . . with surviving eighteenth-century records . . . it would appear that one-man households were decreasing, while large households with more than five tithables were increasing.[39]

Morgan then concludes: "The status of poor whites rose not merely in relation to blacks but also in relation to their white superiors."[40] And while it would appear that some "yeomen" and their families were indeed heading for the frontier as Allen indicates, white freed servants were also going that way, in addition to putting down stakes where they already were and trying to eke out a living.

But Allen counters that freed whites were coerced into this new social formation called whiteness: "Though the squeezing out of such a poor planter to the 'frontier' negated the assumption of a common interest with the gentry, he was still 'made to fold to his bosom the adder that stings him' the bondage of African-Americans."[41] Allen suggests here that the forced migration was accompanied by both resentment and forced white racial solidarity. In doing so he minimizes the opportunity created by this system for increased white social mobility and frontier mobility, which meant even greater white racial solidarity.

There was certainly a material basis that made up the "public and psychological wage" of being white despite their low wages, as W. E. B. Du Bois said of the white workers' situation in post-Civil War America. (Du Bois included in that list of "social wages" better schools and parks, public functions, voting, leniency in the courts, and police jobs, in addition to public deference.)[42] The promise in colonial America for white bond servants of "mere freedom" after an average of five years of indentured servitude was recognized by both white authorities and the bond servants themselves to be insufficient as severance pay, and the "freedom dues" of whiteness therefore were deemed as something requiring negotiation.

Not only was "freeholding" considered a desirable and feasible goal for any white person, but, for example, in South Carolina the possibility of a white former bondservant becoming a self-employed urban artisan was good, with the additional prospect of possibly rising to the level of planter.[43] There is evidence that such a freed servant in that colony " 'out of his time'—might simply hang out his own shingle."[44]

8

Aspirations to achieve slaveholding status by both poor as well as better-off white farmers and artisans in the antebellum South existed side by side with resentment toward the slavocrats, but overall the social discipline of a "caste consciousness" or "caste loyalty" was successfully achieved. It was a problematic loyalty to be sure, one that required constant maintenance and peer pressure.[45] But social control always functions best when it is self-inflicted. Allen has demonstrated how colonial laboring-class Southern whites were the effective social force in policing the slaves and, in doing so, to the detriment of their class interests, policing themselves.

Historian Warren B. Smith points out that white bond servants were originally valued highly "as a defense against possible slave insurrections"[46] and notes the colonial legislative resolutions to import even more white servants to maintain a "safe equilibrium of population."[47] Both he and Allen chronicle the subsequent "quotas" (usually a ratio of one to ten, white to black) established by the South Carolina Assembly in 1712, 1716, 1717, 1722, 1725, 1726, and 1740 for the express purpose of preventing black insurrection.[48]

In colonial Georgia, the same law in 1750 that repealed the ban on slavery also included a "deficiency" provision that required one "white man Servant" on each plantation for every four blacks employed.[49] In 1758, Georgia passed a law limiting what occupations slaves or free blacks could be employed in, so as "to encourage White Tradesman to Settle in the Several Towns within this Province of Georgia by preventing the employing of negroes and other Slaves being handicraft Tradesman in the said Towns."[50] By the nineteenth century, white skilled artisans in Virginia and South Carolina—many either former bond servants or their progeny—were seeking to ban blacks from the skilled trades.[51] White autonomous movement to protect privilege had already become an American tradition. The earliest uses of "preferences and quotas," as affirmative action is often characterized today, emerged with slavery itself and were embellished with the legislated protection of white labor.

IV

Within servitude was born a dichotomy still difficult for many to accept as both historical and still relevant: white privilege is implicated in black subordination. No matter how poor you were, being white meant *not* being a slave. In the North slavery was both practiced and legally sanctioned with various slave codes similar to those in the South. Early antislavery movements included violent uprisings like the 1741 New York City revolt that included black slaves and free whites. Those movements figured largely in the subsequent late-eighteenth-century Northern abolition of slavery, with New Jersey being the last Northern state to do so in 1804. However, most Northern states also passed "Black Laws" that restricted the movement and rights of free African Americans.[52]

White supremacy (or simply "whiteness" which from its origins has always implied a hierarchy) had been further upheld in the Northwest territorial ordinances of 1784–87. Land awards were made to white Revolutionary War soldiers in the years preceding the Northwest Ordinance of 1787 that divided future slave and free territory in the Ohio River region.[53] In fact, in 1780 Virginia James Madison even proposed (though ultimately rejected) to award black slaves to white recruits as an incentive for them to join the Continental army.[54]

Also rejected was Thomas Jefferson's proposal to eliminate all property or taxpaying qualifications for voting in the Northwest Ordinance of 1784 in order to broaden white citizenship privileges. In the debate to draft the first Virginia constitution, Jefferson had even argued for lowering the property qualifications for voting, granting fifty acres to landless white males to make them eligible for suffrage, and waiving property qualifications for all military service veterans, thus anticipating twentieth century federally legislated veterans' preferences.[55]

The irony of the 1776 American Declaration of Independence decrying English King George III's treatment of the Anglo-Americans as "slaves" and blaming him for the transatlantic slave trade, as well as the explicit antislavery clause that Jefferson deleted after protest by slaveholding delegates, has already been noted by John Hope Franklin and many other historians.[56] Jefferson, like the French Enlightenment philosopher Jean-Jacques Rousseau, regarded property as a civil, not a natural or "unalienable" right. For Jefferson, the key words "Life, Liberty, and the Pursuit of Happiness" were synonymous with John Locke's "Life, Liberty, and Property," with property coming to include slaves as individual and collective property of whites—whether whites embraced or merely tolerated the institution.[57] Moreover, the vital corollary was that white skin itself implied freedom.

Useful here is that often-quoted apotheosis of nineteenth-century white bigotry, United States Supreme Court Chief Justice Roger Taney, a historian of early whiteness. The title of this chapter, in fact, is taken from Taney's infamous

1857 *Dred Scott* decision where Taney, in siding with John Sandford, the Missouri owner of fugitive slave Dred Scott, declared that "they [African Americans] had no rights which the white man was bound to respect." But this was much more than mere racial prejudice. That declaration was intended as both a judgment and an attempt, as Taney himself said, to sum up "the public history of every European nation" who ever treated blacks as an inferior caste and to resolve the question of black citizenship once and for all.[58]

Chief Justice Taney argued that it was obvious from looking at both colonial and republican laws that no African Americans had ever been intended citizenship in any of the United States (an erroneous assertion on Taney's part, as pointed out by Justice Benjamin Curtis in his dissent).[59] Citizenship, Taney declared, was both implicitly and explicitly "white," from New Hampshire's militia laws to the United States Naturalization Law of 1790, which granted citizenship to "any alien, being a free white person. . . ."[60] His opinion was unequivocal:

The words "people of the United States" and "citizens" are synonymous terms, and mean the same thing. . . . They are what we familiarly call the 'sovereign people,' and every citizen is one of this people, and a constituent member of this sovereignty. The question before us is, whether the class of persons described in the plea [African Americans] . . . compose a portion of this people. . . . We think they are not, and that they are not included, and were not intended to be included, under the word "citizens" in the Constitution. . . .[61]

What emerges from a close reading of this declaration (besides its inaccuracy) is not simple exclusion of blacks from the citizenship norm, but also an aggressive activist posture that holds that citizenship would be somehow devalued if it lost its white exclusivity, as would whiteness itself. As morally appalling and false as Taney's words sound to us today—as they did to many who objected at the time—we should also consider their popularity and acquiescence among many white people at the time, both in the North and the South.[62]

Overturning the decision in fact would ultimately require Civil War and Reconstruction. We also need to consider the lingering white collective memory that still sees white citizenship as the norm and potentially undermined by affirmative action, suggesting that Taney's ghost still walks among us today.

The drawing up of the Constitution by the American elite in Philadelphia in 1787 (and its subsequent ratification by the states in 1788) 1789 that was cited positively by Taney as an affirmation of white citizenship marked the culmination of a moral as well as a political compromise over slavery that involved whites of all classes, both North and South.[63] This is not to say that there was no opposition to the denial of human rights to African Americans. Some Massachusetts town councils, for example, had objected to this trend—like the town meetings in Hardwick and Essex Counties that voted by large majorities to request that the state constitutional convention declare: "All men, whites and blacks, are born free and equal."[64] Protest petitions were also aggressively brought forward by free blacks in that state.[65]

Nearly half a century later, one can see in the proceedings of the 1835 North Carolina state constitutional convention (four years after the Nat Turner slave rebellion in Virginia), one sees the ingrained identification of whiteness with citizenship in the anger expressed by white delegates over "free colored" people enjoying any citizenship rights at all—combined with doubt over how unfair that sounded.[66] Not only are they undeserving, some delegates argued, but any civil rights extended to blacks would bring down the property value of white citizenship.[67] Is a "black citizen" not a contradiction in terms, a Mr. Bryan of coastal Carteret County wanted to know?[68]

Bryan expressed the overwhelming majority view of the convention: "This is, to my mind, a nation of white people, and the enjoyment of any civil or social rights by a distinct Class of individuals is merely *permissive*, and unless there is a perfect equality in every respect, it cannot be demanded as a *right*. . . ."[69] But a few delegates were still unsure: how can we justify denying citizenship to "free coloreds" who already enjoy it?[70] We may wonder why in 1835 this question was still being debated by white constitutional convention delegates in a slave state.

The problem with Taney's 1857 declaration of a resolute "white citizenship" concept was that it obscured the actual lack of a definition of "citizen" among Constitution builders, combined with the contradictory status of African Americans in the various states. As 1787 Constitutional Convention delegate James Wilson of Pennsylvania had asked, "Are they (Negroes) admitted as citizens? Then why are they not admitted on an equality with white citizens?"[71] (Fifty years later, free blacks in the state of Pennsylvania would be presenting protesting their imminent disenfranchisement by that state's legislature.)[72] Frederick Douglass would later claim in 1865: "At the time of the formation of the Constitution the Negro had the right to vote in eleven States out of the old thirteen."[73] However, the only states to enter the Union without voting bans against blacks or color distinctions for suffrage were Vermont, Maine, Kentucky, and Tennessee.[74]

The legal as well as popular term "white" was omitted from the Constitution but was implied in the expression "free persons." On the one hand, Barbara Jeanne Fields has written that "the terms black and white—or, for that matter, Negro and Caucasian—do not appear anywhere in the Constitution, as is not surprising in a legal document in which slang of that kind would be hopelessly imprecise."[75] However, as labor historian David Roediger has countered, that did not stop the first Congress from later enacting the 1790 Naturalization Act that specifically privileged "white" by its "slang" name, leaving the courts, he adds, to sort out that "hopelessly imprecise" term into the twentieth century.[76]

With regard to the 1777 Articles of Confederation that predate the Constituion, Du Bois maintained: "In 1778 the Congress of the Confederation twice refused to insert the word 'white' in the Articles of Confederation in asserting that free inhabitants in each state should be entitled to all the privileges and immunities of free citizens of the several states."[77] But the word "white" actually *does* appear in this document—specifically in Article VIII under the provisions for a navy and army "to make requisitions from each state for its quota, in proportion to the number of white inhabitants."[78] The implication of an inherently "white citizenship" can be seen in the combination of Article VIII with the "privileges and immunities" in Article IV extended to "free inhabitants" and "free citizens."[79] Land, citizenship, and military service were the exclusive rights that legally made up this white republic in formation.

This precedent having been set, the Constitution, conceived of as a permanent document as opposed to its predecessor, does not deserve the compliment of utilizing "precise language" as much as it does the opprobrium of using tortured English in many instances. For example, Article I, Section 2.3, provides for representatives to be elected "according to their respective numbers, which shall be determined by adding to the whole number of free persons, including those bound to service for a term of years, and excluding Indians not taxed, three-fifths of all other persons."[80]

Notice here that indentured servants are included under "free persons," while black slaves become "all other persons." Section 9.1 similarly beats around the bush on the messy subject of the transatlantic slave trade: "The migration or importation of such persons as any of the States now existing shall think proper to admit shall not be prohibited by the Congress prior to the year one thousand

13

eight hundred and eight. . . ."[81] In fact, the only specific reference to a particular group of people were Native Americans referred to earlier, as well as in Article I, Section 8.3, which states that the Congress shall have the power "to regulate commerce with foreign nations, and among the several States, and with the Indian tribes."[82]

On the other hand, should any slave or indentured servant think of disrupting "normal" commerce or the domestic slave trade, Article IV, Section 2.3, provides a more specific injunction than Article IV of the Articles of Confederation, which had declared that commercial "restrictions shall not extend so far as to prevent the removal of property imported into any state, to any other state of which the Owner is an inhabitant. . . . If any person . . . shall flee from Justice . . . he shall . . . be delivered up and removed to the state having jurisdiction of his offence."[83] The Constitution combined those two clauses and, in doing so, for all practical purposes criminalized black labor, since by that time indentured servitude was practically extinct and the only unfree white workers were convicts. Article IV, Section 2.3, reads: "No person held to service or labor in one State, under the laws thereof, escaping into another, shall, in consequence of any law or regulation therein, be discharged from such service or labor, but shall de delivered up on claim of the party to whom such service or labor may be due."[84]

Despite the Articles of Confederation suggestion of punishment for runaway white indentured servants or convicts, late colonial-era newspapers indicate that only a fraction of the dwindling supply of white servants were running away compared to the constant stream of slave runaways.[85] White servant runaways who were caught did not face lifetime bondage and could still even become slaveholders after completing their time. In the making of the Constitution, did the omission of the word "white" reflect "avoidance of slang" in a permanent document, shame over compromise with the slave system and the control of black slave labor, or a tacit recognition that some free blacks were voting in the Northern states? These were probably all factors, but most important the omission indicates a white elite consensus that indeed full citizenship *implied* whiteness.[86]

Writing under the pseudonym "Publius," James Madison spelled out in *The Federalist Papers* (his combined polemic effort with Alexander Hamilton and John Jay to secure passage of the Constitution) exactly how he thought the new republic would handle the legal "dual status" of Africans as both humans and chattel:

> The federal Constitution, therefore, decides with great propriety on the case of our slaves, when it views them in the mixed character of persons and of property. This is in fact their true character. It is the character bestowed on them by the laws under which they live; and it will not be denied that these are the proper criterion; because it is only under the pretext that the laws have transformed the Negroes into subjects of property that a place is disputed them in the computation of numbers; *and it is admitted that if the laws were to restore the rights which have been taken away, the Negroes could no longer be refused an equal share of representation with the other inhabitants.*[87]

As with the Constitution, nowhere in *The Federalist Papers* does one encounter the word "white." What, then, was the point in writing that term into the 1790 Naturalization Act and not those prior documents? There is a clue contained in the earlier quotation from Justice Taney in *Dred Scott*: "white" is what the "Founding Fathers" *meant* by "citizen" in a document intended to be permanent. Furthermore, Taney argues that white inclusion and black exclusion were implied in both the preamble to the Declaration of Independence's passage "all men are created equal" and in the Constitutional provisions for returning fugitive slaves to their masters and sanctioning the transatlantic slave trade until 1808:

> Yet the men who framed this declaration were great men-high in literary acquirements-high in their sense of honor, and incapable of asserting principles inconsistent with those on which they were acting. They perfectly understood the meaning of the language they used, and how it would be understood by others; and they knew that it would not in any part of the civilized world be supposed to embrace the negro race, which, by common consent, had been excluded from civilized Governments and the family of nations, and doomed to slavery. They spoke and acted according to the then established doctrines and principles, and in the ordinary language of the day, and no one misunderstood them. *The unhappy black race were separated from the white by indelible marks,* and laws long before established, and were never thought of or spoken of except as property, and when the claims of the owner or the profit of the trader were supposed to need protection. This state of public opinion had undergone no change when the Constitution was adopted, as is equally evident from its provisions and language.[88]

If Taney was right, then the "Founding Fathers" did not believe that they had to be any more specific regarding what constituted a citizen except where "aliens" were concerned. In other words, according to this formulation, if you were already here and European, you were assumed to be a "member of the club," so to speak. On the other hand, if you were an alien desiring admission both to the country and to the white racial club, you must be first deemed "white"—a status bestowed upon some (like the Irish) over time and with grudging acceptance.

Yet "grudging acceptance" would be an understated description of the so-called anomaly of the "free Negro" in addition to the anomaly of the slave's status that was also commonly discussed at that time. Southern whites obsessed constantly over the threat "free Negroes" posed to white caste unity: how could the lowest white be exalted, after all, if some blacks were free?[89]

Free blacks in the South, said Du Bois, formed "an unstable, harried class, living on the sufferance of the law, and the good will of white patrons, and yet rising to be workers and sometimes owners of property and even of slaves, and cultured citizens."[90] Nor was the status of free blacks in the North stable or in any way comparable to that of whites. Kidnapping, for example, could transform free blacks overnight into slaves, something that would never happen to whites who were free by definition.[91] Taney's decision that declared freedom and citizenship were exclusively white domains.

V

The question arose: who was "black" when white slaveowner rape and sexual coercion made the bodies of African American slave women the common property of white men—and their "issue" or "product" (as slave children were called, using legal-sounding commodity terms) now became referred to, along with children of African and European parents in consensual relationships, as "mulatto" or "mixed?"[92] Black abolitionist Charles Lenox Remond confronted contradictory white notions of "blackness" when he proclaimed to a committee of the Massachusetts legislature in February 1842: "Sir, it happens to be my lot to have a sister a few shades lighter than myself; and who knows, if this state of things is encouraged, whether I may not on some future occasion be mobbed in Washington Street, on the supposition of walking with a white young lady."[93]

For that matter, who was "white" besides the English? Were the Scots, Irish, Germans, French, and Swiss automatically accepted as "fellow Europeans"? In fact, their status could better be described as "conditional whites" awaiting social promotion. As such their "probationary period" was then considered satisfied after demonstrating "loyalty to whiteness" with their either active or passive participation in the denial of freedom and free labor to African Americans.[94] But not all whites agreed to just "go along to get along."

For example, the early abolitionist leader Abby Kelley attacked the white supremacist status quo in a lengthy pamphlet entitled "The Constitution, a Pro-Slavery Document," where she quoted from the Madison papers to show how "with deliberate purpose our fathers bartered honesty for gain and became partners with tyrants that they might profit from their tyranny."[95] With the issues of citizenship rights and slavery very much subject to debate, social control and labor needs did not automatically translate overnight into repressive white supremacist law but were continuously refined to both meet the demands and garner the support of the entire white population of the colonies and the young Republic.[96] What made this problematic was both the potential and the actual revolt of black workers combined with the objections of free black citizens and their white supporters to slavery and the color-caste system.[97]

For their part, white abolitionists were not merely acting on their consciences, sense of justice, or revulsion at the world that whites had made. They were primarily inspired by the defiant antislavery activity on the part of free and slave black people. In 1831, the year of Nat Turner's slave rebellion, many antislavery activists began abandoning colonizationism (sending blacks back to Africa) for abolitionism, and abolitionists like William Lloyd Garrison and Angelina Grimké linked abolitionism to the fight against race and gender prejudice as well as workplace exploitation. Some white workers with roots in the Thomas Paine radical democrat tradition joined this new movement or signed antislavery petitions.[98]

The clash between these white people and those who exhibited no empathy or notion of reparations for theft of black labor and life chances directly informs today's affirmative action debate and contains some uncanny parallels. Not only did many whites believe that the slaves "had it better" than they did and were somehow responsible for degrading all work, but many of these same white working people also resented the threat free black workers posed to their exclusive caste status. Addressing Southern women in the 1830s, Angelina Grimké concluded: "[G]reat numbers [of Northern whites] cannot bear the idea of equality," because, she said, they feared that consequently blacks "would become as intelligent, as moral, and as respectable and wealthy" as whites. "Prejudice against color is the most powerful enemy we have to fight with at the North."[99]

John Hope Franklin found in his research on antebellum North Carolina that there was greater white worker hostility toward free black artisans than toward slave artisans. Free black women apparently did not encounter the same opposition from either white women or men to independent labor that black men did, given that the women were restricted by convention to spinning, weaving, and dressmaking.[100] Among white men, however, there were continual objections. White river pilots in and around New Bern petitioned the colonial government in 1773, protesting against black pilots who "by unjust and unlawful means take upon themselves to pilot Vessels."[101] The "mechanics" (a nineteenth-century term for blue-collar workers) of Rowan County in 1851 revealed their objections to free black labor to the state legislature as something that challenged their white caste status, there being, as Franklin notes, "no evidence other than that of the Rowan County mechanics that free Negro artisans were employed at wages lower than those paid to white artisans."[102] From their very first phrase here the mechanics reveal their primary concern being one of status:

> Free negroes are with us a degraded class of men, living in a condition but little better than that of the brute creation. . . . Negro Mechanicks should by law be bound to an apprenticeship . . . and that they should only be permitted to work at such trade under the direction and controul of the master to whom they are bound.[103]

But if there was so much conformist white supremacist opinion, then what was stopping whites from eliminating all human rights for African Americans? The answer is: there actually never was a "solid South" or a "solid white America" in that respect. Legalistic euphemisms as well as "scientific" and theological rationalizations were not enough to keep white consciences from being occasionally or even often troubled with the contradictions in this world they were creating on the backs of African labor and culture. We can glean this from the writings and public debates of the period, from white politicians to the white antislavery activists and preachers like Rev. Daniel Wilson in North Carolina.[104]

Within this repressive atmosphere one is struck additionally by the fortitude of the slaves who sued their masters for freedom, despite the judges' repeated assertions that "there is no law . . . by which slaves . . . can obtain freedom, or enjoy the rights of free persons, only by deed in writing, or the last will and testament of the owner. . . ."[105] A slave named Isaac in Virginia, for instance, began suing his master Peter Corbell for freedom in 1799 and was finally freed in 1816 after losing and appealing six times.[106] Also during this period there was developing an African American oratorical tradition for freedom characterized by both militancy and uplift.[107] A common theme was a challenge to the hypocrisy of Independence Day, the Constitution, and the lofty pronouncements of freedom emanating from both institutions.[108]

On the one hand we have Absalom Jones, the first black Episcopalian priest, preaching "On Account of the Abolition of the African Slave Trade" in 1808 and forecasting later nineteenth-century uplift writings by optimistically suggesting:

> Let us conduct ourselves in such a manner as to furnish no case of regret to the deliverers of our nation. . . . Let our conduct be regulated by the precepts of the gospel. . . . Let us teach our children the rudiments of the English language, in order to enable them to acquire a knowledge of useful trades. . . .[109]

By contrast, Frederick Douglass can be heard in 1852 listing dozens of black occupations and declaring: "Is it not astounding that, while we are plowing, planting, and reaping . . . having among us lawyers, doctors, ministers, poets . . . we are called upon to prove we are men!"[110] Prior to that, in 1843 Samuel H. Davis had argued before the National Convention of Colored Citizens in Buffalo that the time for petitioning was over and the time for black unity was at hand—and that unity with any whites depended upon their unconditional support for abolition.[111] An earlier similar challenge was directed at white people by the North Carolina black abolitionist David Walker in his revolutionary 1829 pamphlet entitled *Appeal to the Slaves of the United States of America* when he noted that slavery operated in the name of and for the benefit of all white people and became inherited stolen wealth that fathers passed on to their wives and children.[112]

Walker's tract was meant to inspire blacks to rebel and to challenge whites over their hypocritical notions of freedom—especially those contained in the writings of Thomas Jefferson who had died three years before. However, in the last three decades there has developed a current of thought at odds with Walker's pronouncement. Specifically, it holds that the political, economic, social, and legal systems (including slavery) in colonial, revolutionary, and antebellum United States only benefited white men of means and not their wives and children.[113]

It is true that women in America had suffered a setback in the late eighteenth century with the legal changes being implemented both here and in England that had women's property in marriage going to the husband.[114] But legal historian Marylynn Salmon's research demonstrates that colonial law had never been particularly favorable to women, and postrevolutionary law actually produced both gains and losses for women's legal rights. Among the most significant gains were the liberalizing of marriage and divorce law, the abolition of primogeniture (traditional English first-born male inheritance), and preservation and expansion of the English law of dower.[115] American widows could also inherit their late husbands' real property (including slaves), just as daughters could be given slaves as wedding presents by their fathers.[116]

With regards to slavery, after examining numerous slave mistress letters and diaries as well as slave narratives revealing white female power and even violence over often-defiant black slave labor, historian Elizabeth Fox-Genovese was moved to conclude: "With some pain I am compelled to express my considered opinion that in some essential respects, they [the plantation slave mistresses] were more crudely racist than their men."[117] Slavery, in fact, had the effect of melding not just *white communities* (never exclusively male) but also *white families*.

Slavery as an industry meant tremendous income and wealth for those families and communities, as well as the nation as a whole, even as it retarded the economic, social, and cultural development of the South and its laboring class. A look at the census figures for any Southern state demonstrates the extent to which the average white farmer or professional—both male and female—was able to gain the privilege of slaveholding. John Hope Franklin notes that, while the slave population along with most of the wealth it produced was concentrated in the hands of a relatively small number of slaveowners (384,884 out of 8 million whites), it is important to remember that (1) 88 percent of all slaveholders in 1860, or 338,000, owned fewer than twenty slaves, although the majority of slaves labored on plantations with more than twenty slaves; and (2) most nonslaveowners aspired to slaveowner status and therefore adopted that mentality before actually joining that class. The socially significant fact here, concludes Franklin, is that "the majority of slaveholding was carried on by yeomen rather than gentry."[118]

As restricted as they were, white women's employment opportunities were still greater than those of African Americans—the vast majority of whom were enslaved. Historian Alice Kessler-Harris has exploded the enduring popular myth that has American women virtually locked in their homes since colonial times and working until there was a demand for their labor in World War II as

"Rosie the Riveter." Since colonial times, she points out, many free women were wage laborers in factories or they did piece work at home. As capital responded to the changes in technology and labor market conditions, these women were often used to replace—and in turn could be replaced by—higher-paid or striking male workers. Male and female workers were played off against each other by employers who used sex stereotypes to lower the wages of both.[119]

Kessler-Harris also notes the growing number of women involved in rationalized industrial labor as early as the 1770s concluding that "America's lack of an adequate supply of workers and ongoing need for cheap labor required that women become the first industrial proletariat."[120] By 1840, with only 4 percent of Americans engaged in manufacturing, there were far more women workers than men, although their choice of industry and work was severely circumscribed, with men doing most of the craft work.[121] In any case, whether or not men (and other women) expected women to work outside the home or felt angry and threatened when they did so, there were no pogroms or hate strikes against white women workers that we have seen conducted by whites against blacks from the antebellum period to the present.

Ultimately, accumulation of wealth, freedom to sell one's labor, and social mobility (all of which did privilege white males) depended upon citizenship privileges like suffrage. Yet Charles Wesley points out that suffrage was not specifically mentioned in the Constitution, leaving it to the states to fight it out internally: white laborers versus white merchants, with African Americans fighting them both for recognition.[122]

VI

The political phenomenon known as "Jacksonian democracy" that began with the inauguration of President Andrew Jackson (1829–37) and included his invention of the "spoils system" represented a re-invention of whiteness. It meant a democratization of white inclusion by implementing a more thorough black exclusion. By expanding the franchise to include more white men—even those without property—it widened the circle of those with a vested interest in the property value whiteness conferred.[123] "The democratizing surge," writes historian Alexander Saxton, "was marked by battles at legislative sessions and constitutional conventions—in Virginia in 1829–1830; Mississippi in 1831;

North Carolina in 1835; Louisiana in 1845; North Carolina again in the late 1840s and Virginia and Louisiana again in the early 1850s."[124] Nor was this a movement limited to the rural South. Proslavery, pro-white Democrats made inroads in urban areas and in the North as well. Historian Richard Ellis notes that constitution-making or revising was a

bitterly fought-over issue in every new state that entered the Union between 1800 and 1840 [along with many of the original thirteen states]; Ohio (1803), Louisiana (1812), Indiana (1816), Mississippi (1817), Illinois (1818), Alabama (1819), Maine (1820), Missouri (1820), Arkansas (1836), and Michigan (1836) . . . Connecticut (1818), New York (1821), Delaware (1831), and Pennsylvania (1838) . . . Massachusetts [1820] . . . Tennessee (1834) . . . Georgia in 1833. . . .

Although the specific issues varied from state to state, they involved the elimination of property qualifications for officeholding and voting, demands for the popular election of governors, more equitable representation in the legislatures, and provisions for the periodic reapportionment in accordance with population shifts, as well as the desire to elect rather than to appoint judges and county officials.[125]

Commenting without irony, historian Chilton Williamson has declared: "Among the democratic achievements of the period between the Revolution and the Civil War, universal white manhood suffrage stands out as a reform of considerable magnitude in the context of the history of the United States and also of the world."[126] This was also no overnight affair, as Williamson chronicles. American colonial authorities borrowed the English concept of "freeholding" as "the backbone of state and society because they were the repository of virtues not found in other classes."[127] Freeholding became the property qualification for voting, either in landowning, wealth, or taxpaying ability. In colonial America, Williamson asserts, about 20 percent of the population were (white) adult males, and of them between 50 and 80 percent were eligible voters.[128] The move toward loosening the property restrictions on voting then began during the Revolution. Speaking of the young, often propertyless militiamen, Williamson notes:

On their shoulders would rest the greater burden of combat. It so happened that a larger proportion of these men was unable to meet the property and freehold tests than any other age group. As [seventeenth-century English Protestant ruler Oliver] Cromwell's men had demanded the right to vote if they were declared fit to fight for their country and its liberties, colonials of military age demanded the same right for the same reason. . . . Here and there along the seaboard, letters, newspapers, and resolutions of public meetings show the current of public opinion running in the direction of suffrage reform.[129]

The impulse to liberalize suffrage eventually defeated the current that still favored restrictions, even as it had fought lax attitudes toward restriction since colonial times. Not only had voter fraud been common throughout the colonies (such as "borrowing" freehold title for election day only),[130] but in South Carolina, for example, it was a simple process to acquire a freehold. Williamson quotes a chronicler of that colony who wrote in 1836: "Everyone upon his arrival obtained his grant of land and sat down upon his freehold. . . ."[131] Furthermore, if one were a resident for two years, paying twenty shillings in taxes sufficed for "freeholding," meaning that "a comfortable majority could vote."[132]

Massachusetts colonial lieutenant governor Hutchinson had once complained that voting qualifications were so loose that "anything with the appearance of a man" was allowed to vote.[133] The *Connecticut Courant* of 18 August 1817 responded to contemporary debates over election reform by affirming suffrage entitlement for more prosperous whites while opposing its extension to the allegedly undisciplined general "populace." In Virginia, as the population became more heterogeneous, the old restrictions came under fire. It was noted with concern that the denial of political and economic privileges to poor whites was encouraging a kind of "white flight" of unenfranchised laborers. Williamson cites the *Niles' Register* as an influential source that in 1821 called upon "the state . . . [for some] practical proofs of that republican spirit and vigilance that she so much boasts of."[134]

Williamson also makes this observation about the 1818 Connecticut state convention to revise the state constitution: "Another indication that the convention was more prejudiced about race than class was its confinement of the suffrage to persons who were white."[135] In the Maryland assembly of 1807, it was noted with disapproval: "since 1798, the number of aliens, Negroes, and women [who] were voting."[136] By 1812, freeholding was only a qualification for all state elections in Virginia and Rhode Island and for some state elections in New York and North Carolina.[137] But in 1831 Virginia was spurred by Nat Turner's rebellion to re-define citizenship, whereby universal white police and military functions would be logically extended to imply universal white manhood suffrage:

Furthermore, Nat Turner's insurrection only recently had shaken the complacency of Virginians as to their own personal security. In combination with intermittent criticism form the north, it led some Virginians to consider democratic suffrage doctrine as a means of creating greater unity among all whites, and achieving greater security for slavery. Unenfranchised white men in Virginia and South Carolina had already declared that if they could be trusted with membership in the white patrols they could be trusted with the vote.[138]

All of this evidence is intended to show that the move first to "hook-up" and eventually enfranchise more whites was parallel with the move to *disenfranchise* free blacks—in some cases *in the very same year*. Even more important, this was a mass white movement as much as is today's white anti-affirmative action back-lash. The two are by no means identical, but the former serves as an early precedent for the latter. As Du Bois observed, free blacks were disfranchised in Delaware in 1792; Maryland in 1783 and 1810; Florida in 1845; Louisiana in 1812; Mississippi in 1817; Alabama in 1819; Missouri in 1821; Arkansas in 1836; Texas in 1845; Connecticut in 1814; New Jersey in 1847; Pennsylvania in 1838; Ohio in 1803; Indiana in 1816; Illinois in 1818; Michigan in 1837; Iowa in 1846; Wisconsin in 1848; Minnesota in 1858; Kansas in 1861; in New York they could vote in 1821 after being disfranchised, but only with a discriminatory $250 property qualification; and in Rhode Island they were written out of the Dorr constitution in 1842, although they were re-enfranchised with Thomas W. Dorr's removal as governor that same year.[139]

In the latter case, a dual power situation had arisen in 1842 after former abolitionist Dorr led a group calling itself the Suffrage Association to call a state People's Convention in Rhode Island in 1841. The purpose of this predominantly working-class white organization was to overturn the state's property qualification laws that kept about two-thirds of the adult white males from voting. The opposition Law and Order Party offered the franchise to black men if they would support their legitimacy and recruited blacks to militia units that were ultimately decisive in militarily routing the Dorr faction.[140]

The uprising in Rhode Island was simply the most dramatic example of how, despite the fact that the Dorr faction appealed in vain to Jackson's arch rival John C. Calhoun of South Carolina, the Jacksonian democratic "revolution" represented a break with late colonial and early republican American tradition.[141] With its acceptance of propertyless working people in this new political coalition of landowners, farmers, artisans, and mechanics, Jacksonian democracy shattered what was left of Thomas Jefferson's dream of an agrarian freeholding society.[142] Under the new formulation, it was determined that white workingmen who lacked real estate property and were forced to sell their labor—whether skilled or not—should at least be given some kind of compensation or currency. That currency (like a credit card today) was their white skin. It literally became a form of "walking around money," as well as something that could also be saved and invested. White "freedom" meant not being black.

Andrew Jackson in his 1837 presidential farewell address declared that this coalition of "freemen" (that included white workingmen) formed the "bone and sinew of the country": These were "men who love liberty," he said, who held "the great mass of national wealth" and furthermore knew that "their success depends on their own industry and economy."[143] There was no doubt that this was a white coalition, as prolabor activist clergyman Theophilus Fisk declared in 1835 in Boston: "It calls upon the philanthropist and Christian to advocate and demand the immediate emancipation of the 'white slaves of the North,' and to declare to the world that the workers are, and of right ought to be, free and independent citizens of these United States."[144]

The widening of the franchise to include more white people also extended the constituency that had to be satisfied to some extent between election days. Theodore Allen has pointed out how historians continue "to ignore the most historically relevant fact about the [Jacksonian] spoils system, namely that it was first of all a 'white-race' spoils system."[145] Despite Jackson's own defense of the institution, the "spoils system" (a phrase appropriated today by conservatives to deride what they call affirmative action's unearned black privileges) actually removed only about 20 percent of government employees, many for incompetence.[146] Its biggest impact, besides inconveniencing those suddenly without jobs, was to serve as a controversial concept not unlike "affirmative action" today. The spoils system came to stand for political patronage across a broader class span that further reinforced whiteness as labor without chains, citizenship without qualifications, and suffrage without real economic and political reform.

The enduring popular image today of Jacksonian democracy is epitomized in Jackson's 4 March 1829 Inaugural Ball, where the "common man" could have a riotous, chaotic party in the heretofore dignified White House (built by slaves). An observer and member of the Washington elite, Margaret Bayard Smith, was horrified at the huge crowd of something less than 20,000, conceding in this grudging account: "But it was the People's day, and the People's

President and the People would rule. . . . The noisy and disorderly rabble in the President's House brought to my mind descriptions I had read of the mobs in the Tuileries and at Versailles. . . ."[147]

Popular enthusiasm for the liberalizing of white male enfranchisement became palpable in ways that showed this ball to be no mere myth but rather an enduring mythology. Indeed, the physical intensity of that Inaugural Ball crowd forced Jackson to leave through a back door or risk being crushed to death, thus simultaneously providing us with an image of an approving patriarch who nonetheless knew when to leave a mob scene. For the "common" white person, that now-legendary Inaugural Ball, to quote today's popular white rap group the Beastie Boys, was the "fight for your right to party."[148] It meant literally eating at the table of the white rich—even if the class represented by the party in power had no intention of sharing any more than a fraction of its wealth with what it still considered to be "the mob."

Jacksonian scholar Robert Remini has pointed out the irony of how Jackson could break strikes and still receive the support of white labor. Additionally, the 1828 presidential election figures reveal his broad national and cross-class support.[149] Finally, not only did the preservation of slavery maintain the superior status of white labor, but Jackson's 1830 Indian Removal Act became the political culmination of his prior military efforts to secure more Indian land for white homesteading and slaveholding. Two other points are worth noting here: (1) the women's massive petition campaign against the act inspired many anti-slavery activists to abandon colonization for abolition,[150] and (2) a Congressional Act of 30 June 1834 also provided for Native American hiring preferences "in all cases of the appointments of interpreters or other persons employed for the benefit of the Indians."[151]

Even more so than the spoils system, universal white male suffrage, access to American Indian land, and the "white job" all represented a kind of "white-affirmative action" that was critical in the building of the tradition and expectations of personal wealth and income for average white Americans—even as their position slipped faster and faster below wealthy white people.[152]

VII

At the 1835 North Carolina constitutional convention discussed earlier, during the height of the Jacksonian era, there was a lengthy debate in which many delegates decried North Carolina's "liberal" 1776 state constitutional allowance of all "freeholding freemen" to vote when at the same time other states both North and South were disfranchising blacks while writing more whites into the constitutional language.[153] A few North Carolina delegates did question the demotion to near-slave status of what they deemed to be respectable black citizens who had loyally fought in the Revolution and could potentially form a buffer class against the slaves. But as Theodore Allen has pointed out, poor whites already formed that buffer class (or "America's mulattoes"), and this gathering of North Carolina's white elite probably wondered why they should extend it and thereby complicate matters.[154]

In the end it was decided to add a section to the state constitution that simply disenfranchised free blacks rather than explicitly define an eligible voter as "white."[155] However, the white privilege of franchise was also extended at this convention to European immigrants by providing in Section 40: "That every foreigner [who owns land, takes the oath of allegiance, and has one year of residency] shall be deemed a free citizen."[156]

The United States Homestead Act of 1862 was another form of privileging "white citizenship." Not only did it make cheap western land available to both male and female "citizens"—which effectively excluded all blacks, as *Dred Scott* had yet to be overturned—but the act also offered land to any immigrant who had filed for citizenship under existing naturalization laws, which still excluded all but "free white persons." (The act also contained veteran's preferences and protections.)[157]

America as a concept since its founding as a "white man's country" was renewed as a republic by the young party that took that concept as its name in 1856. During one of his famous 1858 Illinois debates with Stephen A. Douglas in their race for the United States Senate, Republican candidate Abraham Lincoln declared:

> Now, irrespective of the moral aspect of this question as to whether there is a right or wrong in enslaving a negro, I am still in favor of our new territories being in such a condition that white men may find a home—may find some spot where they can better their condition—where they can settle upon new soil and better their condition in life. I am in favor of this not merely (I must say it here as I have elsewhere) for our own people who are born among us, but as an outlet for *free white people everywhere*, the world over—in which Hans, and Baptiste, and Patrick, and all other men from all the world, may find new homes and better their conditions in life.[158]

Even the Civil War itself, with slavery as the principal cause, began as a struggle between white men to determine the fate of slavery, as Frederick Douglass reflected in Boston in 1865: "The South was fighting to take slavery out of the Union, and the North fighting to keep it in the Union; the South fighting to get it beyond the limits of the United States Constitution, and the North fighting for the old guarantees;—both despising the Negro, both insulting the Negro."[159] It would take the entrance of black soldiers beginning in 1862 and then in large numbers the following year to transform it into a war of black liberation (and America's liberation from slaveholding power) that would enable the United States to begin reconstructing itself in ways that forecast today's struggle over affirmative action and civil rights law.[160]

If slavery gave birth to "white" ideology and the legal separation of black from white workers in rights and privileges, then "white citizenship" became the legal reification of the "white race."[161] The denial of free labor and full citizenship to all blacks (but extended to all whites) was first a colonial, then a state and federal institution that was often enforced by popular violence and ultimately had to be overthrown with first a civil war and subsequently with constitutional and other legal measures.

What the abolitionist movement in the antebellum era initially had to contend with in seeking to build support for emancipation and equality was convincing an internally conflicted white American public. On the one hand, this public was avidly buying, reading, and in some cases even weeping over Harriet Beecher Stowe's antislavery novel *Uncle Tom's Cabin*, published in 1852.[162] On the other hand, white mobs had been rioting regularly against black people in cities all across the country in the previous four decades.[163]

In 1835 in Charleston, South Carolina, and New Orleans, Louisiana, militias had to stop white mobs protesting "employment of slaves in the mechanical arts." Riots broke out in Baltimore in 1812; St. Louis in 1836; Albany, New York, in 1832; Washington, D.C., in 1835; Pittsburgh during the 1830s; Boston in 1826 and 1843; New York City in 1834; Providence, Rhode Island, in 1831; and Cincinnati and Philadelphia from 1834 to 1842 almost annually. "If the riot was the ultimate expression of the city's violent nature," writes historian Leonard P. Curry, "to the urban black (when he was the target) it was the ultimate expression of racial prejudice."[164]

Jacksonian-era rioting was in fact state-sanctioned autonomous working-class activity, as historian Noel Ignatiev illustrates: "Francis Grund, a Jacksonian publicist, wrote that direct action by a mob 'is not properly speaking an opposition to the established laws of the country . . . but rather . . . a supplement to them—as a species of *common law*. . . .' "[165] Ignatiev then concludes: "Every institution in American life takes on a new hue when examined through a color-sensitive lens. So with the riot: in antebellum America a citizen (or potential citizen) was distinguished by three main privileges: he could sell himself piecemeal, he could vote, and he could riot."[166]

White riots against black people were especially prevalent during the Jacksonian era when universal white manhood suffrage, abolitionism, and slave rebellions were on the rise and the nation was simultaneously experiencing a "severe economic depression."[167] The sudden explosion on the popular theater stage of blackface minstrelsy in the late 1840s, in what would become one of America's leading forms of popular entertainment for almost a century, simultaneously combined racial romanticism and hostile revulsion—what historian Eric Lott calls "love and theft."[168] (Those shows were especially popular among the immigrant Irish, who became minstrelsy's earliest and predominant performers.)[169] Full-scale rioting would not break out again in New York until 1863, but as labor historians Sterling D. Spero and Abram L. Harris point out: "The new immigrants undercut the Negro scale and pushed the black workers out of their jobs. A deadly hatred resulted which constantly manifested itself in quarreling and fighting between the two groups."[170]

"White people" in nineteenth-century America were in fact the end product of a colonial and republican "melting pot" of white "privilege" that included both opportunity and poverty. Small wonder then that European Americans often viewed slave insurrection, abolitionism, and the existence of free blacks as a threat to their superior (yet paradoxically insecure) social status.[171] The "quarreling and fighting between the two groups," however, was never a fair or even match (or "level playing field" in today's terminology). Through such venerable institutions as the trade union, the Democratic Party, and the Catholic Church, and through the isolation of pro-black white sympathy, urban white workers ensured a white victory as the outcome of these labor and social "quarrels."[172]

If elected officials and slaveholders had stumbled in recruiting mass white support for the Indian Removal Act, this was not to be the case in the 1840s Mexican land grab for slaveholders and white settlers.[173] Despite strong opposition from abolitionists and many working people—including those who deserted the army for political reasons—there was a substantial amount of white enthusiasm at the annexation of Texas in 1845, the invasion of Mexico in 1846, and the eventual forcing of Mexico in 1848 to sign the Treaty of Guadalupe Hidalgo ceding the northern half of their country to the United States.[174] The latter event made Mexican citizens into United States citizens and deprived many of them of land that had been in their families for generations as well as the franchise. Mexicans overnight became a "minority" suffering discrimination in another country.[175]

While Mexican Americans were often popularly regarded by whites in the United States as both an "inferior race" and culture, their social and legal status since the nineteenth century has alternated between "white" and "nonwhite."[176] The combination of this historical and ongoing oppression would emerge in often-nationalistic 1960s activism based on land and political self-determination as well as a campaign for Chicano (Mexican American) civil rights, inspired by the black civil rights and Black Power movements.[177] Subsequent affirmative action programs, ranging from employment to voting rights, would often list Mexicans (usually as "Latinos" or "Hispanics") second after African Americans among groups to be compensated, ironically following a format set by civil rights and leftist groups of the 1960s.[178]

The 1848 colonization of half of Mexico and its people was intimately tied to the extension of slavery. It added another category of people to be denied white privilege as well as adding a future ally to the black struggle for equality.[179] And both native-born and immigrant European Americans simultaneously saw their labor degraded as well as being afforded some privilege at the expense of those of African, Mexican, and Indian descent. Anticipating Du Bois's remarks eighty years later concerning European immigrants advancing ahead of native-born African Americans, Frederick Douglass in 1853 said of the Irish:

> Every hour sees us elbowed out of some employment to make room for some newly-arrived immigrant from the Emerald Isle, whose hunger and color entitle him to special favor. These white men are becoming houseservants, cooks, stewards, waiters, and flunkies. For aught I see they adjust themselves to their stations with all proper humility. If they cannot rise to the dignity of white men, they show that they can fall to the degradation of black men.[180]

While the Irish of the Northern states were aspiring to white status and the Democrat and Republican Parties were torn between compromising with slaveholding capital to hold the nation together and promoting the interests of Northern capital and free Northern labor, the Southern slaveholding forces had their own issues and agenda on the status of whiteness. With Lincoln's election as president in 1860 the ultimate in a series of perceived threats to their absolute power, the Southerners' solution was to call a constitutional convention in February 1861 in Montgomery, Alabama, to plan secession.

Tired of compromising over how much they could use federal power to protect and expand slavery and alarmed at the extent of Northern sympathy for abolitionist John Brown and his revolutionary brigade's failed 1859 raid (and subsequent execution of Brown and six others) on the federal arsenal at Harpers Ferry, Virginia, these proslavery forces declared their intention to reconstruct the United States. This "new" nation would invite the states of the "old" nation to join them on the explicit and fundamental bases of slavery and white supremacy—not the "states' rights" postbellum myth that endures to this day—although plenty of nonslaveholding Southern whites clearly had other ideas about supporting what many called this "rich man's war and poor man's fight."[181]

A reading of the text of the Confederate Constitution, ratified on 11 March 1861, reveals just how much the delegates who were involved in crafting the original 1787 United States Constitution compromised with the "Slave Power," as slaveholders were collectively referred to by abolitionists. The Confederate version is practically a carbon copy of the original—with some notable exceptions that include the explicit protection of slavery and the substitution of the word "slaves" for the earlier euphemism "all other persons." In Article I, Section 2.3, the apportionment clause for determining representation includes "three-fifths of all slaves"; in Article IV, Section 2.1, the citizenship privileges and immunities clause includes the right to transport "slaves and other property"; Article IV, Section 2.3, provides that "no slave or other person held to service or labor . . . escaping . . . shall . . . be discharged from such service or labor"; and Article IV, Section 3.3, states, "In all such [new] territory, the institution of negro slavery, as it now exists in the Confederate States, shall be recognized and protected by Congress. . . ."[182]

Backed by the majority of white Deep South politicians, newspapers, and popular opinion, newly elected Confederate vice president Alexander H. Stephens gave voice to this new constitutional philosophy in a February speech to the assembled Confederate delegates in Montgomery. He proudly proclaimed that the establishment of an explicitly slaveholding republic finally corrected those erroneous "prevailing ideas" of Thomas Jefferson "and most of the leading statesmen at the time of the formation of the old Constitution" who, according to Stephens, believed that that slavery was wrong because of the "equality of races" and would eventually "pass away."[183] Stephens declared to the contrary:

> Our new government is founded upon exactly the opposite idea, its foundations are laid, its corner-stone rests upon the great truth that the Negro is not equal to the white man. That slavery—subordination to the superior race—is his natural and normal condition. This, our new government, is the first in the history of the world, based upon this great physical and moral truth.[184]

If antebellum Southern white enslavement of blacks was ultimately to be stopped only with the force of arms by blacks and whites in uniform in the Civil War, then getting whites in general to recognize black citizenship rights after the war was over would take a combination of cajoling, coercion, and the invocation of a moral imperative by the abolitionists, all backed up by the threat of armed force during Reconstruction: America's "first affirmative action program."

Chapter 2

"THE SPECIAL FAVORITE OF THE LAWS"

Civil War, Reconstruction, and America's First "Affirmative Action Programs," 1861–77

I

It is plain that the Fourteenth Amendment was not intended to prohibit measures designed to remedy the effects of the Nation's past treatment of Negroes. The Congress that passed the Fourteenth Amendment is the same Congress that passed the 1866 Freedmen's Bureau Act, an Act that provided many of its benefits only to Negroes. . . . After the Civil War our Government started several "affirmative action programs."[1]

Writing in his separate opinion in the landmark 1978 *Bakke* decision, United States Supreme Court Justice Thurgood Marshall cited Reconstruction as precedent, arguing in vain for stronger, more active civil rights measures. *Bakke* ultimately recognized such rights, but it also curtailed affirmative action in higher education, except in what have come to be called "diversity" initiatives.[2] Indeed, Reconstruction-era congressional debates, abolitionist discourse, and the activity of the Freedmen's Bureau and the freedpeople themselves all have a direct bearing on today's affirmative action debate, especially as these elements revolved around whether and how much whites needed to be coerced into accepting black citizenship with its implications for truly free labor. This chapter examines these antecedent and parallels.

The programs known collectively as Reconstruction (1865–77) were actually conceptualized during the Civil War (1861–65) and represented a fusion of elements in much the same way that affirmative action operates today— although affirmative action is a compromise civil rights enforcement effort while Reconstruction was much more assertive. Every federal law cited in this chapter, from the 1862 Confiscation Act to the 1875 Civil Rights Act, was designed to protect African Americans specifically (as well as white Unionist refugees) in the South and to serve as a first-time creation of federally guaranteed equal protection for all citizens. While modern critics and opponents of affirmative action insist that the Fourteenth and Fifteenth Amendments were "color-blind"—and contemporary advocates in fact did insist on the amendments' universality—it is also true that both advocates and opponents during that time knew and argued on the basis of the corrective, pro-black nature of the amendments.

The most crucial debates in the United States in both the Civil War and Reconstruction periods revolved around the Freedmen's Bureau (whether blacks could own land), the nature of citizenship (whether blacks could enjoy equal protection in that status), and the unrestricted labor for African Americans that Frederick Douglass called for. The latter two issues were the subject of debates and even riots within the Union while the Civil War was raging against the Confederacy's attempt to create a base for a new slave empire with white supremacy as its ruling ideology. With the end of the Civil War, Reconstruction represented the first attempt to rectify the effects of slavery and white supremacy and in that sense serves as the first antecedent to affirmative action.[3]

Was there ever actually a Reconstruction-era usage of the phrase "affirmative action"? John David Skrentny has maintained that

the phrase *affirmative action* first appeared as part of the 1935 National Labor Relations Act. Here, it meant that an employer who was found to be discriminating against union members or organizers would have to stop discriminating, and also take affirmative action to place those victims where they would have been without the discrimination.[4]

Yet this phrase and others like it can be found in the Reconstruction debates. During the 1871 Ku Klux Act debate Rep. John Coburn (R-Indiana) cited the newly enacted Fourteenth Amendment's power both to protect blacks as well as restrain white terrorist mobs led by the Ku Klux Klan primarily in the South:

Where there is domestic violence and aid is asked by the State, the nation must exercise its authority. Before the Fourteenth Amendment, it could not unless that violence amounted to an overthrow of republican institutions . . . but now, where the equal protection of the law, as in the case of an overthrow of republican institutions, is denied by domestic violence or any other case, the nation may interpose to afford it, by legislation, directing the use of military power and the interposition of the courts of the United States.[5]

Coburn then invoked a legal term that has today become a bitterly controversial and racialized political expression to the point of achieving folkloric and archetypal status:

Affirmative action or legislation is not the only method of a denial of protection by a State, State action not always being legislative action. A State may by positive enactment cut off from some the right to vote . . . to do business . . . to bear arms . . . and many other such things. . . ."[6]

This is the earliest date that I have encountered the term "affirmative action." In other Reconstruction-era debates the word "affirmative" was actually used in the context of *protecting* black civil rights. But here it is linked to safeguarding black civil rights from the *white affirmative action* of state-sanctioned discrimination and refusal to stop white supremacist terrorism. Coburn's remarks challenged a form of white privilege assumed under the rubric of white citizenship from colonial times: the "right" of whites to harass blacks with impunity.[7]

Yet whiteness as a supremacist ideology had also helped create slavery's opposition: abolitionism. During the Civil War abolitionism acquired allies in the military and Congress, and following the war there was a split over disbanding the movement versus fighting for equality legislation.[8] In the postbellum period the legislative and military institutionalization of the latter was referred to as "Radical Reconstruction," which tended to be protective of blacks and white Southern Unionists (or "refugees") and punitive toward defiant whites.

Radical rhetoric combined coercion, strict equality measures, black uplift, white guilt, and black reparations in opposition to expressions of white denial of privilege, charges of innate black inferiority, and white anger at losing exclusive citizenship rights.[9] That white-affirmative reaction would find vindication in the United States Supreme Court's blunting of the Fourteenth Amendment in its 1883 *Civil Rights Cases* opinion that it was time to make freedpeople "mere citizen[s]" and no longer "the special favorite of the laws."[10] But until Reconstruction's overthrow in 1877, social change was both sweeping and included challenges to whiteness.

II

Individual abolitionists both black and white played a major role in the postwar struggle for equality.[11] There were some like the tireless freedom fighter William Lloyd Garrison who concluded that the struggle was over. (Garrison was not particularly active during the Reconstruction era after the dissolution of the American Anti-Slavery Association.)[12] In contrast, Lydia Maria Child, one of many still active in the movement, was like "most Garrisonians [who] . . . believed in some form of reparations for slavery," including planter land confiscation.[13] Abolitionists like Charles Sumner, Frederick Douglass, Major Martin Delany, and Thomas W. Higginson were actively involved in Congress, the military occupation of the South, the Freedmen's Bureau, self-help organizations, and the general agitation for equality.[14] Grassroots black abolitionist leaders in the South like Abraham H. Galloway and Robert G. Fitzgerald had fought in the war and now participated in Freedmen's Bureau schools, black-owned business, armed self-defense against the Ku Klux Klan, and constitutional conventions aimed at reorganizing the oligarchy into a democracy.[15]

There were deep misgivings on the part of most abolitionists and anger on the part of many white female suffragists over the exclusion of female suffrage in both the Fourteenth and Fifteenth Amendments. But opposition from even most Republicans to female suffrage made it extremely unlikely that the amendments would pass with female suffrage clauses included. Most abolitionists, including Lydia Maria Child, Abby Kelley, and Harriet Tubman, agreed with Frederick Douglass on the primacy of at least black men obtaining the franchise to achieve some desperately needed progress for African Americans, and as a defense against white reaction both North and South.[16]

The women's suffrage movement, however, born in large part out of the abolitionist movement, not only split with abolitionism over the Fifteenth Amendment but then enacted its own "devil's bargain" with white supremacists in promoting white women's suffrage as an antidote to black political power. In later years there would evolve a contradictory relationship between black and white women activists (like the one between Ida B. Wells-Barnett and Susan B. Anthony).[17] A precedent was set as well for splits among proponents in today's

36

affirmative action debate by white suffragist leader Elizabeth Cady Stanton's declaration in 1860, when 4 million black men, women, and children were still in slavery and another half a million free blacks lived on the cusp of bondage: "Prejudice against color, of which we hear so much, is not stronger than that against sex."[18]

On the question of labor, Wendell Phillips for his part was convinced that the cause of the freedmen was linked to the larger class struggle and after the war became an eloquent spokesperson on behalf of the labor movement— which continued to see white unions excluding or segregating blacks. Ironically, some of these same white union men were probably among those who applauded him in the Tremont Temple audience in Boston on 23 April 1865, where Phillips attacked the white "caste" and called for Southern land confiscation and distribution to the freedmen: "Confiscate every dollar and acre they own. [Applause.] These steps the world and their followers will see are necessary to kill the seeds of *caste*, dangerous State rights, and secession. . . . Land and the ballot are the true foundations of all governments."[19]

But there is probably no better subject for studying affirmative action antecedents during Reconstruction than Frederick Douglass, the runaway slave who became a prominent abolitionist leader, speaker, writer, and newspaper editor. Some of his most incisive social, political, and legal commentary comes from this period.[20] In reading his letters and speeches from that time we find him maintaining the abolitionist cause through the crucial years of civil rights bills, Reconstruction amendments, and white supremacist attacks—while pursuing a political path that was both confrontational and circumspect. His positions, similar to the positions and paradoxes of affirmative action today, summed up the differing positions, contradictions, and paradoxes of the day within the movement: black political power, federal protectionism, egalitarianism, and even Social Darwinism.[21]

On the one hand Douglass would lecture white audiences to let blacks sink or swim on their own and that character, not color, was all that mattered.[22] But on the other hand he would argue for special federal protective and coercive legislation for safeguarding the rights of African Americans until such time as that protection would become unnecessary.[23] He refused the opportunistic tokenism of President Andrew Johnson in 1867 in turning down an appointment to the Freedmen's Bureau.[24] Yet ten years later Douglass accepted the District of Columbia United States Marshall's position as a kind of "role model" to both whites and blacks, while at the same time maintaining silence on the 1877 Hayes-Tilden compromise.[25] Douglass did not support ex-slaveholder land confiscation with redistribution to ex-slaves in the South.[26] However, he did "urge Congress to enact legislation enabling the Negro masses to purchase land on easy terms."[27] He also was asked to help rescue the ill-fated Freedmen's Bank.[28]

If one were to take Douglass's arguments out of context (the former of each of the three preceding examples), one could even make him sound conservative and politically "color-blind," as historian Paul Moreno has attempted to do in his rebuttal to Justice Marshall's arguments in *Bakke* that Reconstruction was an early form of affirmative action.[29] Moreno bases his claim that Douglass opposed any such "race-based preferences" for African Americans on Douglass's declaration that they desired equal opportunity and not pity in his April 1865 speech in Boston, called "What the Black Man Wants." Toward the end of this speech, Douglass declared:

> What I ask for the Negro is not benevolence, not pity, not sympathy, but simply *justice.* . . . Everybody has asked the question . . . "What shall we do with the Negro?" Do nothing with us! Your doing with us has already played the mischief with us. . . . And if the Negro cannot stand on his own legs, let him fall also.[30]

For that matter, this attempted color-blind "makeover" of Douglass could also have conceivably been done with a document not noted by Moreno: Douglass's 1871 open letter in the *New National Era* to black nationalist leader Major Martin Delany, with whom he had served as coeditor of the abolitionist newspaper *North Star*.[31] In responding to an earlier letter written by Delany to that same paper, Douglass defends the track record of President Ulysses S. Grant's administration in hiring black federal employees against Delany's charges that there were not enough of them—and that Grant had only hired light-skinned African Americans. While Douglass acknowledged that Delany's proposal of a one-eighth black presence in every aspect of political life was the ideal, he argued that, rather than Delany's statistical formula, enforcing federal antidiscrimination law was the only protective measure worth pursuing. Douglass chided Delany:

> The mulattoes, on a solid census basis, ought to have so many offices, the blacks so many, and the whites so many, the Germans so many, the Irish so many, and other classes and nationalities should have offices according to their respective numbers. The ideal is equal and admirable in theory; but does it not already seem to you a little absurd

as a matter of practice? . . . Upon your statistical principle, the colored people of the United States ought, therefore, not only to hold one-eighth of all the offices in the country, but they should own one-eighth of all the property, and pay one-eighth of the taxes of the country.[32]

Douglass's differences with Delany on this question were actually more tactical than philosophical. Both demanded that whites live up to the egalitarian ideals of the Constitution, but while Douglass was willing to take a chance and "let the chips fall where they may," Delany wanted tangible concessions from whites to begin establishing official representation traditions. Despite their pro-black advocacy, their working-class roots, and Douglass's former slave status, however, both men were also known to display exasperation and even condescension toward the freedpeople in ways that reflected the contemporary popularity of Social Darwinism and the Protestant work ethic as well as a middle-class outlook. Douglass's solution was to give "them" time, and he urged Delany to be patient with the freedpeople, arguing

that natural equality is a very different thing from practical equality; and that though men may be potentially equal, circumstances may for a time cause the most striking inequalities. Look at our newly emancipated people, read their history of ignorance and destitution, and see their present progress and elevation.[33]

Moreno ignores these complexities in addition to bypassing other Douglass speeches and writings, such as this 1870 article in support of the Fifteenth Amendment's protection of black voting rights: "We certainly hope that the time will come when the colored man in America shall cease to require special efforts to guard their rights and advance their interests as a class. But that time has not yet come, and is not even at the door."[34] Was Douglass being hypocritical as many modern civil rights proponents of affirmative action are accused of being? Or do his apparently conflicting comments reveal a paradoxical unity of color blindness and color consciousness?[35]

The evidence shows that Frederick Douglass was struggling to change white attitudes while simultaneously using the protective and transformative power of the federal government—the same government that had been successfully won over to transforming a civil war into a war for emancipation in crushing the resistance of recalcitrant Southern states.[36] He knew that creating egalitarian institutions in a land of white privilege was problematic to say the least. "The white people of this country have in one thing been remarkably consistent," he told Delany. "They have hated and persecuted Negro blood wherever they have found it."[37]

While lauding postwar progress for African Americans, Douglass at the same time could be heard expressing bitterness at contemporary white weariness with the fight for equality (or "compassion fatigue" as it is often called today). He advocated racial unity and amalgamation, while maintaining the need for separate black political and labor organizations to advance black interests in a hostile white environment.[38] And he had no illusions that white behavior would change simply with the passage of time, as evidenced by his calls for the full weight of federal law, troops, and firearms to enforce civil rights using whatever means were necessary.[39]

In fact, in Douglass's own words, the "cartridge box," which was responsible for the respect and gains that blacks had won during the Civil War, led to the "ballot box," and he argued that they should now pursue military pensions and homesteading.[40] To his chagrin, he also saw the nascent labor movement already excluding black labor and splitting the working class.[41] He marveled: "Let any man claim for the Negro, or worse still, let the Negro now claim for himself, any right, privilege or immunity which has hitherto been denied him by law or custom, and he will at once open a fountain of bitterness, and call forth overwhelming wrath."[42]

To Frederick Douglass's way of thinking, it was not so much fear or hatred of "difference" that provoked white resistance.[43] Rather, it was the historical identification of citizenship with whiteness that was at the heart of the opposition to the black franchise and, it could be said, to affirmative action today. The resistance was (and is) not so much with the idea of sharing citizenship as it was (and is) with the prospect of the devaluing of whiteness.[44]

That resistance was implied in the reasons given by President Johnson for vetoing the 1866 Civil Rights Act, which he complained established "for the security of the colored race safeguards which go infinitely beyond any that the General Government have ever provided for the white race."[45] He said that it favored blacks, discriminated against whites, upset the balance between capital and labor in the South, and paved the way for black citizenship.[46] The report issued by Johnson's emissary, Carl Schurz, following the latter's postwar trip south in 1865, obviously did not shake Johnson's notion that there actually existed such a thing as white discrimination. Schurz wrote in amazement at what he saw and heard:

> Wherever I go . . . I hear the people talk in such a way as to indicate that they are yet unable to conceive of the Negro as possessing any rights at all. Men who are honorable in their dealings with their white neighbors, will cheat a Negro without feeling a single twinge of their honor. . . . The people boast that when they get freedmen's affairs in their own hands, to use their own expression, "the niggers will catch hell."
>
> The reason for all this is simple and manifest. The whites esteem the blacks their property by natural right, and . . . they still have an ingrained feeling that the blacks at large belong to the whites at large.[47]

III

Despite different political landscapes, a reading of the debates between Reconstruction-era abolitionists and their opponents reveal similar and in some cases even identical arguments as those used today or during the 1964 Civil Rights Bill debate—or for that matter those of the 1930s and 1940s when the civil rights movement renewed itself.[48] White popular opinion in the post-Civil War period was divided on the question of equality.[49] Postwar debates, whether in Congress or labor newspapers, included familiar-sounding issues like social and political equality, freedmen compensation and protection, the end of racism, black favoritism, black inferiority, and discrimination against Southern whites.[50]

When antiblack white workers were not actually speaking out in supremacist terms, they were also telling (familiar to modern readers) an opposite story: that freed blacks were getting preferential treatment—even as those same whites were actively or passively supporting Jim Crow laws and labor formations.[51] Voices of "moderation" like the *Workingman's Advocate* of New York City that often argued in print with confirmed racists nonetheless also agreed with them on labor's interest in opposing "social equality."[52] This only further highlighted the *Boston Daily Evening Voice* for what it was—a truly exceptional labor newspaper and the only one to champion both equality and solidarity, forthrightly declaring: "On what is our movement based? On one idea—JUSTICE. . . . We hope there is more intelligence among workingmen than to persist in the indulgence of an old prejudice when that indulgence is the ruin of their cause."[53]

In 1865, both the House and the Senate were predominantly Republican.

Many of the members were pro-black, especially the Radical Republicans. However, many moderate (or "Liberal") Republicans were at best ambivalent in their racial attitudes, and often split during the contentious debates over such issues as integrated schools, integrated streetcars, and Freedmen's Bureau appropriations.[54] The Democrats, mostly from Border and Northern states, were concerned not only with Southern "white rights" but also with what they saw as challenges to the privileges of their own white constituents.[55] They were later joined by ex-Confederate Southern Democrats who—genuinely or not—had taken the Union loyalty oath while remaining hostile to emancipation and equality.[56]

Radicals like Sen. Charles Sumner (R-Massachusetts) and Rep. Thaddeus Stevens (R-Pennsylvania) argued a strong, active federal stance in defense of African American civil rights. The fourteen black representatives and two black senators who served between 1869 and 1876 were no less confrontational against the opposition.[57] In retrospect it seems amazing that so much progressive legislation was engineered through Congress between 1865 and 1875 against so much white hostility and ambivalence—both in Congress and among the general population. This came despite compromises on such important items as female suffrage and school integration—which were made in order to pass the bills since Republicans sensed that time was running out. They were right: Reconstruction was betrayed in 1877 by political compromise with the Democratic reaction.[58]

It has been argued that Republican sympathy was largely the result of a desire for black votes, and federal legislation was necessary to protect that newly won franchise.[59] The party had already been "on a roll," so to speak, enacting a large volume of progressive legislation after secession took many reactionary Southern Democrats out of Congress.[60] Just as important a factor as political opportunism driving this settling of accounts against former slaveholders on behalf of their former slaves (approximately 200,000 of whom had just served the Union army in the winning effort) was the tradition and cultural logic of Anglo-American common law combined with a moral imperative, anger, and a denial of guilt.[61]

As debate moved from the Thirteenth to the Fourteenth and Fifteenth Amendments, the arguments became more contentious.[62] There were, to be sure, some diehards in the abolition debate like Rep. Chilton A. White (D-Ohio) who continued to maintain: "The right to service in slaves, then, is recognized as property," which he said could only be abolished by the states.[63] In fact, it took the intervention of President Abraham Lincoln (1861–65) to get the Thirteenth Amendment passed—just three votes over the two-thirds majority needed in the House.[64] Nonetheless, the overwhelming tide was antislavery, even if qualified by majority legislators like Rep. Thomas T. Davis (Unionist-New York), who asserted that abolition did not mean equality.[65]

However, the debates over "due process" protection for African Americans, the franchise, and the civil rights bills (including the 1871 Ku Klux Act) were stickier affairs. On the one hand, as W. E. B. Du Bois pointed out, the growing popularity of equality compelled Democrats to rely more on euphemism than direct attacks on black suffrage.[66] On the other hand, Democrats put Republicans on the defensive by raising the specter of integrated schools, cemeteries, public accommodations, interracial sex and marriage (called "miscegenation"), and "unqualified" and "bloc voting" by blacks.[67] They often did this merely by using the accusation of "social equality," a phrase that was still in use as late as the 1960s.[68]

The phrase "social equality" is comparable to "affirmative action," "forced integration," "forced busing," or "political correctness" today. Its usage was both specific and ambiguous code language that also suggested a "sexual slippery slope."[69] Opponents of equality who had grudgingly given ground on abolition with the passage of the Thirteenth Amendment now argued often bitterly against the Fourteenth and Fifteenth amendments. There was no need, they maintained, to create explicit "equal protection" language for blacks because that amounted to special protection for them and not for whites—not to mention the abrogation of "states' rights." (This latter phrase was invoked invariably to mean that it was the "states' rights" to regulate or even deny civil rights to African Americans.)[70] The Fourteenth and Fifteenth Amendments passed only after it was recognized that not only were blacks entitled to political rights as citizens, but they also needed them to break their servile status in the South.

The civil rights bills and their supplements caused the biggest outcry over the prospect of African Americans (often portrayed as filthy and abusive) "forcing" their way into hotels, inns, streetcars, railroad cars, and occupations. With this specter of "social equality" one can see the origins of Jim Crow and *Plessy v. Ferguson* in 1896.[71] If some Republicans (both black and white) seemed rattled by accusations of "mongrelizing" America, radicals like Sumner and Stevens were not afraid to ridicule opponents' claims that whites were suffering discrimination as a result of federal protection of blacks as a class.[72] The black legislators' arguments also provoked race-baiting by white legislators—even if the blacks had soft-pedaled the "social equality" issue.[73]

For example, black representative John Roy Lynch (R-Mississippi) rose to the floor on 3 February 1875 to respond to arguments made by those like Rep. William E. Niblack (D-Indiana) concerning the unfairness of social equality to whites in the debated civil rights legislation. Lynch retorted that "social equality" attacks were a smokescreen for white supremacy and turned his opponents' arguments upside down:[74]

> I can then assure that portion of my democratic friends on the other side of the House whom I regard as my social inferiors that if at any time I should meet any one of you at a hotel . . . do not think that I have thereby accepted you as my social equal. . . . But if any one should attempt to discriminate against you for [your] . . . race or religious sect, I would regard it as an outrage. . . .[75]

Far from exhibiting similar empathetic outrage at racial injustice, however, Lynch's "democratic friends" across the aisle were quick to respond to examples of discrimination by denying them, justifying them as local prerogatives, or countering with anecdotes about deprived whites who in at least one case allegedly "could not get a berth in the sleeping-car in Tennessee because it was filled with colored people."[76] The following day, black representative James T. Rapier (R-Alabama) also spoke up for the Civil Rights Bill. The way that he posed this question sounds remarkably familiar to some of today's arguments for affirmative action and sums up as well the abolitionist hope for reconstructing American democracy by changing laws, enforcing them, and thus breaking white supremacist behavior patterns:

> Suppose there had been no Reconstruction Acts nor amendments to the Constitution, when would public opinion in the South have suggested the propriety of giving me the ballot? . . . The only law that we have any regard for is *uncommon law of the most positive character.* And I repeat, if you will place upon your statute books *laws that will protect me in my rights, that public opinion will follow.*[77]

On the other hand, Sen. Hiram R. Revels (R-Mississippi), America's first black senator, in speaking against an amendment allowing segregated schools in the District of Columbia, added a disclaimer similar in tone to one used by some cautious proponents in today's affirmative action debate. It was (and is) a disclaimer with historical roots in circumspect black oratory that sought to improve life chances for African Americans while recognizing the implicit threat to white privilege implied in that improvement. Directly addressing the president of the Senate, Revels can be seen here reassuring skeptical white opponents:

> Sir, the white race need not be harmed in order to build up the colored race. The colored race can be built up and assisted, as I before remarked, in acquiring property, in becoming intelligent, valuable, useful citizens, without one hair upon the head of any white man being harmed.[78]

What need was there for Revels and other African Americans to raise the issue of "harm" to whiteness if they did not recognize the importance of that elevated status to most white people? Beginning in the next historical period we will see uplift ideology being used by the black middle class to mediate the struggles of black workers. (Uplift ideology would eventually inform the modern civil rights movement and the affirmative action debates as well.) While acknowledging what they believed were social and moral shortcomings in the black working class, uplift proponents also defended black workers, protested against discrimination, and challenged whites to live up to their egalitarian ideals.

IV

What was the actual intent of the Fourteenth Amendment: black protection or universal citizen protection? According to legal scholar Derrick Bell, its primary purpose was "to end doubt about the constitutionality of the Civil Rights Act of 1866."[79] In doing so it drove a stake through the heart of Justice Taney's 1857 *Dred Scott* decision.

Yet even during the 1870 debates over the franchise, the *Dred Scott* decision remained pivotal as it was both passionately praised and denounced by legislators from the floor of Congress. Among the latter was Sen. James W. Nye (R-Nevada), who declared: "Its author and the decision itself have sunk so deep into oblivion that the bubbles will never rise over them."[80] (Thaddeus Stevens had been even more explicit in December 1865, when he declared on the floor of the House: "Sir, this doctrine of a white man's Government is as atrocious as the infamous sentiment that damned the late Chief Justice to everlasting fame;

and I fear, to everlasting fire.")[81] White Democratic congressmen in 1870 none-theless attempted to deny Hiram Revels the Senate seat from Mississippi by invoking *Dred Scott* on the grounds that Revels could not have been a citizen because *Dred Scott* said he was not.[82] Revels's supporters countered by arguing that the Fourteenth Amendment now automatically made citizens of all persons born in the United States.[83]

Justice Thurgood Marshall would later point out in his 1978 *Bakke* opinion the incongruity of white politicians in the Reconstruction era condemning black "special protection" measures that were in fact designed as partial remedies while ignoring the political protections that even the lowliest poor white al-ready enjoyed.[84] Rebutting Taney's white supremacy of more than a century earlier as well modern-era arguments that have tried to de-contextualize the Fourteenth Amendment into one that was somehow never meant to protect blacks as a class, Marshall further pointed out how many benefits of the Freed-men's Bureau were reserved exclusively for the freedpeople.[85]

The 3 March 1865 law providing for a "Bureau of Refugees, Freedmen, and Abandoned Lands" (known as the Freedmen's Bureau) was in fact a vital and integral part of Reconstruction legislation.[86] Besides providing for the "freed-men," its resources were open to "loyal refugees" (white Unionists and any ex-Confederates eligible to take the loyalty oath).[87] But this fact did not deter opponents from denouncing the Freedmen's legislation as "solely and entirely for the freedmen, and to the exclusion of all other persons. . . ."[88] During the 1864 debate on the proposed Freedmen's Bureau, a House minority report in-credulously proclaimed:

> A proposition to establish a bureau of Irishmen's affairs, a bureau of Dutchman's affairs, or . . . those of Caucasian descent generally . . . would be looked upon as the vagary of a diseased brain. . . . Why the freedmen of African descent should become these marked objects of special legislation, to the detriment of the unfortunate whites, your committee fail to comprehend.[89]

Doubtless the members of this uncomprehending committee would have also failed to see the federal government behaving throughout its history as a kind of "Bureau of Caucasian Affairs," with white people as the *real* "marked objects of special legislation." More recent examples included the 1862 Home-stead Act with its free land for (white) "citizens," the 1862 Morrill Act that provided states with land-grant colleges that opened their doors to white students. The 1866 Southern Homestead Act, passed by Radical Republicans frustrated in their drive to confiscate plantation lands, unintentionally opened the door for whites (including ex-Confederates) to claim almost 80 percent of the land applications.[90]

For that reason, President Andrew Johnson (1865–69) signed the Southern Homestead Act, although he vetoed the Freedmen's Bureau Act that same year because he said that it would favor blacks as a "class" and make them "dependent" and that local bureau courts were unfair to whites.[91] (His veto was immediately overridden by Congress.)[92] Johnson's stated concern with the potentially crippling effects of compensation upon the freedpeople predates modern criticisms of affirmative action's alleged stigma imposed upon its recipients. No study, however, has confirmed such a thing—either during Reconstruction or since then—nor is there evidence of large numbers of white people disquieted by the inheriting of privileges based on skin color and not merit.

Protection for blacks during this period, Justice Marshall argued, was asserted both in a constitutional and legal sense, as well as in an aggressive extension of previously exclusive "white rights" to African Americans. For their part, conservatives objected that any form of black "protection" was both a threat to white supremacy and equality, disingenuously calling such "special treatment" unnecessary. Rep. Niblack, for example, was appalled at the prospect of the federal judiciary's "extraordinary machinery" being utilized with the 1875 Civil Rights Bill to levy fines of $500–$1,000 for civil rights violations.[93] Rep. Roderick Butler (R-Tennessee) responded by justifying monetary compensation for African Americans whose rights had been violated, because "owing to the fact that a class of persons in this country have taken away his wages from generations to generations, he does not have the means to carry on a suit, and as we have given him these rights it becomes our duty to give him the means of enforcing those rights. . . ."[94]

In even stronger language, Charles Sumner spoke out explicitly against the white racial "caste," calling it the "oligarchy of the skin."[95] In speeches both on and off the Senate floor he ridiculed the notion of "white racial oppression" as ahistorical and oxymoronic, while calling for federal benefits and protections explicitly for the freedpeople. Here is part of his exchange five years earlier with fellow Republicans during the 7 March 1870 debate on the Supplementary Reconstruction Bill. It shows even members of his own party being reluctant to make anything that appeared to be special provisions for African Americans, despite the fact that the Freedman's Bureau had gone out of existence two years earlier and the Homestead Act had seen the best public land already being taken by whites (mostly speculators):

Mr. [James W.] Grimes [R-Iowa]: Have we not done that [provided homesteads to blacks] under the Homestead Law [of 1862]?

Mr. Sumner: The freedmen are not excluded from the Homestead Law; but I would provide them with a piece of land where they are.

Mr. [William P.] Fessenden [R-Maine]: That is more than we do for white men.

Mr. Sumner: White men have never been in slavery; there is no emancipation and no enfranchisement to be consummated. . . .[96]

During the debate over the 1875 Civil Rights Bill (which eventually passed and became law), Rep. Charles Eldredge (D-Wisconsin) made these typical claims: blacks had become the "pet" and "especial favorite of the law," federal protection "must necessarily humiliate and degrade him," and Congress could not legislate equality anyway.[97] Those remarks echoed his plaintive rhetorical plea made earlier against the 1871 Force Act: "By conferring suffrage upon the colored race have we lost the rights our fathers secured to us by the Constitution? In giving freedom to the slaves have we become slaves ourselves?"[98] Why, asked other legislators with words familiar to today's debate, are blacks singled out for special treatment? Are not these protections for everyone? What about white protections?[99]

The Freedmen's Bureau, debated at the same time as the Civil Rights Act, represented the efforts of abolitionists, Republicans, military and civilian officials, and the freedmen themselves to carve out a land base that would give real meaning to emancipation. While some Republicans promoted black land ownership in the South to ease white Northern labor fears of "black competition,"[100] Freedmen's Bureau legislation was considered a key part of reconstructing the South by Sumner and the forces of abolition-democracy. Thaddeus Stevens warned other legislators in 1866 that if they did not approve "forty acres and a hut" for the freedpeople, they "shall receive Censure of mankind and the curse of Heaven."[101] The more common phrase "forty acres and a mule," like Stevens's variant, passed out of Freedmen's Bureau legislation and Reconstruction debates into African American folk wisdom as well as white mythological and historiographic ridicule.[102]

Similar to today's widespread white anger at even the phrase "affirmative action," Du Bois in 1903 would write of the Freedmen's Bureau: "The *very name* of the Bureau stood for a thing in the South which for two centuries and better men had refused to even argue,—that life amid free Negroes was simply unthinkable, the maddest of experiments."[103] By contrast, today's white anger considers providing traditional Anglo-American legal compensation mechanisms for African Americans as now being "unfair," "preferential," and too far removed from slavery to be applicable. White historical memory is still hostile to the perceived degradation of whiteness by any elevation of African Americans' social status: substantial black compensation automatically means white skin currency devaluation.

Notions of black land compensation expected by the freedpeople themselves actually began with the Confiscation Acts of 1861 and 1862, continued with the Freedmen's Department of the United States Army, and became federal law under the Freedmen's Bureau Act of 1866.[104] The land (awarded exclusively to blacks and loyal whites) was usually apportioned in forty-acre or "double minimum" eighty-acre plots. In some instances this land was confiscated from former slaveholders and sometimes set aside exclusively for use by blacks—although frequently the freedpeople were forced at gunpoint by federal authorities to accept unfavorable one-year contracts from planters.[105] There was even a scheme to provide transportation for freedpeople to settle along the Union Pacific Railroad land in the West.[106]

But the former slaves were not passive recipients of activity by abolitionists, politicians, or the Union army. Black soldiers, as well as the former slaves who either flocked to Union base camps or began cultivating liberated plantations, were the reason for the Confederacy's fall and the subsequent acceptance of African Americans both as citizens and as human beings. As Du Bois declared: "But when he rose and fought and killed, the whole nation with one voice proclaimed him a man and a brother. Nothing else made emancipation possible . . . [or] made Negro citizenship conceivable. . . ."[107]

Personal narratives, letters, and testimony of former slaves show their attempts to negotiate wages, own land, form their own political associations, call strikes, and hold office in places like the Sea Islands and coast of South Carolina, Georgia, and Florida, as well as Fortress Monroe, Virginia, and New Orleans.[108] Abolitionist officers like General John C. Frémont and Colonel Thomas W. Higginson, nonabolitionist officers like General William T. Sherman, and abolitionist missionaries such as those in the Port Royal Experiment in South

Carolina like Charlotte Forten, responded to the black refugee movement. Coming from diverse backgrounds, they were both empathetic and condescending, believing that the "downtrodden" former slaves needed "uplifting" as well as a chance to show the world their abilities to become productive workers and citizens.[109]

There were also wage disparities between black women and black men doing the same agricultural work as whites through the Freedmen's Bureau.[110] Historian Kevin K. Gaines notes the "competition between emancipated black and white workers, whose social identity was predicated on racial slavery, intensified with the Panic of 1873, and persisted in the economically depressed South."[111] He cites historian Gerald Jaynes's study of the development of a quota system that guaranteed half the jobs in the Southern port cities to whites. "Indeed," concludes Gaines, "the emerging racial hierarchy in the labor market paralleled that of fusion politics, which allocated political offices and patronage to whites despite black political majorities."[112]

The "black labor competition" thesis still popular with many historians today was addressed as if it were real in a July 1862 House committee report, and these representatives recommended Caribbean "colonization" (or deportation).[113] Noting this conceptualization of them as a problem, a plaintive letter from forty ex-slaves to Congress three months earlier requesting federal assistance to settle in Haiti concluded with this passage: "If we are regarded as an evil here (and we may become so by our competing with your white labor while here for the necessities of existence), send us where, instead of being an evil, we may be made a blessing. . . ."[114] Ironically, most of those rioters against black people in cities like New York and Boston during the so-called draft riots of 1863 were Irish Catholics who themselves had been subjected to centuries of "religio-racial" oppression.[115] How could white Irish-American workers, particularly those who had known oppression in their own country, simultaneously fear black competition for jobs while deriding black labor and black military service as incompetent? Noel Ignatiev, Theodore W. Allen, and David Roediger have chronicled a rapid transition: from Irish to "white" in one generation.[116]

The Irish made up most but not all of the working-class whites in New York and Detroit who were rioting against being called up in the July 1863 draft, six months after Lincoln formally committed the Union to pursuing the war to end slavery with the signing of the Emancipation Proclamation.[117] They had already been disinterested or even committed to preserving black workers' inferior status in the North by throwing blacks out of skilled jobs that whites coveted—as white workers had done in the South since slavery.[118] The affirmative action debate today goes back to those color-caste labor struggles as well as the subsequent Reconstruction-era attempts to reconstruct American citizenship without regard to skin color.

What ultimately makes capitalist rule possible, according to Karl Marx and Frederick Engels, is competition between the workers.[119] Since the colonial era native-born workers have clashed with immigrant groups (as well as with each other), and strikers and strikebreakers have managed to fight each other as well. But those mid-century struggles by white workers against black labor (rooted in colonial slave codes and indentured servitude laws and practices) were unique, ubiquitous, and effective. They were directed at *black labor*, not black strikebreakers or black "labor competition." There was actually more potential labor competition coming from the thousands of European immigrants pouring into American cities than from black workers.[120]

In fact, African Americans formed a small minority in Northern cities and were not the only ones used as strikebreakers. But it was not the Germans or other Irish who were massacred in their homes, had their genitals cut off and stuffed in their mouths, and driven from the docks and other workplaces, as well as their own neighborhoods. It was black people alone who were the victims of this ritual purification of whiteness.[121] Clashes between immigrant groups (or among the Irish themselves) notwithstanding, no German or other European workers or strikebreakers faced such massive organized murderous attacks.[122]

The July racial pogrom in New York City and elsewhere represented the last attempt to derail the war for slave liberation in the Union, as well as setting a "white" standard for the future of the American labor movement. That standard, ostensibly based upon "merit," for the most part relegated blacks to unskilled jobs, removed them from skilled crafts that they had excelled at and even dominated, excluded them from craft unions, or confined them to powerless Jim Crow locals.[123] The massacre represented something far worse than simply fear of "labor competition." It reflected extreme caste anxiety by those aspiring to become accepted as white or fearful that emancipation would lower the currency value of whiteness.[124]

51

V

Two of the greatest achievements by abolitionists and the freedpeople during Reconstruction were black education and the black male franchise—both of which provided a brief window of progress for African Americans as well as American society generally.[125] The debates and struggles over those issues with their overtones of Social Darwinism and the Protestant work ethic have much relevance to today's debates over affirmative action. For example, John G. Fee, the founder of Berea College in Kentucky, which admitted black students in the antebellum era, told freedpeople that "before public sentiment will cede to you equal positions, you must demonstrate not only equal capacity, but equal merit." Even Wendell Phillips told a black organization in 1873: "The world worships but one thing—success."[126] James McPherson notes the double-edged sword reflected in those two popular philosophies of the period:

> This belief in the Protestant Ethic as the route to success was widely shared in the nineteenth century, by blacks as well as whites. It was the basis of the antislavery conviction that all men must be free to make the most of their God-given talents. It motivated the self-help societies of antebellum free Negroes. It was the taproot of the free-labor ideology described so lucidly by Eric Foner. In the hands of social Darwinists, of course, this ideology of equality of opportunity could become a callous rationalization for inequality of condition.[127]

In other words, white legislators (among others) were challenging the alleged unfitness of the freedpeople, arguing that the "privileges and immunities" of citizenship really meant *whiteness*. While most white abolitionists measured the progress of black former slaves by white standards (not uncommon for that period and similar to "merit" judgments today), they also objected to "progress" and "advancement" being defined by opponents as something unattainable for African Americans.[128] Erstwhile abolitionist sympathizers like the influential *Nation* magazine urged a white Southern counterrevolution of standards to restore "good government" to the supposedly capable hands of white ex-Confederates and out of those of "newly-emancipated field-hands . . . barbers and barkeepers" and their white Northern "carpetbagger" allies.[129] But as McPherson has pointed out, "The few ignorant, bribe-taking black politicians did not inflame white hatred so much as did the large numbers of intelligent leaders whose effectiveness threatened to revolutionize the South."[130]

Reconstruction-era legislation was neither solely black exclusivist nor universalist but both. Although some today are loathe to call that legislation black-focused, blacks then were being contemptuously dismissed as "the special favorite of the laws" even before the Supreme Court's 1883 *Civil Rights Cases* decision made that explicit declaration.[131] Pro-black legislators had argued for coercion in the Reconstruction Acts, the Enforcement Act, the Ku Klux Act, the Force Act, and the Fourteenth and Fifteenth Amendments in protecting black voting rights nationwide.[132] And in defending the harshness of the proposed second section of the Fourteenth Amendment that penalized states that disfranchised black male voters, Thaddeus Stevens optimistically made this prediction of coercion's eventual positive effect on Southern white voters: "True it will take two, three, possibly five years before they conquer their prejudices sufficiently to allow their late slaves to become their equals at the polls."[133]

In fact, the substantial black presence in state legislatures as well as in Congress was testimony to black voting power. It also represented a kind of affirmative action corollary to the disfranchisement of many ex-Confederates, which was done to prevent the reestablishment of the slavocracy.[134] This small window of black political power furthermore encouraged the more progressive Southern whites—many of whom had fought for or sympathized with the Union during the war or were otherwise relieved to see slavery abolished.[135]

But without land, suffrage, opportunity, and legal protection, African Americans were left at the mercy of white Democratic Southern reaction that was already mobilizing to sweep blacks and sympathetic whites from office.[136] The reaction was consummated when the last troops were withdrawn from Louisiana and South Carolina in 1877. Without enforcement power, Reconstruction was finished.[137] Yet within the abolitionists' language can also be seen today's paradoxical affirmative action defense. Abolitionists believed it necessary to combine encouragement and coercion to make white people "share" citizenship rights and responsibilities while simultaneously ensuring that there should be nothing unfairly preferential to blacks or discriminatory against whites in those measures that ultimately benefited everyone. Coercion of whites was necessitated by guerrilla warfare, terrorism, and general intransigence symbolized by the Black Codes of 1865–66 and the Ku Klux Klan.[138]

The opportunity to achieve citizenship, productive laborer, and landowner status—which laid the basis for future generations of inherited wealth among average white families—was something that was ultimately denied to the freedpeople. Yet this had not been the sole intention of the Black Codes: ultimately they were designed to control black labor power.[139] Vagrancy statutes were enacted for blacks caught not working—which could mean fines or involuntary labor on the chain gang. An apprenticeship law also enabled whites (with "preference" going to former masters) to take over the custody of black orphans or black children whose parents could not support them.[140]

The white reconstruction of Redemption (as it was called) embodied in the Compromise of 1877 reestablished white control, locally overturning the effects of the Freedmen's Bureaus, the Fourteenth Amendment, and the Civil Rights Act.[141] Equality's gains were also retarded by growing Northern appeasement of the South and white institutions generally, such as the labor unions.[142] Eric Foner has noted that the Redemption statutes, similar to the earlier notorious Black Codes in repressing and controlling black labor, also had a new feature: "As required by the Fourteenth Amendment, the statutes were, on the surface, color-blind. . . ."[143] Embracing white privilege, then as now, apparently requires losing an appreciation for irony.

One significant irony rarely noted among historians was the precedent set by white New Orleans butchers in the United States Supreme Court 1873 *Slaughterhouse Cases* decision for today's opportunist use of the Fourteenth Amendment by white litigants who have used it to attack affirmative action as discriminatory toward white people. Not only did that white New Orleans labor monopoly claim that their rights as workers had been violated under the 1866 Civil Rights Act when Louisiana granted a monopoly to a slaughterhouse corporation, but they even claimed involuntary servitude under the Thirteenth Amendment.[144]

The court rightfully dismissed that claim, declared black representative Robert Browne Elliott (R-South Carolina) in a speech to the House on 6 January 1874 in favor of the Civil Rights Bill.[145] Elliott decried the likening of black people "in legal view to 'unwholesome trades,' . . . 'offensive collections of animals,' [and] 'noxious slaughterhouses.'. . ."[146] He defended the *Slaughterhouse* decision against opponents of black civil rights who interpreted the decision as a blow to antidiscrimination law. Elliott then drew a parallel between the decision's protection of the New Orleans slaughterhouse monopoly and the Fourteenth Amendment's protection of African Americans: "The only ground upon which the grant of exclusive privileges to a portion of the community is ever defended is that the substantial good of all is promoted; that in truth it is for the welfare of the whole community that certain persons should alone pursue certain occupations."[147]

Elliott had also earlier made this declaration: "It is true that only the fifteenth amendment in terms mentions the negro by speaking of his color and his slavery. And it is just as true that each of the other articles was addressed to the grievances of that race, and designed to remedy them, as the fifteenth."[148] Elliott additionally reminded his audience to consider the disparity between blacks and whites in literacy rates and in determining who was allowed to board railroad cars, stay at inns, or be buried in public cemeteries.[149]

During Reconstruction, the unfulfilled promises of the franchise, education, land grants, and antidiscrimination law established precedents for today's affirmative action debate, including the implications for black reparations, the omnipresence of white preference, and the "birthright of white jobs."[150] As Du Bois put it: "It must be remembered that the white group of laborers, while they received a low wage, were compensated in part by a sort of public and psychological wage."[151]

The "white race," as we have already seen, was invented in the colonial era as a social control mechanism and to resolve the contradiction between black slavery and white liberty.[152] Abolitionists and Reconstruction activists utilized language and activity encompassing both compensatory preferences and egalitarianism to try to dislodge white supremacy. But while "white citizenship" was challenged to some degree with Reconstruction legislation, the United States Supreme Court's 1883 *Civil Rights Cases* decision led to an undoing of those corrective measures, paving the way for the 1896 *Plessy v. Ferguson* and 1906 *Hodges* cases, which legalized and extended white privilege and black exclusion in transportation, employment, and all forms of social and political activity.[153] Citizenship guarantees once again became white-only.

Modern white hostility to affirmative action can therefore be said to have its basis in the *un*reconstructed ideology of the "white citizenship and free labor birthright."[154] If white labor could not be coaxed or coerced into accepting black labor in an equal status that would have strengthened the working-class movement, it found itself supporting the coercion of black labor into a subordinate status. As white empathy began to fade, the law both preceded and followed custom and popular prejudice in ending Reconstruction as America's first effort at "affirmative action." Today's black ambivalence toward affirmative action can be traced to abolitionist arguments that simultaneously embraced formal equality, compensatory preferences, and middle-class condescension as part of the overall opposition to white supremacy.

Reconstruction, said Du Bois paradoxically, represented "a splendid failure" to "make black men American citizens," provided "seven mystic years" when "a majority of thinking Americans in the North believed in the equal manhood of black folk,"[155] and established footholds, paradigms, and precedents for future struggles.

Chapter 3

BLACK NADIR, WHITE LABOR

Segregation, Immigration, and How the Polish
Became "White" in America, 1877–1933

I

"The last decade of the nineteenth century and the opening of the twentieth
century marked the nadir of the Negro's status in American society," wrote the
pioneering Howard University historian Rayford Logan in 1954.[1] From the end
of Reconstruction to the beginning of the New Deal African Americans were
subjected to the cementing of segregation across the country and especially the
South—at a time when some whites were enjoying prosperity and opportunity
while others experienced grinding poverty and labor repression. The black
community responded by both withdrawing into itself as well as continuing its
historic struggle for equality.[2] And just as there is a popular modern expression
"A white recession is a black depression," there is a similar historiographical
apartheid with regard to naming and imagining this particular period.

The "black nadir" that ran roughly from the end of Reconstruction to the
First World War coincided with Redemption, the Gay Nineties, the Gilded
Age, and finally the Progressive Era. Other optimistic and inclusive-sounding
names used by political movements of the period, like "populism" and "fusion,"
similarly conceal the betrayal of black people by those movements.[3] This was
an era that saw large-scale national white race riots, lynchings, black disfranchisement, black exclusion from federal employment, and black rural Southern

57

peonage.[4] As part of the roots of today's affirmative action struggle, this period reflects not a passive atrophy of rights and civil rights protest but losing battles for equality that would eventually give birth to new forms of black-led protest and organization against white privilege.

The most salient characteristic of this *American* nadir was the white affirmative action of race riots and lynchings. "Between 1893 and 1904," writes Kevin Gaines, "more than 100 blacks on average were lynched each year, compared to an average of twenty-nine whites."[5] Altogether, at least 3,386 African Americans were lynched between 1882 and 1930 in what was a steady reign of terror, while the number of white lynching victims drastically fell. The vast majority of black victims were in the South, with the only drop in mob violence coming after the "Red Summer" of 1919, then picking up again with the onset of the Great Depression. The figure is actually higher, notes historian Jacquelyn Dowd Hall, if one includes legal lynchings that white mobs demanded of the criminal justice system.[6]

While ostensibly conducted for maintaining the "purity" of white women or against the "threat" of black labor competition or strikebreaking, these were spurious reasons for lynching. The practical purpose that emerged for whites generally was one of both absorbing what wealth and occupations African Americans had been able to attain as well as to redefine the boundaries of what social activity would be allowed to the black caste. As the African American journalist and activist Ida B. Wells-Barnett wrote in her autobiography: "This is what opened my eyes to what lynching really was—an excuse to get rid of Negroes who were acquiring wealth and property and thus keep the race terrorized. . . ."[7] In 1929 a young black investigator for the National Association of Colored People (NAACP) named Walter White, who would one day become the organization's president, concluded after ten years of studying lynchings in the South that "lynching is much more an expression of Southern fear of Negro progress than of Negro crime."[8]

Precedents for affirmative action in this larger period include the promotion of white labor and retarding of skilled black labor, as well as the black middle-class' contradictory relationship with rich white elites and poor Southern black emigrants, the notion of "special treatment" whenever African Americans were involved, and an immigration "crisis" that excluded the Chinese in 1882 and privileged northern and western Europeans in the 1921 and 1924 Immigration Acts.[9] These latter laws became the first combined use of the catchwords "preferences and quotas" that determined who could enter among the restricted groups.[10] The "not quite white" eastern and southern Europeans became "Americanized" through a combination of both a new-found patriotism, support for militant unionism as the American Federation of Labor (AFL) became mainstream, and hostility to black workers as a way out of their own ethnic discrimination. This was a process similar to the white assimilation experienced by the eighteenth-century Irish-Americans as described by Noel Ignatiev and discussed in the first chapter.[11] At that same time, the "race science" of eugenics and the field of intelligence testing had their peak and origin, respectively, leaving us with a muddled so-called scientific criteria for establishing "merit" as a basis for job entry and promotion or college entrance.[12]

It could be said that what was left over from the Republican commitment to Reconstruction was a mixture of half-hearted habit from that party, as well the patronizing expectation that blacks would be satisfied with the new "compromise." The party of Reconstruction replaced the fight for equality with an acquiescence to Jim Crow and provided for the tiny black middle class the tokenism of appointment to certain designated federal jobs.[13] During this period, the Republicans exhibited some concern with losing black votes to the Democrats, while advocates of white supremacy like the Democratic Party and the AFL were making a paper commitment to equality even as they were cementing this new system of white racial privilege.[14] The political story of this period, according to Logan, was one of hypocrisy, betrayal, and counterattack:

> The nadir was reached, however, not because of lack of attention. On the contrary, the plight of the Negro worsened precisely because of the efforts made to improve it. The Republicans, [in 1889] once more in the White House and with a majority in both Houses for the first time since 1875, introduced two major pieces of legislation to protect the right to vote and to provide expanded educational facilities. The resurgent South, supported by old allies in the North and by new allies in the West, not only defeated both these measures but launched a counter-attack that further curtailed the already diminishing rights of Negroes.[15]

In this climate of "reuniting" white people North and South, any measures to improve the quality of black life and safeguard African American citizenship rights were commonly regarded among whites as "special treatment" to be avoided (a phrase generally studiously avoided, however, when it came to philanthropy or patronage).[16] The *Civil Rights Cases* decision promoted that concept of "special favorites" as it reversed the 1875 Civil Rights Act, after which the Fourteenth Amendment would then be used primarily by corporations and not find use again as a civil rights tool until the New Deal era.[17] That decision made no bones about why the Court found black civil rights litigation so annoying and insisted on referring to it as "special treatment." Even during slavery, the Court's majority proclaimed innocently (and incredibly), free blacks had enjoyed the *rights* of white citizens but not all the *privileges*:

> When a man has emerged from slavery, and by the aid of beneficent legislation has shaken off the inseparable concomitants of that state, there must be some stage in the process of his elevation when he takes the rank of a *mere citizen, and ceases to be the special favorite of the laws*, and when his rights are to be protected in the ordinary modes by which other men's rights are protected. There were thousands of free colored people in this country before the abolition of slavery, enjoying all the essential rights of life, liberty, and property the same as white citizens; yet no one, at that time, thought that it was *any invasion of their personal status as freemen because they were not admitted to all the privileges enjoyed by white citizens, or because they were subjected to discriminations in the enjoyment of accommodations in inns, public conveyances, and places of amusement*.[18]

Justice John Marshall Harlan, the former Kentucky slaveholder and Union army veteran who delivered the famous "color-blind" dissent in the 1896 *Plessy* decision, also dissented alone in *Civil Rights Cases*:

> It is, I submit, scarcely just to say that the colored race has been *the special favorite of the laws*. What the nation, through congress, has sought to accomplish in reference to that race is, what had already been done in every state in the Union for the white race, to secure and protect rights belonging to them as freemen and citizens; nothing more. The one underlying purpose of congressional legislation has been to enable the black race to take the rank of *mere citizens*. The difficulty has been to compel a recognition of their legal right to take that rank, and to secure the enjoyment of privileges belonging under the law. . . . At every step in this direction the nation has been confronted with *class tyranny*. . . .[19]

Reminiscent of the declarations of "affirmative prohibitions" by the Radical Republicans against black disfranchisement during the Reconstruction congressional debates, Justice Harlan made similar assertions in his dissent that are still relevant today. At one point Harlan declared:

> The fourteenth amendment presents the first instance in our history of the investiture of congress with affirmative power, by legislation, to enforce an express prohibition

upon the states. . . . The citizenship thus acquired by that ["colored"] race, in virtue of an *affirmative grant* by the nation may be protected, not alone by the judicial branch of the government, but by congressional legislation of a primary direct character. . . .[20]

Did the courts consciously play an activist role during this period? Rayford Logan argues that the Supreme Court was clearly fishing for loopholes in Reconstruction legislation in order to overturn it, causing Harlan to dissent in exasperation that the letter of the law was being obeyed to the detriment of the spirit, its original intent "sacrificed by a subtle and ingenious verbal criticism."[21] Derrick Bell locates decisions like this within a general probusiness historical context:

> In the final decades of the nineteenth century, American courts had become first the espousers and then the creators and propagators of a conservative ideology that permeated all aspects of American life. Called upon to decide pressing questions concerning the relations of labor and capital, the power of state legislatures, and the rights of big business, the courts forswore impartiality and came down heavily on the side of economic interests.[22]

Within this context, "whiteness" as property, political status, and economic interest was clearly favored over what could only be imagined by the justices as a desire for "special treatment" by blacks wanting to step out of caste definition and into prohibited free territory, so to speak. "Within this framework," concludes Bell, "racial law became an important conduit for the preservation and legitimation of the established order."[23] The *Civil Rights Cases* decision was the perfect "fit," as Bell calls it, whereby the North could put aside its differences with the South, giving the latter free rein to pass Jim Crow laws that ensured that both whitest and elitist boundaries and rituals would be enforced and protected.[24]

The United States-as-meritocracy—a vital component of anti-affirmative action discourse—is a "myth" not just in the sense of being a falsehood but also in terms of what mythologist Joseph Campbell has referred to as the "sociological" function of mythology "supporting and validating a certain social order."[25] Besides supplanting the predominantly white spoils system of government patronage jobs with the 1883 Pendleton Civil Service Act, "meritocracy" during this period also took on overt white supremacist and imperialist dimensions. Social Darwinist ideology—adapted by philosopher Herbert Spencer from the scientific work of Charles Darwin—became popular during this time as an explanation and rationalization for tremendous wealth discrepancies and living conditions in the American population.[26] Much-quoted millionaire monopolist John D. Rockefeller once told a business dinner audience: "The growth of a large business is merely a survival of the fittest. . . . This is not an evil tendency in business. It is merely the working out of a law of nature."[27] (Presumably this included machine-gunning strikers and other similar acts committed by workers' "natural predators.")

Another archetypal icon of wealth and power of this period was Andrew Carnegie with his aptly titled popular essay "Gospel of Wealth" (a work that Booker T. Washington once solemnly advised W. E. B. Du Bois to read and take to heart).[28] Contending with traditional proletarian grumbling over "fat cats" who inherited old money and never had to do any real work was the Horatio Alger "self-made man" myth that served as a "democratic capitalist" ideal fusion and actually had some basis in fact similar to that of the early Southern slaveholders arising from the ranks of the yeomen farmers and mechanics.[29] However, Alexander Saxton points out that the promotion of a collective white meritocracy actually came from *another* Social Darwinist, Josiah Strong, whose "Social Gospel" was distinct from Carnegie's promotion of individual talent being its own reward and with class mattering more than race. Strong had more of a relationship to the frontier Anglo-Saxon expansionist optimism of colonial and early republican times than did Carnegie's throwback to the old Whig Party with its emphasis on national prosperity and social order.[30]

Rayford Logan further points out the omission in Richard Hofstadter's classic work on Social Darwinism concerning the racial views of Spencer disciple William Graham Sumner, a professor in political and social science at Yale from 1872 to 1909.[31] "An examination of Sumner's writings prior to 1900 throws additional light on the effect of the new 'science of sociology' in convincing American thought of the inherent inferiority of the Negro," declares Logan.[32] According to Logan, Sumner pointed to Reconstruction law as an example of the inevitable failure that occurred "everywhere in history from coercive legislation enacted by one community against another."[33] Conflating "persons" into "races" and politics into social relations, Sumner elucidated a Social Darwinist rationalization of Jim Crow that evoked Justice Roger Taney and also forecasted the 1924 immigration debates:

No two persons were ever born equal. They differ in physical characteristics and in mental capacity. . . . Thus if you asked Thomas Jefferson, when he was writing the first paragraph of the Declaration of Independence, whether in "all men" he meant to include negroes, he would have said that he was not talking about negroes. Ask anyone who says it now whether he means to include foreigners—Russian Jews, Hungarians, Italians—he would draw the line somewhere. The laws of the United States draw it at the Chinamen.[34]

As discussed in the previous chapter, even the abolitionists (including Frederick Douglass) were influenced by Social Darwinism, clearly one of the most influential ideas of the age.[35] On the other hand, the egalitarian alternatives espoused by anarchists, communists, and socialists, as well as labor organizations like the Knights of Labor, by and large promoted color-blind class-consciousness, not specific opposition to white supremacy. At best, groups like the Knights made impressive gains in pulling black and white workers together into a common cause, but at worst these movements would come to characterize blacks as problematic and eventually yield to Jim Crow convention.[36] By and large, white workers continued to sacrifice progress for all for their own short-term gains.

II

It is hard to find anyone today who does not feel sympathy in retrospect for all the victims of corporate violence during this period, such as those who died in the 1892 Homestead, Pennsylvania, steel strike (in a plant owned by Andrew Carnegie), the Pullman railroad strike in Chicago in 1894, or the massacre at the Rockefeller-owned Ludlow, Colorado, coal mine during the strike of 1914.[37] In the many violent strikes during this period, dozens of workers were killed, hundreds injured, and many more driven from their jobs and homes, and into poverty. Those who survived were expected to tolerate the daily violence that was industrial work. In the aftermath of the Homestead strike, workers who had struck against the 18 to 26 percent wage cut (skilled workers made about $280 a month, unskilled workers about $200 a month) saw their wages drop to as low as $40 a week fifteen years later.[38]

It is also quite natural to feel anger today looking back at that repression as well as feel vindicated that labor eventually won the right to organize and be represented. In one form or another this is essentially what many of us learned in this country from a young age: that labor peace was won through a now-archaic class war. What does not seem natural, however, is the deliberate ignoring or downplaying of the persecution and forced segregation of black workers by white workers that is found in so much labor historiography.

This shameful fact of American labor history is often presented as being a question of misunderstandings, mutual hatred, or even the understandable rage of white strikers toward black strikebreakers, even while acknowledging that it was unfortunate for the labor movement and social progress generally that whites blocked blacks from jobs. According to this formulation, white and black workers were being used and divided by management, and whites did not know any better than to be exclusionary—but a workers' movement, albeit one with racist elements or tendencies, is still better than none at all. This view ignores how the pro-white element turned every forward movement of labor in this country into a reactionary one.[39]

That same pro-white element created new variations on its white supremacist origins—never finding the will to shake off that legacy. The isolation, failure, and even violence that often greeted attempts to organize black and white workers in the same union daunted postbellum labor activists in the Knights of Labor and played a part in that organization's downfall. In fact, during this period only the Industrial Workers of the World (IWW, or Wobblies) made opposition to white supremacy an organizing reality as well as a fundamental principle. In doing so, both the IWW and the Knights insisted (in what will sound familiar to readers today) that only class, not race, should matter. But the hostility of so many working-class whites to *any* challenge to white supremacy proved that race indeed mattered very much—as it still does today.[40]

Theodore Allen, quoted in chapter 1 on the essential white racial component of the Jacksonian spoils system of the early nineteenth century, makes the same point with regard to the late nineteenth century "reconstructed system of social control" known as the Cotton Mill Campaign. Mill towns were established throughout the South as exclusively white communities built around the textile factory itself, which employed entire families, many of whom were former sharecroppers or tenant farmers.[41] The express purpose of these Jim Crow mills, testified to by the mill owners themselves in 1901 before the U.S. Industrial Commission, which had been investigating the industry, was, in the commission's uncritical words, "that the white mill workers ought to be saved from negro competition; that this field ought to be reserved for white labor."[42] Low-paying, dirty, and dangerous as these jobs were, they represented a concrete racial preference, as Allen concludes: "In earnest thereof, the mill owners had awarded the poor white an annual income differential *vis-à-vis* the African-American equal to the difference between the share-tenant's $525 and the mill-worker's $900."[43]

Lynchings and race riots were only the most glaring examples of an overall hostility to the attempt by black workers to overthrow their degraded caste. They represented the will of a determined white minority (deferred to by an acquiescent white majority that generally only reined in that minority's "excesses") to enforce that caste law through terror.[44] Frederick Douglass addressed this issue with an 1884 pamphlet called *The Lesson of the Hour* in which he asked the question, "Why is the Negro Lynched?" His answer was that it was to terrorize and control black labor. Douglass's solution in turn was: "Let the white people of the North and South conquer their prejudices. Let the Northern press and pulpit proclaim the gospel of truth and justice against the war now being made against the Negro."[45]

Why were urban race riots against blacks considered necessary among whites in the South even after Reconstruction ended? "Blacks not only continued to vote in large numbers in most parts of the South, however," writes historian H. Leon Prather Sr., "they also held public offices. Thus the political riots were destined to continue until total black disfranchisement became a fait accompli in the South."[46] Too often forgotten is that riots represent explosions, not exceptions within social life. Lynchings were collective and frequently even many times festive family affairs where white people dressed up like they were going to church (they were often held on Sunday).[47]

Lynchings involved rural Southerners across class lines, while white race riots were urban as well as national in scope. Both became a kind of "festival of the oppressors."[48] The key element in both forms of violence was white anger at black wealth, employment, and trade. The most revealing race riot of this period occurred in the port city of Wilmington, North Carolina, in November 1898, where dozens (possibly even hundreds) of African Americans were killed and hundreds more were injured.[49]

Neglected by historians for nearly a century, the event is now more accurately described as a planned racial massacre and coup d'état than a riot—a word that implies spontaneity.[50] As Prather noted, even with the departure of federal troops in 1877, blacks continued to vote and hold office in the South—despite threats, violence, and the absence of federal or state protection.[51] In the last decade of the century, a political coalition in North Carolina (similar to that in other Southern states) between Republicans and disaffected Democrats called Populists produced the Fusion ticket that won victories statewide in the 1894 and 1896 elections.[52]

The problem with "biracial" (as they are commonly called) social and political movements in the United States is that they almost always have been on white terms, with whites jettisoning or even turning on blacks when sympathetic whites find the white supremacist reaction problematic for sustaining their movement. However much Populism and Fusionism have been praised since then as models of embryonic integrationism tragically cut down in their prime, they never were more than a marriage of convenience for whites in North Carolina, according to historian Helen G. Edmonds.[53]

Similarly, in his examination of Southern Populism—focusing especially on Texas and the Georgia movement led by Tom Watson— ethnic studies scholar Robert Allen reached these conclusions on that alleged biracial movement: it continued to support white supremacy, which led to its easy collapse when Southern Democratic politicians made their move to divide it; and its overtures to black workers and farmers on the basis of shared class interests were attractive to blacks but were never actually predicated on political or social equality.[54]

In fact, black activists, who were tired of being taken for granted by the Republicans, had formed even during the closing days of Reconstruction what could also be called marriages of convenience or desperation with either erstwhile or "closet" Southern Democrats in order to try and secure some political power as reaction began to take hold. Major Martin Delany, for example, ran (but lost) in the race for lieutenant governor of South Carolina in 1874 on one such fusion ticket with John T. Green, an ex-Confederate General.[55] After ex-Confederate General Wade Hampton won the governor's race in 1876 on the Democratic ticket, he appointed Delany as trial justice, along with eighty-five other black officials during his 1876–78 term as part of what today might be called that party's "diversity" policy, which in fact only involved black selection, not representation.[56]

Meanwhile, in 1890s North Carolina white supremacist diatribes continued to appear in the state's main Populist organ, and Fusion leaders never found a way to counter the vicious and divisive white supremacist propaganda campaign of the Democrats.[57] But for a time there was election reform as well as a political voice for blacks and poor whites. The subsequent wrenching of political and economic power that blacks accumulated by a coalition of wealthy and working-class whites serves as an appropriate backdrop for the compensatory aspects of the affirmative action debate today. And the courage of those white fusion advocates who maintained their commitment to equality even to the point of risking life, limb, and property is relevant to today's human rights activists.

The events of 1898 that led to the Wilmington massacre included a highly publicized rebuttal by black newspaper editor Alexander L. Manly to a call by a white Georgia feminist, Rebecca L. Felton (later the first woman to serve in the United States Senate), to lynch black men "by the thousands" and thereby "save white womanhood."[58] Manly, a descendant of an antebellum North Carolina governor and a female slave, who to all appearances was "without the slightest earmark of negroid features," also served as deputy registrar of New Hanover County.[59] There was considerable resentment by Wilmington whites of the black numerical majority, black wealth (there were a number of successful merchants), black political power, and black factory jobs. The *Wilmington Messenger*, a white Democratic newspaper, advised in September:

> There is a great injustice done to a highly respectable portion of the whites. . . . White mechanics by the dozens have walked our streets without money and without work often, while negroes were given steady employment. There have been instances when six, ten, twenty or more negroes were employed to work upon houses, even public buildings—while genuinely worthy white men had to stand around and look on hopeless and helpless.[60]

This was the perfect atmosphere for the statewide Democratic white supremacy campaign to invoke "Negro domination." A mass movement demanded that all whites join white supremacy clubs. Election day, 8 November, saw Democrats winning statewide and in Wilmington, as whites mobilized and also used fraud and the threat of reprisals to keep blacks from voting. Two days later some members of the white elite combined with a white supremacist labor movement called the White Government Union (many of them Irish) and the terrorist Redshirts to torch Manly's newspaper office. They attacked and drove blacks and their white allies from their homes, businesses, trades, jobs, and political office (where some Fusionists remained, their offices not up for election until 1900), with millions of dollars in property going up in smoke or passing into the hands of whites.

Ironically, Prather notes, after the massacre and political turnaround, coup leaders like Mayor Alfred Waddell established white preferences in municipal jobs—and promptly cut wages drastically as they enriched themselves.[61] A further irony was that "employers were soon complaining that the whites were poor workers. . . . [T]hey could not count and pile the lumber and run the mills."[62] African Americans had not been originally employed simply because of their willingness to work for lower wages than whites, points out Prather in countering a commonly held view of black labor. Large numbers of blacks *and* whites had been kept unemployed or underemployed to maintain a surplus of labor.[63] But now poor Wilmington whites, many of whom had hoped to profit from their revolt against black wealth, jobs, and political power, were left with nothing but low-waged "white" jobs and the "psychological wage" of their whiteness. One could speculate how part of that psychological wage included guilt and self-disgust as part of its collective memory.[64]

Was Wilmington an isolated incident or a "watershed," in the words of historian Thomas R. Cripps, whereby "white violence against blacks for the next quarter of a century would be organized, collective in strength and in daylight, and marshaled against concentrations of blacks in their own ghettos?"[65] Was the Progressive-era race riot indeed emblematic? Or was Swedish scholar Gunnar Myrdal right that "their devastation and relative fewness make them landmarks in history?"[66]

Besides Wilmington, post-Reconstruction white supremacist pogroms occurred in such cities as Danville, Virginia, in 1883; Phoenix, South Carolina, in 1898; New Orleans and New York in 1900; Springfield, Ohio, in 1904; Atlanta and Greenburg, Illinois, in 1906; and Springfield, Illinois, in 1908.[67] Judging by the violence and the demands for tighter caste restrictions, lynchings and race riots can be seen as representing merely the most egregious examples of the overall hostile climate that saw white workers frequently organizing strikes against the hiring of blacks: at least fifty such incidents between 1882 and 1900.[68] Even in sports, black players were run out of professional baseball by white players in 1889, and black jockeys were forced out of horse racing by white jockeys.[69]

This was not simply a case of extreme prejudice, "false consciousness," or capitalist manipulation at work. It also represented autonomous mainstream whites acting decisively when they saw official institutions hesitating in the protection of their dominant caste status. For example, it was not a fear of "labor competition" that drove white mobs to attack blacks in East St. Louis, Illinois, in 1917, killing nearly two hundred, injuring hundreds more, and driving six thousand from their homes. Contemporary accounts indicate there was a labor shortage in that city and throughout the North, as blacks migrated from the South to fill the space left by the decline in European immigration due to World War I in what could be called "black flight" from terror, lynchings, economic hardship, and the near bondage of sharecropping.[70] Helping to organize this white anger against the black refugees was the AFL.

The founder and president of the AFL from 1886 to 1924 (except in 1895), Samuel Gompers, was an English Jewish immigrant and president of the all-white Cigar Makers International Union. The consolidation of the AFL came about through black exclusion as well as nationwide anti-Asian hysteria that began in California. His union produced a campaign in 1874 called "Look for the union label" that is still used as a slogan today. But originally it was meant to indicate that the product was made by white, not Chinese, cigar makers who belonged to the white-only union.[71] By 1885 they had successfully driven Chinese cigar makers out of the trade, and similar campaigns were also conducted in the boot, shoe, and other trades.[72]

Gompers was outspoken over what he called the "racial problem created when Chinese and white workers were brought into the close contact of living and working side by side," as he later wrote in his autobiography.[73] He had voiced the same sentiments in 1901 when he coauthored a virulently racist pamphlet entitled *Some Reasons for Chinese Exclusion: Meat vs. Rice, American Manhood Against Asiatic Coolieism, Which Shall Survive?*, which combined a peculiar mixture of racial, gender, and dietary chauvinism.[74] Additionally, Gompers published an article in the February 1898 issue of the *American Federationist* that maintained that blacks lacked the "character" to be union members.[75] Finally, in an editorial in the June 1904 issue of that publication an organizer in the South warned that "the greatest competition we have in this section is the negro."[76]

The domination of organized labor by the AFL involved seizing the right to work exclusively for the white race, which was still under construction, so to speak. The issue of new European immigration still had to be dealt with. As Gompers later reflected in his autobiography: "The first step in Americanizing them [Bohemian workers] was to bring them to conform to American standards of work, which was a stepping stone to American standards of life."[77]

This "American" privilege was explicitly defined as exclusively white. Gompers declared in a Minnesota speech in 1905: "But the caucasians are not going to let their standard of living be destroyed by negroes, Chinamen, Japs, or any other."[78] Despite the fact that organized labor today ostensibly supports the ongoing campaign for equality, autonomous working-class whiteness through the sheer weight of conscious historical habit continues to exert a stronger force against black advancement through affirmative action than any conservative political party or ruling class formation.

III

Black protest in this period clashed with accommodation—with the response to white violence a crucial dividing issue. The ideology of uplift mixed protectiveness with defensiveness and embarrassment by the black middle class for the black urban and rural working class, and it could be seen in both the accommodationists as well as the "new abolitionists," as the black and white founding members of the NAACP called themselves.[79] In his 1899 seminal work of urban sociology, *The Philadelphia Negro*, Du Bois himself adopted the uplift perspective at the same time that he was refuting the scientific racism of Herbert Spencer and Francis Galton in promoting his radical notion that social problems like poverty and white supremacy were the result of environment not heredity. "How long," Du Bois asked rhetorically, "can a city teach its black children that the road to success is to have a white face?"[80]

Years before the New Deal social welfare state, black women's clubs like the National Association of Colored Women and the National Council of Negro Women combined uplift and service as they "erected a nationwide network of institutions and organizations welding together the entire black population."[81] This uplift ideology, an outgrowth of abolitionism in the antebellum era, can be heard in the rhetoric of civil rights leaders of the 1960s and affirmative action proponents today. But however similar this widespread uplift ideology was to that of Washington's, the latter's approach represented both a tactical retreat and a surrender, not a continuation of the struggle, and it could not have been expected to last indefinitely.

Washington's philosophy reflected an optimistic faith in the eventual emergence of humanity among white people: as a tactic for the times it could be also accused of representing extreme naiveté or even denial.[82] Furthermore, Washington's answer to discrimination against blacks in public accommodations and at the ballot box was to propose that discrimination instead be based upon *class*.[83] But for his pains Washington was met with this rebuff by Mississippi

Governor James Vardaman: "I am just as much opposed to Booker T. Washington as a voter, with all his Anglo-Saxon reinforcements, as I am to the cocoanut-headed, chocolate-covered, typical little coon . . . who blacks my shoes every morning. Neither is fit to perform the supreme function of citizenship."[84]

Washington's 1895 "Atlanta Compromise" speech did not contain new ideas, Rayford Logan has argued, but was notable in its symbolic surrender to the terms of a racial caste society by a leading black spokesperson.[85] Yet for Washington, it has also been argued, this represented a tactical compromise wherein African Americans could achieve a truce with white America by abandoning the fight for equality in exchange for more "even-handed treatment" now and eventual equality once blacks had somehow against all odds proven themselves to be deserving citizens. To Washington's way of thinking this meant more money for black education (in the manual, not liberal arts) and black acceptance of disfranchisement in exchange for a "share in the economic growth that Northern investment would bring."[86] "Cast down your buckets where you are"— Washington's classic phrase from the 1895 Atlanta speech—was also part of a suggestion that blacks should be considered for jobs over European immigrants.[87] It was an idea that the white establishment never took seriously.

The abolitionist movement had never quit fighting but was clearly on the defensive until the freedom movement was reestablished with the Afro-American League (1890), the Afro-American Council (1898), the Niagara Movement (1905), and the NAACP (1910).[88] Legal and social protections during this period were often cautiously proposed by Republicans but ridiculed by Democrats as unnecessary or representing a privileging of blacks and a return to the oppression of Southern whites.[89] "Separate but equal" was a necessary fiction in maintaining the "white republic," as Alexander Saxton calls it. There was no better example of this gross fiction than the public black college.[90]

The public black colleges—the normal, teachers', or land-grant colleges—were limited to manual and industrial education that would not cause graduates to compete with white skilled workers or professionals.[91] The old antebellum shibboleth of black "inferiority" that was used to drive Jim Crow laws was also accepted by white academics, particularly in the South, as justification for underfunding, understaffing, and woeful lack of resources for black public colleges compared to white public colleges. The black school was designed to "train a better servant" and avoid "ruining a good field hand" with an education that might increase social mobility or social awareness. Its institution in the form of the 1890 Second Morrill Act, which provided for black land-grant colleges to be established and receive equal funding as white schools, actually predated the 1896 *Plessy v. Ferguson* decision as federal recognition of Jim Crow segregation.[92]

For years, black public colleges were mainly boarding schools for primary and secondary students, while white public colleges offered opportunities to the sons and daughters of white middle- and working-class Southerners in schools that were rapidly rising to the prestige and academic level of liberal arts institutions. As late as 1928 the seventeen black land-grant schools had two-thirds of their students enrolled at the elementary and secondary level. By contrast, the white Southern institutions by the 1920s "had been transformed by the diversity of the land grant curriculum. In addition to their schools of agriculture, the white land grant colleges offered their students broad opportunities in schools of engineering, the sciences and medicine, the professionals and business, and the liberal arts."[93]

In the black colleges certain academic subjects, like civics and the social sciences, were studiously prohibited by Southern state legislatures. White students were taught the privileges and duties of citizenship and the Constitution; black students were given courses in "character building."[94] Additionally, in North Carolina until 1960, anyone who died without a will had a portion of his or her estate automatically sent to the University of North Carolina or North Carolina State University.[95]

The schools themselves were carefully designed to replicate the rigid caste system: its proponents freely acknowledged that fact. A past president of the Georgia Institute of Technology once declared:

> When the colored race all become bricklayers, somebody will have to carry the mortar. Whey they all become plumbers, who are going to be the helpers, the men who carry the tools? When they become scientific farmers, who are going to be the laborers? Are Southerners, we Southern whites? No. We have settled that question long ago.[96]

Governor William C. Oates of Alabama (1894–96), a former Confederate army officer, was even more blunt. Speaking at a graduation ceremony at Tuskegee University, he declared:

> I want to give you niggers a few words of plain talk and advice. You might as well understand that this is a white man's country as far as the South is concerned, and we are going to make you keep your place. Understand that. I have nothing more to say.[97]

By the mid-1930s, most students at black land-grant colleges entered at the college level but faced a curriculum that offered little but education courses. There was rarely any technical or professional training; the mechanic arts were represented by auto mechanics, tailoring, carpentry, and printing; and courses were still being taught on shoemaking and repair.[98] But in midst of this deliberate inequality, the preserving of black history and culture and the nurturing of black professionals (especially teachers) were the primary benefits of these separately unequal learning institutions.[99]

Meanwhile, at the NAACP annual convention in 1924—the same year of the new restrictive Immigration Act—Du Bois and the NAACP challenged the AFL by defending the affirmative practice black workers were using to gain entry into industries where white unions had excluded them: "The Negro . . . broke the great steel strike [of 1919]," read a resolution from the 1924 NAACP national convention directed specifically at the AFL. "He will soon be in a position to break any strike when he can gain economic advantage for himself."[100] And for perhaps the last time in a major national work stoppage, the Great Steel Strike of 1919 also witnessed divisions based on "old" and "new" European immigrants.[101]

IV

America's first definition of eligible naturalized citizens as "free white persons" (defined as "Anglo-Saxons" originally) in the 1790 Naturalization Act was already problematic to the English majority surrounded by growing numbers of German and Irish settlers.[102] Industrial expansion after the Civil War meant great opportunities for European Americans and European immigrants to America, as well as great opportunities to become impoverished and exploited in the fantastic enrichment of capital. The "right" to become "white" for eastern and southern European immigrants required overcoming first opposition and then hysteria from nativist western European Americans that culminated in the bigoted and prejudicial Johnson-Reed Act—better known as the 1924 Immigration Act. In a process similar to Irish experience, the requirements for acceptance of the Poles, Italians, and Russians into the white social club involved a demonstration of enmity for African Americans combined with rapid social and cultural assimilation through English language mastery, intermarriage, integration, and industrial unionism.[103] Herbert Hill has noted:

By the end of the nineteenth century the American working class was an immigrant working class. European immigrants held power and exercised great influence within organized labor. By 1900, Irish immigrants or their descendants held the presidencies of more than 50 of the 110 national unions in the American Federation of Labor (AFL).[104]

Between 1819 and 1900 over 19 million immigrants entered the United States—92 percent of them from Europe, and until the mid-1880s 95 percent of them from northern and western Europe (including Germany, Ireland, Britain, and Scandinavia).[105] In the mid-1880s, a "new" immigration movement began from southern and eastern Europe. Answering the call for factory workers in the East and Midwest were single males as well as entire families from countries like Italy, Russia, Hungary, Austria, and Poland—countries that were also seeing political and economic turmoil.[106] During the last decade of the century, "new" immigrants outpaced "old" immigrants' arrival by 1.9 million to 1.6 million.[107]

This second great immigration wave produced another crisis in American nativism, theorizes historian Matthew Frye Jacobson, pointing to a "fundamental revision of whiteness itself."[108] The 1911 Senate Committee on Immigration, chaired by William P. Dillingham (R-Vermont), compiled something that it called *A Dictionary of Races and Peoples*.[109] Eighteenth-century German anthropologist Johann Friedrich Blumenbach's five-race hierarchy was now superseded by a staggering 45 "races"—36 indigenous to Europe, with some considered "better" or more Anglo-Saxon than others.[110] Among other things the *Dictionary* stated:

> While darker than the Lithuanians, the Poles are lighter than the average Russian. In other words, they show more of the Teutonic and little or none of the Asiatic element of eastern Europe. In temperament they are more high strung than are most of their neighbors. In this respect they resemble the Hungarians farther South.[111]

This passage is a typical one, both for that publication and that debate, illustrating the convoluted and contradictory attempts of the day to define "pure" and "mixed" "races." Racial classification being the inexact "science" that it is caused these esteemed public officials and "scientists" searching for certainty to waver between hysterical fears of being overrun by "polluted European races" and acceptance of most them as being "close enough for the white race." The latter principle, of course, is nearly opposite the notorious "one drop" rule that has been used for centuries to both legally and socially classify African Americans.[112] That fact is certainly not accidental.

Furthermore, a kind of "rite of passage" (from "inferior race" to "white") can be seen here in the classification of the Irish as "Nordic" in this official public document.[113] For non-English-speaking Europeans, however, the rite (or right) of passage in real terms meant being herded like cattle through overcrowded federal immigration facilities on Ellis Island in New York City and humiliated by rude, overworked customs officials, who frequently, either out of contempt or convenience, "Anglicized" the last names of the immigrants on official documents as a prelude to their "Americanization" or "whitening."[114]

The leading proponents of the "race science" of eugenics were a major influence in the writing of the new 1924 immigration legislation.[115] The foremost eugenicist at the time in America was Charles Davenport, a member of the New England elite. His "laboratory" based on Mendelian genetic principles received contributions from such prominent figures as W. W. Astor, David Guggenheim, J. P. Morgan, the Rockefellers, the Vanderbilts, and Andrew Carnegie.[116] Other leading and influential eugenicists like Madison Grant, Harry Laughlin, and Lothrop Stoddard held forth before congressional committees on their theories of the critical differences between the "Nordics" (which included Anglo-Saxons) and the inferior "Alpines" and "Mediterraneans."[117]

Immigration hysteria combined with "Negrophobia" and was reflected in the surge of popularity of eugenics theory. Along with those already mentioned, another noted eugenics proponent was Carl Campbell Brigham, the principal originator of the Scholastic Aptitude Test (SAT)—today's leading entrance examination used by American colleges and universities. An outspoken white supremacist, Brigham opposed integrated education because he believed that blacks were "very inferior."[118] In his 1923 book, *A Study of American Intelligence*, he warned against diluting allegedly superior European genes with those of blacks and immigrants.[119] As legal scholar Richard Delgado points out: "Two years later, he became director of the College Board's testing program. He based his first test on Madison Grant's *The Passing of the Great Race*. Its purpose was to confirm the superiority of white test-takers pure and simple. It is no different today: merit is up-to-date bigotry."[120] In fact, the general use of standardized testing in the 1940s and 1950s coincided with the increasingly successful efforts by the NAACP to gain either the admission of blacks to colleges or the establishment of separate facilities for them if admission to white schools was not forthcoming.[121]

An earlier development of intelligence testing that so heavily informs the affirmative action debate today began in 1905 when French educator Alfred Binet created a diagnostic test to help French schoolchildren. English and American educators, however, translated his "intelligence quotient," or IQ test, into a kind of genetic performance measurement. The United States Army used this IQ Test during World War I to demonstrate "Nordic superiority," which figured largely in the 1924 congressional immigration debates. (One example of the culturally biased test questions: Polish, Italian, and Jewish immigrants were asked to identify American professional baseball team nicknames.)[122]

Also cited as part of this "scientific evidence" of intellectual racial disparities were the 1912 IQ tests given to a sample of Ellis Island immigrants that claimed to prove that the vast majority of Jews, Hungarians, Italians, and Russians were "feeble-minded."[123] Dr. Harry Laughlin of the "Eugenics Record Office of the Carnegie Institute" was the eugenics expert for the House Committee on Immigration, impressing them with his "findings" of mental and physical deterioration of Americans because of unrestricted immigration.[124]

For the industrialists, this new nativist concern with the "pollution of the national character" did more than unite them with Anglo-American working people. It provided an explanation and rationale (which they discussed frankly in their trade journals) for increasing labor turmoil, which they could blame on anarchists and other "foreign" trade union militants.[125] Noel Ignatiev noted a similar restriction as having been implemented just over a century earlier with the passage of the Alien and Sedition Acts of 1798 against the feared onslaught of what some Anglo-Americans called "hoardes of wild Irishmen."[126] The early-twentieth-century anti-immigration demagoguery that frequently conflated anti-Semitism with anti-Communism while simultaneously arousing fears of higher unemployment and recession made immigration restriction a popular cause.[127]

This is not to say that there was no opposition. Social scientists Franz Boas and Earnest Hooten spoke against the proposed restrictions and their underlying white supremacist, anti-immigrant bias, as did immigrant groups,[128] the New York congressional delegation led by Fiorello LaGuardia (D-New York), as well as Rep. Robert H. Clancy (R-Michigan).[129] In addition, immigrants themselves, Matthew Jacobson reminds us, "were often as quick to recognize their racial distance from the Anglo-Saxon as vice-versa."[130] For example, rock musician Frank Zappa remembered as a child growing up in the 1940s hearing his Italian immigrant parents derisively referring to the odd behavior of the native-born "white people" in this strange new land.[131] And David Roediger has noted how "Poles in the Chicago stockyards community initially saw the post-World War I race riots there as an affair between the whites and the Blacks with the Poles separate and uninvolved."[132]

Following on the heels of the 1921 Quota Act, the 1924 Immigration Act was passed in a vote that was not even close.[133] President Calvin Coolidge solemnly stated as he signed it in June: "Biological laws tell us that certain divergent people will not mix or blend. The Nordics propagate themselves successfully."[134] A happy immigration commissioner proclaimed later that year that new arrivals from Europe once again "looked exactly like Americans."[135] The act also injected "preferences and quotas" into the official language long before that phrase became derisively associated with black civil rights.

The new law established beginning 1 July 1927, a 164,667 total immigrant limit, using a 2 percent "quota" based on the number of a country's inhabitants counted in the United States 1890 census. (This represented a revision from the 3 percent quota based on the 1910 federal census and a 350,000 limit contained in the 1921 Quota Law.) For example, Italy's quota was now 5,677; Greece's was 310; Poland's was 6,524; and Cameroon, Ethiopia, and Japan each received 100. Great Britain, by contrast, had a quota of 65,721; Germany, 25,957; and Ireland, 17,853. Western and northern European countries were allotted 85 percent of the total. "Aliens ineligible for citizenship" were the Chinese under the Chinese Exclusion Act of 1882. Within the quotas, "preferences" were established for unmarried children under twenty-one, parents, spouses of United States citizens twenty-one and over, and immigrants twenty-one and over (along with wives and children under sixteen) with agricultural skills. "Preferences and quotas" in the 1924 Immigration Act combined to both qualify and quantify predominantly European immigration—the greatest overall preference going to those deemed "white."[136]

With the development of "race science" in the early twentieth century there came to be an assurance that no matter what one's family or individual shortcomings were, there was a predestination recognized by government, science, industry, labor, and society generally if one was "white." Years would pass and few immigrants or their descendants would remember or understand the process by which that happened. But they would alternately "remember" either that they or their immigrant ancestors had to "work hard" to be assimilated—or that it was no work at all. Either way they would be right.

It is a profound and bitter cultural irony that "criminal" and "drug user" are still common white euphemisms for black people—America's first working class. Meanwhile the archetypal proletarian has "his" name iconified in the mass media as "Joe Sixpack," the honest, hard-working, beer-drinking (providing us with the name), unassuming, slightly overweight, outspoken (yet potentially violent if pushed too far) blue-collar worker with a Chicago accent and a consonant-heavy Polish last name—the latter having once served as a marker of a "non-white" people.[137]

Yet one quote that stands out from this era should give pause to the face value popularity of "whiteness" today: "Race," said eugenicist Lothrop Stoddard, "is what people physically think they are."[138] (It could be added that race is also what *others* think "they" are.) Stoddard further theorized that the "Asiatic hordes" for centuries had "swept down on" eastern Europe, "mongrelizing its blood."[139] Stoddard's colleague Madison Grant made reference to white worker cultural bias in ridiculing the popular "melting pot" thesis of the day (similar to today's "multicultural and diversity" attempts to undercut white supremacy) that posed a polite opposition to anti-immigrant hysteria: "It is true," Grant concluded, "that they [native American "white" workers] will not work alongside of Negroes or Slovaks or Mexicans."[140]

But the frequency with which white workers referred to eastern Europeans as being "not white" during this period has been all but forgotten, as Noel Ignatiev points out. More important, Ignatiev explains, their eventual "transformation" into the white "racial status, far from being the natural outcome of a spontaneous process, grew out of the decisions by the immigrants themselves and those receiving them."[141] The Committee for Industrial Organization (which later became the Congress of Industrial Organizations, or CIO), founded in 1935 as a challenge to the AFL's conservative craft unionism, was, according to labor historian Thomas Göbel, "based on the mobilization of ethnic workers and on their willingness to join unions."[142] For once-despised European immigrants, this represented an interesting by-product of the 1924 Immigration Act:

> The process of assimilation had significantly speeded up after the quota laws of 1924, which lead to a disintegration of the ethnic communities and to a growing "Americaniza-

tion" of their members. This discontinuity in ethnic history explains much of the turbulent labor history of the 1930s. . . . The people most eager to unionize were second-generation Poles . . . who were trying to overcome the discrimination their parents had experienced.[143]

V

We have seen in the first chapter how the machinery of indentured servitude and racial oppression was something first "tried out" by the English on the Irish at home and in America before the invention of slavery in America as a color-coded caste. A similar process happened in the United States with the eugenics and immigration debates resulting in the passage of the Immigration Act of 1924—and the absorption of some of the previously "unassimilables." It was as if war had been declared, won, and then suddenly a "new" (or rather an "old" standby) enemy had been discovered to take the brunt of assumptions of inferiority and bad behavior, while the European immigrant became both ally and *American*. As Matthew Jacobson notes:

The period from the 1920s to the 1960s saw a dramatic decline in the perceived differences among these white Others. Immigration restriction, along with internal black migrations, altered the nation's racial alchemy and redrew the dominant racial configuration along the strict, binary line of white and black, creating Caucasians where before had been so many Celts, Hebrews, Teutons, Mediterranean's, and Slavs.[144]

Once again black people, both in official and in popular white formulations, became for whites "the alien in our midst," as eastern and southern Europeans were forgiven any possible racial sins they may have committed. Significantly, the landmark 1896 *Plessy v. Ferguson* decision that has come to symbolize the dawn of the Jim Crow era was initially pursued by Homer Plessy, a Louisiana man of one-eighth African American ancestry who was phenotypically white and did not even identify himself as black.

Plessy's arrest in 1891 for refusing to move from a "white" to a "colored" car was actually orchestrated with the cooperation of New Orleans railway officials, annoyed with the cost of having to provide separate railroad cars for blacks and whites.[145] Contrary to popular notions of the origins of this important decision, Plessy pursued this in the courts more as a case of mistaken identity than as a civil rights case. This is notwithstanding Justice Harlan's impassioned dissent on behalf of Plessy that is so well remembered today or the fact that Plessy's attorney was former North Carolina Reconstruction lawyer, judge, and abolitionist Albion Tourgée or, most important, the role played by the black "Citizens Committee to Test the Constitutionality of the Separate Car Law" in challenging the "Jim Crow Car Act of 1890."[146]

In fact, as Cheryl Harris has pointed out, Tourgée disagreed with organized black leadership, who objected to Tourgée's deliberate selection of a light-skinned African American for a Jim Crow test case, their fear being that a legal victory would only benefit those with light skin.[147] Also not commonly known or considered is the following argument made by Tourgée to the Court. Tourgée argued that most property and business opportunities were in white hands and that most whites would rather die than be black: "Under these conditions, is it possible to conclude that *the reputation of being white* is not property? Indeed, is it not the most valuable sort of property, being the master-key that unlocks the golden door of opportunity?"[148]

But the Court rejected this reasoning, saying that Plessy or anyone so aggrieved could certainly sue to have their "white reputation" compensated: if indeed he or they *were* white. "Upon the other hand," the majority continued, "if he be a colored man and be so assigned, he has been deprived of no property, since he is not lawfully entitled to the reputation of being a white man."[149]

This background makes it even more fascinating to note how regularly Justice Harlan's famous dissent is invoked out of context in the modern affirmative action debate. It is quite possible that if the context and the whole text were consistently brought to that discussion, opponents would never mention it again. "Our Constitution is color-blind," Harlan indeed declared, "and neither knows nor tolerates classes among citizens."[150] But it becomes obvious upon reading the rest of this famous dissent as well as his dissent in *Civil Rights Cases* (with its references to *Slaughterhouse*) that he considered this to be the ideal state that was still far from reach. More important, Harlan considered "color blindness" and zero "tolerance" of legal "classes" to be the result of the Reconstruction-era Constitution as opposed to the previous document, which he declared to have been especially compromised as proslavery by *Dred Scott*.[151]

Shortly after making his "color-blind" reference, Justice Harlan concluded: "It is therefore to be regretted that this high tribunal, the final expositor of the fundamental law of the land, has reached the conclusion that it is competent for a state to regulate the enjoyment by citizens of their civil rights solely upon the basis of race."[152] Harlan did not pretend that there were no such thing as legal classes in the United States. But his earlier dissent in *Civil Rights Cases* (quoted in the preceding chapter) echoed the words of Frederick Douglass: blacks need the special protections contained in the Reconstruction amendments and civil rights law just to become "mere citizens" because of a "class tyranny" exercised by white people.[153]

Yet Harlan offered this reassurance to whites in the same breath that he declared his impatience with white privileges and the fact of constitutional color blindness: "The white race deems itself to be the dominant race in this country. And so it is. . . . But in view of the constitution . . . there is in this country no . . . ruling class of citizens. There is no caste here."[154] How could Harlan have expected white people to behave any different legally than they did socially? Harlan himself apparently was no exception: in the latter case he framed his sympathy for blacks (which he would abandon three years later) within this anti-Chinese diatribe:

> There is a race so different from our own that we do not permit those belonging to it to become citizens. . . . I allude to the Chinese race. But by the statute in question, a Chinaman can ride in the same passenger coach with white citizens . . . while citizens of the black race . . . are yet declared to be criminals . . . if they ride in a public coach occupied by citizens of the white race.[155]

On the question of race during this era, many white Americans feared light-skinned African Americans "passing" and "corrupting" the "white race" almost as much as they feared blacks leaving the caste system entirely through equal opportunity in employment, civil affairs, and social life. H. Leon Prather points to Alexander L. Manly and other light-skinned "blacks by choice" who declared themselves proudly "Negro" and became leading proponents of civil rights, while Kevin Gaines quotes Alice Dunbar-Nelson's estimate that about 20,000 African Americans passed into the "white race" annually by the 1920s.[156]

Meanwhile, Booker T. Washington's brand of racial accommodationism lost its political grip with his death in 1915. While the movement for equality that succeeded him rejected white charity, its campaign also contained his uplift ideology tradition of apologizing for the "underdeveloped" black proletariat as well as laying claim whenever possible to political appointments where they thought they could exert some influence. Whether to salve their guilt or as an admission of cluelessness in personal relations, the practice of "tokenism"

81

marked official white concessions to representative advocacy. It represented a kind of super-democratic surrogate as well as the exception that proved the "rules of democratic meritocracy and black underdevelopment." Tokenism was an accepted political device that would serve as an antecedent for later affirmative action struggles—-along with the violent white reaction to even these small emblems of advancement. Kevin Gaines notes:

> Southern intolerance of even this limited tokenism was illustrated in 1898, when Frazier B. Baker of Lake City, South Carolina, was lynched by a local mob after being appointed postmaster. Here, again, by failing to intervene, federal authorities permitted the subversion of this spoils system for blacks.[157]

The Woodrow Wilson administration (1913–21) beginning in 1913 instituted segregation within federal government, calling it a "rational, scientific policy."[158] When black activist leader William Monroe Trotter led a delegation from the National Independent Rights League on 13 November 1913 to the White House to present President Wilson with a petition signed by African Americans in thirty-eight states protesting federal Jim Crow, Wilson told them that "segregation was caused by friction between colored and white clerks" and was therefore for their "benefit."[159] An account of this confrontation (reminiscent of that in the Johnson White House almost half a century earlier) was printed in the *Crisis*, the journal of the NAACP, which two years earlier had printed a statement signed by thirty-two prominent African Americans protesting Booker T. Washington's public denial of systematic white racial prejudice in the United States during his 1911 European tour. Here are two striking examples in a list of grievances that pointed to widespread systemic black discrimination and white privilege in education, housing, employment, suffrage, law, and everyday social life:

> No sooner, however, had we rid ourselves of nearly two-thirds of our illiteracy and accumulated $600,000,000 worth of property in a generation, than this ballot, which had become increasingly necessary to the defense of our civil and property rights, was taken from us by force and fraud. . . .
>
> We are forced to take lower wages for equal work, and our standard of living is then criticized. Fully half the labor unions refuse us admittance, and then claim that as "scabs" we lower the price.[160]

The response to this appeal by the mainstream press varied widely, but this one from the *New York World* could have been lifted verbatim from some of today's affirmative action critics after substituting retired United States Army General Colin Powell's name for Booker T. Washington's:

Undeniably, the black population of the United States has just grievances. So also has the white population in the United States.

Race prejudice is here as it is in Europe, and blacks are not the only sufferers. Three is brutal tyranny in industry, but the blacks are not the only victims. There are social limitations that are cruel and inexcusable, but the blacks are not the only ones against whom the gates are shut.

This is a world in which true men give and take. It is a world in which all must make allowances. It is a world in which, after all, men are judged not so much by race or nationality or possessions as by personal merit. Otherwise, how could a Booker Washington, born a Virginia slave, have "stood before kings" and associated for the greater part of his life with the earth's greatest and best?

We do not condemn the American men of color who have made this protest. We simply remonstrate with them. They are asking more than a white man's chance, and in the circumstances that is inadmissible.[161]

Somehow the "job competition" bogey returned with the black servicemen after World War I to afflict the white imagination—despite low unemployment and an actual labor shortage. The black challenge to an exclusively white armed forces led to white race riots nationwide in 1919—so violent and bloody that James Weldon Johnson, NAACP field secretary at the time, referred to them collectively as the "Red Summer."[162]

Also during this period the "price of the ticket" (as James Baldwin used to say)[163] for white women in the form of the right to vote (finally won in 1920 with the Nineteenth Amendment) was the jettisoning of some of the most ardent activists for women's suffrage: black women and men. A number of famous feminists (some of whom had once been abolitionists) like Elizabeth Cady Stanton and Susan B. Anthony made political alliances with Southern white supremacists and increasingly couched their arguments for women's suffrage in terms that white women deserved to be placed on a more equal footing with their men, as opposed to the undeserving and uneducated black men and women.[164] Rosalyn Terborg-Penn draws this conclusion: "Racism aside, many white women suffragists sought the vote only for themselves. Conversely, African American women were universal suffragists in the sense that their voices called for the vote for all citizens, not just for themselves."[165]

Despite the security that white caste status is supposed to confer, it also remains constantly insecure and requires constant "border patrols," so to speak—both internally and externally. Even in the midst of a general class conflict, the instruments for this caste policing were the latter-day "patrollers"— white labor. The truce between organized labor, management, and government during this period that would eventually become part of a New Deal partnership under President Franklin D. Roosevelt had for its legacy bitter, often bloody, struggle as well as white privilege and white exclusion of workers of color. Only the bravest white workers would raise the issue of protecting rights of black workers—and away from the monopoly enjoyed by ostensibly "fellow" white workers. As Du Bois observed in 1933:

> Thus in America we have seen a wild a ruthless scramble of labor groups over each other in order to climb to wealth on the backs of black labor and foreign immigrants. The Irish climbed on the Negroes. The Germans scrambled over the Negroes and emulated the Irish. The Scandinavians fought forward next to the Germans and the Italians and "Bohunks" are crowding up, leaving Negroes still at the bottom chained to helplessness, first by slavery, then by disfranchisement and always by the Color Bar.[166]

As we have also seen, adopting "whiteness" while abandoning empathy as well as their native culture and language became the price of admission to "American-ness" that was paid by southern and eastern European immigrants— even by the most militant industrial workers. Southern white workers moving north added their white racial solidarity to join with the immigrants in a volatile mixture. Consider, for example, how the Ku Klux Klan revived itself during World War I and enjoyed a national mainstream presence in the 1920s during economic boom times by targeting African Americans as well as immigrants and Roman Catholics as threats to American white identity, supremacy, economic security, and conformity.[167]

A common theory for this phenomenon explains it as a matter of the mass popularity of the 1915 white supremacist film *Birth of a Nation* by D. W. Griffith, based on the novel *The Clansman* by Thomas Dixon. There is no doubt that the film was a significant national mass white event. While blacks and their allies held protests, 25 million people (probably half of whom had never seen a film before)saw this motion picture. Historian Wyn Craig Wade has commented on the power of myth: "In an astonishing few months, Griffith's masterpiece had united white Americans in a vast national drama, convincing them of a past that had never been."[168]

Wade further relates the film inspired white civic and social groups to begin talking about reviving the Klan. But in fact, historian David Chalmers has documented how Alabama Klansman William J. Simmons had long dreamed of reestablishing the Klan as a fraternal organization and began laying the groundwork for a nationwide organization in anticipation of Griffith's film release. This time it would not be exclusively Southern but, in Simmons's words, one of "comprehensive Americanism."[169] By 1917, when the Klan assumed a paramilitary stance, it began to take hold among average white Americans in state after state both North and South, in both urban and rural areas. Thanks to Simmons's "vision" and the mass advertising techniques of Edward Young Clarke and Elizabeth Tyler, the spontaneous upsurge gave way to a concerted and organized movement. That movement counted millions of members nationally and for a decade controlled local civic organizations, college student groups, local labor unions, state legislatures; elected governors and five members to the United States Senate; and brought 40,000 members to march on Washington, D.C., in 1925.[170]

Returning black veterans were both cheered and attacked by white crowds following the end of the war.[171] For many whites, the fear of white status devaluation accompanied the fear of the status elevation of blacks through military service during World War I. There was anxiety among whites, especially in the South, over the rising expectations of black veterans after returning home. Generic conformist xenophobia that the Klan exploited was still based fundamentally on pro-whiteness and antiblackness. Resistance to the Klan had to contend with its violent nature, which, according to Chalmers, was paradoxically the very thing that both brought it to popularity and helped to undo it for the second time.[172]

The Klan claimed to hate immigrants and Catholics in the 1920s (besides their traditional targets, African Americans and Jews). They derisively referred to these European arrivals as "hyphenated Americans"—a common term used during this era. Not only did the Klan support anti-immigration legislation, but their Imperial Wizard claimed credit for the passage of the Immigration Act of 1924.[173] One historian considers their mainstream lodge format as evidence that they were "not primarily southern, terrorist, or white supremacist,"[174] but their literature and paramilitary activity contradicts this supposition.[175] As exponents of patriotic American Protestantism, what they invoked was the famous Protestant work ethic that was anything but meritocratic or color-blind. Yet they self-consciously promoted what they considered to be traditional American values of the Jacksonian era, including the pre-Reconstruction Constitution.[176]

By 1943 what was left of the Klan was encouraging Poles and other "hyphenated Americans" to join Southern whites—already incensed at black protest finally making gains in employment and housing—to combine in a pogrom against the black Sojourner Truth Housing Project in Detroit. This white violence organizing came after a series of "hate strikes" had already rocked the defense industry.[177] Looking back at 1924 Detroit (the year the mayor's race was almost won by a Klan member), Chalmers notes how "when well-to-do Negroes attempted to move from the crowded ghettoes of Paradise Valley, they met violent resistance. The Klan took the lead in organizing various neighborhood improvement associations to stand guard against such unwanted intruders. . . ."[178] A decade later, those same nonviolent associations as well as federal agencies and realtors would accomplish the same task, but nonviolently and more effectively—and even white opponents of the Klan would acquiesce in this white affirmative action in the area of housing.

VI

Years after first publishing *The Negro in American Life and Thought*, Rayford Logan published a revised edition entitled *The Betrayal of the Negro* in which he noted some other prominent black historians' opinions of the nadir as not having ended until after the First World War.[179] Logan himself did not answer the question directly but suggested a revision from the earlier date of 1901 to its gradual disappearance after World War I. "The most significant gains have of course resulted from federal intervention," he maintained, while also noting that the government's abysmal civil rights record during World War I contributed to the civil rights explosion of the 1960s.[180]

Significantly, the end of World War I saw the reemergence of black militance. It also witnessed the beginning of the decade-long Harlem Renaissance, which as historian Nathan Irvin Huggins has pointed out, "stands for something more than the actual works of art it produced." Even if that cultural movement itself was elitist, as historian David Levering Lewis has contended, it still represents an aesthetic expression of reawakening social and political consciousness in the black community.[181] If during this period even the most militant immigrant European worker was "becoming white," anti-white supremacist protest was becoming more self-consciously *black,* as can be seen, for instance, in the pages of the *Messenger* newspaper, published by two young black labor activists, Chandler Owen and A. Philip Randolph, or the Marxist African Blood Brother-hood or Marcus Garvey's popular black nationalist Universal Negro Improve-ment Association (UNIA).[182]

After the stock market crash of 1929 threw the American economy into a massive economic depression and the later recovery largely excluded blacks, the new black consciousness was ready to confront white labor, industry, and the federal government to correct this situation. For example, a black Chicago journeyman plumber named Edward L. Doty would later testify before the Fair Employment Practices Committee (FEPC) in 1942 how during World War I he had worked in the stockyards as a pipefitter's helper because the white pipefit-ter's union would not admit him: "We were used to training young white fellows and refugees who were brought from Europe over here—and after these refu-gees worked here for six months, they became foremen, and we colored men, we worked there year in and year out."[183]

Later, Doty and other black plumbers would form their own union after being refused entrance to white unions, but in 1933 contractors in government-financed housing projects only honored bargaining agreements with white con-struction unions. "Thus Negroes most severely affected by the Depression," writes Herbert Hill, who interviewed Doty in 1967, "were denied jobs on many construction projects that were created to relieve the effects of the Depres-sion."[184]

It is important to remember, however, that New Deal labor policy did not represent so much a liberal Democratic salvation of labor held down by hope-lessly probusiness Republicans. As labor historian Ruth O'Brien has shown, Democrats got the National Labor Relations Act idea from the "Republican notion of responsible unionism."[185] This was also a formulation that the AFL was coming to, exemplified in their no-strike pledge during World War I in return for an administrative agency that would endorse their right to organize (in contrast to the IWW opposition to both the war and to labor peace based on compromise).[186] The difference between the AFL and the Republican Party on this question was that Gompers thought the state should grant the same rights and privileges to labor as it gave to capital.[187] But Republicans "forced organized labor to sacrifice its organizational autonomy,"[188] laying the founda-tion for the 1935 National Labor Relations Act that would give the state discretion over labor-management relations through the quasi-judicial agency called National Labor Relations Board.[189]

What evolved during the Calvin Coolidge administration (1923–29) was a compromise in the form of the 1926 Railway Labor Act. O'Brien argues that the act imposed collective bargaining on the labor movement.[190] But as Herbert Hill points out, it also "sanctioned and strengthened" the power of the railroad unions, including the power to exclude and eliminate black workers—which they proceeded to do with relish—including terror tactics by white members to deprive black firemen and trainmen of their seniority rights.[191] Before we consider the New Deal, it would help to look briefly at one significant and also often overlooked piece of legislation enacted during the Herbert Hoover administration (1929–33) that epitomizes the compromise organized labor made with the state in a kind of "whiteness protection program," the Davis-Bacon Act.

In 1931 the AFL gave its support to a bill sponsored by Rep. Robert Bacon (R-New York). Signed into law that year, the Davis-Bacon Act ensured that every federal construction contract over $5,000 would require workers to be paid *"not less than the prevailing wage."*[192] "The stated rationale for the Davis-Bacon Act. . . ," concludes Armand J. Thieblot Jr., "was one of protecting local contractors and local labor from the predations of itinerant, low-wage contractors."[193] But Thieblot suggests further:

> It was a "Jim Crow" position, motivated by fears of job loss to blacks. One of the supporters of the bill testified as to the employees of one of the itinerant contractors, calling them "cheap colored labor," and noting with implied horror that it "it is labor of that sort that is in competition with white labor throughout the country."[194]

The bill's origins go back to 1927, when an Alabama contractor brought a crew of black construction workers with him to build a Veteran's Bureau hospital in Long Island, New York. Bacon was appalled that black workers were working on a federal project in his district and introduced the first of a series of over a dozen bills over a four-year period, finally teaming up with Sen. James J. Davis (R-Pennsylvania) to pass the Davis-Bacon Act. "Cheap," "transient," and "migratory" were thinly veiled euphemisms that were used in both houses of Congress along with explicitly bigoted references to black labor. One result of the act was to reinforce the construction unions' exclusion of blacks from skilled jobs and apprenticeship programs. Black construction workers, many of whom were then migrating north and beginning to practice skilled trades outside the Jim Crow unions, lost that chance with the act's provisions that workers be paid union wages:

The measure passed because Congressmen saw the bill as protection for local, union-ized white workers' salaries in the fierce labor market of the Depression. In particular, white union workers were angry that black workers who were barred from unions were migrating to the North in search of jobs in the building trades and undercutting "white" wages.[195]

Like the original conception of citizenship as one of "responsible" participa-tion in republican affairs by white men of property, Jim Crow "responsible unionism" (that also often rode by night) would cast a pall over the labor re-forms of the next decade—further ensuring the property of whiteness. Oppos-ing them were black and white latter-day abolitionists who could be found in the NAACP; the Urban League; the CIO; various black labor, social, civic, and religious organizations; and the Communist Party of the United States of America (CPUSA). The pro-black revolt against the reconstruction of white-ness that emerged with the advent of the New Deal in 1933 gives us the most immediate context for today's affirmative action debate.

Chapter 4

"WE WANT SOMETHING THAT IS . . . AFFIRMATIVE"

Black Labor Confronts the New (White) Deal,
1933–45

I

In August 1935, an unusually titled article appeared in *Opportunity*, the monthly journal of the National Urban League. It was written, the journal's editor noted, by "a Southern white man" named Harold Preece, and was called "Confession of an Ex-Nordic: The Depression Not an Unmixed Evil."[1] In this personal narrative, the author describes his change of consciousness from youth to adulthood: from early prejudice, to revulsion with racism, to colonization as the solution, to romantic racialism, to insights gained from being laid off from his white-collar job as a result of the Great Depression. But hard as it was, Preece experienced joblessness as a kind of epiphany in a way that sounds very familiar to us today in its "class unity and color transcendentalism" theme: "Outside the 'slave markets' of the Southern and Middle Western cities," he wrote, "I waited in line with other men—white and black—who spent their days frantically wandering to obtain the same tawdry necessities. Forgetful of Jim Crow, we discussed the appalling debacle and shared crumbs of cheap tobacco."[2]

While "black meets white during hard times" is an old and familiar theme in American historiography, what is unique here is that this unemployed white man was not commiserating with other white workers about their "really" being the ones in chains, nor was he making the hackneyed claim that all workers are exploited regardless of color—with some being exploited just a little more than others based on color. Instead, right from the subtitle we hear Preece actually finding some satisfaction with this socioeconomic and personal catastrophe. The Great Depression finally signified the leveling—or so he thought—of the American working class. White skin, Preece seemed to be saying, had lost its superior social status in the aftermath of the stock market crash of 1929.

Now, Preece declared, with this new-found activism he found himself walking with blacks in hunger marches, speaking out in black churches on behalf of the Scottsboro Boys, shedding his guilt, and discovering: "To me, white and black no longer exist. There are only oppressors and oppressed."[3] But Preece had already spoken too soon. The second phase of the New Deal actually strengthened whiteness and provoked black frustration to the point of laying the groundwork for the black labor and civil rights movements of the 1950s and 1960s, which were themselves antecedents to the later compromise that would be called affirmative action.

For all the inflamed rhetoric of the 1920s denouncing the "inferior races" of Europe polluting America's "pure" racial stock, the 1930s saw the once-reviled "melting pot" thesis (including sexual amalgamation) gradually being hailed as a positive good—as far as European Americans were concerned. It was somewhat akin to the North-South post-Reconstruction white reconciliation, only this time the rapprochement was a transatlantic East-West phenomenon. The term "Nordic" was becoming just another euphemism for "Caucasian" or "white" and no longer a marker of "better Europeans." In fact, there was no longer any such thing as the latter.

The social club known as the white race had expanded just in time for a devastating economic depression that saw the federal government eventually stepping in to provide jobs, housing, and relief in line with the traditional American racial differential. But this time it would do so on the basis of a more solidified partnership with organized labor. In effect, government was offering a compromise against a tremendous nationwide surge of strike activity in 1934 when about 1.5 million workers—from textile workers to teamsters to longshoremen—went on strike.[4]

The acceptance of this compromise by both organized labor and organized management, if grudging on the part of some, reflected both effective government coercion as well as recognition of the current impasse.[5] The institutional-ization of this compromise through the mechanism of supervised collective bargaining in turn forced black labor to move, along with its allies, into direct confrontation with capital, the labor movement, and the federal government, even as it was appealing to the latter two for aid, compensation, and representa-tion in the fight for equality.

The actual origin of modern affirmative action advocacy and policy came about as a result of pressure exerted by the mass movement led by black labor and civil rights leader A. Philip Randolph, who in 1941 had called for an all-black March on Washington.[6] The most telling omission in the history of af-firmative action was white labor's refusal to share the benefits of the first law to contain "affirmative action" provisions: the 1935 National Labor Relations Act (NLRA; also known as the Wagner-Connery Act, or simply the Wagner Act). The act established frameworks and procedures for workers' rights to union representation and defense against unfair labor practices, as well as a mandate for unions to behave responsibly with this new franchise. Section 10(c) provides that any victim of an unfair labor practice can report it to the National Labor Relations Board (NLRB), which may then "take such *affirmative action*, including reinstatement of employees with or without back pay."[7]

More important, actually, was Section 7, which guarantees that "employees shall have the right to self-organization, to form, join, or assist labor organiza-tions, to bargain collectively through representatives of their own choosing."[8] But the even more significant part of this law was Section 9. That section, as Herbert Hill indicates:

established labor unions as the *exclusive collective bargaining agents* through a process of governmental certification by the National Labor Relations Board. . . . [M]ost of the unions affiliated with the American Federation of Labor either excluded Negro workers from membership . . . thus preventing their employment in union-controlled jobs, or engaged in other discriminatory practices. . . .[9]

What became a victory for trade unions in fact constituted a defeat for Afri-can American workers when in 1935 Congress adopted and President Franklin D. Roosevelt (1933–45) signed into law the Wagner Act without the antidis-crimination amendment supported by civil rights groups.[10] Subsequent redress for black workers, as Hill points out, had to be found in civil rights legislation and court decisions not directly related to labor issues.[11] What is most ironic here is the fact that modern civil rights law has drawn not just from the 1866 Civil Rights Act, the Reconstruction amendments, and the interstate commerce clause of the Constitution, but also from the Wagner Act. (That act, which actually had begun to be used with regard to labor in the courts from 1890 to 1930 and with Republican railroad labor policy in the 1920s, made the temporary legal relationship between any voluntary association and its members, known as "principles of agency," a permanent part of labor law.)[12]

Despite the demands of the NAACP, the Urban League, and civil rights groups nationwide for an antidiscrimination clause in the Wagner Act, which its sponsor, Senator Robert F. Wagner (D-New York), supported, the AFL successfully fought against its inclusion. NAACP board member Harry E. Davis had warned NAACP President Walter White that "it is not a 'closed' shop which is in the offing, but a 'white' shop."[13] But President White's telegrammed plea to President Roosevelt—"we rely on you to prevent [the] sacrifice of [the] Negro to Jim Crow unionism"—went unheeded.[14]

Even with subsequent restraints placed on organized labor like the 1947 Taft-Hartley Act or the "right to work" laws passed in many Southern states, organized labor was now nonetheless firmly established and recognized on a *white* basis with the government's sanction.[15] As labor historian David Montgomery states in general terms: "The point to bear in mind is that this governmental activity was simultaneously liberating and cooptive for the workers."[16] Similarly, while a minority of white workers (especially those associated with the CPUSA and the CIO) understood the liberating potential of pro-black activity in building working-class solidarity, the vast majority would go the other way into co-optation.

II

Historians differ somewhat on the impact of the New Deal on black America. Some who offer critical examinations of Roosevelt's policies toward African Americans still believe that New Deal-era federal intervention "aided blacks to an unprecedented extent."[17] Others maintain that, despite the morale boost of that intervention, "most blacks were ignored by the New Deal programs."[18] Most agree that black protest was responsible for whatever gains were made. More recently, however, some historians have taken another look at New Deal policies and found that they actually constituted a new social contract with angry white workers whose impact is still felt today. An attempt was made, according to this argument, to relieve the economic misery of white workers at the expense of black workers—whose protests and demands in many ways forecast compensatory programs presently known as affirmative action.[19]

Roosevelt's New Deal indeed represented a federal sanctioning of white privileges and black discrimination in employment, housing, schools, and the franchise. This came despite the fact that his administration provided a forum for black grievances, and the Supreme Court during his tenure undermined segregation with its positive responses to black litigants fighting discrimination.[20] During this period white workers continued to acquiesce in and demand job preferences over blacks. White "hate strikers" sometimes had to be threatened by the federal government, their employers, and their own union leadership with firing, loss of union membership, and even loss of draft deferment.[21] As a traditional form of white labor protest the "hate strikes" provoked more protest by black workers and their allies, and pro-black demands now embraced equal opportunity, quotas, preferences, black representatives, and appeals boards in the fight against racial discrimination at the workplace and within the unions.[22]

The New Deal and World War II saw the federal government both saving and nationalizing capitalism, while simultaneously sanctioning whiteness and in effect nationalizing Jim Crow even as it was being compelled by black protest to begin dissolving racial discrimination.[23] The credit that Roosevelt got at the time and still receives today for challenging racist law was primarily the result of pressure from his more liberal wife, Eleanor, as well as confrontations with groups and individuals like Randolph and the March on Washington Committee.[24] During a time when the effects of a virtually unregulated capitalism had already begun to create massive social upheaval, a state-sanctioned set of programs in two parts reasserted what could be called a "re-invention of whiteness." These programs elevated white status in all spheres of social life as they further degraded the status of "blackness." It was this reinvention of the time-honored system of white preferences and quotas during one of America's most profound economic, social, and political crises—the Great Depression—that is just one of the many important stories not ordinarily told in today's affirmative action debate.

Popular notions of the New Deal are important to consider as part of the mythology as well as the academic discourse on that period. Generally the New Deal is seen as having served as an antidote to the Great Depression.[25] This is true even among conservative critics who today call for drastic cuts in New Deal survivals like Aid to Families with Dependent Children (AFDC), first established in 1935 under the Social Security Act. According to these critics, those policies were necessary but temporary measures and are no longer needed (especially, the subtext seems to read, with so many black people now utilizing them).[26]

Some of those programs—Social Security, unemployment compensation, and exclusive collective bargaining rights for unions—remain intact today, and some still carry discriminatory baggage from that period. The Federal Housing Administration (FHA), for example, established in 1934, continues to subsidize white wealth through the development of the white suburb.[27] The prototypical universal employment scheme through service and vocational training known as the Civilian Conservation Corps (CCC) overwhelmingly gave preference to unemployed young white males in both hiring and training opportunities.[28] A number of scholars, including Melvin Oliver, Thomas Shapiro, Gwendolyn Mink, and Jill Quadagno, have pointed out that the Social Security Act of 1935, the New Deal's hallmark, left out most African Americans and Latinos by exempting agricultural and domestic workers and marginalizing low-wage workers. In 1935, for reasons that included lower wages and a lower rate of unionization and military service (all products of discrimination), "42 percent of black workers in occupations covered by social insurance [including Social Security and unemployment compensation] did not earn enough to qualify for benefits compared to 22 percent for whites."[29]

Not only did the New Deal itself bequeath a legacy of white privilege, but the period also saw black demands for compensatory justice based on reparations for three centuries of American white supremacist practice—demands that were at times successful. In some cases those demands for equal opportunity included black representation and preferential hiring, as well as federal oversight boards.

How was the New Deal crafted as an instrument of white privilege and social control that required such protest? Were Roosevelt's hands tied by white Southern Democrats, or was his commitment to equality that thin? Was this a "Southern Strategy" or one for the whole nation? How successful was grassroots black-led resistance in attacking this white social contract? And how do the social struggles of that era relate to today's debate over affirmative action?

The New Deal era actually had two phases. The first (1933–34) provided relief from the Great Depression with programs to regulate agriculture and business and established public works and emergency organizations like the National Recovery Administration (NRA). The second phase (1935–41) provided social and economic legislation to benefit most working people.[30]

However, several of Roosevelt's programs survived until 1941–43, and it could be argued that were it not for World War II, they might have survived longer and those "war years" of 1941–45 that stimulated the economy might have instead been referred to as a continuation of the New Deal era. The postwar veterans benefit programs of his successor, President Harry S. Truman (1945–53), in effect represented an extension of New Deal politics. Those programs ostensibly provided for all veterans but in actual practice discriminated against black veterans, which provoked a struggle that ultimately led to the desegregation of the military during Truman's administration.[31]

The Great Depression, which in fact ended with the beginning of World War II, began in 1929 with the crash of the stock market: "At the depth (1933) of the Depression, 16 million people—a third of the labor force—were unemployed. . . . The policies of the New Deal relieved the situation, but complete recovery came only with the heavy defense spending of the 1940s."[32] In addition to those New Deal reforms already mentioned, its farm programs included the 1933 Agricultural Adjustment Administration (AAA), the Resettlement Administration (1935), and the Bankhead-Jones Farm Tenancy Act (1937); labor legislation like the minimum wage and child labor protection of the Fair Labor Standards Act (FLSA) of 1938; welfare programs like the Public Works Administration (PWA, 1933), Civilian Conservation Corps (CCC, 1933) and the Works Progress Administration (WPA, 1935);[33] and the Glass-Steagall Act of 1933, which was intended to reform the banking structure and was opposed by most of the banking community.[34]

The New Deal actually represented a vast differential in benefits that enabled white people to recover better than blacks could—even as it was giving aid to all the desperate and hungry.[35] W. E. B. Du Bois later acknowledged: "Any time people are out of work, in poverty, have lost their savings, any kind of 'deal' that helps them is going to be favored. Large numbers of colored people in the United States would have starved to death if it had not been for the Roosevelt policies."[36] But in a 1935 essay that was supposed to be published by Alain Locke in a series for Howard University (but was replaced by one more favorable to the New Deal by T. Arnold Hill of the Urban League), Du Bois had also pointed out that Roosevelt's policies promoted employment, higher wages, and landholding for whites over blacks.[37] If the second half of the New Deal was aimed at restoring labor peace and white employment, the first half of the New Deal aimed to rebuild the white property status quo, as summed up by sociologist Charles Abrams:

> The federal recovery program that began in 1933 sought primarily to correct economic imbalance not social inequalities. The emphasis on housing and land was no accident, for the groups chiefly affected by the economic collapse were homeowners, farmers, farm tenants, slum-dwellers, mortgage-lenders, and cities dependent upon tax revenues. No real pump-priming could be done without restoring these groups to a functioning role in the economy.[38]

As the federal government intervened to bring capitalism more completely under its authority, it also gave further sanction to white institutions in response to white labor rebellion. That included converting white members of the working class from renters to homeowners.[39] Consider the example of just two New Deal programs: the 1933 Home Owners Loan Corporation (HOLC) and the 1934 FHA. From their own documents we see that their business was not merely regulating housing but racial discrimination.[40] Both agencies not only respected existing segregated neighborhoods and racial housing covenants, they encouraged and institutionalized them while paving the way for the postwar white suburbanization of America. As Abrams points out:

> FHA adopted a racial policy that could well have been culled from the Nuremberg laws [Hitler's definition of what constituted "a Jew"]. From its inception FHA set itself up as the protector of the all-white neighborhood. . . . Racism was bluntly written into FHA's official manual [against allowing blacks, Mexicans, Chinese, and indigenous peoples in white neighborhoods].[41]

The New Deal represented a watershed in terms of resolving years of cyclical capitalist crises—including chronic depressions and class upheaval—with a new Keynesian social contract between the capitalist class and the working class. Named after British economist John Maynard Keynes, this new political model promised more security against chronic depressions with a program calling for full employment through massive government spending, subsidized growth, and welfare intervention. This effectively countered the Left's call for more workers' control, as well as blunting white labor insurgency generally.[42] But what about black workers? How far would they be pushed before fighting back, and how does that directly inform today's affirmative action debate?

III

As a key liberal Democratic New Deal centerpiece, the FLSA excluded most black workers from its child labor, minimum wage, and overtime protections for the same opportunist political reasons as other employment-related black exclusions (this applied to both industrial and agricultural workers).[43] For example, while the AAA rescued white farmers with cash grants for plowing under crops and slaughtering hogs, it was also misappropriating black farmers' grants, allowing many black sharecroppers to be cheated out of their checks, and subjecting black Southern sharecroppers and tenant farmers to local white control. Jill Quadagno observes:

> Roosevelt sought to stabilize his unwieldy coalition of northern workers and white southerners by refusing to back legislation abolishing lynching or poll taxes and by weaving racial inequality into his new welfare state. This was accomplished by excluding agricultural workers and domestic servants from both old-age insurance and unemployment compensation and by failing to provide national standards for unemployment compensation. These omissions were not random. Rather, they reflected a compromise reached with southern Democrats over the structure of the welfare state.[44]

The AAA sought to help cotton farmers by paying them not to grow their crop, thus creating a shortage and forcing cotton prices up. This program soon became a scam whereby plantation owners shared little or none of their subsidy checks with sharecroppers and saved even more money by evicting sharecroppers and replacing them with (usually white) day laborers.[45] This mass eviction (a third of African American agricultural workers: over half a million people), along with mechanization and wage cuts, became an incentive for blacks to leave the agricultural South for the industrial North and West where they would soon play a key role in the labor movement.[46]

The resistance by both all-black and integrated sharecropper unions to attacks on their livelihood produced not only an example of whites joining with blacks in a mutual effort and in some dramatic struggles like the famous 1939 Missouri highway encampment protest. It also inspired a struggle for black autonomy within the Southern Tenant Farmers Union (STFU) that reveals an affirmative action element with deep roots in the Black Belt South—complete with white rural workers complaining of black special privileges even as their lot began to improve.[47]

In 1938, E. B. McKinney, a black minister elected as vice president of the STFU, was threatened with expulsion after being accused by STFU President J. R. Butler of "agitat[ing] for a separate office set-up for himself for the purpose of allowing him to handle all business of the Union that anyway affects the Negro membership."[48] As noted by labor historians Philip S. Foner and Ronald L. Lewis: "McKinney became the spokesman for disgruntled blacks who believed that they should have a stronger voice in policy-making, while Butler demanded adherence to class-conscious principles."[49]

Before ultimately retracting certain "insubordinate" statements having especially to do with pro-black advocacy, McKinney had declared: "But we stand ready for a treaty with any fair minded concern. But [we] shall endeavor to retain race autonomy."[50] Yet despite the fact that the number of black sharecroppers dropped between 1930 to 1940 (from 392,897 to 299,118) and the number of white farm owners increased during this period, white sharecroppers during this period generally still complained that landowners replaced whites with blacks.[51]

Blacks migrating North were soon confronted with other New Deal drawbacks: "The minimum wage provisions of the National Recovery Administration (NRA) codes permitted white employers to replace their black workers, who had been paid less than the new rate, with whites."[52] The NRA, ostensibly set up to improve living conditions by establishing and regulating labor codes, in fact excluded over 3 million blacks (domestics, farm workers, laborers) from many of its codes and recognized a racial wage differential. That differential was being defended by Labor Secretary Frances Perkins, according to one critic, because "the low wage rates in the southern districts are based upon the predominance of Negro labor."[53]

Black writers did not hesitate to blast such excuses. Writing in *Opportunity* in 1934, Ira De A. Reid cataloged some of the more typical ones: blacks were "dull-witted," had a lower standard of living, lower skill level, fewer economic needs, and so forth.[54] Robert C. Weaver wrote that same year in the *Crisis*:

It was pointed out above that the most damnable feature of racial prejudice in America is the tendency to judge all Negroes by the least able colored persons. Obviously a racial minimum [wage] is an expression of such an attitude. Were this not true, why should Negroes be singled out for a special—and lower—rate of pay? . . . The efficiency of a worker depends upon his native ability, environment and specific training. These factors differ between individuals rather than between races. A racial differential, on the other hand would say, in effect, that efficiency is based on race and the individual black worker—because he is a Negro—is less efficient.[55]

After NRA Labor Advisory Board official Gustav Peck defended that agency's work in the September issue of the *Crisis* as actually having "narrowed" the black-white wage differential and even proportionately benefited blacks more than whites, he came under fire the following month in those same pages. Attorney John P. Davis declared that the NRA should have begun by first eliminating the racial differential altogether. He countered that Peck had used no statistics in arguing his position and criticized him for justifying differentials out of fear of upsetting white labor—Peck's fear being the subsequent replacement of all black labor. Davis also made this observation of the board itself: "Packed—as the Board was—with reactionary A.F. of L. leaders of unions, whose members were highly skilled— and practically all white—its interests lay in grasping advantages for these unions."[56]

With wage differentials by race codified by the federal government, it is small wonder that the NRA was referred to by many African Americans as the "Negro Removal Act," "Negroes Rarely Allowed," "No Rights at All," and "Negro Repressive Act." But whites opposed to equal pay in general for black workers still ridiculed the NRA, calling it the "Negro Relief Act" and promised "No Roosevelt Again."[57] While these opposing views might be dismissed today by some as simply prejudice that went with the time, "false consciousness," ill-advised narrow self-interest by both parties, or even another example of the success of divide-and-rule tactics, they are actually more indicative of white resistance to any black compensation as being somehow "privileged" and black resistance to the privileges of white compensation.

Far from being a quaint archaic anecdote, the example of these black and white opposing portrayals of the NRA very much informs today's affirmative action debate. We are still interested in examining as much evidence as possible that points to modern white opposition as having historical roots within any and all prior challenges to the American racial caste system. We have already seen white impatience with black demands for equality following the Civil War and will see more of it in the discussion of the civil rights movement of the 1950s and 1960s as well as the subsequent affirmative action debate. In these

Depression-era debates, we hear similar historical echoes from the nineteenth century as well as from the end of the twentieth: fear of upsetting white labor as well as whites predetermining the impossibility of blacks achieving that elusive goal called "merit."

Although black and white workers were at times operating in joint opposition to the NRA, writer B. D. Amis made this revealing observation in 1934: "At the same time that the low level living conditions of the Negroes are being attacked by the NRA, lynchings are increasing. Over 40 were lynched in the first year of the Roosevelt 'New Deal.' "[58] Scoffing at the often-raised excuse that white workers who bought into reaction were simply the pawns of a ruling class intent on dividing the working class, Du Bois laid the blame squarely on white labor's shoulders:

And while Negro labor in America suffers because of the fundamental inequities of the whole capitalistic system, *the lowest and most fatal degree of its suffering comes not from the capitalists but from fellow white laborers.* It is white labor that deprives the Negro of his right to vote, denies him education, denies him affiliation with trade unions, expels him from decent houses and neighborhoods, and heaps upon him the public insults of open color discrimination.

It is no sufficient answer to say that capital encourages this oppression and uses it for its own ends. This may have excused the ignorant and superstitious Russian peasants in the past and some of the poor whites of the South today. But the bulk of American white labor is neither ignorant nor fanatical. It knows exactly what it is doing and it means to do it.[59]

IV

Before the Civil War black people had formed "the traditional working class of the South."[60] Africans were originally brought to America as slaves not just as free labor but for their skilled artisanry, animal husbandry, and agricultural labor,[61] working as tailors, shoemakers, blacksmiths, weavers, tanners, carpenters, cattle herders, and every imaginable craft. Following the Civil War, blacks began to learn new industrial trades as well as continuing their monopoly over others. By the end of the nineteenth century white trade unions had forced them out of the skilled trades and blocked them from apprenticeships.[62] Writing in a 1936 economics journal, George Sinclair Mitchell observed that "the Southern trade unionism of the last thirty-odd years has been in good measure a protective device for the march of white artisans into places held by Negroes."[63] Black labor nationwide lost jobs as streetcar drivers, railroad firemen, switchmen, shopworkers, construction workers, shipbuilders, hotel service workers, and barbers, among others.[64]

Similar to the federal subsidizing of the segregationist housing industry and the ceding of local control to discriminatory Southern welfare agencies, Washington put its imprimatur on Jim Crow trade unions with the 1935 Wagner Act, making them a partner with government and business. That left it up to black workers and their white allies to take the initiative in challenging the trade unions' white-only constitutions, "rituals," and exclusionary as well as manipulative use of the seniority system, which was a key part of any collective bargaining agreement. Was seniority (which governed promotion, job assignment, and layoffs based on the order hired) truly the egalitarian innovation of modern labor legend, or was it actually founded as a "white jobs" mechanism. Or was it both?[65]

"Seniority itself," declares David Montgomery, "emerged from the confluence of twentieth-century managerial practice with the demands of workers in depression-born industrial unionism. Few nineteenth-century workers harbored any sense of long-term attachment to a particular company."[66] Montgomery goes on to point out how seniority in layoffs, not often seen in union contracts before the 1930s, represented both a welcome change for workers tired of arbitrary dismissals as well as a built-in barrier to black employment and advancement.[67]

Herbert Hill studied of some of the earliest of these modern-day seniority systems in the railroad industry. In the early 1900s the Georgia Railroad actually granted equal seniority rights to black firemen and other workers, which meant that many of them got the better runs. (Blacks by custom could not be engineers, which was a white-only classification.) In 1909 the Brotherhood of Locomotive Firemen and Enginemen struck the railroad to evict the black workers but failed.[68] The following year many railroad brotherhoods established contracts with railroads and made their aim the elimination of equal pay and black workers from the higher job categories. By 1940, the National Mediation Board was approving agreements with language like this: "Engines in preferred service shall be manned by fifty-five percent white firemen, regardless of their seniority."[69]

Seniority by and large meant fairness and equality *within whiteness*. Affirmative action as public policy actually got its start with black workers battling this and other industrial versions of "formal equality" that had the New Deal stamp of approval. Hill sums up the reality of seniority in this way:

> In many industries and trades, including jobs in the public sector such as in police and fire departments, white workers were able to begin their climb on the seniority ladder precisely because nonwhites were systematically excluded from the competition for jobs. Various union seniority systems were established at a time when racial minorities were barred from employment and union membership. . . . A seniority system launched under such conditions inevitably becomes the institutionalized mechanism whereby whites as a group are granted racial privilege.[70]

By 1940, over a quarter of the American population consisted of first- or second-generation immigrants—mostly those considered "white." Part of the naturalization (and assimilation) process for European immigrants and their offspring came in the form of governmental as well as labor concern with remedying the effects of discrimination against them, while blacks were having to wage their own campaigns for entrance into the unions, industries, and government employment.[71] With whitening came the access to seniority that now included both white and "newly white" European immigrants, while still excluding workers of "color."

The CIO emerged in the middle of the Depression and became a radical alternative to the conservative, older AFL. The 1936–1937 Flint sit-down strikes in the Michigan automobile plants were led by a CIO affiliate, the United Auto Workers (UAW).[72] With its expansion and name change in 1938, the CIO in many instances made inroads in black worker recruitment and advancement into industry and the unions. The black president of the United Transport Service Employees wrote an article in the October 1943 issue of *Crisis* called "Citizen CIO," in which he declared:

> One of the bright spots, in an otherwise dark picture of race riots, lynching, job discrimination, and the brutal treatment of the Negro in the armed services, is the aggressive fight being waged by the Congress of Industrial Organization [*sic*] along the racial front. Today the CIO has two new powerful weapons in its battle against discrimination—the Committee to Abolish Discrimination, formed to eliminate discrimination within its own ranks; and the National CIO War Relief Committee, set up to administer the collection of war relief funds from organized labor.[73]

But the CIO was also becoming part of the white labor establishment in privileging whiteness through occupational hierarchy, seniority, and even the union contract itself.[74] This was especially true "in steel, where the white majority insisted on maintaining its privileged position."[75] Black worker militancy was "conveniently ignored or contained during the mid to late 1940s," during which time the CIO also sided with white supremacist workers in Birmingham in 1949 who violently ousted the "the biracial local unions built by Mine, Mill and Smelter workers."[76] A year later the CIO helped break up the multiracial Food and Tobacco Workers local in Winston-Salem, North Carolina.[77] In Detroit,

[white] . . . hate strikes . . . were evidence that anti-Negro sentiment among the whites was so pervasive that a black candidate could not be elected to the International Executive Board through normal procedures. . . . Accordingly Negro [UAW] union leaders decided to press forcefully . . . for a specially designated seat for blacks.[78]

The NAACP and Urban League, acting in their role as black labor advocates, at times supported "quotas" as a necessary temporary tool for black inclusion. Take the case of the St. Louis Negro Housing Project with its "3.2 percent Negro skilled craftsmen clause, based on the 1930 census percentage of Negro craftsmen within the total St. Louis population."[79] With the white carpenters' local refusing membership "until all white craftsmen were employed," the Urban League joined with the Brotherhood of Sleeping Car Porters (BSCP) and the government and "forced the carpenters' local to give examinations to 15 Negro carpenters. . . ."[80]

The NAACP was also involved along with black workers in putting pressure on the Tennessee Valley Authority (TVA), which including the setting of hiring and training quotas to include black workers in that mammoth New Deal project that constructed sixteen dams within twelve years and brought electricity, employment, labor skills, and access to labor unions to thousands.[81] Using a mathematical formula in hiring became a logical way of imposing fairness by coercion upon recalcitrant whites in government, management, and labor. Its roots lie in Reconstruction experience as well as representing lessons learned from the failure of Reconstruction to impose fairness standards until they had become second nature in a society accustomed to discrimination as the status quo.

V

Black resistance literally began at the grassroots and employed a number of different tactics to fight discrimination. This was true whether it was Southern black sharecroppers who remained in the South and wrote letters to Franklin and Eleanor Roosevelt concerning discriminatory local welfare practices or those who headed for Chicago, New York, Kansas City, or Los Angeles to find factory or retail work by any means necessary—including strikebreaking.

When Du Bois was writing his seminal work *Black Reconstruction in America* in 1935, he noted that out of a total black population of 12 million, 3 million now resided in the North (largely as a result of the great black migration begun during World War I), while 9 million remained in the South.[82] In response to this challenge some CIO unions like the UAW recruited black members and in a few cases supported black demands for special representation and hiring in proportion to their numbers in the population.[83] Many blacks were finding work in the Northern automobile plants. But most CIO unions (including the UAW) failed to follow through on fighting white supremacy. In fact, after the 1955 AFL-CIO merger, numerous affiliates from both sides of that hyphen would become targets of discrimination lawsuits by black workers.[84]

There were also instances of African American workers demanding inclusion in neighborhood workplaces based on their percentage of the local population.[85] Examples of the new aggressiveness include the "Don't Buy Where You Can't Work" campaigns in Harlem, Baltimore, and Washington, D.C.[86] In Washington, D.C., the picketers for proportional hiring against Sanitary Stores (a grocery store chain in the black community) were taken to court and initially lost, but they ultimately won before the Supreme Court in 1938.[87] As historian William Harris relates:

> Also in 1938 blacks forced New York merchants to accept the first affirmative action plan in the country. In August the New York Uptown Chamber of Commerce agreed with the Greater New York Coordinating Committee for Employment to grant one-third of all retail jobs—executive, clerical, and sales—to blacks. Whites currently employed would not be fired to make room for blacks, but blacks were to receive preferential hiring until they held at least one-third of the jobs.[88]

The national offices of organizations like the NAACP and the Urban League were either ambivalent about these kinds of protests or downright opposed to them, just as they were initially slow in responding to rising militancy of black workers who were now joining and pressuring the CIO and the UAW.[89] An issue of the *Crisis* in 1934 saw a debate between Vere E. Johns and George Schuyler over the efficacy of the boycott weapon in black protest. On the one hand Johns chronicled the grassroots evolution of an earlier "Don't Buy" campaign, whereby Harlem community residents chose the Rev. John H. Johnson, vicar of St. Martin's P. E. Chapel, to lead a delegation to Blumstein's department store armed with $7,000 in sales receipts collected from black customers.[90]

Calling themselves the Citizens League for Fairplay, this black delegation asked for "fair representation" in black employment. Owner L. N. Blumstein, who admitted that he received 75 percent of his business from African Americans, refused. He was then confronted by a campaign that included leaflets, orators, newspaper editorials, community meetings, and a planned "monster demonstration parade and mass meeting." Johns declared: "Never before in the history of Harlem was such united action seen and it was not long before Blumstein's began to feel the pinch" and began to hire black clerks.[91]

But the other side of the *Crisis* debate found black columnist George Schuyler denouncing the boycott tactic.[92] Forecasting many conservative black and white "color-blind" arguments today, he declared:

> Mouthy minorities in the black belts of Chicago, Washington, Richmond, Baltimore, and New York, to name a few communities, have thus embarked upon a dangerous campaign of urging the substitution of black for white workers purely on a color basis without regard to either justice or fitness. This is the same type of rabid race chauvinism ballyhooed by Negro-phobic white elements in the South and which Negroes continually and rightfully condemn.[93]

Schuyler further chided blacks for not having secured enough training and establishing their own businesses or forming consumer cooperatives. He also warned of repression that he thought blacks were unprepared for and uncannily predicted today's white anti-affirmative action backlash, employing his characteristically bitter humor: "This is plainly war. . . . An insistence upon employment on a racial basis alone will be re-echoed with avidity by jobless whites and professional Anglo-Saxons."[94]

Despite being on record as opposing "preferences and quotas," both the NAACP and the Urban League also approved New Deal agencies that aggressively promoted black employment in the face of white employers' and white workers' own white preferences and quotas.[95] Minimum quotas for black construction workers in the PWA were promoted by Secretary of the Interior Harold Ickes, a former NAACP branch president in Chicago, and by black economist Robert C. Weaver.[96]

The CPUSA was also very instrumental in laying the groundwork for modern-day activist affirmative action, according to historian Mark Solomon:

> The Communists advocated special measures to compensate for generations of special oppression. The concept of "super-seniority," pressed upon the emerging industrial union movement, was a forerunner of affirmative action. At the same time, such measures were linked inseparably to the need for economic reforms to assure employment for all—thus grounding support for special steps to end discrimination in the overarching interest of the entire working class.[97]

Solomon cites African American CPUSA official William L. Patterson as an example of this activist paradigm:

> Within the Depression context, Patterson projected a two-layered 'affirmative action' for the working class in general and for the black masses in particular. Thus, the needs of blacks were now on the table as the most compelling aspect of the needs of all working people. By 1932, the unemployed movement in general was pressing special consideration for doubly burdened blacks. An Unemployed Council group burst into the San Diego City Hall to demand a special quota for Negroes in hiring for work on a proposed dam project.[98]

Another affirmative action antecedent with roots in late-nineteenth-century tokenism was black representation in the Roosevelt administration. For African American activists, these were not mere tokens but rather a corollary to the campaigns going on in the community and on the shop floor. Ickes's and Weaver's presence in the Roosevelt administration, along with Mary McLeod Bethune's position in the National Youth Administration (NYA), formed part of an ongoing demand for black representation by appointment to help promote black interests in an indifferent or hostile environment.[99] As Herbert Hill has stated:

And the so-called "Black Cabinet," consisting of about two-dozen Negro advisers, did succeed in obtaining some assistance for at least a portion of the black community not, in fact, by abolishing discrimination but by managing on occasion to make it less flagrant. Several members of the Black Cabinet agreed later that at best the emergency assistance they obtained was on a segregated basis.[100]

While noting the pitfalls of tokenism and black entrepreneurial opportunism, Du Bois reprinted in a 1935 essay the purported minutes of a 1933 Roosevelt administration "Special Industrial Recovery Board" meeting that included a fascinating and revealing exchange. In this official discussion of the need to respond to black protest by appointing a black advisory committee, the following passage sums up the effectiveness of grassroots struggle as well as the social control aspect of what years later would be called affirmative action programs:

> Chairman Ickes: I think Negroes have to be dealt with as individuals.
>
> [Labor] Secretary [Frances] Perkins: The Negroes are treated differently as workers than any other group of people and it is just possible that one who has not experienced discrimination against Negroes and who has the necessary training in other fields is not qualified to follow up their complaints. Other things being equal, a Negro investigator sent out would be able to bring back the facts better than anybody else.
>
> General [Hugh] Johnson: If the Board thought well of it, we could appoint a Negro Advisory Committee. They are becoming very clamorous.[101]

VI

The apotheosis of black protest during the New Deal era was the March on Washington Movement (MOWM) organized by A. Philip Randolph against Jim Crow in the defense industry. Randolph was an organizer and leader in three militant black working-class organizations—the BSCP, the MOWM, and the Negro National Labor Congress (NNLC).[102] With a war on against European fascism, white racism at home was not only embarrassing to the Roosevelt administration, but the threatened black revolt against it was considered potentially disastrous.

According to Randolph's biographer, the idea for the March on Washington by 10,000 African Americans was Randolph's. After he first raised the idea during his lectures around the country, however, the response grew like wildfire to the extent that he soon felt compelled to raise that figure to 100,000.[103] Weary of the interminable, fruitless forays by black leaders to the White House to remedy this situation, Randolph proposed a mass activity by black people that would dramatize their exclusion from the war effort, both in segregated military units and on the shop floor. Finally, at a June White House meeting just weeks before the projected July 1941 march, Roosevelt suggested that he could simply make some phone calls to the heads of the defense plants and ask them to ensure black hiring:

"We want you to do more than that," Randolph said. "We want something concrete, something tangible, definite, positive, and affirmative."

"What do you mean?"

"Mr. President, we want you to issue an executive order making it mandatory that Negroes be permitted to work in these plants."[104]

Roosevelt balked—but he soon relented, unwilling to gamble on a potentially massive black protest march being simply a bluff by Randolph.[105] A committee was then formed to write up what became Executive Order 8802. Much of the wording came from Randolph himself, as can be seen even in the first words of the title: "Reaffirming Policy of Full Participation in the Defense Program. . . ."[106] The order banned discrimination and established the Fair Employment Practice Committee (FEPC), although Randolph tactically decided to save the fight over Jim Crow military units for a later date.[107] The FEPC was a weak federal agency with no enforcement powers, was opposed by the AFL, and was dissolved right after the war, but Herbert Hill notes:[108]

Yet the important fact is that the March on Washington Movement had forced the federal government to admit publicly that blacks suffered from discrimination in employment and that the government had a responsibility to remedy it. The action forced an end to official racism in one important sector of American life.[109]

The FEPC represented a symbolic as well as a material victory that paved the way for other legal challenges and mass protests against Jim Crow. Historian Manning Marable concludes: "This executive order not only greatly increased the number of African-Americans who were employed in wartime industries, but expanded the political idea that government could not take a passive role in the dismantling of institutional racism."[110] In fact, there were state FEPCs that outlasted the federal FEPC.[111] The latter, never very popular in Congress, came under Southern filibuster attack in 1946 and was abolished that year.[112]

We will never know, as historian Louis Ruchames points out, how much of an effect the FEPC actually had in opening up the defense plants to black workers, because employers soon began hiring black workers out of economic necessity.[113] Full employment at livable wages was a product of the war economy of 1940, the same year the military draft was instituted. While the defense industry begged for workers and instituted emergency training programs, the number of blacks on WPA rolls actually rose from 14.2 to 17.5 percent from 1939 to 1942.

Surveys revealed that 51 percent of new manufacturing jobs would be white-only.[114]

It could be that Roosevelt's executive order and the establishment of the FEPC provided the official rationale that employers needed against their own bigoted members as well as against recalcitrant white workers who opposed the entry of blacks into their plants. But most significantly, "the committee's existence had served to spur militancy among black workers."[115] And the fruits of black protest were far from minimal, although even the gains reveal obvious and familiar shortcomings:

> By March of 1942, black workers constituted only 2.5 to 3 percent of all war production workers, most of whom were relegated to low-skill, low-wage positions. The employment picture improved more rapidly after 1942: by April of 1944, blacks made up 8 percent . . . [and] the number of black workers in trade unions increased from 150,000 in 1935 to 1.25 million by the war's end . . . [mostly in] unskilled, menial jobs.[116]

Demonstrating both the pluses and minuses of centralized political leadership in social struggles, A. Philip Randolph, who had combined black nationalism and trade unionism in organizing the BSCP, acted on behalf of the mass movement of African Americans as well as made executive decisions for it. Notably, the eight-point "Program of the March on Washington Movement" not only demanded enforcement of the Reconstruction amendments but also included demands for "colored and minority group representation on all administrative agencies" and "representation for the colored and minority racial groups on all missions . . . to the peace conference. . . ."[117] These demands were promoted during a series of mass rallies called in 1942 to protest the slow pace of enforcement of the new Executive Order: 20,000 participated in New York City, 16,000 in Chicago, 9,000 in St. Louis. The rallies were responding to Randolph's question (one that was commonly heard then in the black community): "What have Negroes to fight for?"[118]

These grassroots questions and demands represented a major advancement from the late-nineteenth-century disempowered tokenism promoted by the two major political parties and Booker T. Washington or the social-control warnings of the New Deal Special Industrial Recovery Board cited earlier. Echoing the words of both Frederick Douglass and Martin Delany during the Reconstruction era, these demands presaged the modern "watchdog" aspect of affirmative action programs and their immediate antecedent, the Black Power demands of the late

1960s at workplaces and on college campuses. Ironically, tokenism and social control combine with the original black grassroots demands for fairness in the making of affirmative action today to the extent that it is hard to know where one ends and the other begins.

Following his successful 1941 confrontation at the White House, Randolph encountered both praise from the black community as well as anger from some of his more radical followers like Bayard Rustin. Radicals charged that Randolph had acted without consulting them and should not have been so quick to cancel the march. The victory that was achieved, namely the short-lived consultative FEPC, was small in comparison to the enormous federal government protections that white workers had begun receiving, starting with the Wagner Act.

VII

With the New Deal there came a climax to an ongoing struggle between civil rights activists and government, corporations, and labor unions over the revision of the social contract with white people that the unions were reluctant to amend in any way.[119] American-ness as whiteness has historically combined both simple exclusion of and outright opposition to black people. Historically, as black protest escalates and finds success, simple black exclusion by whites gives way to overt white vocal and physical opposition, which challenges other whites to either acquiesce or take a principled stand against white supremacy—as many did during the dozens of costly World War II "hate strikes." The challenge to whites' privileged position and their justification for maintaining it provides even more fuel for black protest.

If the New Deal represented the government's response primarily to white workers who had made enough of an ideological break with capitalism to threaten the legitimacy of its rule, these workers' white supremacy in turn was challenged by black workers with few illusions about capitalism who had themselves made the ideological break with "knowing their place" and staying out of politics.[120] Despite skepticism and derision by some in the black media toward A. Philip Randolph's declaration that Executive Order 8802 represented "the Second Emancipation Proclamation," Randolph's pronouncement summed up the hopes of many African Americans.[121] Much as Lincoln had to be pushed to take any progressive steps toward emancipation, Roosevelt had to be pressured to take a position instituting a federal investigative agency—the FEPC—while he still allowed for local control in the South of his New Deal programs.

"Whiteness" is not a uniformly practiced ideology. Its participants have historically vacillated at times when confronted with its antidemocratic nature. This is a weakness that generations of pro-black activists have tried to exploit.[122] Viewed in this context, white concessions when they do occur become almost more amazing than the persistence and resiliency of white supremacy itself. Forgotten in all the modern legends of white-looking "Rosie the Riveter" (based on the popular poster of the time) filling vacancies in defense plants while the men went off to war was the chronic and desperate shortage of skilled and unskilled labor—a shortage that black labor could have easily helped to fill.[123] In 1946, Robert Weaver could only marvel:

> That a nation at war would delay the use of its total manpower resources for three long years is the most striking instance of the tenacity with which America has clung to its established color-caste system in occupations. Yet this is what happened in the United States in World War II.[124]

One the other hand, labor historian Richard Steele has noted a stark but typical differential between the federal government's handling of discrimination complaints by African Americans and Polish Americans:

> While the pressure for ending discrimination against blacks came mainly from Afro-Americans themselves, the impetus for taking on the problems of white minorities came from inside government. Officials seem to have believed that remedying ethnic employment problems was both easier and more important to the nation's defense than similar efforts on behalf of blacks. Anti-Negro prejudice was thought to be a complex sociological problem requiring years of effort to eliminate, while anti-ethnic discrimination was largely seen as the result of federal policies and solvable with the mere stroke of a pen.[125]

The acceptance of black labor—both in factories and in the military—also represented the climax of the Roosevelt administration's efforts to save the capitalist economy and preserve social peace and white consensus at home, while simultaneously trying to win the world war against the Axis powers.[126] And while civil rights was being catapulted onto the national agenda, the American social caste system based on white supremacy was actually entering a new phase of government approval.

The biggest irony of affirmative action today lies in its institutionalized attempt at federalizing national and local antidiscrimination initiatives (inaugurated by black workers) in a reform tradition that specifically harkens back to the New Deal: an era that also saw a more complete federalizing of Jim Crow and the government subsidizing and sanctioning of whiteness. The postwar, post-New Deal era, besides representing a step backward in implementing civil rights, saw government pressure on unions to expel their left-wing members as well.[127] This pressure limited the power of organized labor while simultaneously making it a more efficient partner in both labor discipline and the implementation of the many forms that white privilege would take in the 1950s.

Chapter 5

"THE EVIL THAT FHA DID...."

White Suburbs, "Negro Quotas," Red Scares, and Black Demands, 1945–55

I

Historical periods are imaginary creations, although what takes place within them is very real. Whether marked by historians or popularly conceived, they are typically distinguished by significant events, tend to overlap with other "periods," and often then become packaged into decades. The historical period running from 1945 to 1955 represented more than an economic rebound from the Great Depression, an emotional and political lift with the end of World War II, and the emergence of the United States as a world power. It also became a prelude to an even larger battle over the domestic racial caste system.

While federal government policy was elevating white people socially in the postwar era, African Americans were challenging those privileges and the denial of equality in schools, labor unions, jobs, housing—and the government itself. They demanded and sometimes received some form of compensatory justice, and later debates over affirmative action would be shaped by these pre–civil rights movement antecedents of the late 1940s and early 1950s. Why, then, is this period generally associated with both social stasis *and* political repression?

The popular image of the postwar era is one of economic progress, stable baby boom families, Jim Crow acquiescence, fierce white supremacy and inquisitional anti-communism, the beginning of the Cold War, fear of nuclear annihilation, and white flight to the suburbs.[1] What could have paved the way for the battles of the civil rights era of the 1950s and 1960s in such a repressive, conformist climate? With so much conformity and fear—how did mass black protest activity suddenly erupt with the 1955 Montgomery, Alabama, bus boycott—which in turn brought white allies and helped inspire other progressive movements? In fact, the civil rights movement that came out of the 1930s even during this lull period never stopped where it had begun confronting government and the white labor movement, even if the terms of the debate caused it to behave in a more circumspect manner.[2]

The notion of the postwar years being static politically has been overdrawn. Even absent the mass protest associated with the civil rights era, there was still activity revolving around race and class issues and confronting political and social conformity. White affirmative action in all aspects of social life—from the workplace to the military—was confronted by black and problack activists with a mixture of demands that were a combination of reliance on popular power, pressure, political embarrassment on the world stage, and a traditional hope that the federal government would complete Reconstruction especially in confronting hostile Southern state governments.[3]

While most postwar civil rights groups continued to press for strict equality measures, we also find rhetoric, demonstrations, and lawsuits calling for some form of black representation as well as remedial action involving some kind of compensatory preferences and quotas. Similar to the perennial debate over fighting for integrated schools versus building independent black schools, there was (and is) no inherent contradiction between demands for equality and compensation.[4] The latter usually represents a mechanism for achieving the former through a combination of mandatory and voluntary measures.

If the white race was invented in colonial America, one could argue that it was reinvented with the post–World War II suburbs. Early suburbs, however, were not composed solely of the white middle class. The majority consisted of white blue-collar households with a fair number of African Americans all living on the outskirts of town, often with no city services.[5] But symbolized by the popular phrase "white flight," the postwar white suburb represented both a collective and individual affirmative desire for some pastoral space away from the crowded city (and sometimes away from older immigrant relatives),[6] the desire to relocate closer to where better-paying jobs were being established, and the negative impulse to flee the incoming black urban migration.

Long before it became a popular phrase in the 1960s, "white flight" in post-war America came to signify, both explicitly and implicitly, the first imagination of whites as "refugees in their own country"—albeit privileged and fleeing to secure the best land and jobs they could find. The end of World War II also meant the beginning of the Cold War and the nuclear age, where there was also some fear of cities being hit by Soviet nuclear bombs. The greatest nonnatural disaster that creates refugees is war. Besides pursuing unequal opportunity, many of these white urban emigrants were hoping to leave behind both the potential for nuclear annihilation and the "war zone of the city"—which to many meant black people. "Responsible" early white republican citizenship had now reemerged in the twentieth century by fusing the property of whiteness contained in "white jobs" with the quarter-acre suburban tract. Its colonial, early republican, and post–Civil War antecedents lay in the often elusive dream of a freeholder's minimum plot of 50 acres of farmland and the homesteader's 160 acre claim.[7]

The chief engine of this flight was the 1944 Servicemen's Readjustment Act (also known as the GI Bill) that gave a boost to all veterans (but especially white veterans) in what was originally intended as a vehicle of social control as well as a compensatory benefits package to help prime the economy.[8] (It must be remembered that the United States armed forces that fought World War II were both restricted and segregated racially.) At the same time, federal intervention in the white supremacist 1944 Philadelphia Transit Strike also set a precedent for government antidiscrimination action and energized the civil rights movement.[9] Finally, despite the FEPC's limited enforcement powers, its collapse as a federal agency in 1946 was preceded by five years of some usefulness as a forum and clearinghouse for black worker protest against Jim Crow trade unionism, as well as being followed by the establishment of similar state committees.[10]

The period that runs from war's end to the AFL-CIO merger and the United States Supreme Court *Brown II* decision in 1955 is especially relevant to understanding the struggle against racial discrimination, including affirmative action. Did the AFL-CIO merger represent progress for black workers and the labor movement in general, or was it more akin to the 1877 abandonment of Reconstruction? How did the pre-1955 civil rights movement resolve the contradiction between "color blindness" and "special protection"? How did its activities begin shaking the federal government and labor unions to action?

While not a period of social upheaval associated with the 1930s or 1960s, this decade was clearly not one of universal conformity but instead saw a continuation of the clash of social forces begun in the 1930s: black-led protest against racial discrimination, white efforts to maintain accumulating privileges, and the contradictory government responses and initiatives in support of both those forces. Those who argue today that affirmative action programs unfairly elevate the black middle class over working-class whites in higher education need to consider the phenomenal postwar propulsion of many working-class white families into the middle class through the GI Bill, NLRB-sanctioned union-management contracts, and the FHA.

II

In 1945, the United States was emerging from war, economic depression, and what was also being called a "Depression Psychosis"—an expression coined by economist John Kenneth Galbraith. There was widespread public fear that mass unemployment would return with peacetime industrial conversion.[11] There was also a fear by government and civic leaders of the potential demands of returning veterans. American Legion National Commander Warren H. Atherton, for instance, predicted that GIs "will be a potent force for good or evil."[12] Earlier Eleanor Roosevelt had warned in 1942 that veterans might create "a dangerous pressure group."[13]

The 1944 GI Bill helped increase distance between blacks and whites by granting government benefits to returning white veterans (also predominantly male) that were beneficial out of proportion to veterans of color in terms of employment, housing, and education. As Hilary Herbold, a researcher into postwar discrimination, put it: "Even though the official specifications of the bill (at least with regard to education) did not discriminate by race, the terms were interpreted one way for blacks and another for whites."[14] Reminiscent of the 1787 Northwest Ordinance, the Jacksonian-era spoils system, and the 1862 Morrill and Homestead Acts, white expectations based on skin color were aroused during this decade just as they had been during those earlier periods, if not more so, with the GI Bill emerging as a prime vehicle of white privilege.

Elements of New Deal programs were actually folded into postwar veterans' policies—sharing the same language and compensatory intent as affirmative action.[15] Preferential veteran hiring, for example, was frankly written into the original GI Bills. There was a readjustment allowance; home, farm, and business loan guarantees; and provisions for every state to have a veterans' representative to ensure that counseling, training, apprenticeships, and employment be made available to veterans.[16] Some labor unions argued over whether returning veterans should enjoy "superseniority rights" (displacing nonveterans with more seniority) at the workplace. Nevertheless, "superseniority" became Selective Service policy until overturned by the 1946 United States Supreme Court *Fishgold* ruling.[17]

Labor leaders were ambivalent about this early form of veterans' affirmative action because, while recognizing the sacrifices their members had made in uniform, they were also anxious not to displace those who had stayed behind. Although industry spokespersons demanded that unions bend their rules to allow the hiring of servicemen, "[t]he UAW and many other unions had already agreed that all servicemen should be credited with employment seniority for the time they spent in uniform."[18] The following exchange between the "CIO veterans' committee" representative and Sen. H. Alexander Smith (R-New Jersey) during the superseniority hearings highlights this contradiction in labor's position and illustrates the paradox of ostensibly "color-blind" seniority rights as a "white entitlement":

> Mr. Bernstein: We insist very strongly that veterans shall be entitled to all their promotions that they would have received had they not been inducted into the service. . . .
> Sen. Smith: That is part of the seniority principle?
> Mr. Bernstein: That is part of the seniority principle.[19]

While white women during this period encountered gender discrimination in employment and education, many also shared homes and children with white men, many of whom were returning World War II veterans and who were receiving unprecedented benefits in the form of free college education, low-cost housing loans, a weekly unemployment benefit called a "readjustment allowance," and jobs in the federal government. But as Herbold notes: "When blacks refused employment at wages considerably below subsistence level, the VA [Veterans Administration] was notified and unemployment benefits were terminated."[20]

Most veterans also wanted better jobs, and the educational opportunities both propelled many working-class veterans into the middle class and raised the hopes and frustrations of black veterans:[21]

Thanks to the first GI Bill, an estimated 2.2 million veterans received education at colleges and universities in the aftermath of World War II. A total of 7.8 million veterans, or 50.5 percent of the World War II veteran population received training or education under the bill. . . . The bill greatly expanded the population of African Americans attending college and graduate school. In 1940, enrollment at Black colleges was 1.08 percent of the total U.S. college enrollment; in 1950 it was 3.6 percent. . . .[22]

College benefits included "tuition, fees, books, and supplies, up to $500 a year, plus a monthly living allowance of $50 for an unmarried veteran and $75 for married veterans."[23] Historian Stephanie Coontz observes: "The GI Bill also fostered employment of wives by offering men incentives to stay in school but paying family allowances so low that wives needed to work in order to supplement them."[24] Furthermore,

one free year of higher education was provided for each ninety days of service and one additional month of paid education for each month of service up to forty-eight months. . . . In 1947, veterans accounted for 49% of U.S. college enrollments [at a cost of] $14.5 billion. . . . In the late 1930s about 160,000 U.S. citizens graduated from college each year. By 1950 that number had increased to 500,000.[25]

Emblematic of the mixed blessing of New Deal and post–New Deal federalism was the explosion of federally subsidized black college education, as well as the federal sanction of white college educational advantage:

The G.I. Bill did not include a bar against race discrimination. . . . Lacking an antidiscrimination ban, and leaving the disbursement of funds to state authorities, the G.I. Bill in effect subsidized continuing and enlarging disproportions between the incomes of white public colleges and universities, and the A&Is and the A&Ms that in some states equaled *black*.[26]

In other words, African Americans could share the benefits of having fought the Axis powers—but far from equally.[27] Until 1949, in fact, the army maintained a "Negro quota" that was finally ended by an outcry led by the African American community.[28] Articles from the *Pittsburgh Courier* in 1946 reveal this campaign: " 'Quota' Halts Enlistments" reads a headline from the 17 August issue, where according to War Department sources "a 10 percent Negro quota" was in effect. Again on 12 October a headline on the *Courier's* front page read: "Army Restricts Colored Youth in Regular Army: High School Grads Only." The article revealed that army officials admitted that Army General Classification Test qualifying scores had been raised to 99 for blacks and 70 for whites in order to limit black enlistees to within their population percentage.[29]

This so-called Negro quota disappeared along with segregation in the military only as a result of Executive Order 9981 by President Truman in 1948. It should be remembered, too, that the order itself was in response to A. Philip Randolph's threat to lead black draft resistance combined with Truman's desire for black votes in what proved to be a close upcoming presidential election with Henry Wallace and Thomas Dewey.[30]

III

Only a third of the nation's population lived in the suburbs in 1940. By 1970, most of the nation's population would be living there—and they would be predominantly white.[31] But even in the quarter century preceding the end of World War II, 75 percent of new owner-occupied developments were being built in the suburbs. And while big cities between 1940 and 1950 were absorbing less than a third of the total national population growth, suburbs grew during this period by 35.5 percent.[32]

A popular film from the postwar era still enjoyed by millions today is the 1947 Oscar-winning classic *Miracle on 34th Street*, where a young white Manhattan single mother (Maureen O'Hara), her daughter (Natalie Wood), and an attorney (John Payne) find the young girl's Christmas wish in the film's dramatic conclusion: a suburban home. As in many films of the period but similar to the real-life emerging suburbs themselves, black people are almost invisible except as maids and janitors.[33]

The "American Dream" of home ownership is an established cliché, one that combines both a sense of modern advancement as well as evoking a general sentiment among United States citizens since colonial times. In his 1955 study *Forbidden Neighbors*, sociologist Charles Abrams cited popular magazines from both the Depression and postwar eras that extolled suburban home ownership—in racially exclusive neighborhoods. "Home ownership was repeatedly referred to as the American ideal (suggesting of course that renting is low class)," he noted. "It was intimated that Washington's ragged troops had bled and died for this cause."[34]

Assuming the role of cultural theorist, President Herbert Hoover gave voice to "this cause" in a speech to the President's Conference on Building and Home Ownership during his administration. (Notice his citing of three sentimental popular songs, the latter two evoking antebellum slaveownership and Native American displacement for white settlement, respectively):

> Those immortal ballads "Home Sweet Home," "My Old Kentucky Home," and "The Little Gray Home in the West," were not written about tenements or apartments. They are expressions of *racial longing* which find outlet in the living poetry and songs of our people. . . . That our people should live in their own homes is a sentiment deep in the heart of our race and of American life.[35]

After the war, low-interest VA loans were made available through the GI Bill to veterans to buy homes in a program that paralleled that of the FHA. Coontz reports that

> FHA policy required down payments of only 5 to 10 percent of the purchase price and guaranteed mortgages of up to thirty years at interest rates of just 2 to 3 percent on the balance. The Veterans Administration asked *a mere dollar down from veterans*. At the same time, government tax policies were changed to provide substantial incentives for savings and loan institutions to channel their funds almost exclusively into low-interest, long-term mortgages.[36]

However, VA/FHA loans were not made available to many black veterans. As the President's Committee on Civil Rights reported in 1947:

> When Negro veterans seek "GI" loans in order to build homes, they are likely to find that credit from private banks, without whose services there is no possibility of taking advantage of the GI Bill of Rights, is less freely available to members of their race. Private builders show a tendency not to construct new homes except for white occupancy. These interlocking business customs and devices form the core of our discriminatory policy. But community prejudice also finds expression in open public agitation against construction of public housing projects for Negroes, and by violence against Negroes who seek to occupy public housing projects or to build in "white" sections.[37]

For veterans and their families, college education, job training, and home-ownership benefits represented the springboard for whites and their families to leave the cities for the segregated suburbs, which meant better jobs, schools, and futures; and for blacks and their families to receive college educations or otherwise move up the occupational ladder and thereby enter the middle class—as well as in some cases enter civil rights activism.[38]

Anticipating Cold War anti-Communist language and hysteria, FHA housing guidelines beginning in the New Deal era safeguarded these new "homogeneous" enclaves against what they called "infiltration of inharmonious racial or nationality groups."[39] The FHA "professional appraisal" was said by sociologists Douglas A. Massey and Nancy A. Denton to be "the most important factor encouraging white suburbanization and segregation of blacks" in the inner-city ghettoes.[40]

The innocuous-looking postwar suburban white family with the station wagon and the ranch or Cape Cod–style houses in reality represented the new all-American Jim Crow system and successor to the moribund Southern variety.[41] The mass-produced identical homes by the Levitt family of developers in New York and Pennsylvania subdivisions (satirized by folksinger Malvina Reynolds in her 1960s popular song "Little Boxes") explicitly excluded blacks from their deeds and leases. Indeed, Blacks were kept out even after the Supreme Court barred enforcement of restrictive covenants (housing exclusions written into real estate titles) in 1948. Black steelworkers who worked in the local steel plant had to find housing in the nearby cities of Trenton, Camden, and Philadelphia.[42]

But if white suburbanization was achieved popularly, it was not achieved entirely peaceably, as seen in riots in Detroit in 1943 and Cicero, Illinois, in 1951. It is not at all outlandish to suggest that lynchings and white riots during this era served as a kind of white affirmative action whereby whites asserted their "right" to keep blacks out of "their" neighborhoods and jobs.[43] The FHA's indirect role in sparking this white mob activity calls to mind official involvement in nineteenth-century pogroms. As Abrams points out:

If FHA policy did not sanction violence, it inspired it. At the time of the [1943] Sojourner Truth riots in Detroit, for example, FHA dogma about values declining with the entry of Negroes was generally believed. Some frightened whites declared that if Negroes moved in, FHA would guarantee no further loans in the neighborhood.

It is difficult to determine why prejudice functions, why mobs of homeowners and their teen-age children stone, bomb, or burn buildings. One thing is certain. The publication of anti-racial doctrine by a federal agency established official justification for prejudice and gave the semblance of right to lawlessness.

The evil that FHA did was of a peculiarly enduring character. Thousands of racially segregated neighborhoods were built, millions of people were re-assorted on the basis of race, color, or class, the differences built in, in neighborhoods from coast to coast.

FHA simultaneously undermined the old pattern of heterogeneous neighborhoods in communities from coast to coast where people of mixed races and mixed religions had been living nearby or in the same block without a qualm or a quibble.[44]

The conclusion of the 1953 NAACP national convention concurred with Abrams's observation: "The chief force and sanction now in support of the maintenance and extension of racial ghettos come from the federal government itself through the operations of the federal housing agencies."[45] It would take problack pressure and protest to strike down the restrictive covenants that had been revived with the black post–World War I migration.[46] The 1948 United States Supreme Court *Shelley v. Kraemer* ruling against restrictive covenants was handed down in an atmosphere that suddenly saw support for their abolition by the attorney general and a number of civic and labor groups (including the AFL).[47] The FHA itself was forced by civil rights group mobilization and the attorney general to abandon its longtime support for restrictive covenants in 1949.[48]

However, even after *Shelley v. Kraemer* and the 1949 FHA reversal, the FHA as late as 1955 was still financing discriminatory housing projects.[49] Ironically, two years later American competition with the Soviet Union's technological advances spurred skilled black recruitment under a program begun under President Truman: the Committee on Government Contract Compliance (CGCC).[50] Meanwhile, better jobs, better schools, and more capital were all heading for the suburbs, along with the white refugees.[51]

The grassroots mechanism for enforcement of the post–New Deal white reconstruction in maintaining exclusively white housing developments came in the form of the greatly expanded real estate industry and the homeowners' associations. Long after restrictive covenants were found unconstitutional, these institutions would still help preserve privilege and prejudice in the formation of the historical memory of the white suburb.[52] That memory (or worldview or ideology) informs much of today's white hostility to, as W. E. B. Du Bois might say, the *very name* affirmative action.

IV

The campaign for justice and equality for African Americans in both the North and South, carrying the seeds for the modern affirmative action debate, was developed within a climate of fear, employing both defiance and deference. In dealing with the white status quo civil rights activists found themselves navigating between suspicion and conformity tendencies on the one hand and a willingness to consider traditional token concessions on the other. The mobilization of black middle- and working-class people after the war came about in large part due to the contradiction between having fought for freedom abroad and coming home to discrimination.[53] The migration of 5 million predominantly rural black Southern sharecroppers to the factories and offices of the North during this period expressed both their hope and frustration.[54]

While the NAACP was pursuing a limited legal strategy, it was also encouraging grassroots activity against discrimination and for the franchise, joined by groups like the Congress of Racial Equality (CORE) and the MOWM.[55] While left-wing unions and organizers suffered repression, it is no coincidence that anti-Communist hysteria especially was applied to African American challenges to white supremacy as "un-American."[56] How could black demands for equality be construed by whites as being subversive? Challenges to the white status quo—even by anti-Communist blacks—were called "un-American." The final resolution adopted by the 1953 NAACP national convention included these observations:

> Already there is discernible a pattern which tends to link the advocacy of full equality for Negroes and other minorities to subversion or "un-Americanism." In some communities, textbooks, courses of study, and teaching techniques dealing with human relations and minority group situations have been condemned or eliminated on the ground that these are not "American." In exams designed to test the loyalty of applicants for or holders of, positions in government, a question frequently asked of persons is whether they believe in the equality of the black and white races or entertain Negroes socially in their homes. In many areas the advocates of low-cost public housing are already branded as socialists, while those advocating non-segregated housing are now being called Communists. Professors and teachers who declare that segregation and discrimination based upon color are un-democratic are suspect, as are those who assert that scientific inquiry supports the thesis of the basic equality of peoples, regardless of race or color.[57]

Pauli Murray, noted black author, legal scholar, feminist, priest, and civil rights activist, spoke for many non-Communist (as well as anti-Communist) civil rights activists in the 1940s and 1950s who desired to be seen as loyal Americans as well as deserving of the rights of Americans. In the 1984 introduction to *Proud Shoes*, the famous biography that she wrote about her family's roots in slavery, abolitionism, and Reconstruction, she recalled the time when she wrote the book in the early 1950s:

> The civil rights movement was gaining momentum. At the same time, the country was gripped by the hysteria of McCarthyism. . . . As a civil rights activist fighting against racial segregation when challengers of segregation policy were few and defeats were many, I found it imperative to declare my American heritage. Not Communism, but the ideals and influences within my own family had made me a life-long fighter against all forms of inequality and injustice.[58]

For Murray, like many African American civil rights activists, there was a contradiction between (1) not wanting to be identified with vilified organizations like the CPUSA and its politically manipulative tendencies, (2) recognizing that many black workers were sympathetic to leftist groups owing to the greater degree of empathy demonstrated by these groups than exhibited by most other organizations that primarily included white people, and (3) feeling competition from leftist organizations with whom they would have preferred not to have to engage.[59]

On the one hand, the 1953 NAACP national convention expressed its concern with loyalty oaths, except for "security sensitive departments," but confessed that they were "alarmed at the mass firing of federal employees many of whom are Negroes." They opposed "communist-controlled" unions and the NNLC but also declared: "The NAACP hopefully calls upon the new leadership of the AFL to take *affirmative action* to end the various forms of racial discrimination practiced by certain affiliated International unions."[60] Such judicious, pro-American declarations, however, were lost on the members of such reactionary groups as the House Un-American Activities Committee (HUAC), although they made a practice of officially denying that they considered the NAACP subversive, as illustrated in this testy 1952 exchange with Coleman A. Young (who would later become the first African American to be elected mayor of Detroit), called to testify about his labor organizing:

> Mr. Tavenner. I understood you to state—you answered a moment ago that this committee had labeled the NAACP as subversive.
> Mr. Young. That is correct. . . .
> Mr. Tavenner. Can you refer to any record of the committee which has so designated the NAACP?
> Mr. Young. I am sure this committee is in possession of its own records. I would suggest a search of those records.[61]

The NAACP, like the CPUSA, was not just considered by the Federal Bureau of Investigation (FBI) and HUAC to be "subversive" for its civil rights activity, but it was also harassed throughout the South. Eight Southern legislatures called it "subversive and communistic" and demanded such things as membership lists—which the NAACP refused to provide, thus tying the organization up in court. In 1957, the NAACP was actually outlawed in Alabama.[62]

The popularity of FBI director J. Edgar Hoover had never been greater—and exceeded even that of President Dwight D. Eisenhower (1953–61).[63] When United Mineworkers (UMW-CIO) leader John L. Lewis made a speech contrasting Hoover's anti-Communist hysteria with the real work that he said needed to be done in combating discrimination at home he found himself in a distinct minority.[64] In fact, from the beginning of his career Hoover had equated the black civil rights movement with subversion, Communism, and anarchy.

According to Mark Ellis, the Palmer Raids that Hoover led in 1919 were as much an attack on blacks who were trying to defend themselves against a nationwide racial pogrom as they were raids against "Bolsheviks." Ellis calls Hoover's attitude "slave rebellion paranoia" and claims that Hoover feared the "dissemination of subversive propaganda among blacks." During that period Hoover had Du Bois and Marcus Garvey investigated, and he helped deport Garvey after he was convicted in a trial for mail fraud on weak evidence.[65] According to historians Athan G. Theoharis and John Stuart Cox:

> The FBI tapped and bugged virtually every civil rights organization challenging racial segregation or seeking to promote equal rights for black Americans. . . . The FBI both tapped and bugged the March on Washington Movement in . . . June 1943. . . . Six months later . . . the FBI tapped the NAACP.[66]

In a survey taken in 1954, shortly after the first *Brown* decision, white Americans ranked Communism near the top of a list of concerns. "Communists" were popularly conceived in these interviews exactly as they were portrayed in the media and by Hoover and by elected officials like Sen. Joseph McCarthy (R-Wisconsin)—as shadowy, nonconformist figures.[67]

This postwar scapegoating of black civil rights and labor activists as "reds" and "troublemakers" was part of a general public antipathy toward certain sections of militant labor being "un-American." This is not surprising in light of Robert Weaver's observation in 1946 that racial attacks by whites against blacks represented a form of racial scapegoating during the war.[68] An extension of this phenomenon can be seen in the large vocal opposition (including among black conservatives) to A. Philip Randolph's threat to organize massive black draft resistance if Truman did not eliminate Jim Crow from the armed forces.[69]

Russians were popularly regarded in this country as being "white" during the Cold War. The Korean war, however, the first actual "war with communism," was not with the Soviet Union but with the racialized, dehumanized, so-called "yellow peril" of China and North Korea—less than a century after domestic white paranoia over the Asian "labor invasion." Reminiscent of the post–World War I anti-immigration hysteria, American Communists were often regarded as being white race traitors, especially in view of Communists' active opposition to Jim Crow segregation.[70]

During this time the NAACP was simultaneously demanding equality in labor issues, challenging American apartheid in educational issues, and at times supporting remedial action in consumer affairs. Amazingly, in today's debate over affirmative action, "color-blind movement" theorists like John David Skrentny and Paul Moreno seem satisfied with their assessments of pragmatism, opportunism, or lapsed egalitarianism as explanations for such apparently contradictory behavior. In fact, the repressive anti-Communist environment during this period made traditionally diplomatic middle-class black appeals to powerful white institutions even more circumspect than usual.[71]

For example, historian Manning Marable notes that Robert L. Carter of the NAACP legal team, in arguing the *Brown* case before the United States Supreme Court in 1954, maintained that "the constitutional rights granted by the Fourteenth Amendment were 'individual rights' and not 'group rights.' "[72] Ironically, the Court's unanimous decision to use federal judicial power to intervene against school segregation (based in large part on their reading of eminent black scholars like historian John Hope Franklin and sociologist Kenneth Clark) suggests protection for African Americans as a legal class based on their history of oppression and discrimination. The Court's recognition of the Fourteenth Amendment's roots in this protection unintentionally provided a basis for affirmative action, as they declared: "In the first cases in this Court construing the Fourteenth Amendment, decided shortly after its adoption, the Court interpreted it as proscribing all state-imposed sanctions against the Negro race."[73]

The notion of "individual versus group rights" has become a cornerstone of conservative arguments against affirmative action. While conservatives rightly point to the Fourteenth Amendment (as well as the Fifth) as a guarantor of individual rights, they both ignore its ongoing protection of African Americans as a class since Reconstruction as well as its role as a guard against what Justice Harlan called the "class tyranny" of the white majority, as he tried to remind his colleagues in *Civil Rights Cases*.[74] These conservative arguments also ignore the historic protection of "group rights" for *white people* by the Constitution until Reconstruction and in legal and social practices since then.

Despite the NAACP's emphasis on court action as a national strategy, local branches and black churches were mobilizing mass actions against Jim Crow school districts and challenging white privileged school systems.[75] Meanwhile, how did white conformity affect race and labor issues?

V

The AFL-CIO merger that finally came about in 1955 is something that is looked back upon by trade union proponents today with a fondness that rivals modern-day popular appreciation for the Continental Congress of 1776 and the Declaration of Independence.[76] But many black workers and problack labor activists (even some who were associated with the CIO) dreaded combining the more sympathetic CIO with the older, more conservative AFL, with its tolerance of Jim Crow affiliates.[77] The NAACP initially had high hopes after the merged organizations adopted resolutions against discrimination and segregation—hopes that would soon be dashed.[78]

The CIO had purged its own leftist unions by this time and felt the need to put distance between itself and anything that hinted of "subversion." Not only did they purge left-leaning unions that were either controlled by or associated with the CPUSA, but when they announced their campaign to organize the South they rejected aid from all other organizations, including civil rights groups. Challenging white privilege in the South or anywhere else was not on the CIO's agenda, despite their documented national opposition to Jim Crow.[79]

Anna Hass Morgan, a CPUSA activist in Columbus, Ohio, during this time, provides an example of privileged white spatial mobility during a 1948 strike during which she ran a relief committee.[80] The strike involved the International Union of Mine, Mill, and Smelter Workers (or simply Mine Mill)—one of the "red unions" expelled by the CIO that also refused to implement President Truman's Loyalty Oath. Looking back Morgan wrote:

Locally the Mine, Mill and Smelters Union (MM&S) had gone on strike because the local American Zinc Oxide plant would not stop polluting the area with its poisonous fumes, which the union claimed were affecting the health of the workers in their nearby village, the American Addition. Gradually all the white workers drifted to other jobs, leaving the Black workers of the American Addition, who were buying their modest little homes at $25 a month, with principal and interest.[81]

Integrated "red" unions like the Mine Mill were often identified in the popular imagination as being "black."[82] Despite sincere antiracism exhibited by individual party members as well as party policy and practice that reprimanded any display of "white chauvinism," the distrust and disillusionment felt by many black activists toward opportunism, dogmatism, and even racism on the part of the CPUSA and the Communist Party of the Soviet Union (CPSU) was understandable. This was true even in those cases where that distrust of the CPUSA (and the left in general) manifested itself in opportunist ways.[83] And among whites, leftists and liberals by no means had a monopoly on antiracism.[84] Furthermore, challenging white preferences while supporting black compensatory justice was not something that either leftists or reformists (black or white) even did consistently. For example:

The NAACP and the CIO fought a proposal for a racial superseniority system by the communist-dominated United Electrical, Radio, and Machine Workers Union (UE) in Bridgeport, Connecticut. When the local, communist-infiltrated NAACP supported the idea, the national office denounced the local, saying that the association never endorsed . . . "special attention because we happen to be Negroes."[85]

We have already witnessed the irony of black civil rights groups being rebuffed in 1935 upon demanding that the Wagner Act (with its "affirmative action" clause) include protection for black workers. Comparable with the defense of affirmative action today, the CPUSA was accused of "Jim Crow in reverse" when during the late 1940s' economic downturn it unsuccessfully appealed to white-dominated labor unions to bend their strict adherence to seniority rules in dealing with layoffs.

While asking unions to amend seniority might be imagined today to be the equivalent of asking a devout religious member to convert, in fact it was not. The CPUSA was merely asking unions to extend to black workers the same kind of work-sharing plans that those unions had frequently enacted to "spread the misery" of layoffs, such as shorter work weeks and even quota systems to

protect older, slower workers. These were already common practices throughout a variety of industries, including steel, mining, service, textiles, and construction.[86]

Black organizations similarly campaigned strongly for state and federal fair
employment practice commissions. One of the few success stories during this
period was the establishment of minimum black quotas for black retail workers
in New York City by Local 65 of the National Council of Distributive Workers.
(Local 65 later became the well-known District 65, which earned the praise of
Martin Luther King Jr., among others, in the 1960s.)[87]

But organized white labor opposition was both adamantly against tampering
with strict seniority when it came to tampering with whiteness—a reaction
similar to today's widespread white anger at "fairness" being compromised by
affirmative action. Clearly, the cyclical crises endemic to capitalism were not
the only thing causing a "white recession" to be a "black depression." White
workers themselves through their unions were thus ensuring the preservation of
that economic color line. If there were any remedial, affirmative measures to be
implemented, they were to be white ones.

Seniority not only protected the jobs of white workers who had worked
longer at a given plant, but it made it easier for white workers to "bid" better
jobs over black workers. This happened because they were not locked into
menial "black" job categories that additionally only possessed department-wide,
not plant-wide, seniority. As promotion currency, black seniority became relatively worthless.[88] The National Alliance of Postal and Federal Employees
(NAPFE) was one black labor organization that voted at their ninth national
convention in Norfolk, Virginia, in 1946 to protest the mass layoffs of women
workers (especially black). All had "war service appointments," they said, and
should keep their jobs "on the basis of their ability instead of their race, color,
creed, or sex," as opposed to the white privilege of seniority.[89]

A good example of white seniority manipulation can be seen with the railroads, where the traditionally "black" jobs of fireman and porter were seized by
whites during this period through a manipulation of the seniority system. An
article in the *Pittsburgh Courier* from 1946 illustrates how a black fireman could
be displaced by a white fireman with less seniority because the latter had Brotherhood of Locomotive Engineers and Firemen (and therefore preferred) membership. This in turn forced the black worker to seek redress in the courts, with
legal aid from groups like the NAACP, against the maximum "Negro quotas" of

the time.[90] Similar in a nonviolent sense to lynchings, workplace terror campaigns, and white race riots, seniority plans (both the manipulated variety and the inflexible types) became an institutionalized as well as a grassroots form of "white-affirmative action" within most AFL unions.[91]

Meanwhile, the NAACP branch in Richmond, California, was challenging the color-blind strategy of their national office during this era with their illegal pickets of white-owned grocery stores in black neighborhoods, demanding demographically proportional hiring of blacks. After two members were arrested, served an injunction, and later convicted, they asked the NAACP to handle their case. Special Counsel Thurgood Marshall eagerly took the case, *Hughes v. Superior Court of California*, which the plaintiffs lost in 1950 before the United States Supreme Court. The Court ruled in part:

> The injunction did not violate petitioners' right of freedom of speech as guaranteed by the Due Process Clause of the Fourteenth Amendment. . . . The Due Process Clause cannot be construed as precluding California from securing respect for its policy against involuntary employment on racial lines by prohibiting systematic picketing that would subvert such policy. . . .[92]

This decision was the reverse a similar 1938 case and sums up the struggle that both the high court and the NAACP encountered over whether the Fourteenth Amendment should apply as a special vehicle for blacks to have guaranteed equal justice or should be read as a "color-blind" federal law.[93] The compensatory demands by problack activists in the postwar era have become almost forgotten antecedents to today's affirmative action debate. These campaigns are highly relevant to today's debate, as activists combined legal tactics and direct action, as well as expressions like "merit employment" and "equal opportunity," in their attempted appeals to reason.

"Merit employment" was the name given to a nationwide campaign to bring qualified black workers into traditionally white jobs as well as increase workplace diversity and was generally opposed by both white workers and employers. One R. J. Reynolds executive labeled the campaign "communistic," and its proponents also acknowledged that its use invited tokenism as a tactical ploy by its opponents.[94] The very name implied that "merit" was something that whites possessed innately (not unlike today), whereas, presumably if the countryside were sufficiently scoured with enough diligence then a suitable "meritable" black employee might be found. Clearly there is a historical basis for

131

generations of African American parents often exhorting their children to perform a "double effort" in any given endeavor in order to receive something approaching normal recognition.[95]

VI

The period known as the beginning of the Cold War that ran from the end of World War II to the launching of the post-*Brown* modern civil rights movement and the merger of the AFL-CIO was actually a prelude to the modern affirmative action debate. As historian Gerald Horne has maintained: "Indeed, it is no longer possible to comprehend the Cold War itself without comprehending its sharp racist edge."[96] Within that "war footing" context, the debate became a multifaceted one over equality, integration, segregation, separatism, domestic and foreign neo-colonialism, Communism, and white privilege.

The relevance of this decade to the modern civil rights and black nationalist movements is finally becoming documented and discussed in the way that it deserves. Failing to look at the relevance of this period (as well as prior legacies of slavery, Reconstruction, and the New Deal) to today's affirmative action debate makes a true understanding of this debate and struggle impossible.

Civil rights group "pragmatism" operated not in a vacuum but in opposition to slowly opening opportunities as well as wider racial differentials. These differentials represented continuations of past white privileges as well as reinventions; actions justified by an enlarged projection of the black subversive Other in popular culture; and discriminatory actions in all spheres of social life—held together with a discipline among whites that recalled the hysteria of World War I, World War II, and the antebellum South.

Both the civil rights movement and the white reaction received encouragement from the *Brown* decisions. The same Supreme Court that with *Brown I* overturned *Plessy* and abolished segregated schools returned in 1955 with *Brown II* with its "with all deliberate speed" injunction to Southern white school districts, which actually allowed them to pick their own pace for change.[97] "Progress" generally designed for the working class with the AFL-CIO merger, veterans' benefits, and federal housing subsidies actually constituted an extension of race-based white preferences. In trying to hold whites to the principle of "formal equality," civil rights activists found that without enforcement "equality" was only a noble-sounding word that white supremacists could hide behind and even throw back at the activists when they demanded effective enforcement mechanisms.

Yet another irony involving *Brown* came fourteen years after that decision. A young white NAACP attorney named Lewis M. Steel was fired by the organization after writing an article that declared that the *Brown* decisions were more palliatives to whites than they were justice for blacks. Steel wrote:

> Never before in the history of the Supreme Court had the implementation of a constitutional right been so delayed or the creation of it put in such vague terms. The Court thereby made clear that it was a white court which would protect the interests of white America in the maintenance of stable institutions.
>
> In essence, the Court considered the potential damage to white Americans resulting from the diminution of privilege as more critical than continued damage to the underprivileged. . . . Worse still, it gave the primary responsibility for achieving educational equality to those who had established the segregated institutions.[98]

With *Brown* ultimately signaling the end of Jim Crow, it was later noted by Du Bois that "no such decision would have been possible without the world pressure of communism."[99] Government, business, and organized labor were all feeling the ideological competition with the so-called Communist world, as well as the independence and liberation movements in developing countries that were so inspiring to American pro-equality activists (and vice versa).[100]

The evil that the FHA, Supreme Court, AFL-CIO, homeowners' associations, and a host of other historically white institutions did in promoting or protecting white privilege was not extraordinary but quite ordinary.[101] It lay not in furtive, conspiratorial terms but rather in those agencies and organizations just doing their job. They helped to ensure that white privilege would be bureaucratically enforced, popularly encouraged, spuriously defended, easily disguised, generally forgotten, but relentlessly duplicated throughout American society.

This evil occurred despite a human rights movement that was organizing in opposition. White supremacist policy and practice could not have happened without widespread white acquiescence that formed a culture of conformity and suspicion anxious to preserve its dominant social status and stifle potential dissenters. Small wonder, then, that white suburban youth in the 1960s would join the global rebellion against white supremacy enacted in their name, as well as rebelling against the personal repression they experienced in that stifling atmosphere. Their rebellion also often included a rejection of white privileges that they had never asked for—privileges that accompanied black discrimination. This rejection represented a significant phenomenon that would not only affect social movements but also create white sympathy and activism against those privileges, both from without and within key institutions.

The danger today, however, is that looking back, white Americas often collectively protest: "We're not the people those other white people were!"—when in fact progress continues to be compromised by reaction. This reaction was substantially institutionalized throughout society during this era—from the military to the factory to the schools to the neighborhoods—and in large part through mass white complicity.[102]

The landmarks that define this decade in United States history helped set the stage for a collection of opposites: tentative steps toward federal intervention in civil rights matters simultaneous with federal promotion of white privilege, especially in housing, labor, education, and veterans' rights; the merging of the two major labor federations under government protection and supervision that institutionalized both white privilege and the further loss of workers' autonomy; the social discipline and homogenization of a European American population that was diverse both in class and ethnic terms; and mass protest as well as mass reaction around civil rights. This collection of potentially volatile opposites suggests not so much a slumbering beast as a ticking time bomb.

Chapter 6

"IT WAS SOMETHING THAT WAS HARD TO DESCRIBE"

Black Movement, White Reaction, and Affirmative
Action from the Civil Rights Movement to
Reagan-Bush, 1955–93

I

The incubator of 1960s social protest was the organized and spontaneous struggle by African Americans in the South against white supremacy.[1] There is, however, a modern fable that holds that the civil rights movement was a black middle-class phenomenon and that affirmative action today is a product of black middle-class integrationist advocacy and liberal Democratic philanthropy. But both the civil rights and Black Power movements, as well as black urban riots and "wildcat" (unauthorized) industrial strikes, had black working-class origins, participation, and focus, even when there was middle-class leadership.[2]

As sociologist Aldon D. Morris has shown, it was the mass working-class movement (including the black churches) that chose the leadership before the charismatic leadership helped galvanize the movement.[3] Riots, rebellions, demonstrations, and strikes during this period represented the frustration and political will by masses of people and by activists to end all manifestations of white supremacy. Affirmative action became the result of the collective—though not always united—black community struggle against white supremacy, rather than a victory for the black middle class at the expense of black workers as is often heard in retrospect.[4] That struggle involved whites as well: becoming directly involved in civil rights organizing, applying those methods to other radical activity such as mobilizing against the Vietnam War and responding to the mid-1960s Black Power challenge to white paternalistic liberalism.[5]

Splits over tactics, strategy, and goals have often revolved around class, but there is no evidence that the black middle-class activists who frequently served as leaders ever intended to fight for themselves alone. Indeed, black professionals in the 1950s only made about 3 percent of the Southern black population.[6] Their high standing in the black community counted for little at white-controlled social and economic institutions, to say nothing of the vast income differential between middle-class blacks and whites. Most of those in the black middle class did not actually achieve that status until subsequent to (and as a result of) the civil rights movement.[7]

However, this is not to say that a certain middle-class agenda did not retard the mass movement to some extent (much as it does today) with legalistic strategies, self-help notions, class distinctions, tendency to compromise, and a de-emphasis on economic equality.[8] But segregation, as Morris has pointed out, "[i]ronically . . . facilitated the development of black institutions and the building of close-knit communities. . . . Cooperation between the various black strata was an important collective resource for survival."[9]

Jim Crow was a symbolic reminder of not just separation but white status superiority. For example, black men and women on their way to the most menial jobs in the city had to yield the most convenient seats on the bus to white people in an important daily ritual of humiliation for blacks and affirmation for whites.[10] Confronting whites' privilege to send their children to better schools than blacks and thus improve their life chances was probably the greatest challenge to Jim Crow.[11] In the affirmative action debate today, modern white resentment at losing the "bottom rail" that was once below them (similar to the abolition of slavery) needs to be considered in the context of historical memory. Benign calls to forgive and forget and to "celebrate diversity" cannot erase the line many white people have drawn beyond which they will yield no more: their very social status as whites.[12]

Too often forgotten about the Cold War that the United States was involved in during this period for political and economic hegemony with the Soviet Union and China are two prominent issues. First, there were also violent and nonviolent class and human rights struggles going on at home in the United States—beginning mainly in the South and then spreading throughout the nation. Second, part of the inspiration for mass antiwhite supremacist and antiwar militancy (and resistance towards involvement in those wars) had to do with the model of those people who were the targets of America's imperial wars in Africa, Asia, and Latin America because of their own resistance.

The 1960s' movements waned as all social movements eventually do, and activity then centered on reforming existing institutions or creating alternative ones. In fact, there was never an "affirmative action movement" per se until after affirmative action had come under attack in the 1990s—long after its first appearance as an antidiscrimination tactic to enforce equal opportunity measures and a state device for regulating discrimination. This chapter looks at how the combined sum of those black movements (including both black nationalism and integrationism) against white privilege produced the compromise with the status quo known today as affirmative action.

The benefits of affirmative action, of course, are generally made available to those individuals broadly termed "minorities and women," not just African Americans. This is a result of the confluence of a number of antidiscrimination movements that reached their zenith in the 1960s, including Latinos, Native Americans, and women. All of these movements, despite their own respective autonomous origins and development, fundamentally owe their inspiration to that of African Americans, and the combined effect of these movements produced a concept of "temporary" compensation for past discrimination for these groups, from suggested hiring minimum quotas to congressional districts drawn in such a way that blacks and Latinos are in the majority. But as this is a historical study of the roots of affirmative action, I will be primarily focusing on how African Americans put affirmative action on the agenda.

II

Was the invention of affirmative action advocacy simply a kind of "big bang" pragmatic confluence of civil rights protest, riots, liberal guilt, and bureaucratic activism, as suggested by John David Skrentny?[13] We have seen the historical impossibility of that notion. Civil rights activists since Reconstruction have wrestled with the ideals of equal opportunity and "color blindness" in civic affairs versus utilizing coercion and compensation to combat the tenacity of white supremacy. Additionally, there is a remarkably similar propensity among both white liberal and conservative scholars either to ignore or dismiss the conundrum for black activists: "speaking truth to power" on the one hand and making conciliatory pronouncements for tactical advantage on the other.[14]

For the most part, during the 1960s the NAACP and the Urban League were able to subsume their doubts and ambivalence into diplomatic language for white audiences. The same goes for sympathetic public officials in 1965 (similar to those of today) who were dismissing quotas as "illegal" while inventing their own euphemisms (for example, "substantial" numbers).[15] However, the constituency and leadership of more radical direct-action grassroots groups like the Congress of Racial Equality (CORE), Southern Christian Leadership Conference (SCLC), and Student Nonviolent Coordinating Committee (SNCC) were not shy about employing compensatory justice formulations.[16]

Even the most conservative of all the civil rights groups, the Urban League, debated the "Marshall Plan" proposed by its president, Whitney Young Jr. Young's proposal was for "indemnification" (another name for reparations) for black America based on the precedent of veterans' preferences, and he argued for it until negative feedback forced him to support a Bayard Rustin–type antipoverty coalition proposal.[17] Yet the language of typical affirmative action plans—from the earliest to the present—not only suggests the integrationist model but *also* historic black nationalist claims for reparations, reflecting the debate going on within black institutions.

Black nationalism among black workers has deep historical roots, as Manning Marable points out, so it should be no surprise that even integrationist civil rights leaders would at times employ the rhetoric of reparations and autonomy.[18] Consider these examples: (1) Martin Luther King Jr.'s 1963 call for America to redeem its "bad check" to black America;[19] (2) the 1966 Black Panther Party program call for the currency equivalent of "40 acres and two mules";[20] (3) James Forman and the 1969 Black Manifesto demand to white churches for $500 million in reparations for their part in propping up slavery and racism;[21] (4) the recommendation by the 1972 National Black Political Convention in Gary, Indiana, that a national majority-black presidential commission be established to award reparations to African Americans based on past and present racial oppression;[22] and (5) black students' demands for "open admissions" programs, higher black enrollment, hiring of more black professors and staff, and more black studies courses and departments.

Most antiwhite supremacist activity during this period took place in urban areas like Birmingham, Montgomery, New York, Detroit, Chicago, Newark, the San Francisco Bay Area, and Los Angeles, all of which became largely black or majority-black working-class cities in the 1960s.[23] But a study of 1960s' protest must begin with the 1955 Montgomery bus boycott. Following by a year the landmark *Brown* decision, the boycott expressed the confluence of movements: labor, black community, and civil rights legal strategy. It was a popular uprising in the aftermath of the NAACP's lawsuit in *Brown* and was initiated by NAACP activists E. D. Nixon and Rosa Parks after Parks's refusal to cede her seat to a white man on a Montgomery city bus.

Nixon's position as regional director of the BSCP with Parks (a professional seamstress) as his secretary also forms a link with the Depression-era struggles against white supremacy in industry and within white trade unions led by BSCP president A. Philip Randolph.[24] According to former NAACP President Roy Wilkins, E. D. Nixon "was the godfather of the boycott; through him all the years of fighting and organizing done by the BSCP and the NAACP came to fruition in Montgomery."[25] It was also, according to boycott organizer Mary Fair Burks,

the women who were trailblazers in the Montgomery Bus Boycott—Rosa Parks, Jo Ann Robinson, Johnnie Carr, and members of the Women's Political Council [as well as] . . . nameless cooks and maids who walked endless miles for a year to bring about the breach in the walls of segregation.[26]

Organized as the Montgomery Improvement Association, the group's initial principal demand would only have eliminated the reserved section in the middle of the bus but would let stand the "black in the back and white in the front" setup. But representing a harbinger of demands that united black community and black labor was the group's demand for the bus company to hire black drivers for predominantly black routes.[27] The national NAACP actually frowned on this wildcat movement for not initially pursuing a full frontal assault on segregation.[28]

But the movement the black community helped launch, along with the 1954 Supreme Court victory in the *Brown* decision, went far beyond the NAACP's legalistic strategy.[29] In accounting for the sudden rise of militancy in that 1955 campaign, Parks told an interviewer years later something that also illustrates that entire era of protest and autonomous political activity in general: "It was something that was hard to describe. It drew the whole community together and this began to be noticed by other people in other sections of the country."[30]

It must not be forgotten that black labor continued in the 1960s to campaign against discrimination, both independently as well as within the AFL-CIO. Also forming part of Montgomery bus boycott history, for example, was District 65 of the National Council of Distributive Workers (NCDW), a black-led union of 40,000 workers that broke with the AFL-CIO because, in the words of its president David Livingston, "it has not faced up to the fight against racism and for liberation."[31] The NCDW, according to labor historians Philip Foner, Ronald Lewis, and Robert Cvornyek,

contributed heavily to the boycott—not from union funds but from gifts solicited from the membership. . . . King attended every District 65 convention from the days of the bus boycott. . . . Speaking at one of the conventions, King once said: "Indeed, you are the conscience of the labor movement."[32]

King himself not only called for the abolition of racial discrimination and segregation in the United States, but his campaign for economic equality became confrontational and at times suggested reparations and remedial black racial preferences. This was true despite the fact that it was often couched in middle-class integrationist rhetoric of "rehabilitating the disadvantaged."

In a January 1965 interview with *Playboy* magazine, King supported black compensation based on slavery, Jim Crow, and the precedent of American Indian settlements and veterans preferences. In doing so, he went beyond his own previous statements, as well as those by other civil rights leaders, comparing needed black urban aid with the federal government's relief programs in Appalachia and in postwar Europe with the Marshall Plan. In answer to the interviewer's query, "Do you feel it's fair to request a multibillion-dollar program of preferential treatment for the Negro, or for any other minority group?" King replied:

I do indeed. Can any fair-minded citizen deny that the Negro has been deprived? Few people reflect that for two centuries the Negro was enslaved, and robbed of any wages—potential accrued wealth which would have been the legacy of his descendants. All of America's wealth today could not adequately compensate its Negroes for his centuries of exploitation and humiliation. It is an economic fact that a program such as I propose would certainly cost far less than any computation of two centuries of unpaid wages plus accumulated interest. In any case, I do not intend that this program of economic aid should apply only to the Negro; it should benefit the disadvantaged of *all* races.

Within common law we have ample precedents for special compensatory programs, which are regarded as settlements. American Indians are still being paid for land in a settlement manner. Is not two centuries of labor, which helped to build this country, as real a commodity? Many other easily applicable precedents are readily at hand: our child labor laws, social security, unemployment compensation, manpower retraining programs. And you will remember that America adopted a policy of preferential treatment for her millions of veterans after the war—a program which cost far more than a policy of preferential treatment to rehabilitate the traditionally disadvantaged Negro would cost today.[33]

Despite King's abhorrence of violence in any form, after the August 1965 Watts "riots" in Los Angeles he nonetheless sympathized with Watts as a class rebellion. During his visit there he referred to it as "a rebellion of the underprivileged against the privileged."[34] King saw Black Power and urban violence as self-defeating and threats to the nonviolent victory over racism that he hoped for, yet the Black Power advocates also influenced King's thinking.[35]

By 1967 King was calling for a nationwide campaign to "dislocate" American cities as an "alternative to rioting," as one newspaper reported his plan: one that would provide for "jobs, improved housing, better education and more intensive enforcement of existing civil rights legislation."[36] In fact, according to Malcolm X, there had been a growing sentiment among African American activists for the 1963 March on Washington for Jobs and Freedom to produce just such a shutdown to stop the Southern congressional delegation's filibuster then going on against the Civil Rights bill:

[T]hey were going to march on Washington, march on the Senate, march on the White House, march on the Congress, and tie it up, bring it to a halt, not let the government proceed. They even said they were going out to the airport and lie down on the runway and not let any airplanes land. I'm telling you what they said. . . . That was the black revolution.

It was the grass roots out there in the street.[37]

Pauli Murray confirmed this sentiment in a letter she wrote to NAACP president Roy Wilkins from Yale Law School in June 1963, where she was working on her doctorate. She proposed that the NAACP coordinate a massive sit-in involving "1,000,000 persons, colored and white," and carry out direct action campaigns during the march, if that became necessary to stop the filibuster.[38] Direct action proposals were abandoned after a nervous President John F. Kennedy (1961–63), reminiscent of President Roosevelt in 1941, called civil rights leaders to the White House just before the march and pledged passage of the bill in exchange for a nonconfrontational rally.[39]

The moral example of Montgomery sparked the civil rights movement, but the black workers' movement of the 1960s could be said to have begun in Birmingham. "Birmingham is the Pittsburgh of the South," wrote black autoworker and intellectual James Boggs in 1963:

> Inside the central city the Negro masses live in the black ghetto. It was these ghetto-ized Negroes who broke through police lines on that memorable day in May 1963. Both the President and the Attorney General immediately recognized and stated that the real problem had now become the danger of explosion from the unemployed Negroes concentrated in the Northern cities. The Birmingham events lit the spark which has since erupted in the struggle by Northern Negroes, in cities like Chicago, New York, and Philadelphia, against *de facto* segregation in jobs, schools, and housing. From the moment *de facto* segregation became the issue, the way in which the American system actually operates also became the issue.[40]

It was during Project C (for "confrontation") that African Americans fought back against police during nonviolent protests against discrimination in Birmingham in 1963.[41] A dual power situation actually arose in which the outgoing defeated city administration refused to cede power to the one newly elected, so the private sector moved to negotiate with civil rights leaders.

The newly elected white mayor, David Vann, later recalled that the accords were almost undone by Rev. Fred Shuttlesworth, who objected to the agreement calling for only three black clerks to be hired immediately in downtown Birmingham stores. Shuttlesworth wanted three blacks hired in each store.[42] He also helped lead black community protests against police repression. But Shuttlesworth was an exception among the middle-class black movement leaders, as Robin D. G. Kelley points out:

> Although Shuttlesworth was far more sympathetic to working people than Birmingham's traditional black bourgeoisie had been, the ACMHR [Alabama Christian Movement for Human Rights]. . . . leadership defined racial equality in employment in terms of civil service and professional jobs for qualified blacks and viewed conditions in the slums as essentially a moral dilemma rather than a product of unequal opportunity.[43]

Too often remembered as only a kind of footnote to the 1964 Civil Rights Act was the Voting Rights Act of 1965 and the multiclass mass movement that inspired it. Hugh Davis Graham has noted King's tactical brilliance in taking the offensive in reviving the voting registration drive in Dallas County, Alabama (where Selma was the county seat), and later staging the 7 March 1965 Selma-to-Montgomery march as part of the campaign to get the bill passed. Citing the internal SCLC debate discussed in David Garrow's biography of King, *Bearing the Cross*, Graham maintains: "The strategic paradox was the realization by King and his lieutenants that nonviolent protest would fail unless it triggered violent repression."[44]

Federal reforms and enforcement had proved ineffective, as there was still "a racial differential in registration of 11 percent to 76 percent [black to white in Dallas County]."[45] Alabama police and state troopers "cooperated" in this scenario of martyrdom by beating and teargassing marchers, and Jimmy Lee Jackson and the Rev. James J. Reeb were killed during the campaign—the former by state troopers, the latter by white terrorists, who also killed Viola Lee Liuzzo two weeks later. (Reeb and Liuzzo were both white.)[46] The often-quoted emotional proaffirmative action Howard University speech by President Lyndon B. Johnson (1963–69) on 4 June 1965 (the "starting line of a race" speech) was actually made to announce the imminent passage of the Voting Rights bill. Additionally, it represents a summation of the classic white liberal quandary: simultaneously empathizing with and paternalistically judging black oppression and black rebellion, capped with a cautious and ambivalent attempt at coercing whites to accept economic and political rectifying of their historical privileges.[47]

It does not require a close reading of Johnson's speech and King's *Playboy* interview six months earlier to spot some apparent similarities between white liberal paternalist integrationism and black middle-class uplift ideology, notwithstanding King's reparations demands. But black demands for immediate satisfaction in the form of timetables and quotas, however modest they may have been, for the most part sprang from a growing militance that demanded immediate results over vague promises. This should come as a surprise to no one, since militant movements generally make demands for tangible results, often as a reaction to past inaction or duplicity on the part of those in power. Reminiscent of the abolitionist "immediatism" that took hold in the 1830s, one could also say that there is in the black community and among its allies both a distant and a recent historical memory of the white status quo not changing without being given a definite plan.

III

The Cold War and fear of domestic anarchy acted as an impetus in the first steps taken toward re-instituting the laws and policies from the first Reconstruction to craft antidiscrimination measures and make African Americans full citizens. These measures included the 1957 and 1964 Civil Rights Laws, the 1965 Voting Rights Act, President Kennedy's and President Johnson's executive orders, and the 1972 Equal Employment Opportunity Act.

President Kennedy used (but did not invent) the phrase "affirmative action" in his Executive Order 10925 in 1961 that forbade government contractors from discriminating in hiring based on "race, creed, color, or national origin."[48] He issued this order at a time when civil rights was barely even on his agenda, but it set a precedent for "affirmative action" programs in both the public and private sectors with the watchdog agency known as the President's Committee on Equal Employment Opportunity (PCEEO).[49] Johnson's Executive Order 11246 in 1965 surpassed Kennedy's order in requiring federal contractors to ensure equal employment opportunity based on race.[50] But it was Title VII of the 1964 Civil Rights Act that finally outlawed all job discrimination, not just by government contractors, and established the Equal Employment Opportunity Commission (EEOC).[51]

Civil rights activists actually thought that Title II (public accommodations) would arouse the greatest opposition from Southern senators and representatives and therefore be the hardest to pass.[52] In fact, arguments from the Title VII debate mainly reflected the debates over "social equality" found in those Title II debates. Opponents' concerns centered over the "right" of employers to hire whomever they saw fit (even if it involved discrimination by race), which was compared to the "right" of innkeepers and restaurant owners to choose their clientele.[53] Some, like Sen. Everett Dirksen (R-Illinois), insisted that their objections were not supportive exclusively of "white employers" and their "right" to hire their own. Dirksen even used the Harlem Globetrotters as an example of black employers who might lose similar rights to "preserve their racial identity" if Title VII were enacted.[54]

Civil rights proponents argued in both cases that certain precedents like the

Fourteenth Amendment and the interstate commerce clause of the Constitution prohibited discrimination based on race, and that jobs, hotels, and restaurants were all within the public domain and therefore subject to federal law.[55] Objections raised to Title VII for potentially establishing "quotas" were dismissed by liberal proponents like Sen. Hubert Humphrey (D-Minnesota) and Rep. John Lindsay (R-New York).[56] However, years later, when United States Supreme Court Justice William Rehnquist wrote his dissent in the 1979 *United Steelworkers v. Weber* decision criticizing federal "bureaucrats" and black "quotas," he cited that very debate—in particular Sen. Sam Ervin (D-North Carolina), who wanted to delete Title VII because he said it "would make the members of a particular race *special favorites of the laws*."[57] Justice Rehnquist also noted that, despite the adamant objections of civil rights supporters Sen. Richard Clark (D-Iowa) and Sen. Edmund Muskie (D-Maine), two Title VII opponents—Sen. Norris Cotton (R-New Hampshire) and Sen. Carl Curtis (R-Nebraska)— actually "expressed dismay that Title VII would prohibit preferential hiring of 'members of a minority race in order to enhance their opportunity.' "[58]

An additional irony came about in the addition of women as one of the protected classes under Section 703 of Title VII.[59] From all outward appearances, the clause prohibiting gender discrimination was added to Title VII to sabotage the entire act by Rep. Howard Smith (D-Virginia), who had once held sympathetic hearings for white supremacist Philadelphia transit workers in 1944 and against the FEPC. Pauli Murray, who was both a contemporary observer and activist, arrived at that logical-sounding conclusion.[60] But a more complete and very revealing explanation is provided by historian Hugh Davis Graham, who discloses that Smith had in fact supported the Equal Rights Amendment (ERA) since 1945. Furthermore, Smith was friendly with Alice Paul's feminist National Women's Party (NWP)—a group that had definite white supremacist leanings. It was actually the NWP that convinced Smith to add that amendment protecting women's employment rights to Title VII. Otherwise, the NWP declared in a resolution unanimously passed at its national convention that year, the bill would not offer "to a *White Woman*, a *Woman of the Christian Religion*, or a *Woman of United States Origin* the protection it would afford to Negroes."[61]

Echoing century-old white supremacist suffragist appeals, a contingent of white female congressional representatives, including Martha W. Griffiths (D-Michigan), Katherine St. George (R-New York), and Catherine May (R-Washington), invoked that same argument in the House debate against the flabbergasted efforts of civil rights and women's rights advocates like Edith Green (D-Oregon) and Emmanuel Celler (D-New York) in the House, who feared that it was being used as a weapon to capsize the Civil Rights Bill.[62] Civil rights proponents, notes Graham, were caught flat-footed and had no substantive counterarguments to make. But if they feared a replay of the Fifteenth Amendment debates nearly a century earlier, they were mistaken, as the Civil Rights Act ultimately passed over the opposition of those like Smith.

Whether Smith meant this performance as a last-minute desperation monkey wrench tactic or simply as a "last laugh" in a losing cause cannot be determined. But to Pauli Murray and other women's rights advocates also opposed to white supremacy, this was a gift from an unlikely source to a women's movement that was still in its infancy.[63] The President's Commission on the Status of Women (PCSW), formed in 1961 by President Kennedy and chaired by Eleanor Roosevelt until her death in 1962, had opposed the ERA and the inclusion of sex discrimination in Kennedy's Executive Order 10925 because "discrimination based on sex, the Commission believes, involves problems sufficiently different from discrimination based on the other factors listed to make separate treatment preferable."[64]

Including a ban on gender discrimination in Title VII constituted what Graham calls Alice Paul's "posthumous revenge" on Eleanor Roosevelt for the latter's opposition to the ERA.[65] In the end, the black-led civil rights movement helped inspire the women's liberation movement—with unintended help from reactionaries creating a more inclusive Title VII. The National Organization for Women (NOW) and the Women's Equity Action League (WEAL) grew nationally out of this battle, followed by feminist groups in the 1970s and the mass campaign against gender wage differentials, promotions, occupations, and admissions to law and medical schools.[66]

Moreover, as Graham points out: "The EEOC's first annual report [in 1966] revealed that only 60 percent of the complaints were racial, and 37 percent charged sex discrimination!"[67] And while that first year saw many black complainants charging discrimination in hiring and firing (37.3 percent), only 5.6 percent of women had those complaints, instead objecting mainly to unequal employee benefits and seniority lines.[68]

In all of the congressional debates over civil rights legislation during this period, there can be heard the distinct echo of the Reconstruction and Redemption eras. Rep. Thomas Abernethy (D-Mississippi) issued both a warning and a prediction in 1964 of a nationwide popular white supremacist movement (often called the "white backlash"):

There was a time when the people of my part of the country stood alone in their opposition to the might of the Federal Government in forcing social change. But now we are not alone. Our support is coming from many places, especially the big metropolitan centers of the North and West—Philadelphia, New York, Detroit, Los Angeles—everywhere that there is a large and concentrated Negro population.[69]

Meanwhile, in the Senate Sen. John Sparkman (D-Alabama) was comparing the Civil Rights Act of 1875 with the present bill, portraying in histrionic terms what he considered to be the "nightmare" of Reconstruction now about to be revisited:

In those days when the Southland lay prostrate, crushed, harshly ruled by military governors, the Congress, in which the South was misrepresented in many cases by residents of Northern States, rammed through the notorious "Civil Rights Act of 1875." This was one of the infamous "force bills" designed to tear apart the very fabric of southern life.[70]

Sen. Humphrey, acting as both floor manager and diplomat, displayed empathy for the standard invocation of "the dark days of Reconstruction" made by Sen. Ervin, who offered this curious comparison: "We [Southerners] have historical recollections of the days of Reconstruction, when Congress passed laws which it would not allow the Supreme Court to pass upon. . . . We are like the Irish, who suffered great injustices at the hands of the British."[71] To this Humphrey responded with his usual manner of studied deference: "I can well understand the Senator's concerns and point of view. . . . The South suffered unjustly and unduly at the hands of the victorious North."[72] However, during a long earlier oration, Humphrey had made this lucid, prophetic, and (for Humphrey) uncharacteristic observation that also reflected liberal domestic concerns in the era of national liberation movements around the world rising up to overthrow European and American colonialism:

In a sense, America is now in the midst of a struggle of anticolonialism. Those of us who seek to impose this yoke of superiority—which is nothing more or less than a refined definition of the ugly practice of colonialism—will find that the yoke of superiority will be ripped from our hands. We can either drop it peacefully and treat our fellow citizens as human beings or it will be torn from us—and rightly it should.[73]

While President Johnson was more "affirmative" (as well as successful) in his efforts to pass both the Civil Rights Act of 1964 and the Voting Rights Act of 1965 than Kennedy had been, both were responding to threats of and actual mass white violence as well as the embarrassment of American racism before the world.[74] Previously, America presidents had to dispatch troops to Arkansas (1957) and Mississippi (1962) to enforce court orders allowing black students to attend previously all-white schools.

Worrying about national prestige and propaganda points being gained by "Communism," President Eisenhower had referred to "demagogic extremists" and "disorderly mobs" in Little Rock, Arkansas, in a national address in which he announced the sending of federal troops to that city. He then added, "Our personal opinions about the [*Brown*] decision have no bearing on the matter of enforcement."[75] Citing that precedent, and as part of a national letter and telegram campaign, John A. Morsell, acting for NAACP chief Roy Wilkins, wrote to President Kennedy in 1962 urging troops to protect James Meredith's attempt to attend the University of Mississippi in Oxford: "[P]ublic officials there are willing to risk plunging the state into anarchy in an effort to deny to the state's colored citizens their constitutional rights."[76]

Within ten weeks of the 1963 Birmingham confrontation, 758 demonstrations were held in 186 cities with 14,735 arrested.[77] Many marches were countered by white race riots and legal activity to tie up the NAACP in court. White defiance against black protest was led by Southern governors, local police, judges, and the middle-class leadership of white supremacist organizations like the Ku Klux Klan and the White Citizens' Councils. During the late 1950s the Klan and White Citizens' Councils in the South were involved in forming "several groups of southern workers committed to racial segregation and white supremacy."[78]

The white middle class was also later instrumental in leading a race riot in the 1975 Boston school bus boycott. Some leaders in that boycott were also working class, and local unions, like those of the police, firefighters, teamsters, and construction workers, also opposed the court order mandating busing (black) students to integrate the public schools. In 1982 the Boston local of the American Federation of Teachers (AFT) opposed the court's order that more black teachers be hired.[79] But despite today's almost complete disappearance of the white race riot, white anger at black demands for equality as well as white fears of black rebellion inform white opposition to affirmative action.

In 1963, demonstrations by African Americans against segregation and for jobs and better housing took place in Birmingham and in Cambridge, Maryland, turned into riots, provoked in part by police repression. Federal troops were sent to Birmingham, and the National Guard was called up to occupy Cambridge as well as other cities during the 1960s.[80] Black community protests accompanied lawsuits against racist construction unions for more apprenticeship programs and black hiring. Sites were picketed and often shut down, as in Newark in 1965 and in Cincinnati, St. Louis, and San Francisco in 1966. In 1968 the black and Latino (mostly Puerto Rican) community of Ocean Hill–Brownsville in Brooklyn—including teachers—fought for community control of schools against the AFT local that resisted the transferring of white teachers deemed to be insensitive.[81] Meanwhile, what was the reaction of the private employers to this social upheaval that, in addition to protests over education, housing, and public sector employment, also related to the workplaces in the private sector?

V

Articles published by the National Association of Manufacturers (NAM) in 1965 show a paternalist attitude toward the breaking down of the color bar in industry similar to that exhibited by white liberals in Congress who authored and supported civil rights legislation. There was a growing popular white sentiment that wanted to abolish overt prejudice without disturbing the status quo.[82] It is important to remember, however, that affirmative action types of programs did not come into being as some kind of white ruling-class pacification conspiracy to pull the black middle class out of the ghetto and into a role of neocolonial leadership—even if those kinds of discussions were actually held at the highest levels of power.[83] Corporations and the federal government did react frantically to black protests, particularly after the 1967 Detroit riots. But what was implemented was never intended to eliminate discrimination. White racial preferences were only revised, never abolished.

As the center of the American automobile industry—itself a vital arm of American industry—Detroit especially was seen as needing "pacifying." After the 1967 riots, as seen in a collection of studies conducted by the Wharton School of Economics, industry moved quickly to give preferences to hiring African Americans in jobs in the auto plants. These were jobs previously denied to black workers, although they were still generally the worst jobs available.[84]

The Commission on Civil Disorders (also known as the Kerner Commission) was appointed 27 July 1967 by President Johnson, during a summer that saw disturbances in 150 cities, and its report was published the following year, just before riots again broke out in more than 100 cities after King's assassination in Memphis on 4 April 1968.[85]

Actual change was not as easy as predicted by the 1965 NAM report. Urban Institute studies have shown the ground-in habits of industry in how they judge job applicants: "merit" still means "white."[86] Despite language in the NAM report about eliminating prejudicial attitudes, nothing was done to change the status quo at the workplace: that whites should have first pick of what was available. In 1969, the *Inner City Voice*, the newspaper of the League of Revolutionary Black Workers (LRBW) in Detroit, revealed that NAM had held a "counter insurgency seminar" in a Detroit auto plant.[87] In 1974, the business community in the form of the national Chamber of Commerce would join with the AFL-CIO in filing briefs opposing affirmative action in the *DeFunis v. Odegaard* case before the United States Supreme Court.[88] The message was clear: blacks should continue to work at the most menial jobs and not advance at the expense of white workers.

In a modern twist of Eric Williams's quotation of a colonial Barbadian slaveowner that "three blacks work better and cheaper than one white man,"[89] black autoworkers called the preautomation days of the auto industry " 'niggermation' (in which one black man does the job previously done by three white men)."[90] "Niggermation" represented an attempt to keep down labor costs while allowing equipment to deteriorate in anticipation of the big investment in automated equipment that was anticipated.[91] It was the black-led general rebellion against these unsafe plants that would provide much of the impetus for the auto industry to retool and institute drastic layoffs.[92] After this challenge, white status throughout all American industry was once again reconstructed—so to speak—both preferentially and precariously.

Organized labor and industry were forced by lawsuits and public protest to implement voluntary affirmative action plans after initial indifference. Although it later came to be part of the broader civil rights movement, the AFL-CIO refused to endorse the 1963 March on Washington and after the Civil Rights Act was passed "did not hesitate to join with anti–civil rights forces to limit the effectiveness of Title VII. . . ."[93] Its opposition to affirmative action in the 1974 *DeFunis* case turned into support for the Supreme Court's *University of California v. Bakke* compromise decision on affirmative action in 1978 and its 1979 *Weber* decision allowing private sector affirmative action plans to employ preferences and quotas.[94]

However, in 1984 the AFL-CIO filed an amicus curiae brief to reverse the *Firefighters v. Stotts* lower court decision in favor of black firefighters in Birmingham, Alabama, who had sued to keep from being laid off over first-hired whites with more seniority.[95] How to account for such a reversal? Did this represent progress and then backsliding or support for two "reasonable" plans followed by an "unreasonable" one? The organization's history in effectively fighting remedial job integration measures suggests two things: an acceptance of the principle of affirmative action for workers of color and women, as well as a recognition that it had for the most part finished its work protecting white privilege in industry through seniority.[96] *Weber*, after all, involved a training program that would upgrade only a handful of workers, and the academic *Bakke* case was considered to be a civil rights case and not a workplace issue, while *Stotts* challenged the seniority system itself. White bias in hiring, promotion, and seniority has particularly been the modus operandi with the construction trades, which was challenged in the late 1960s by the Philadelphia Plan. Understanding that plan's origins is crucial to understanding affirmative action history, and the plan actually goes back to the beginning of the civil rights era that saw clashes between pro-black and pro-white autonomous movements.

VI

The Philadelphia Plan evolved in a manner similar to compensatory programs fashioned during the New Deal. In 1967, "activist blacks and liberal white reformers" within the Office of Federal Contract Compliance (OFCC) in the Johnson administration looked for ways to force the construction trade unions to include more people of color in government contract work.[97] This effort was itself the product of black protest. As early as 1963 the NAACP had led a picket line against a Philadelphia school construction project. The protest later turned into a violent confrontation with white hardhats and police.[98] Actually, five years earlier, Philadelphia white-owned businesses that discriminated against blacks found themselves the target of a Selective Patronage campaign organized among black churchgoers by Rev. Leon Sullivan and the Philadelphia Four Hundred, as that alliance of black ministers called themselves.

Combining protest and uplift, the ministers established a training center for African Americans to take jobs opened up by the selective patronage campaign, and the movement spread to other cities like Atlanta, Detroit, and New York.[99] Rev. Sullivan's own account of their successful struggle in Philadelphia is refreshing in its candor and forthrightness on what has become the very contentious subject of "preferences and quotas." When he realized that the Youth Employment Center that they had initially created was not getting jobs into the community, Rev. Sullivan preached a sermon at his Zion Baptist Church entitled "The Walls of Jericho Must Come Down," that began the Selective Patronage campaign. He later recalled the quota debate of the time, how it emerged from movement activity, and its role in forcing changes in company policies:

> As a result of Selective Patronage the discussion of quotas became quite prevalent. . . . Quotas would have been justified, in view of the fact that black people had been "quotaed" out of the company's employment as long as the company existed. . . . But . . . quotas were not enough. Our desire was not only to get black men and women into sensitive positions they had never held before, but also to break the company's entire pattern of discriminatory employment practices. After meeting the minimum request, the company had to continue hiring [to discontinue the boycott].[100]

Rev. Sullivan goes on to discuss how their success was due to pressure from the black community along with support from some whites as well as the media, particularly the black press. There were twenty-nine such campaigns between 1959 and 1963, and Sullivan estimated that as a result over 2,000 skilled jobs were opened directly to black workers and probably many more indirectly. (He maintained that the movement was inspired by the biblical verse found in Matthew 7:7 that declares "seek and ye shall find.") In considering the "reverse discrimination" accusation that was common even then, Rev. Sullivan added this rejoinder that combined an assertion of black job reparations with his assessment of the white preference status quo:

> Sometimes the cry was heard "You are asking for discrimination against white people!"
> Our answer was, "Yes, we are asking for discrimination against white people in upgrading a black man over a white man into a job classification where blacks have been excluded or were employed in insufficiently large numbers. In time that white man will be promoted into the higher job classification anyhow. Black men have been waiting for a hundred years; white men can wait for a few months!"[101]

In cities like St. Louis, San Francisco, and Cleveland, programs similar to the Philadelphia Plan had been tried and failed because of an absence of standards to which employers could be held.[102] In 1967, the Federal Executive Board (FEB) hatched a plan to force change upon the unions by pressuring the employers. It represented part of a growing general frustration among civil rights advocates within the government concerning problems with antidiscrimination enforcement.[103] After finding that only a tiny fraction of Philadelphia's skilled construction union members were "minorities," the OFCC acted on the FEB's plan to require detailed tables for how many "minority workers" would be employed in each craft.[104] Despite these attempts by liberal bureaucrats to circumvent the quota prohibition against "preferential treatment" contained in Section 703(j) of Title VII, U.S. Comptroller General Elmer Staats ruled in 1968 that the Philadelphia Plan was illegal because it imposed preaward conditions.[105]

But the Philadelphia Plan was revived a year later during the Richard Nixon administration (1969–74) by an African American former professional football player, Arthur A. Fletcher, Nixon's assistant secretary of labor for employment standards.[106] Fletcher was explicit about the need for "quotas and timetables" to correct for past and present discrimination.[107] He evolved a plan that skirted the "quota ban" by requiring that in all the major cities OFCC area officials request a "target range" from employers that included not the *numbers* of prospective black workers but the number of *hours* to be worked by blacks.[108] In a fascinating account, Fletcher tells of convincing Nixon and his top officials that they could utilize "existing government regulations" and the "ingrained bureaucracy" rather than writing new civil rights law: "They had no idea that existing procurement laws could be used to write blacks in, to give us a piece of the American pie."[109]

Comptroller Staats then ruled that the new Philadelphia Plan was also illegal after construction contractors and unions protested. This set up a truly bizarre scenario whereby conservative Republican Nixon administration officials like Secretary of Labor George Schultz (much like liberal affirmative action proponents today) found themselves testifying before congressional committees and awkwardly defending compensatory justice for blacks against affirmative action opponents.[110] There was even the spectacle of Schultz teaming up with Fletcher during this debate to ridicule the opposition's color-blind model as unsatisfactory and unpragmatic. The opposition by now included some Northern civil rights proponents as well as conservative Southerners who had opposed but now demanded strict adherence to the formal equality of Title VII. Observers and historians of the modern affirmative action debate might find surprising not just the alignment of political forces on quotas in 1969 but that the opposition felt constrained not to attack the Philadelphia Plan directly but did so through a rider to a hurricane relief bill.[111]

In 1969, Nixon was eager to promote "black capitalism" as well as to calm the militant and often violent black protests against job discrimination.[112] At the same time he wanted to hold on to his "white backlash" blue-collar worker constituency, many of whom had voted for Alabama Democratic Governor George Wallace for president in the 1968 general election when Wallace ran as an independent.[113] This constituency approved (as did white people generally) of Nixon's attacks on the use of school busing for integration.[114] There is a large body of evidence indicating that Nixon wanted to become a "consensus George Wallace," while simultaneously positioning himself as a latter-day Theodore Roosevelt in search of a new Booker T. Washington.[115]

But through his white supremacist appeal Wallace accomplished what Nixon was never able to do: create a combination of what Dan T. Carter calls "as much religious exorcism as political exercise."[116] In 1968, for instance, Wallace spoke to wildly enthusiastic crowds of 70,000 at Boston Commons, 15,000 in Pittsburgh, 16,000 in Baltimore, 12,000 in San Francisco, 10,000 in San Diego, 15,000 in Detroit, 16,000 in Cincinnati, and 20,000 in New York's Madison Square Garden.[117] At the latter "performance" he took off his jacket like a prize-fighter and, combining sex, race, and violence themes (reminiscent of Rebecca Felton's prolynching appeal seventy years earlier), he painted the unmistakably black Other to a crowd now going berserk: "We don't have riots in Alabama," he cried. "They start a riot down there, first one of 'em to pick up a brick gets a bullet in the brain, that's all."[118] Wallace demonstrated how the working-class autonomous reactionary element historically associated with fascism could be aroused by such popular demagoguery when fear of black domination (white privilege's worst nightmare) was invoked.[119]

Meanwhile, congressional Democrats had been split on the Philadelphia Plan of 1969 (which was Nixon's aim: to provoke a fracture between pro–civil rights liberals on the one hand and labor and Southerners on the other). In the end, enough Democrats joined Nixon and sympathetic Republicans to force a standoff in Congress, thus enabling the Philadelphia Plan to survive.[120] Yet by 1972 the two parties had actually switched sides, both on the Philadelphia Plan and "affirmative action" generally, as it was becoming more popularly known. Most Republicans now opposed it altogether, while most Democrats supported it.

VII

The Equal Employment Opportunity Act that was passed in 1972 provided for an expanded EEOC far beyond the Nixon administration's more circumscribed limits. More private workplaces would be covered as well as all government workers, and the agency would now be able to issue cease-and-desist orders as well as file pattern-or-practice suits.[121] And despite the fact that the new voluntary "hometown" plans were ultimately undermined by labor opposition and Labor Department enforcement failure, the Philadelphia Plan—conceived in black protest but implemented primarily by the Nixon administration—became both precedent and paradigm for other affirmative action plans.[122]

One of those grassroots affirmative action initiatives was the Harlem Fight Back organization led by Jim Haughton, a veteran of the Negro American Labor Council. This was a grassroots campaign by African Americans and Puerto Ricans "to get jobs in New York City's multibillion-dollar construction industry."[123] Fight Back had begun in the mid-1960s picketing or conducting sit-ins at construction sites. Contractors tried to meet this protest with token response, while the community escalated its protests and traditional civil rights and job rights groups like the NAACP and the Workers Defense League pursued the struggle in the courts and in developing alternative apprenticeship programs to those traditionally handed down by white males to younger family members. After violent protests at construction sites in 1963, 3,000 minority applicants were screened for trade jobs: only 31 got in.[124]

The New York Plan that was devised by union leaders as one of the hometown plans in reaction to the Philadelphia Plan "seemed so inadequate that even the O.F.C.C. director in Washington, John L. Wilks, could not approve it."[125] But after a meeting in 1970 between state Construction Trades Council President Peter Brennan and President Nixon in which Brennan pledged labor support for the Vietnam War, Wilks suddenly approved the plan, which was denounced by civil rights groups. When three construction unions refused to abide by its terms, "Mayor John Lindsay reacted in March, 1971, by freezing $200-million in city construction awards."[126]

After seven months, two of the unions capitulated, while one was still adamant. The freeze expired, and the plan was under way with a goal of a thousand trainees that was not even a quarter of the way filled. Herbert Hill, then labor secretary of the NAACP, said at the time:

> There is only one way—numerical goals. You can call it quotas or ranges, but it must be fixed in writing. Not a token 1,000 trainees in some amorphous scheme to get them books, but so many union journeymen working by such a date. And the bid specifications for contractors must reflect population percentages.[127]

A sympathetic *New York Times Magazine* article in 1972 summed up that job struggle and drew an inference of the logical extreme of the community's deferred demands—one that most liberals and conservatives in today's affirmative action debate would consider unthinkable:

> Ultimately, it seems, the job discrimination crisis must be resolved through a combination of governmental action, social commitment and minority pressure. After community people in the South Bronx stormed the courthouse site, the number of trainees there was suddenly trebled. But that still was regarded as insufficient and the day is approaching when militant groups will draw their issue plain: *In minority sections, white men must be laid off to make places for blacks and Puerto Ricans.*[128]

Finally, not to be forgotten as a pivotal event in the evolution of affirmative action is the landmark AT&T settlement of 1973. Historian Robert Weiss notes how within a year of the EEOC receiving new enforcement powers in 1972 (which included increasing its staff from 40 to 222 attorneys), the agency responded to hundreds of minority and female discrimination complaints against the world's largest private employer. The resulting agreement fused those complaints into one that included $23 million worth of modifications (including goals and timetables for hiring and promoting minority and female workers, with seniority "overrides" in some cases to meet those goals), as well as the distribution of $17.5 million in back pay to minority and female workers by 1975. But this agreement and a similar one with the steel industry in 1974 (awarding $30 million in back pay to about 4,000 minority and female workers, as well as agreeing to hiring goals and "plant seniority") represented the zenith of EEOC's activist role.[129]

VIII

In trying to analyze the reasons for the Watts uprising in Los Angeles in 1965, the "[Kerner] Commission had to misinterpret the Black Nationalist rhetoric of many rioters themselves, and impose an integrationist view of racial justice."[130] "Black Power" was more than a slogan, but like "affirmative action," it also meant different things to different people. For black nationalists like Kwame Ture (Stokely Carmichael) and Malcolm X it meant autonomous black political, economic, and social power—both separate from and within the American political framework. For Richard Nixon and black conservatives it meant "black capitalism" as a partnership form of labor exploitation.[131] Despite this ambiguity, "Black Power" more so than "affirmative action" had strong connotations of black self-determination and compensation in addition to its psychologically liberating defiance of circumspect "race relations" rhetoric—and it was not that much of a stretch from the defiant spirit of the so-called New Negro thesis of organizing in the 1950s.[132]

The Black Panther Party, for example, in addition to its community control and self-help campaigns, also called for a United Nations–sponsored plebiscite for black separation and carried out discussions with groups like the Republic of New Afrika on its call for a black nation in the South, which was similar to that of the Nation of Islam.[133] As historian Nikhil Pal Singh concludes in his contribution to a recent collection on the Black Panther Party:

> Most importantly, the Panthers were effective in projecting themselves as an outside force that was also inside the nation because they refused the terms of Black inclusion and citizenship in the American polity at precisely the point of African Americans' greatest augmentation and reform since the Civil War and Reconstruction as a result of the Civil Rights Act of 1964, the Voting Rights Act of 1965, and Johnson's War on Poverty programs.[134]

The Nation of Islam, for its part, in its early newspapers throughout the 1960s featured such headlines and articles as "Separate Black States" and "Land of Our Own," in addition to articles on racism, religion, culture, and black pride. Elijah Muhammad, the organization's leader, spoke to enthusiastic audiences of thousands in New York and Chicago on the subject of reparations.[135]

Despite King's commitment to integration and opposition to the Black Power slogan, he also appears to have been intrigued by the idea of black "dual unionism" (alternative unions) as a protest weapon, notwithstanding his many appearances at AFL-CIO functions and union leaders' official appearances at civil rights functions. A letter to King from black civil rights activist C. Sumner Stone Jr. in 1967 suggests decertifying racist unions with the help of the Negro American Labor Council.[136] During King's last campaign in Memphis, Tennessee, while organized labor dawdled in coming to the aid of black city sanitation workers, King was calling for a black "general strike" in Memphis in response to black militancy and white intransigence.[137] The strike itself began as a walkout against white privileges and escalated into a community struggle that involved students, the black churches, and a riot that began over police provocation during a nonviolent march.[138]

Rioting and looting are not civil rights protests, declared President Johnson in an address to the nation after the late July 1967 Detroit rebellion,[139] but in looking back, Roger Wilkins (then a Justice Department official) disagrees: "Having watched all the riots from '64 to '67 it was quite clear to me that the riots were an extension of the civil rights movement, not something different."[140] Blacks in Northern cities followed the events in the South, contributing support and feeling frustration with the slow pace and betrayals of promises made to the movement. Civil rights demonstrations occurred daily in New York City in 1963.[141] The 1964 Harlem rebellion began after a rally called by CORE to protest Mississippi lynchings "developed into a march on a precinct police station. The crowd clashed with the police. . . ."[142]

In addition, there were demands for black autonomy in urban areas where blacks were increasingly centered and becoming a majority. In July 1967, riots in Newark, New Jersey, broke out after police beat a black cab driver. But other issues were also involved that made this riot political, like most other black urban rebellions: police repression, unemployment, community control of schools, and the passing over of a black candidate for school superintendent.[143] Long before "urban" became a euphemism for "black," a popular viewpoint during this period held that the cities were part of the emerging "black nation," as wholesale black migration to the North had long since rendered moot the CPUSA's "black nation in the South" thesis of the 1930s.[144]

Sociological studies and the Kerner Commission report itself point to unemployment as the primary cause of rioting by citing statistics showing a high rate of unemployment among riot participants. But in *The Politics of Violence*, a study of the 1965 Watts rebellion, one figure stands out: 22 percent of self-described rioters interviewed answered that they were "middle or upper class," 21 percent were "working-class," and 29 percent called themselves "lower class."[145] Not only were community issues important, but menial and token jobs were not enough. Riots can also be read as part of black efforts to end the "white job" category itself.

Evidence of this challenge to the white "hook-up" is provided in the number of lawsuits against "virtually every industrial union" for discrimination during this same period.[146] Sit-ins at construction sites frequently turned into fistfights. Black "dual unions" like the LRBW and Dodge Revolutionary Union Movement (DRUM) flourished, as well as caucuses within the major industrial unions during this period, the latter coming together as the Coalition of Black Trade Unionists (CBTU).[147] The Black Economic Development Conference (BEDC) was a coalition of black nationalist workers and activists who put together the "Black Manifesto" James Forman presented to white churches in 1969 for reparations.[148] Three years later, the National Black Political Convention, a broad coalition of political and social groups and individuals from across the country, declared:

> The economic impoverishment of the Black community in America is clearly traceable to the historic enslavement of our people and to the racist discrimination to which we have been subjected since "emancipation." . . .
>
> Therefore, an incalculable social indebtedness has been generated, a debt which is owed to Black people by the general American society. . . .
>
> It is against the background of such realities that we move to a Black Agenda for economic empowerment.
>
> RECOMMENDATION: That there be established a presidential commission, with a majority of Black members (chosen by the Black Convention or its successor body) to determine a procedure for calculating an appropriate reparations payment in terms of land, capital and cash and for exploring the ways in which the Black community prefers to have this payment implemented.[149]

Amazingly, little has been written on the influential nationwide Black Power student movement of the late 1960s in academia and the precedents that it set for affirmative action. I will consider two examples: Duke University in the South and the University of Wisconsin-Madison (UW) in the North.

At Duke University in Durham, North Carolina, thirty to forty black students took over the Allen Building on the morning of 13 February 1969. Members of the Afro-American Society (AAS), many had just returned from "Black Week," a cultural awareness conference at historically black Howard University in Washington, D.C. They left the building after the National Guard was mobilized and just before local police began moving in. A crowd outside of between 1,000 and 2,000 mostly white students formed a shield for the black students as they left the building.¹⁵⁰ The AAS demands included a black studies department, the right to a black dormitory, a black student population commensurate with the black population of the state (29 percent), "financial reassurance," a black adviser selected by black students, black student fees earmarked for a black student union, an end to "white middle-class criteria" for "determining academic potential" among applicants for admission, and "an immediate end to the tokenism of black representation in university power structure."¹⁵¹

In Wisconsin that same month, the demands upon UW by the Madison Black People's Alliance (some of whose members had also attended Black Week at Howard) included "[t]hat at least 500 Black students be admitted" by the fall 1969 semester, and "[t]hat 20 teachers be allocated for the initiation of the Black Studies Department. . . ."¹⁵² The governor called out the National Guard to assist local police after hundreds of black and white students marched and disrupted classes for two weeks following a weeklong conference on the "Black Revolution." UW's initial response was positive on admissions and hiring but negative on a new and autonomous department: that would have to wait for some years.¹⁵³

It can be fairly stated that without Black Power at the workplace, in the communities, and on the college campuses there would be no such thing as affirmative action today. The same can be said for other movements (like those of Native Americans and Latinos) against oppression and white privilege that combined civil rights and nationalism in the pursuit of such goals as increased hiring and promotions, college admissions, official appointments, and majority-minority voting districts.¹⁵⁴ And while the final result never fit the initial demand, once again the call for timetables and minimum quotas became a prominent marker within both the civil rights and Black Power movements. But it was exactly these kinds of enforcement initiatives that were blocked in the 1978 *Bakke* case.

In 1974, Allan Bakke, a working-class white male, sued the University of California–Davis (UC–Davis) medical school after his application was rejected despite relatively high test scores. Bakke claimed discrimination as a white male, and that his rights under the Equal Protection Clause of the Fourteenth Amendment were violated by the university's special admissions program. That program reserved sixteen spaces out of a hundred for "economically and/or educationally" members of a "minority group" ("Blacks," "Chicanos," "Asians," and "Native Americans").

The university's medical school faculty established this special admissions program in 1971 after the first class in 1968 contained three Asians but no African American, Latino, or Native American students. Between 1971 and 1974, twenty-one African American, thirty Mexican American, and twelve Asian American students (sixty-three in all) were admitted through the special admissions program, which included minority members on the admissions committee itself. The regular admissions program admitted one African American, six Mexican American, and thirty-seven Asian American students, for a total of forty-four. Many whites, including Bakke, applied to the special program under the "disadvantaged" category (similar to today's proposed "class-based" affirmative action programs) but were rejected.[155]

Regardless of whether the medical school set up the program as a result of black community pressure, fear of losing federal funds under Title VI of the 1964 Civil Rights Act, or as a reaction to the general atmosphere of militant black protest in the late 1960s and early 1970s (or all the above), what is important to note is the school's voluntary establishment of a plan that, even if not intentionally, posed a modest challenge to white privilege. While most of the decision's language spoke in terms of "minority handicaps," the Court also acknowledged the preferences that many whites typically enjoyed that it did not consider unconstitutional (such as veterans' preferences and "legacies"—or students with alumni parents).[156] Moreover, in this case, using legal precedent to justify a moral imperative, we can see legal scholars, attorneys, and jurists speaking the language of reparations.

In fact, Justice Brennan, in a dissent joined by Justices White, Marshall, and Blackmun, noted that "Davis had a sound basis for believing that the problem of underrepresentation of minorities was substantial and chronic, and that the problem was attributable to handicaps imposed on minority applicants by past and present racial discrimination."[157] Brennan noted that the majority had at least salvaged "diversity" as a basis for admissions with their decision, while insisting nonetheless that the UC–Davis program had indeed been constitutional. "Congress was empowered under that [enforcement] provision [of the Fourteenth Amendment] to accord preferential treatment to victims of past discrimination in order to overcome the effects of segregation," he wrote, and later added something we have heard earlier, especially by those defending restorative "make-whole" provisions under civil rights and labor law:

> The constitutionality of the special admissions program is buttressed by its restriction to only 16% of the positions in the Medical School, a percentage less that that of the minority population in California. . . . *This is consistent with the goal of putting minority applicants in the position they would have been in if not for the evil of racial discrimination.*[158]

The Court, of which Warren Burger was Chief Justice, ruled five to four that while the university could allow race to be used in considering admissions, it could not reserve slots for "minorities." It also ruled that Bakke had been excluded because of his race, which was a violation of the Constitution's Equal Protection Clause, and the school was therefore ordered to admit him.[159] While some liberal legal scholars breathed a sigh of relief (and some to this day argue that it was a victory for affirmative action), others like Derrick Bell have argued that *Bakke* was the beginning of a downhill slide for affirmative action programs. In that sense it served as a harbinger of future decisions. With its "strict scrutiny" of discrimination claims, the more conservative Rehnquist court in fact safeguards what Bell calls "protection of whites' race-based privilege":

> A paradigm example presents itself in the case of . . . *Bakke.* Relying heavily on the formalistic language of the Fourteenth Amendment and utterly ignoring social questions about which race has power and advantages and which race has been denied entry for centuries into academia, the court held that an affirmative action policy may not unseat white candidates on the basis of their race. By introducing an artificial and inappropriate parity in its reasoning, the court effectively made a choice to ignore historical patterns, to ignore contemporary statistics, and to ignore flexible reasoning. Following a Realist approach, the court would have observed the social landscape and noticed the skewed representation of minority medical students.[160]

Additionally, Cheryl Harris and cultural historian George Lipsitz have both noted how, given that Bakke never challenged the five "legacy" admits to the UC–Davis medical school or his rejection from medical schools without special admissions programs that nonetheless favored younger applicants than himself, his case was based upon a demand to not have to compete with *minorities*, just other whites. In the majority opinion written by Justice Powell, the Court obliged. The Court acknowledged Bakke's nonminority status but was concerned that in similar cases white people might *perceive* that they had suffered racial discrimination. In doing so the Court obviously ignored Charles Sumner's century-old admonition that without a history of slavery or racial oppression there was "no emancipation or enfranchisement to be consummated" for white people—least of all at the expense of black people.[161]

IX

In 1980, the black neighborhoods of Liberty City and Overtown in Miami erupted for five days in protest of what was referred to by many as "another lynching."[162] An all-white jury had just acquitted four white Miami police officers who had beaten a black businessman to death—in a city where adult black unemployment was already 50 percent and urban renewal had decimated Overtown.[163] The subsequent election of Ronald Reagan as president in 1980 with traditionally Democratic white worker support was not the first time that reasserting the "white status quo against black anarchy" was invoked in a national election. Richard Nixon had done the same in 1968 and 1972, as had Barry Goldwater in 1964.[164] But this time the scapegoats were unmistakably identified as black. President Reagan set in motion at the federal level a process that treated race-based affirmative action as both outmoded and an attack on white people that must be eliminated.[165]

It has been commonly observed that the affirmative action legacy that Reagan intended to repudiate included what was inherited from fellow Republican Presidents Nixon and Gerald R. Ford (1974–77).[166] One of those legacies was the broadening of the 1965 Voting Rights Act by the Supreme Court in 1969, as noted by historian Steven F. Lawson:

> Beginning in 1969, it decreed that the statute . . . was also meant to include "all actions to make a vote effective." In a series of decisions the judiciary empowered federal authorities to strike down electoral rules that had the purpose or effect of diluting the strength of black ballots. The conversion from single-member districts to at-large elections, the expansion of municipal boundaries through annexation of largely white areas, and reapportionment plans that produced racially gerrymandered districts were regulations of this type.[167]

Although Republican policies were much more tokenistic than those of Democratic President Jimmy Carter (1977–81), there is controversy over whether he deserves to be called progressive in his civil rights attitudes, policies, and appointments. In support of Carter's record, Robert Weiss points to

Carter's appointments of prominent African American civil rights activists like Eleanor Holmes Norton as chairperson of the EEOC. The federal equal opportunity apparatus was restructured, observes Weiss, and Norton was given the task of reducing the tremendous backlog of 130,000 complaints. However, the EEOC's success at the latter endeavor received mixed reviews from some civil rights groups, which believed investigations had become less efficient and full relief to complainants frustrated. Meanwhile, the already overburdened Office of Federal Contract Compliance Programs (OFCCP) took over contracting enforcement from EEOC, and while in 1978 it collected more in back-pay settlements ($9 million) than the previous year, it allowed too many firms to slide in civil rights violations on the job.[168]

Manning Marable's assessment of Carter's civil rights policies is more blunt: "Once he had assumed office, Carter began to rescind many of the basic achievements of the Second Reconstruction."[169] Carter, he notes, did not fight to save the Full Employment Bill and in 1977 cut black college support to 53 percent and in 1980 down to 18 percent of the 1976 allocation.[170] Ironically, after the Miami riots, Carter told a 4 August 1980 press conference: "I went to Miami [after the riots] . . . and helped put together a package, working with those black leaders there, that would give them some economic assistance. . . . And we've tried to provide jobs." But studies show that effort to have been a failure.[171]

As soon Ronald Reagan took office in 1981, he began to dismantle affirmative action programs as well as all entitlement programs deemed *"black."* "In 1981, for example," writes policy analyst Linda Faye Williams, "the Labor Department proposed revised OFCCP regulations to reduce the number of contractors covered."[172] The Departments of Labor, Justice, and Education as well as the Federal Communications Commission (among others) virtually shut down the antidiscrimination enforcement process. "In sum," notes Williams, "the Reagan and Bush administrations virtually eliminated the threat of sanctions for discrimination in employment."[173]

Not only did President Reagan and his successor, George Bush (1989–93), dismantle much of the federal antidiscrimination enforcement machinery, but they did so with a considerable amount of broad-based active white support.[174] A *Washington Post* survey conducted during Reagan's first year in office concluded: "The white men's unions of 1970 remain the white men's unions of 1981."[175] The Philadelphia Plan and other "hometown" plans were undermined by circumvention, and the combined Reagan and Bush Republican administrations rolled back affirmative action programs from 1981 to 1993, combining white reaction with black conservative support to blunt any future challenges to white privilege as it manipulated the black "self-help" tradition in this new compromise.[176] Another "white reconstruction" had been re-affirmed—not simply by executive or congressional fiat but with both active and passive white support. Nonetheless, these early attacks on affirmative action came at a time when many white people were also beginning to accept the notion of black compensatory justice in some form:

> A 1972 survey had indicated that 82 percent of whites opposed affirmative action plans that favored blacks over equally qualified whites. Nevertheless, 77 percent of those polled approved of job-training programs for blacks. . . . These attitudes were hardened by the [deteriorating] economic situation of the 1970s, which heightened competition for increasingly scarce jobs and spaces in graduate and professional schools.[177]

This popular interpretation by Steven F. Lawson, like other "black-white labor competition" theses, ignores what could better be described as "white caste anxiety." While on the one hand we can see progress in those polls as well as those today that indicate support for "training programs" as a kind of compensation, on the other hand we seem to be spinning our wheels in that most whites still adamantly resist any change in the *end result* of those programs, as Rev. Sullivan noted earlier in his discussions of boycotts and forms of coercion. Black preferential or compensatory hiring that superseded the white "hook-up" would necessarily involve a devaluation of whiteness as an employment criterion—or as a criterion for other social activity.

One can chart the lull following the intense activity of the Black Power movement that followed the civil rights movement in watching both eventually lose their offensive momentum and be forced to go on the defensive with regards to issues of equality. But the combined movements certainly helped change Thurgood Marshall's thinking from arguing against black preferences and quotas as NAACP counsel in the postwar period (or that race had no place in the deliberations on the 1954 *Brown* case) to his 1978 arguments in *Bakke* where he explicitly argued for race-based remedies to counter centuries of white privilege.[178] The late 1960s and early 1970s were similar in many ways to those "seven mystic years" that was W. E. B. Du Bois's description of Reconstruction in terms of the role of black initiative (within a general societal upsurge) in influencing changes in white attitudes and behavior. Substantial numbers of white students and workers became supporters and activists in ways that exposed them to ostracism and even violence at the hands of hostile whites.[179]

The civil rights movement had embarked upon a strategy based on making real the seemingly impossible: abolishing Jim Crow through a direct action campaign against the white-privilege caste system while simultaneously ensuring that ideologically this campaign stayed within accepted bounds of "formal equality." But so pervasively had whiteness been woven into the social fabric that this movement would eventually witness the "splendid failure" (as Du Bois also called Reconstruction) of the 1960s "Second Reconstruction"—after all pro-black movement had finally subsided. As Justice Marshall mused in his 1978 *Bakke* opinion: "I fear that we have come full circle."[180]

Chapter 7

"AND THE LAST SHALL BE FIRST"

Black Reparations, White Ambivalence, and
Historical Memory, 1993–2000

I

Almost four centuries after the founding of the European colonies that later
became known collectively as the United States of America, the most contentious sociopolitical debates and struggles in this country still involve racial caste
status and work. The fact that even the mere mention of affirmative action
provokes such hostility proves that those caste and work issues fought over
during slavery and Jim Crow still remain unresolved.

Work is not just a creative act, additionally subject to alienation and exploitation by those who own the means of production. It also implies chances for
individual and family survival, elevated wealth and social status for individuals
and families, and improved overall life chances. Improving life chances for people of color in the United States has always involved some form of protest
against job and other discrimination. Grievances to rectify the effects of past
or present discrimination can be affirmed, denied, or redressed by executive,
legislative, or judicial action—usually in response to some expression of popular
will—and involve both individuals and "classes." Frustrating those grievances is
the very thing that first caused them: white entitlement, along with denial that
such a thing exists.

167

Does the historical unwillingness of whites to recognize and repudiate their privileges without some kind of pressure or coercion imply the need for more active measures—including the practically taboo subject of "preferences and quotas?"[1] Furthermore, does affirmative action imply mere tokenism or reparations to black victims of the legacy of slavery and segregation by a white population that has benefited from that oppressive institutions? Can fairness ever be confronted as a class issue that favors the wealthy under capitalism without first abolishing white privilege—or more to the point, whiteness itself? Finally, does affirmative action actually reify whiteness if it does not explicitly challenge white privilege?

During Reconstruction official coercive actions were at times deemed necessary against supremacist whites bent on denying black civil rights.[2] Affirmative action as a modern institution actually began coming under attack as early as 1969, as soon as it began to show signs of effectiveness, due in large part to its combination of coercion and growing (if grudging) acceptance by the white majority.[3] After the entity known as the "white race" had been constructed, large corporations, the federal government, the military, the trade unions, and organized religion continually found themselves obliged either to intervene forcefully to discourage whites from defending (sometimes violently) privileges they were always taught were theirs or give in to white hostility.[4] Roger Wilkins reminds us that

> It is insufficient to vilify white males and to skewer them as the whiners that journalism of the kind practiced by *U.S. News and World Report* invites us to do. These are people who, from the beginning of the Republic have been taught that skin color is destiny and that whiteness is to be revered.[5]

Late-twentieth-century surveys conducted by pollster Louis Harris demonstrate that a majority of white Americans support affirmative action as long as there is no sacrifice on their part—sacrifice being implied in loaded words generally used in the media and many polls like "preferences" or "strict quotas." Harris has also criticized the media conflation of "affirmative action" with "preferences and quotas" that paints a distorted picture of mass white revulsion with affirmative action.[6]

But as poll analysts W. Richard Merriman and Edward G. Carmines have indicated: "Even when whites pass the test of racial tolerance . . . this in itself does not mean that they will support compensatory efforts on behalf of blacks."[7]

Conservative opponents understand better than liberal proponents that this is not merely a semantic or marketing war. It concerns the very essence and identity of whiteness as privilege, or "What good is being white if it doesn't mean being number one?"

Will a poll ever be conducted that confronts rather than tacitly accepts the white status quo in its questioning? What if, rather than pose questions to whites-as-the-norm and inquiring as to what (if any) allowances they would extend to people of color, a poll instead asked whites directly if they favored maintaining or scrapping a system based on whiteness?

II

While it has been asserted that affirmative action and civil rights legislation have not been particularly effective,[8] affirmative action has made unmistakable gains in employment, education, and voting rights—all of which have historically been integral elements in creating social progress.[9] Those gains, however, have coexisted with a perpetuation of white privileges like the word-of-mouth hiring practices, suspicion of (not white) racial considerations in college admissions, and Supreme Court rulings against majority-minority congressional voting districts.[10] Furthermore, as has been often pointed out, current affirmative action programs have little value for the black poor despite the roots of those programs in the labor and community struggles of black working people.[11] Astonishingly, this has often been cited as a reason to scrap those programs entirely—simultaneously and contradictorily with the claim that the goals have been reached rendering those programs unnecessary.

The divided consciousness of whiteness has always labored to maintain the contradiction of claiming liberty in an unfree land, has resented and feared black protests against that contradiction, and has been haunted by both the protests and the contradictions. Thomas Jefferson, who claimed to hate slavery even as he prospered from it, wrote in 1785 the much-quoted phrase that has been used to suggest a guilty conscience and an apocalyptic fear of slave insurrections: "I tremble for my country when I reflect that God is just: that his justice cannot sleep forever." Yet equally revealing are his very next words:

that considering numbers, nature and natural means only, a revolution of the wheel of fortune, an exchange of situation, is among possible events: that it may become probable by supernatural interference! The Almighty has no attribute which can take side with us in such a contest.[12]

Abraham Lincoln, who quoted Jefferson's "God is just" phrase in one of his 1858 debates with Stephen Douglas,[13] also concurred with Jefferson's opinion that black people were not needed in this country and were too much trouble.[14] Yet Lincoln also revealed his own divine retribution fantasy during his Second Inaugural Address in March 1865, when, with the Union army poised on the verge of victory (mostly due to the entrance of black soldiers, as he himself admitted), he declared:

> Yet, if God wills that it continue, until all the wealth piled by the bond-man's two hundred and fifty years of unrequited toil shall be sunk, and until every drop of blood drawn with the lash, shall be paid by another drawn with the sword, as was said three thousand years ago, so still it must be said "the judgments of the Lord, are true and righteous altogether."[15]

On the other hand, John C. Calhoun—antebellum slaveowner, United States Senator from South Carolina, and proslavery spokesman—expressed in 1849 (a year before his death) a deep-rooted white fear that slavery's demise also meant white supremacy's demise. Losing both, he predicted, implied by definition not equality but black supremacy—there could be no other alternative.[16] And the history of lynchings and white race riots demonstrates that the targets were primarily blacks who were doing comparatively well financially despite Jim Crow.[17]

In his 1920 essay "The Souls of White Folk," W. E. B. Du Bois exposed the abstractness and artificiality of whiteness without exploring the split consciousness in the white ideology or worldview.[18] But the modern affirmative action debate has exposed this white "twoness": "we're sorry/not sorry," "you're entitled to compensation/you don't deserve it," "you deserve protection/do it yourself," "no, we don't receive privileges/yes we do—don't mess with them," and so on. There is a contradictory "white" folklore that has expected and been rewarded with white racial favoritism (which it generally does not admit), while at the same time claiming to abhor nepotism and favoritism. White-dominated trade unionism simultaneously built a seniority system into union shops to fight "hook-up" types of preferential systems that failed to reward merit and years served, utilizing among other things the "affirmative action" provisions of the 1935 National Labor Relations Act.[19]

The "twoness" of whiteness does not, however, correspond directly to Du Bois' black "twoness"—which was to be American and black.[20] White "twoness" has merged American-ness with whiteness in a way that requires a justification of the contradiction between egalitarian ideology and caste superiority. White racial superiority notions have for the most part been exiled to the margins of society, leaving black racial inferiority conceptions to be worked out in more polite terms than their cruder antecedents. An expert in the field of professional counseling, Tracy L. Robinson points out:

> There seem to be at least two conditions that intensify obliviousness to unearned privilege in its many forms. The first, albeit unconscious, is anticipated benefit of the pervasive privileges to which one has become accustomed. . . . The second condition pertains to the inherent difficulty, shame in, and fear of admitting to the unearned properties of group membership. . . .
> Privilege creates confusion about identity.[21]

An essential part of the black freedom struggle has been the direct challenge to the system of white privileges. That challenge is either implicit in demands for equality or explicit as part of an intellectual critique of a "white problem" in opposition to the prevailing "black problematic" paradigm.[22] If within black discourse explicit demands are muted, either for diplomatic and tactical reasons or to concentrate on remedying the immediate effects of discrimination, this should not be seen as a license to continue portraying discrimination as one-sided without having white beneficiaries.[23]

It is also important to recognize that affirmative action is not just an old Anglo-American legal concept adopted by African Americans as part of the "acculturation" process. It also represents a distinct form of antisubordination politics historically thrown back at white society in "Signifying" fashion (as literature professor Henry Louis Gates Jr. calls it)—similar to David Walker's critique of Thomas Jefferson's hypocrisy.[24] As American folklore, this use of that legal conception known as "affirmative action" furthermore has roots in African religion and worldview, most notably the West African Yoruba concept of *àshe,* or "the-power-to-make-things-happen."[25] "Like the prophetic or progressive traditions in Christianity and Marxism," explains theological scholar Theophus H. Smith, "the African American folk wisdom tradition also features practices for negating and transforming imposed realities."[26]

Along these lines, note that the well-known biblical passage found in Matthew 19:30 ("But many *that are* first shall be last; and the last *shall* be first") and continuing through Matthew 20:1–16, actually had to do with the last parable of Jesus of Nazareth concerning the compensation paid by a vineyard owner to the victims of job discrimination. The owner pays those who had worked all day the same as those who had only worked an hour. When the all-day workers complain of unfairness, the owner defends his actions on the grounds that no one else would hire the workers whom he had hired late in the day, owing to the fact that they had been available to work all day.[27] In 1831, the black slave revolutionary leader Nat Turner conflated that verse with the apocalyptic vision contained in the New Testament book Revelation, telling attorney Thomas R. Gray:

And on the 12th of May, 1828, I heard a loud noise in the heavens, and the Spirit instantly appeared to me and said the Serpent was loosened, and Christ had laid down the yoke he had borne for the sins of men, and that I should take it on and fight against the Serpent, for the time was fast approaching when *the first should be last and the last should be first.* . . . And on the appearance of the sign, (the eclipse of the sun last February) I should arise and prepare myself, and slay my enemies with their own weapons.[28]

While this country is certainly not headed back to antebellum slavery, the status of the "free black" (so to speak) is still precarious today, much as it was over a century ago when that was an actual social status. There are some who have therefore argued for a more radical affirmative action—one that involves completing not just Southern but American Reconstruction, implies reparations, and proposes abolishing "whiteness as property."[29] Yet an affirmative action movement based mainly in the middle class arose in the last decade of the twentieth century to defend what was left of antidiscrimination compensatory programs. Its goals ranged from narrow to radical, sometimes even including reparations.[30]

But the narrow defensive posture assumed by this movement accounts for the fact that this issue has so far failed to galvanize masses of people in a grassroots nationwide effort comparable to the civil rights or Black Power movements of another era. Legal scholar Kimberlé Crenshaw has noted how the 1978 *Bakke* case helped define and shape the subsequent affirmative action movement and limit it to considering "diversity issues."[31] "Diversity" as an argument has led to an defense of affirmative action as something that would enrich the experience of whites at workplaces and campuses, rather than being promoted principally as a black compensatory measure.

III

The struggle over affirmative action has its immediate roots in the pro-black labor struggles that followed the Harlem Renaissance—which themselves were preceded by the post-Reconstruction nadir where, with few exceptions, white labor used its advantage to further distance its social status from black labor by severely restricting the latter's job mobility.[32] In a sense another nadir has arrived as the century and millennium turned, representing white weariness with conscience, subconscious, contradictions, and a shameful historical legacy as well as a desire to maintain its advantages.[33] By conflating affirmative action with issues like reparations and apologies, opponents have both recognized the potentially radical implications of affirmative action and portrayed it as more radical than it actually is in present practice.

Former Reagan Justice Department official William Bradford Reynolds has even referred to affirmative action as a "racial spoils system" for black people—a popular and unintentionally ironic reference by affirmative action opponents to the Jacksonian white preferential spoils system of the nineteenth century.[34] In fact, whether through "networking," accepted middle-class social skills, or culturally biased testing credentials, the highly touted concept of "merit," as legal scholar Richard Delgado puts it, "is basically white people's affirmative action."[35] Herbert Hill and others have documented the fact that the only "merit" lacking among qualified black workers or students—from slavery times to the current battle for affirmative action—is in their not being white. In this tautology, whiteness constitutes "merit" and therefore "fairness."[36]

But how can we prove that the opposition to affirmative action among whites is driven by a desire to protect privileges—especially when most white Americans would probably deny that both the privileges themselves and the drive to maintain them exist?[37] That protective impulse has actually been the subject of several sociological and psychological studies.[38] If it cannot be proven it can at least be demonstrated, as this historical study has done. White behavior has its own collective memory, including anecdotes blurted in public or furtively among other "whites," mass events like the angry white reaction to the 1994–95 O. J. Simpson murder trial and his acquittal by a mostly black jury,[39] the popularity of white rights lawsuits, and widespread complaints of "reverse discrimination" based on skin color but seldom on gender, family legacy, or military veteran status.[40]

White public denial makes "proof" of such a connection a slippery affair. However, labor historians like Herbert Hill have provided ample evidence of a dominant white hegemony as the historical basis for the hostility shown to even the most modest black compensation.[41] Reminiscent of Albion Tourgée's 1896 defense in *Plessy*, political scientist Andrew Hacker, in a well-known study almost a century, later found white college students actually unwilling to hypothetically change skin colors unless a huge sum of money was involved ($50 million was actually proposed).[42] Additionally, George Lipsitz, citing the study of desegregation in schools by education professor Gary Orfield, notes that among many white suburban parents "the superiority of suburban schools is taken for granted as a right attendant to home ownership, while desegregation is viewed as a threat to a system that passes racial advantages from one generation to the next."[43] Orfield himself describes the evidence of this contradictory white "twoness":

> Whites tell pollsters that they believe that blacks are offered equal opportunities, but fiercely resist any efforts to make them send their children to the schools they insist are good enough for blacks. . . . [while] the people who oppose busing minority students to the suburbs also tend to oppose sending suburban dollars to city schools.[44]

A typical 1997 national poll indicated that most adult whites interviewed claimed they were willing to acknowledge past discrimination, favoring laws to "protect minorities against discrimination in hiring and promotion" (65 percent, compared to 88 percent of blacks). A majority of whites also supported "special [college] educational programs to assist minorities" (59 percent, compared to 82 percent of blacks) and "government financing for job training for minorities . . . in industries where they are underrepresented" (64 percent, compared to =95 percent of blacks). But white opposition to "diverse work forces" (57 percent, compared to 17 percent of blacks), "preference in hiring . . . to make up for past discrimination," (57 percent, compared to 23 percent of blacks), and calls for abolition of affirmative action programs (52 percent, compared to 14 percent of blacks) has to represent something more than "media and conservative propaganda against preferences and quotas."

It makes more sense to see it reflecting what might be called white conventional wisdom. Of course, this is not to suggest that all white people think alike, but that there is an ideology whiteness that says that black disadvantage exists through a combination of blacks' own failings and some past discrimination that is now gone and in any case should not interfere with white positions that were presumably earned.[45]

During the last decade of the twentieth century, the United States Supreme Court's attitude toward antidiscrimination lawsuits constituted an important benchmark of majority white opinion. The high court under Chief Justice William Rehnquist has moved steadily rightward since *Bakke* in 1978 on a variety of issues related to affirmative action—a reflection of both the weakness of the pro-black movement as well as the strength of the pro-white movement.[46] *Missouri v. Jenkins* (1995) was a blow to *Swann v. Mecklenburg* (1971) on the issue of publicly financed court-ordered county-wide school integration.[47] *Shaw v. Reno* (1993) and *Shaw v. Hunt* (1996) undermined much of the Voting Rights Act of 1965 by overturning minority-majority congressional districts created in the 1990s while ignoring the history of gerrymandered white districts and white bloc voting against black candidates.[48] *Richmond v. Croson* (1989) and *Adarand v. Peña* (1995) overruled *Fullilove v. Klutznick* (1980) and *Metro Broadcasting v. FCC* (1990) on the constitutionality of minority contract set-asides to promote equality and racial diversity.[49] *Wards Cove v. Antonio* (1989) undid *Griggs v. Duke Power* (1971) on the question of workplace discrimination.[50] Finally, the breach in historically white-privileged seniority systems seen in *United Steelworkers v. Weber* (1979) was eroded substantially in *Wygant v. Jackson* (1986) and in an earlier overturning of a court-ordered affirmative action layoff plan in *Firefighters v. Stotts* (1984).[51] And Supreme Court decisions, like other legal and public policy initiatives, have also affected other populations who had previously made gains under affirmative action.

IV

It is only recently under the Rehnquist court that Native Americans—whose historical removal from or imprisonment on their ancestral lands accompanied the "white affirmative action" of colonial and republican settlement—have now come to be considered as a *racial* group rather than their previous *political* category. In a situation that parallels that of historically black public colleges (discussed at the end of this chapter), the "political" category at one time actually protected American Indians' preferential hiring on reservations while leading many in official positions to question their right to affirmative action benefits off of reservations. Yet the "racial" category has now been invoked as more Native Americans are being considered eligible for affirmative action outside reservations at the same time that official and popular sympathy builds for restoring the alleged lost "rights" of whites both on and off reservations.[52]

Moreover, as Harry Pachon has stated, Latinos have until recently not been treated by the government and the private sector as victims of discrimination. "In the 1960s, for example," he recalls, "it was Latinos' protests over the lack of inclusion in the Equal Employment Opportunity Commission and the lack of Hispanic representation in the federal bureaucracy that led to the forging of a common issue among Hispanic leaders from different regions of the country."[53] Pachon notes that in many federal agencies Latino employment has actually dropped in the last decade. But he raises a key point about Latinos' contradictory social position:

Another reason for low Latino visibility is the historical focus on the problem of race. From the onset of the modern civil rights movement in the 1950s until recently, "minority" by and large meant black and "majority" meant white. Hispanics, having characteristics of both groups, did not fit neatly into either categorization.[54]

Part of the reason for this, as historian David G. Gutiérrez written, has to do not only with class differences in the Latino community but with a change to a posture of assimilation adopted by Mexican American civil rights groups after World War I, such as the large and still influential League of United Latin American Citizens (LULAC). This stance, which distinguished LULAC from Mexican expatriates, became especially pronounced "after the great Mexican repatriation campaigns of the early 1930s (when as many as six hundred thousand Mexican nationals and their United States–born children were compelled or coerced into returning to Mexico). . . ."[55] Yet most Mexican Americans, Gutiérrez continues, found themselves caught between cultural preservation and assimilation: "And most of them clearly were not 'white.'"[56]

However, as sociologist William Javier Nelson (of Dominican descent) has observed, many Latinos—both foreign and native-born—quickly catch on, as do all American immigrants, to the operative system in the United States of white advantage. Having brown skin, a Spanish surname, or a Spanish accent or being a native Spanish speaker has historically been the basis for discrimination. But the United States racial caste system is simultaneously familiar and different from Latino immigrants' experience with the way African ancestry is regarded in their home countries. Nelson asserts that not only are there options open for light-skinned Latinos to "join" (or at least become honorary members) of the white race and partake of some of its benefits, but there also exists what he calls "the Indian escape hatch" for Latinos of indigenous ancestry who would also deny what for many of them is also their African ancestry. Those who utilize the "escape hatch" choose the ostensibly lesser discrimination based on Indian ancestry over being discriminated against as "blacks" in the United States:

> In the U.S., African ancestry . . . is something that converts the holder (of whatever percentage of African ancestry) into a person who is 100% black, and therefore 100% in a "genetically-defined" out-group. Latinos with African ancestry, highly cognizant of this dictum, will be so treated—unless they can use the Indian escape hatch.[57]

One of the key United States Supreme Court decisions that has stalled the progress of affirmative action involved a Mexican American highway guardrail contracting firm in Colorado called Gonzales Construction Company. Yet a reading of the 1995 *Adarand v. Peña* decision reveals no discussion of the particulars of Latino discrimination in the writings of the Court's majority but rather a critique of the merits of affirmative action in public contracting. (The plaintiff, Adarand Constructors, Inc., was a white-owned company whose owners believed that they should have been awarded the guardrail contract because they had submitted the lowest bid. The respondent, Secretary of Transportation Federico Peña, was the first Mexican American mayor of Denver.) In fact, in this decision Justice Antonin Scalia defiantly discounted any compensation or reparations basis for affirmative action. The fact was, Scalia declared,

> that government can never have a "compelling interest" in discriminating on the basis of race in order to "make up" for past racial discrimination in the opposite direction. Under the Constitution there can be no such thing as either a creditor or a debtor race. We are just one race in the eyes of government.[58]

Writing for the minority, however, Justice William Souter (joined by Justices Ruth Bader Ginsburg and Stephen Breyer) noted the 1990 Urban Institute Report whereby "Anglo applicants sent out by investigators received 52% more job offers than matched Hispanics." Souter, not normally known for radical pronouncements on civil rights issues, candidly countered Scalia's outright rejection of white culpability:

> When the extirpation of lingering discriminatory effects is thought to require a catch-up mechanism, like the racially preferential inducement under the statutes considered here, *the result may be that some members of the historically favored race are hurt by that remedial mechanism, however innocent they may be of any personal responsibility for any discriminatory conduct.*[59]

Besides the necessity of reversing historical white entitlements to level society's playing field as Souter pointed out, two additional ironies regarding "race" must also be addressed here. The first has to do with Asian Americans being occasionally historically promoted by some sectors of whites as "model minorities" and "honorary whites" until they either became expendable or were seen as both assimilable and "white."[60] An example of the latter was revealed by historian Charlotte Brooks in her study of the Japanese Americans, or Nisei, who had been confined to World War II internment camps but were able to win release to resettle in Chicago beginning in 1942. There they encountered an "in-between" status where they experienced some of the same workplace, housing, and social discrimination that they had encountered living on the West Coast. At the same time, they received an extension of white privileges by white working people as part of the latter's antagonism toward blacks—privileges that the Nisei in many cases came to embrace.[61]

Legal scholars Theodore Hsien Wang and Frank H. Wu, among others, have challenged the "model minority" myth as an exploitative one that conceals class divisions within the Asian community and ignores anti-Asian prejudice, which has often been framed in racial terms. Based on historical discrimination specifically in California, Asians were among the "minority" categories (along with Chicanos, Native Americans, and African Americans) that the pre-*Bakke* University of California special admissions program was trying to promote.[62] Examples of modern anti-Asian racial prejudice include white students at the University of California–Los Angeles (UCLA) referring to their school as "United Caucasians Lost Among Asians" and white students at the Massachusetts Institute of Technology (MIT) calling that school "Made in Taiwan." Anecdotes like these reveal that many whites are trying to have it both ways on the question of "merit." Wu notes that the "selective nature of immigration ensures that Asian immigrants arrive with significant educational and professional advantages. . . .

Comparing equally qualified individuals [however], and controlling for immigrant status, Asian-Americans consistently earn less than whites."[63]

Wu also points to a government investigation of how Asian American college students, despite their increasing test scores, have run into maximum quotas (similar to those many universities applied to Jews in the United States until the 1960s) and "hit the plateau" because "the definition of merit had shifted."[64] A sociology survey completed in 1997 at the University of California–Berkeley by Howard Pinderhughes (and featured in a book by David T. Wellman) finds white social support for anti-Asian roadblocks: "In the case of Asian Americans, the meritocratic yardstick white students apply to African Americans and Latino-Hispanics is switched. The criteria for merit are literally changed. Applied to Asian Americans, meritocracy has its limits and new standards are therefore invoked."[65]

Some of the sample white student opinions in this study are worth citing here: " 'There's a lot of tension between white students and Asian students,' observed a sorority member. . . . 'The Asians throw the curve and they study all the time,' added one of her sororal sisters. . . . 'I mean, it's the people like us who belong at the university,' said one young woman candidly as heads bobbed up and down in agreement, 'the people who are at the very top, who have fun, and are involved in all these things.' . . . 'Well-rounded people,' added someone else, 'not the classic high school nerd who has been transformed into an ethnic group at college.' "[66]

Another "racial irony" in the United States has to do with the official practice of defining Arab Americans as "white" simply because many are phenotypically white (white-appearing).[67] But contradicting that white phenotyping is a combination of traditional white American notions of "white" being synonymous with "European" along with the common ant-Arab prejudice and discrimination that negatively defines Arabs as brown and synonymous with "terrorists." The popular practice seems casual: calling all Arabs either "white" or "brown" for want of a better term (and subject to current mood) regardless of their national or ethnic origin. But this ambiguity in fact is symbolic of the conditional or honorary white status assigned by European Americans to Arab Americans, as well as reflective of a desire by many Arab Americans to assimilate as (white) Americans while still holding on to their culture.[68]

The two terms of Democratic President Bill Clinton (1993–2001) have been marked by compromise and weakened enforcement of antidiscrimination law.[69]

Between 1992 and 1998, race-based discrimination charges received by the EEOC averaged just under 30,000 annually, yet those thrown out for "no reasonable cause" continued to climb from the Reagan-Bush era average of 60 percent to 68.6 percent in 1998.[70] Despite widespread claims that discrimination is a thing of the past, the "NAACP Legal Defense and Education Fund . . . says it doesn't have the resources to handle the thousands of calls it gets each year describing discrimination in hiring, promotion, job assignments and racial epithets."[71] Tests done by groups like the Urban Institute continue to show that whenever a black (or Latino) and a white applicant are sent out with identical credentials to apply for jobs and housing, the results invariably indicate discrimination against applicants of color and a privileging of whiteness.[72]

Despite the fact that gender discrimination is challenged by affirmative action plans, the expression "affirmative action" still popularly and historically has come to connote race, while support for the idea by those who have benefited most from it—white females—has been generally lukewarm among those not sympathetic to or politically active in feminist organizations like NOW.[73] The major emphasis on affirmative action plans dismantled or attacked to date have been primarily those based on race, not gender. These include the Supreme Court decisions that require greater proof ("strict scrutiny") of racial discrimination,[74] or the decision by the University of California Board of Regents not to take race into account in admissions to all its schools beginning in January 1997.[75]

The question of gender has been consistently and ingeniously finessed by conservative white opponents: "gender" now joins "class" as yet another euphemism for "white rights."[76] The subtext proclaimed here is that blacks are somehow never actually working class (contrary to history and census figures) but are either privileged middle class or hopelessly underclass. Either way, they are held in this determination to be undeserving of any further "special attention." In examining the new-found conservative sympathy for "poor whites" in academia, Andrew Hacker analyzed one of the ways that a "race-blind" system might be opportunistically used:

> In 1993, of the 1,044,465 high school seniors who took the Scholastic Aptitude Test, 148,319 came from families with incomes under $20,000. . . . (less than 15 percent). . . . Much like the Asians, the largest contingent among poor whites were raised in middle-class households and attended middle-class high schools. What makes them poor is that their parents have divorced and they are now living with their mother.[77]

With so many people benefiting from affirmative action, why does the debate continue to mainly revolve around African Americans, why is there so much black ambivalence on the issue, and what larger issues are implicated in the debate over affirmative action's survival? Manning Marable made this cogent observation about the limitations of reformist affirmative action:

> About half of all Hispanics, according to the Bureau of the Census, term themselves "white," regardless of their actual physical appearance. Puerto Ricans in New York City have lower media incomes than African-Americans, while Argentines, a Hispanic group which claims benefits from affirmative-action programs, have mean on-the-job incomes of $15,956 per year. The Hmong, immigrants from Southeast Asia, have mean on-the-job incomes of $3,194; in striking contrast, the Japanese have annual incomes higher than those of whites. None of these statistics negates the reality of racial domination and discrimination in terms of social relations, access to employment opportunities or job advancement. But they do tell us part of the reason why no broad coalition of people of color has coalesced behind the political demand for affirmative action; various groups interpret their interests narrowly in divergent ways, looking out primarily for themselves rather than addressing the structural inequalities within the social fabric of the society as a whole. [78]

Poll results among African Americans consistently show a majority supporting affirmative action to help correct the effects of past and present white supremacist practice. Yet commentator Earl Ofari Hutchinson has pointed out that one in four blacks voted for California's 1996 anti-affirmative action Proposition 209. He maintains that this was not just because of the deliberately deceptive wording of the measure, as many like Kimberlé Crenshaw and George Derek Musgrove have argued, or because of a new conservatism in the black community.[79] Instead, Hutchinson argues that it was based on a "traditional" black conservatism that feels insulted by white charity and "government handouts."[80] Actually, both explanations are credible.

There has been skepticism and even scorn in the black community toward examples of black middle-class opportunism that uses the "minority set-aside" contracting bid award process as a model for affirmative action, when it is actually closer to the white "hook-up" paradigm than the principle of compensation. For example, in their study of the events leading to the pivotal 1989 *Richmond v. Croson* decision, W. Avon Drake and Robert D. Holsworth note:

> Our study of the set-aside program in Richmond offers little consolation to liberal defenders of affirmative action. . . . While our examination of the set-aside program

demonstrates that the ordinance helped to funnel money to black entrepreneurs and may have even improved the psychological climate for minority businesses, it is also true that the extent of the program's benefits were limited. Just two contractors received the majority of the money spent on the entire set-aside program. Moreover, the program could not guarantee that blacks would be more widely employed in the construction industry or that the money would be distributed more evenly. . . . Prior to the formation of the policy, there was a debate within the African American community about the extent to which set-asides could actually foster black economic development.[81]

On the other hand, a 1997 Urban Institute report documented the direct correlation between affirmative action in government contracting and black economic development.[82] A close reading of this report reveals that, far from being a marginal issue, contracting actually embodies a number of issues discussed here.[83] These include black aspirations toward economic autonomy as an antidote to black vulnerability in white-owned or white-dominated workplaces where most blacks work,[84] and the contract business world essentially still being monopolized by exclusive white business and union apprenticeship networks, higher loan approval rates for whites, and residential segregation that translates into capital and educational advantages for whites.[85] The authors draw two stark conclusions: "We find substantial disparity in government contracting"[86] and *"disparity is greater when there are no goals programs in place."*[87]

Put another way, even with modest constrained affirmative action measures in place, the government still bears responsibility for inhibiting black business formation and participation by allowing the white business club to go unreconstructed. Finally, there is growing concern among African Americans over how erosion of affirmative action in such areas as government contracting not only retards black entrepreneurship, economic development, and social opportunity but also conceals even more serious attacks on the black community.

V

The de-industrialization of America has hit African Americans the hardest. Poverty and unemployment remain at higher rates than among whites and issues of societal discrimination and police harassment affect blacks of all classes. While the gap in educational attainment between whites and blacks has shrunk by half since 1960, the unemployment gap remains roughly the same: 5.0 percent to 9.8 percent in 1993 and 5.4 percent to 10.8 percent in 1996.[88] This has made the issue of higher education all the more urgent as many new higher-skilled jobs require a college education—itself an economic challenge more so for blacks than whites.[89] Preferential admissions for African American college students are challenged in court times by both white males and females, while the chances for African Americans to be admitted to colleges have declined and the number of African Americans receiving advanced degrees has dropped since the 1970s according to a 1989 study by the National Research Council. Obviously, this shrinks the pool of future African American professionals.[90] Moreover, notes Allen S. Hammond IV:

> More than 60 percent of the new jobs being created today require computer skills. Children in poor inner cities, near suburban and rural schools are least likely to have access to learner-centered, skill-enhancing computer hardware and software. According to a 1994 report by the U.S. Census Bureau, only 39 percent of African-American students and 56 percent of European-American students use computers in school. Statistics on home-computer use are even more dismal. Fifteen percent of African-American students and 36 percent of European-American students reported using a computer at home. Because so many jobs in our economy are going to require some computer skills, children without such skills will be increasingly left behind.[91]

This also means that those with such skills—predominantly whites—will leap far ahead. Unfortunately, like all the other so-called hot-button issues (including drugs, crime, welfare, immigration, and prisons) white reactions to affirmative action too often revolve around what white society thinks it should collectively "do" about people of color—reminiscent of the colonization debates during the Civil War. This reaction conveniently and maddeningly forgets how fast whites have to keep running to "keep from falling behind" in a capitalist society, how white labor is degraded every time black labor is, and how any black advances compel "white upgrades."

A different situation prevails today from the time when the federal government waged war against the system of chattel slavery, against European fascism during the Second World War, or against Communism during the Cold War and worried about its international standing over official treatment of African Americans. There are now no unified competitive global social systems to count on for political leverage. There is also evidence that many whites who complain of being "tired of hearing about racism" are actually and ominously *tired of black people*: another old and familiar theme in American history—especially when blacks protest the status quo.[92]

The high rate of black imprisonment and the reintroduction of chain gangs in some Southern states have brought forth comparisons with antebellum slavery or the postbellum chain gangs that served as cheap labor on public works projects.[93] Less obvious and less frequently analyzed is white labor's latest demand for greater discipline of black labor. White labor often finds itself now united in a new white entitlement program that itself evokes the antebellum slave patrollers or the postbellum rural lynch mobs and urban white race rioters.

African American journalist, activist, and Pennsylvania death-row prisoner Mumia Abu-Jamal has characterized President Clinton's 1994 crime bill (now law) as "in essence, a $30+ billion dollar public employment program for predominantly white workers, a social program if ever there was one that reflects the changing face of America's sociopolitical and economic reality."[94] Massive incarceration of black labor has possibly become the fulfillment of James Boggs's grim forecast thirty-five years ago, one that helps explain white working-class hostility to affirmative action and complicity in the re-creation of a black prison labor force:

> Meanwhile, a technological revolution of automation and cybernation has been taking place in the United States; its main accomplishment, as of now, has been the systematic elimination of the menial, unskilled, and semi-skilled jobs which have been left to Negroes. There are no jobs in agriculture. The old basic industries no longer need Negroes. Even the white workers are being thrown out of the coal mines, the steel mills, the auto plants. Where then are the Negroes to go as they press for equality? The only places they can go are those places which are filled by white workers.[95]

Not only has the state taken over the black labor discipline function formerly employed in large part by white civilian violence, but America's growing majority-black penal population is once again working for that time-honored oxymoron—"slave wages"—in a further degradation of black labor and labor in general.[96] Private prisons are growing in this re-criminalization of black labor, and state and federal penitentiaries have begun to "contract out" their captive workforce:[97]

> Today, North Carolina inmates work on a wide variety of jobs. . . . on prison farms and Department of Transportation road crews. . . . Inmates employed by the state's Correction Enterprise program manufacture items like paint, soap and office furniture, which are then sold to state agencies. . . . Expanding inmate work programs is a popular way to offset spiraling corrections costs.
>
> Some states have begun selling inmate labor to private corporations. . . . In South

Carolina, prisoners sew graduation caps and gowns for Jostens. In Texas, they assemble circuit boards for a subcontractor who serves IBM and Texas Instruments. In California, prisoners have replaced striking workers to take reservations for TWA.[98]

The so-called drug war is mostly responsible for the ballooning United States incarceration rate that "has more than quadrupled, from 200,000 prisoners in 1975 to 1.6 million in 1996," in spite of the fact that crime rates fell over that same period.[99] Despite studies that show that blacks use proportionately fewer illegal drugs (13 percent) than whites, blacks are jailed at a much higher rate, making up 74 percent of drug sentences.[100] Citing the Washington, D.C.–based Sentencing Project, historian Barbara Ransby reports that in 1995, principally as a result of more arrests, harsher sentences, and poorer quality counsel imposed on black than white defendants in drug cases, "there were more Black men in US prisons than white men, 43 per cent and 42 per cent respectively, despite the fact that Blacks comprise a mere 13 per cent of the entire population. . . . Incarceration rates for Black women have risen 20 per cent in the last decade."[101]

As Abu-Jamal has written, the new crime law "outlaws knowledge, because it prohibits government funds for college courses. . . ."[102] Those imprisoned are frequently jobholders or students, and after being convicted of felonies they can no longer hope to advance in the job market or even vote upon being released. Ransby sums it up this way:

> Black imprisonment constitutes a reversal of many of the voting rights gains won by the civil rights movement of the 1960s. Prisoners, now mostly Black, are essentially deemed non-citizens. Poor Blacks, therefore, are being systematically disenfranchised and reduced to a non-citizen status reminiscent of slavery. . . . Nearly all states deny prisoners the right to vote, over half deny voting rights to individuals on probation, and nearly a third of states deny even ex-offenders the ballot. Today, this racially biased disenfranchisement affects 14 million Americans, disproportionately Black.[103]

Prison, then, has become the site for new reserve army of labor: the ultimate exploitation site for black labor by modern postbellum capitalism. Chained and isolated from the general population, no longer able to "compete" with free labor in the job marketplace, prison laborers are far less able to join the struggle against capital. In this full circle harkening back to antebellum white workers' movements, predominantly white trade unions object to losing union jobs to prison labor but rarely to the exploitation itself, the penal system's endemic white supremacy, or the degradation of all labor involved in this throwback to postbellum peonage. "White affirmative action" at the start of this century includes being able to buy, sell, and use illegal drugs while enjoying the odds of probably *not* finding oneself exiled to the American gulag.[104]

In a further irony, one of the United States' original affirmative action plans has been updated in the "Veterans' Employment Opportunities Act of 1997" (also known as the "Veterans' Preference Act") with support from the postal clerks union that had earlier been concerned that the bill compromised union seniority.[105] Previous veterans' benefits and preference laws contain references to (or imply) "affirmative action" for veterans.[106] Sponsors of this bill included two traditional opponents of affirmative action and black civil rights in general: Republican Senators Jesse Helms and Lauch Faircloth, both from North Carolina.[107]

Supporters of the act have taken pains to distinguish veterans' preferences from affirmative action. "Veterans preference is an earned right and not an affirmative action program," testified American Legion official Eric Naschinski at a 1997 congressional hearing, further claiming that veterans do not enjoy the "protection from discrimination" that "women and minorities" have with the EEOC.[108] House Civil Service Subcommittee chair John L. Mica (R-Florida) similarly proclaimed that veterans' preferences were "an earned right not a gift."[109] This represents a marked departure from the 1946 testimony of Rep. Gerald R. Ford (R-Michigan) at a similar hearing. Backed by the major postal unions, Ford decried veterans' "discrimination,"[110] declaring: "If this committee . . . and the Congress as a whole fail to take *affirmative action* for the benefit of the many veterans of World War II who are employees of the Post Office Department, we will be remiss in our duty to those who fought on the fields of battle. . . ."[111]

Notable among the many ironies here concerning how affirmative action has been viewed by white public officials and private administrators relating to veterans and blacks, the previous reference was to the post office (reorganized as the United States Postal Service, which became a quasi-governmental agency in 1971 after the successful 1970 nationwide postal worker wildcat strike). For years the post office represented the one federal agency where African Americans stood a good chance of finding employment, although equal advancement opportunities would not be available until after the civil rights movement appeared and affirmative action went into effect in the late 1960s.[112]

186

Meanwhile, what are the larger issues behind affirmative action today? Is the issue of compensation and reparations to African Americans threatening to whites because it involves white shame and denial? Is there a fear that such a program would be never-ending given the sheer mass of past injury? Or is there a sense that this will lead to an identification and subsequent termination of ongoing white privilege?

VI

There are some definite similarities between reparations, compensation, and affirmative action.[113] Affirmative action is a legal fixture in the former British colonies of South Africa, Canada, India, Malaysia, and Northern Ireland.[114] It is important to note that, as with the United States, a medieval common law antecedent was revived in these other former British colonies as an institutional remedy for historical oppression based on race. Even more striking today is the popularity of heralding (or bemoaning) the coming "minority status" of whites in the United States in the twenty-first century—forgetting the apartheid option of white minority rule that South Africa only recently dismantled.[115]

Compensation, a prominent feature of American law and political practice, represents in a sense a circumscribed form of reparations, limited to victims directly affected by a particular case. The arguments dismissing reparations as impractical and impossible are contradicted by notable national and international examples: these include payment by the German government and corporations to Israel for the World War II Holocaust, payment by the United States government to the families of Japanese Americans interned in United States concentration camps during that war, payments by the federal government to American Indian tribes for land theft and treaty abrogation, and the 1994 payment by the Florida legislature to black families who survived the Rosewood massacre by a white mob in that small all-black town in 1933.[116]

It is certainly appropriate that we find a legal precedent for black reparations in the same Reconstruction debate where we first encountered the legal concept of affirmative action being invoked to protect the rights of blacks under the Fourteenth Amendment. Boris Bittker has noted that a legal precedent exists for black reparations in the United States in the form of Section 1983, Title 42, of the United States Code, found in the 1871 Ku Klux Act, which reads:

Every person who, under color of any statute . . . of any State or Territory, subjects . . . any citizen of the United States . . . to the deprivation of any rights . . . secured by the Constitution and laws, shall be liable to the party injured in an action at law, suit in equity, or other proper proceeding for redress.[117]

There is also the economic aspect of reparations to consider. Richard F. America has collected essays by other economists who debate the logic, precedents, and limitations of this important issue, although America himself muses that "it really is the stuff of fantasy to imagine white America turning more than $1 trillion of wealth over to black America."[118] In this collection, one economist argues that affirmative action programs are a form of reparations,[119] while others argue that such programs are not exclusively for African Americans, do not transfer income disproportionately to African Americans, and are more in the nature of "compensation for current damages" than reparations.[120] But regardless of what it is called or whether affirmative action implies or merely suggests reparations, contends David H. Swinton, "equality is not likely to be obtained without some form of reparations."[121]

Much of the basis for popular white anger with affirmative action is based on the specter of black reparations. "We shouldn't have to pay for what previous generations did" is a familiar objection—one that fails to recognize how whites have benefited socially in a myriad of ways from their physical appearance both before and ever since the Civil War.[122] But the disparity based on race in fact is staggering in terms of sheer numbers: "40 to 60 percent of racial income inequality is due to discrimination," as Swinton points out.[123] Lester Thurow has estimated the range of "annual white benefits from labor market discrimination" alone in 1969 at $15 billion "plus or minus $5 billion."[124] Between 1969 and 1974 it was estimated that blacks lost $61 billion in income "because of racial differences in job assignments and wage differentials."[125] Swinton concludes:

Rough calculations suggest that to repair the damages of slavery and discrimination would require expenditures of $650 billion. Programs of the past two decades to benefit blacks provided no more than $150 billion in current value. Thus, reparations of more than $500 billion would still be required to compensate for the damage slavery and discrimination did to capital stocks owned by the living black population.[126]

How, in fact, would such reparations work? Robert S. Browne suggests a formula that includes cash transfers to individuals as well as to the African American community collectively, based upon the claims of payment for unpaid slave labor before 1863 . . . for underpayment since 1863 . . . to compensate for denial of opportunity to acquire land and natural resources when they were widely available to white settlers and investors. . . . [and] to provide the black community with the wealth and income it would by now have had if it had been treated as other immigrants after importation ceased.[127]

Job and wage differentials, however, only tell part of the story. Sociologists Melvin L. Oliver and Thomas M. Shapiro have extensively studied the continued vast differential in white and black wealth (asset accumulation) in the United States. A "racialization of state policy," as they call it, exists in the tax codes that favor predominantly white homeowners (lower capital gains tax rate plus home mortgage and real estate tax deductions); discriminatory banking, real estate, and insurance policies; educational and occupational mobility; and status inheritance.[128] Drawing on the 1987 Survey of Income and Program Participation (or SIPP, consisting of extensive interviews with thousands of American adults), they found that blacks control only 1.3 percent of the nation's financial assets while whites control 95 percent.[129]

The massive transfer of wealth to the rich from the working class during the Reagan administration also benefited average whites—including those in the working class. For example, the average white home in this same study was valued at $45,000, while the average black home was valued at $31,000.[130] Whites were more likely to be homeowners and enjoy higher housing values than blacks. This was true even for those white families earning less than black families, yet these white families were still more likely to qualify for a housing loan.[131] Middle-class status for African Americans, having increased in numbers since 1970, was nonetheless more tenuous for blacks than it was for whites and even more dependent than for whites on there being two incomes within the same family.[132] Furthermore, the SIPP study found that a "lower-blue-collar" white worker averaged $38,850 in net worth and $3,890 in net financial assets, compared to an "upper-*white*-collar" black worker's net worth of $21,430 and $230 in net financial assets.[133]

White wealth, then, despite vast income disparities among white people, is a state-sanctioned family legacy that operates through a network both visible and invisible (including friends, relatives, and total strangers) but is nevertheless consistently tangible in its rewards. When one considers the history of this country from slavery to Jim Crow to the present white "hook-up," the subject of reparations necessarily presents itself for consideration.

The payment of black reparations not only is politically controversial, but it also carries the disadvantage of closing the book on future claims were it actually to be consummated. This is not to argue against the justice of reparations claims and lawsuits being pursued, however, but to posit affirmative action as it already exists as a kind of open-ended form of reparations—a kind of "Reconstruction Act of 2001." And like reparations, affirmative action would also share the drawback that the award could never possibly compensate the damage. On the other hand, a strengthened reparations-based affirmative action would enjoy the advantage of having a judicial, political, and moral imperative, as well as the existing framework of compensatory justice.

If we agree that affirmative action does not constitute reparations per se but nevertheless contains key legal and philosophical elements of it, then there is an advantage to strengthening affirmative action on the basis of reparations rather than "diversity." Diversity suffers the weakness of being determined by and beneficial to whites, and for that reason many have concluded that diversity is not a compelling argument for affirmative action. Affirmative action on the basis of reparations contains the essence of why those programs should exist in the first place as part of replacing the "oligarchy of the skin," as Charles Sumner called it, with reconstructed democracy.[134]

This approach, of course, undermines the temporary nature of these programs often insisted upon by proponents. But even more important, it is an approach that would necessitate much more active support for abolishing all forms of white affirmative action. Just as it has taken whites far longer than Thaddeus Stevens's 1866 prediction of it taking only "two, three, possibly five years" for whites to accept black representation, I am talking about compensatory programs whereby whites are persuaded to assume both the past and present costs of their privileges extending for an indefinite time period—possibly several generations. But we have the legacy of Reconstruction as evidence that even as that sociopolitical program was weighted to benefit the freedpeople and African Americans generally, it was ultimately beneficial to all working people.[135]

Nonetheless, there is both an implicit and explicit objection by affirmative action proponents to such confrontational tactics. The question is raised: "Why arouse the sleeping giant of white reaction and violence when so much more can be accomplished by appealing to humanitarian and multicultural instincts?"

However, whiteness, exclusive by definition, is neither humanitarian nor multi-cultural but is the opposite of both of these.

Furthermore, whiteness as ideology and social category is perpetually reactionary and requires constant individual and collective effort to counteract. To forestall any more reaction—whether popular or governmental—the more that affirmative action programs are designed at the grassroots level and defended openly as being *antiwhiteness*, the better, quicker, stronger, and more effective those programs will be in advancing social progress. Absent this kind of strategy, the "affirmative action movement" will fail to excite sufficient mass support to save the institution and will have to settle for traditional tokenism.

CONCLUSION

A conundrum for the movement for justice and equality has always had to do with its ultimate reliance on federal power—the same power that brought into being and still perpetuates injustice and inequality. Whether it was Reconstruction or the civil rights era and its aftermath, this movement has always found itself asking or demanding through lobbying or mass protest that the state revamp its historically white supremacist institutions as well as discipline the supremacist behavior of white people. An endless cycle occurs when there is a failure of grassroots activity to adequately confront white privilege but is still able to win some measure of progress with federal coercion—until autonomous white reactionary activity regains the upper hand, causing an erosion of the initial compromise policy that was won by pro-black activity.

The results of mass protest in general rarely resemble the initial demands that were made. This happens because of compromises felt to be tactically necessary or because certain elements both within the movement and the reaction gain or lose strength. "Affirmative action," which came into being in the late 1960s as a state-sanctioned social reform and control mechanism, is just such a result. Its erosion at the end of the twentieth century suggests that reaction has sensed a strengthening of its position and the weakness of its opponents. The future of affirmative action or anything resembling it will be a gauge of whether the movement for or against white privilege has prevailed.

The more one studies the past, the clearer it becomes that the forces opposed to affirmative action and antidiscrimination measures will continue to have the upper hand in the debate until proponents acknowledge affirmative action's historical roots in black-led protest to end white supremacy and achieve substantial compensation—whatever the name. Both the lobbying and legal campaigns of mainstream civil rights groups as well the grassroots demands of black nationalist groups and black workers, by implication if not by design, have actually constituted radical challenges to white privilege, which is really what the "affirmative action debate" is really about.

Just as there is no inherent contradiction between the campaign for integrated schools and independent black schools, there is no similar legal or moral contradiction between a historically oppressed social group like African Americans in the 1940s opposing "maximum ceilings" (seen the United States Army's "Negro quota") while simultaneously advocating "minimum floors" (as the Washington, D.C., Lucky Stores pickets did).[136] Given that three special amendments were required after the Civil War to prevent the denial of civil rights to blacks, "deviations" from "color blindness" cannot possibly be said to represent pro-black opportunism in any general sense, especially when "white affirmative action" has long cornered that market.

Proposition 209 was upheld by the United States Supreme Court on 3 November 1997—yet a day later voters defeated a similar ballot initiative in Houston, Texas.[137] There is no inexorable slide backwards toward Jim Crow even if the trend appears to be in that direction. That is because affirmative action is both potentially radical and traditionally tokenistic and therefore exists as a kind mainstream scapegoat. Affirmative action has become a safe euphemism for antidiscrimination law as well as a potentially potent challenge to white privilege. It represents an advance over existing civil rights law, yet it still suffers from the same Achilles heel in failing to consistently challenge white privilege.[138]

In highlighting the limitations of Title VII, Stephanie Wildman has observed: "Antidiscrimination law has not addressed privilege, the flip side of disadvantaging, subordinate treatment."[139] Cheryl Harris further argues that affirmative action "implicitly challenges . . . the property interest in whiteness,"[140] concluding:

> But affirmative action is more than a program: it is a principle, internationally recognized, based on a theory of rights and equality. Formal equality overlooks structural disadvantage and requires mere nondiscrimination or "equal treatment"; by contrast affirmative action calls for equalizing treatment by redistributing power and resources in order to rectify inequities and achieve real equality.[141]

Yet affirmative action is still no more than a limited compromise reform measure born in response to the black freedom struggle. In a sense it actually reifies whiteness by not dismantling it the way the Confederacy and Jim Crow were taken apart. Affirmative action accepts whiteness as the norm within the historically prejudiced standards of formal equality. Whiteness, it could be said, knows everyone's name but its own, as seen in John David Skrentny's strange contention that the racial reporting (EEO-1) forms that the EEOC began sending to employers in 1966 to tabulate the race of their employees "mark[ed] the benign institutionalization and reification of blackness in America."[142]

Oliver and Shapiro argue that "formal equality" actually preserves existing inequalities: "Equal opportunity, even in the best circumstances does not lead to equality . . . [given] the historically sedimented nature of racial wealth disparities. Blacks will make some gains, but so will whites, with initial inequalities persisting at another level."[143] Even the accelerated opportunity of affirmative action does not go far enough: its black "exceptions" still prove (and simultaneously obscure) the continuing white "rule."

Both of what have been called "America's Reconstructions"—in the 1860s and the 1960s—provoked white hostility, encouraged white acceptance of the ideals of justice and equality for all people, and promoted black activism—which set off yet another round of white reaction. The essence of the struggle remains the same; only the particulars keep changing. The historical precedents and parallels are both uncanny and instructive.

Given what we know about the reactionary tenacity of whiteness, can it still be honestly said (as many do) that "progress for some is better than no progress at all"? When did we stop having choices? What if, for example, the Depression-era labor movement had stood fast against all manifestations of Jim Crow unionism? For that matter, imagine if the refusal to accept the Union army's Jim Crow wages by the white officers of the Fifty-fourth Massachusetts Regiment had become a commonplace action by workers from that day to the present.

What would have happened if President Franklin Roosevelt had refused to back down on antilynching legislation, thus putting his New Deal on the line and risking plunging the country into economic and social chaos? What if he and the labor movement had then declared, like President Lincoln, that they were doing so because "the judgments of the Lord are true and righteous altogether"? Someone would have had to budge—someone other than black people.

193

Models for uncompromising and productive grassroots activity against organized white privilege have been suggested throughout this book: the abolitionists cited in chapters 1 and 2; the IWW activists cited in chapter 3; the white CPUSA and CIO activists in the 1940s and 1950s who were willing to confront and reprimand rather than placate or ignore their recalcitrant white coworkers' white supremacy, as cited in chapters 4 and 5; the white workers and students who demonstrated in support of civil rights and Black Power demands in the 1960s and 1970s, as cited in chapter 6; and pro-affirmative action and related protests of the last twenty years that have been based on reparations and justice more than diversity and formal equality.

What are some recent examples highlighting the limitations and perils of relying on diversity and formal equality? In September 1999, a district court struck down school busing for integration in Charlotte, North Carolina. A group of white parents led by Bill Capacchione, a white insurance consultant (who has since relocated his family to California) successfully sued the Charlotte-Mecklenburg School (CMS) district. The court's ruling has threatened the 1971 *Swann v. Mecklenburg* decision that sanctioned busing to eliminate segregated, unequal schools that themselves are products of government-sponsored neighborhood segregation since the New Deal.[144] Reminiscent of all the "black favoritism" charges during Reconstruction, Capacchione claimed in a December 1998 deposition that his daughter's constitutional rights were violated because, in being turned away from her chosen magnet school (a product of the school desegregation era), she "was not permitted to compete equally with similarly situated black people because she is not of a preferred race under CMS policy. . . . In effect, CMS hung a 'no nonblacks need apply' sign on its black-only seats and racially segregated its nonblack applicants."[145]

On the other hand, in a throwback to Republican Party tokenist politics of a century ago, the California state Republican Party chair announced in May 1999 that state party funds would only go to "minority" candidates (including women) in state primary election campaigns until a proper "diversity" balance was achieved.[146] Additionally, the Glass Ceiling Commission of the United States Department of Labor that found ongoing corporate discrimination toward "women and minorities" and issued recommendations for change was initiated by Republicans like former Labor Secretary Elizabeth Dole and her successor Lynn Martin in 1991.[147]

However, the ultimate irony yet with regards to affirmative action and diversity issues has to do with what has been called the "whitening" of America's 109 historically black colleges and universities (HBCUs).[148] While black enrollment at HBCUs grew 26 percent from 1976 to 1994 largely in response to the anti-affirmative action backlash at traditionally white institutions (TWIs), white enrollment at HBCUs grew 70 percent during that same period.[149] But America's fifty public HBCUs, originally founded like all HBCUs from 1837 to 1964 as alternatives to exclusively white higher education, are being held to higher integration standards than TWIs.[150]

For example, thirteen HBCUs nationwide are now at least 20 percent white. The five public HBCUs in the North Carolina system have been pressured to increase their white enrollment (currently at 16.5 percent).[151] A Mississippi school desegregation lawsuit victory was transformed by the United States Supreme Court in *U.S. v. Fordice* into one that many black legal scholars now argue threatens that state's three public HBCUs' autonomy.[152] Bluefield State College (BSC), a HBCU in Bluefield, West Virginia, has a 92 percent white enrollment, no black faculty, no black fraternities or sororities, and only one black history course, yet it still receives about $1.6 million in federal funds earmarked for black colleges. (BSC's response has been a one-time diversity task force and an ineffectual "Multicultural Advisory Committee.")[153] Tennessee State University (TSU) was ordered by a federal court to raise white enrollment to 50 percent by 2000. A white fraternity was scheduled to open there in the fall of 1999. And a year earlier a white parent had complained when the school alumni association magazine ran an article protesting the whitening of black public colleges.[154]

It would appear that the movement to save affirmative action on the basis of diversity rather than reparations has done worse than simply handcuff itself. Diversity as a rationale for affirmative action has actually backfired into something that represents tolerance for minimal black enrollment at TWIs as a way of enriching the white collegiate experience while simultaneously insisting that HBCUs be made more "tolerable" for whites. Until the built-in currency of whiteness is devalued, both diversity and race-neutral schemes will actually encourage more whites not only to demand "their" slots back at TWIs[155] but also more white space at HBCUs, the very shelters that African Americans erected against the storm.[156]

Equally laden with irony have been the late 1990s' public pronouncements of the AFL-CIO: that it will only survive if it learns to support affirmative action and embrace diversity. Meanwhile, other organizational documents describe the "right-wing Republican" threat to affirmative action and the Davis-Bacon Act as being one and the same and that African American construction workers would suffer if the latter were repealed—indicating how much privilege AFL-CIO officials know white workers will be willing to give up—namely, very little, if any.[157] But discrimination and privilege are not merely abstract external evils that legislation, speeches, workshops, and "training programs" alone can eliminate. Together they make up both sides of an unequal everyday equation, still maintaining themselves as tenacious popular and official institutions in jobs, in education, and in every other aspect of American social life.

Public and private sector diversity plans and discussions, notwithstanding their usefulness in the loosening and questioning of the so-called old-boy network through establishment of voluntary programs that try to sidestep the "preference and quota" issue—avoid the underlying causes of conflict and reaction over affirmative action.[158] As we saw in the second and third chapters, post-Reconstruction government in the United States under the leadership of both ex-Confederates and lapsed Republicans employed some diversity in their political appointments but nevertheless kept power in white hands. Diversity notions in the past have reflected whatever minimal concessions white America believed necessary when confronted by black-led protest.

Despite the privileges of whiteness (which however much they may be denied still are commonly regarded as worth fighting for and require daily work to maintain)—how much does white working America really benefit from identifying themselves and being identified as "white"? Manufacturing jobs continue to flee the country. Well-paying jobs require more education, are highly sought, and are in limited supply. Families depend more on two incomes as well as multiple jobs per adult. Despite a decade-long capitalist expansion and "booming economy," real wages for working Americans continue to fall as they have since 1974, while social services like health care and public education continue to deteriorate.[159] As Derrick Bell Jr. has mused:

> One wonders. What kind of miracle or—more likely—how enormous a catastrophe will be required to get whites to realize that their property right in being white has been purchased for too much and has netted them only the opportunity, as historian C. Vann Woodward put it in *Reunion and Reaction*, to hoard sufficient racism in their bosoms to feel superior to blacks while working at a black's wages.[160]

Perhaps the answer lies in W. E. B. Du Bois's observation in his biography of the white abolitionist martyr John Brown. It is one that also fits the overall struggle for equality today—including affirmative action—and particularly applies to those white workers who identify more with their corporate masters who look white than with their fellow wage-slaves who look black:

This is the situation today. Has John Brown no message—no legacy, then, to the twentieth century? He has and it is this great word: *the cost of liberty is less than the price of repression.* The price of repressing the world's darker races is shown in a moral retrogression and an economic waste unparalleled since the age of the African slave-trade. What would be the cost of liberty? . . . It would cost something. It would cost something in pride and prejudice, for eventually many a white man would be blacking black men's boots. . . .[161]

The "white race" is not a passive demographic fact but an invented voluntary social institution whose only utility is oppression. It is one that continues to be collectively reinvented in a vain attempt to resolve the contradiction between white political and social freedom and the denial of same to African Americans, while simultaneously blurring class differences between capitalist and working class among those who share the coincidence of looking white.

Abolishing white preferences and quotas really means abolishing this social club known as the white race with all its "badges and incidents" that confer privilege. American Reconstruction is still unfinished. To complete it, however, requires not simply restructuring institutions to ensure equality and social progress. Ultimately this is a question of reconstructing "white people" from "the special favorite of the laws" into "mere citizens."

NOTES

Chapter 1

1. Frederick Douglass, *The Life and Writings of Frederick Douglass*, ed. Philip S. Foner, vol. 4, *Reconstruction and After* (New York: International Publishers, 1955), 158.

2. See Theodore W. Allen, *The Invention of the White Race*, vol. 1, *Racial Oppression and Social Control* (London: Verso, 1994), introduction, for his concept of the "invention" of the white racial construct, which he calls "a political act" (22). Allen's extensive research shows both slavery and the white race as evolving institutions, not ones that arrived prefabricated from Europe. However, "synthesis" might better express the process of the creation of the "white race." "Invention" implies a conscious policy, whereas the early Anglo-American colonial ruling class that devised slavery as an economic choice similarly created whiteness as a social division in reaction to the challenge posed to their rule by African and European indentured servants. Nevertheless, Allen's thesis is groundbreaking in contradicting racial prejudice origin theories held by such prominent historians as Winthrop Jordan and Carl Degler—theories based largely on speculation about "natural" and even genetic white predisposition to antipathy toward blacks. Allen, *White Race*, vol. 1, 4–14. See also Lerone Bennett Jr., *The Shaping of Black America* (New York: Penguin, 1993; 1975), 76–78; Barbara Jeanne Fields, "Slavery, Race and Ideology in the United States of America," *New Left Review* 181 (May–June 1990): 95–118; Winthrop D. Jordan, *White Over Black: American Attitudes toward the Negro, 1550–1812* (Baltimore: Penguin, 1969); Carl Degler, *Out of Our Past: The Forces That Shaped Modern America*, rev. ed. (New York: Harper and Row, 1959); and Oscar Handlin and Mary F. Handlin, "Origins of the Southern Labor System," *William and Mary Quarterly*, 3rd series, vol. 7 (April 1950): 199–222.

3. Herbert Hill, *Black Labor and the American Legal System: Race, Work, and the Law* (Madison: University of Wisconsin Press, 1985; 1977), 1.

4. Cheryl I. Harris, "Whiteness as Property," *Harvard Law Review* 106 (1993): 1709–91.

5. The fundamental difference between the colonial slave codes and all subsequent antiblack legislation was that the former represented ruling-class policy, while the latter, in expanding white privilege and black discrimination, represented both a response to mass white supremacist demands and ruling-class efforts to blunt developing black-white alliances. See Theodore W. Allen, *The*

Invention of the White Race, vol. 2, *The Origin of Racial Oppression in Anglo-America* (London: Verso, 1997), chapter 13; Charles H. Wesley, "Negro Suffrage in the Period of Constitution-Making 1787–1865," *Journal of Negro History* 32 (April 1947): 143–68; Lawrence C. Goodwyn, "Populist Dreams and Negro Rights: East Texas as a Case Study," *American Historical Review* 76, no. 5 (December 1971): 1435–56; J. Morgan Kousser *The Shaping of Southern Politics: Suffrage Restriction and the Establishment of the One-Party South, 1880–1910* (New Haven, CT: Yale University Press, 1974); and C. Vann Woodward, *The Strange Career of Jim Crow*, 3rd rev. ed. (New York: Oxford University Press, 1974; 1954).

6. John David Skrentny, *The Ironies of Affirmative Action: Politics, Culture, and Justice in America* (Chicago: University of Chicago Press, 1996), 6. See also Lawrence M. Friedman, *American Law* (New York: W. W. Norton, 1984), 70–71; Thomas C. Cochran, *Frontiers of Change: Early Industrialism in America* (New York: Oxford University Press, 1981), 23: "Equity—the placing of justice ahead of doctrine—became in the hands of American lawyers and jurists a means of upsetting or avoiding jury verdicts hostile, often from ignorance, to the needs of business . . . [but] by the 1840s equity was being absorbed into the common law." Cochran adds that in many states judges still set aside jury verdicts.

7. Also operating here was the ancient tradition of rewarding soldiers. See Harold M. Hyman, *American Singularity: The 1787 Northwest Ordinance, the 1862 Homestead and Morrill Acts, and the 1944 G.I. Bill* (Athens: University of Georgia Press, 1986). The 1784–1787 Ordinances reserved about 2.7 million acres for veterans to be decided by rank and lottery. The 1862 Homestead Act waived the age minimum (twenty-one) for veterans. President Lincoln noted in his 1863 Annual Message to Congress that about 1.5 million acres had been dispersed by that act. See Abraham Lincoln, *Abraham Lincoln Complete Works*, ed. John G. Nicolay and John Hay, vol. 2 (New York: Century, 1902), 445–56.

8. Cited in James C. Foster and Mary C. Seegers, *Elusive Equality: Liberalism, Affirmative Action, and Social Change in America* (Port Washington, NY: Associated Faculty Press, 1983), 143 n 1.

9. Nijole V. Benokraitis and Joe R. Feagin, *Affirmative Action and Equal Opportunity: Action, Inaction, Reaction* (Boulder, CO: Westview Press, 1978), 1.

10. Eleanor Holmes Norton, "Affirmative Action in the Workplace," in *The Affirmative Action Debate*, ed. George E. Curry (Reading, MA: Addison-Wesley, 1996), 39. Directly related to affirmative action and work are the implications contained within job training or "mentoring" programs for those previously denied opportunity or based on assumptions of their inexperience—in contrast with "apprenticeships" as a historic form of white entitlement. See Hill, *Black Labor*, 14 and passim.

11. Peter H. Wood, *Black Majority: Negroes in Colonial South Carolina from 1670 through the Stono Rebellion* (New York: W. W. Norton, 1975), 18–19.

12. Harris, "Whiteness as Property," 1721 and n 45. See also Herman Melville, *The Confidence Man* (New York: Airmont, 1966), chapter 26, "Containing the Metaphysics of Indian-Hating, According to the Views of One Evidently not so Prepossessed as Rousseau in Favour of Savages."

13. See John Hope Franklin and Alfred A. Moss Jr., *From Slavery to Freedom: A History of Negro Americans*, 6th ed. (New York: McGraw-Hill, 1988; 1947). See also Bennett, *The Shaping of Black America*, 5–14; and Allen, *White Race*, vol. 1, 3, 234 n 8. Jamestown was founded in 1607.

14. Franklin and Moss, *From Slavery to Freedom*, 54; Edmund S. Morgan, *American Slavery, American Freedom: The Ordeal of Colonial Virginia* (New York: Norton, 1975), 216–18, 328–31. American Indians in Virginia were exempted from slavery in 1670, but after the 1676 Bacon's Rebellion any American Indian could be enslaved. See infra note 29. See Peter Kolchin, *American Slavery 1619–1877* (New York: Hill and Wang, 1993), 8–13.

15. Fields, "Slavery, Race and Ideology," 107. Maryland had allowed slavery since its settlement in 1634 but first recognized it legally in 1663. Maryland established slavery on the basis of the father's condition in 1664 and then that of the mother in 1681. See Franklin and Moss, *From Slavery to Freedom*, 54–55. Virginia reckoned slavery by maternity in 1662.

16. Fields, "Slavery, Race and Ideology," 101, 106. See also Bennett, *The Shaping of Black America*, 78, where he notes that "the white sense of identity developed in response to the forced degradation of blacks."

17. Morgan, *American Slavery*, 329–31. See also A. Leon Higginbotham Jr., *In the Matter of Color: Race and the American Legal Process* (New York: Oxford University Press, 1978), 38. See infra note 30.

18. Helen T. Catterall, ed., *Judicial Cases Concerning American Slavery and the Negro*, vol. 1 (New York: Octagon, 1968; 1926), 53. Native American slaves were the first slaves in America under the Europeans American chattel system. Ibid., 63.

19. Walter Clark, ed., *The State Records of North Carolina*, vol. 23, *Laws 1715–1776* (Goldsboro: Nash, 1904). "Severance pay" in 1715 included "three Barrells of Indyan Corn & two new Suits of Apparell [or] . . . a good well-fixed gun. . . ." Ibid., 6.

20. For the earliest colonial references to "whites" found in the writings of English Quakers on a missionary tour of the American colonies, see Terrence W. Epperson, "Whiteness in Early Virginia," *Race Traitor: journal of the new abolitionism* 7 (winter 1997): 9–20.

21. Jordan, *White Over Black*, 75, 93–98. John Hope Franklin said of this incident: "That was the beginning of discrimination." John Minter, "Racism Benefits Whites: Franklin," *Charlotte (NC) Post*, 30 October 1997, 1; and Allen, *White Race*, vol. 1, 235 n 17, 261 n 77.

22. Jordan, *White Over Black*, 123.

23. Allen, *White Race*, vol. 2, 252. See also Wood, *Black Majority*; Morgan, *American Slavery*; and Lerone Bennett Jr., *The Shaping of Black America* (New York: Penguin, 1993; 1975), which also discuss the export, import, and use of American Indian slaves by European Americans in the early American colonies. But the best discussion of the use of American Indian slave labor as well as the decision to export it is contained in Allen, *White Race*, vol. 2, 40–45. Allen dismisses popular notions that bondage of Native Americans was discontinued because they were somehow unfit for agricultural labor by arguing that "the reasons were rooted in three intractable problems of 'white race' social control: (1) resistance. . . ; (2) the necessity to maintain nearby friendly . . . Indians in the buffer role. . . ; and (3) . . . preserving 'white skin' privileges of laboring-class European-Americans *vis-à-vis* all non-European-Americans." Ibid., 41.

24. Allen, *White Race*, vol. 2, 249–50.

25. Ibid., 251.

26. Ibid., 250–51, 360 n 63. See also Higginbotham, *In the Matter of Color*; and Warren B. Smith, *White Servitude in Colonial South Carolina* (Columbia: University of South Carolina Press, 1961).

27. John Anthony Scott, "Segregation: A Fundamental Aspect of Southern Race Relations, 1800–1860," *Journal of the Early Republic* 4, no. 4 (winter 1984): 433–41; and Allen, *White Race*, vol. 2, 252. See Allen, *White Race*, vol. 2, 361 n 85, on the prospects of a "financial windfall" for whites who apprehended runaway slaves in the antebellum era. Allen's source is Kenneth M. Stampp, *The Peculiar Institution: Slavery in the Ante-bellum South* (New York: Knopf, 1956), 153. Also on slave patrols see Wood, *Black Majority*, chapter 10; and Herbert Aptheker, *American Negro Slave Revolts* (New York: International Publishers, 1974; 1943), 67–70.

28. Frederick Douglass (5 July 1852, Rochester, NY), "What to the Slave, Is the Fourth of July?," in *Lift Every Voice: African American Oratory, 1787–1900*, ed. Philip S. Foner and Robert James Branham (Tuscaloosa: University of Alabama Press, 1998), 256.

29. See Allen, *White Race*, vol. 1 and vol. 2.

30. Ibid., vol. 2, 179.

31. Ibid., 120–21.

32. Ibid.

33. John Lawson, *A New Voyage to Carolina*, ed. Hugh Talmage Lefler (Chapel Hill: University of North Carolina Press, 1967; 1709), 246.

34. See Allen, *White Race*, vol. 2, chapter 8; James Axtell, *The Invasion Within: The Contest of Cultures in Colonial North America* (New York: Oxford University Press, 1985), chapter 13; and Alexa Silver Cawley, "A Passionate Affair: The Master-Servant Relationship in Seventeenth-Century Maryland," *Historian* 61, no. 4 (summer 1999): 751–63. See also Ron Sakolsky and James Koehnline, eds., *Gone to Croatan: Origins of North American Dropout Culture* (Brooklyn: Autonomedia, 1993).

35. Morgan, *American Slavery*, 330.

36. Ibid., 254–70, 327–28. One of the last bands of Bacon's Rebellion to surrender was comprised of eighty blacks and twenty whites. See also Allen, *White Race*, vol. 2, 204–7, 210.

37. Allen, *White Race*, vol. 2, 248; and Jackson Turner Main, "The Distribution of Property in Post-Revolutionary Virginia," *Mississippi Valley Historical Review* 41 (1954–55): 241–58.

38. Morgan *American Slavery*, 344–45.

39. Ibid., 341.

40. Ibid., 338.

41. Allen, *White Race*, vol. 2, 257. Allen is including the following quotation (362 n 115): "George W. Summers of Kanawha County, speaking in the Virginia House of Delegates, during the debate on slavery, following Nat Turner's Rebellion (*Richmond Enquirer*, 2 February 1832)." See also Marvin L. Michael Kay, review of *The Invention of the White Race*, vol. 2, *The Origin of Racial Oppression in Anglo-America*, by Theodore W. Allen, *Journal of American History* 86, no. 3 (December 1999): 1326–27.

42. W. E. B. Du Bois, *Black Reconstruction in America 1860–1880* (Cleveland: Meridian, 1968; 1935), 700.

43. Smith, *White Servitude*, 89.

44. Ibid., 88.

45. James M. McPherson, *Battle Cry of Freedom: The Civil War Era* (New York: Ballantine, 1989), 199–200.

46. Smith, *White Servitude*, 30.

47. Ibid., 31.

48. Ibid.; and Allen, *White Race*, vol. 2, 252.

49. Allen, *White Race*, vol. 2, 253.

50. Higginbotham, *In the Matter of Color*, 264–65.

51. Allen, *White Race*, vol. 2, 253.

52. There were even in some cases explicit white worker and white land quotas in the colonies of Georgia, South Carolina, and Virginia. See Ibid., 252–53. On the differences between black and white in social and labor status in the North during the colonial, revolutionary, and antebellum periods, see Franklin and Moss, *From Slavery to Freedom*, 59–63, and chapters 5, 6, and 9, as well as page 135 for discussion of antebellum white Southerners who aided slave revolts; and Lerone Bennett Jr., *Before the Mayflower: A History of Black America*, 5th ed. (New York: Penguin, 1984; 1962), 441–50. Massachusetts was the first colony to legally recognize slavery in 1641, with Connecticut following in 1650, New York and New Jersey in 1664, and Rhode Island and Pennsylvania in 1700.

In the South slavery was first sanctioned in Virginia in 1661, followed by Maryland in 1663, South Carolina in 1682, North Carolina in 1715, and Georgia in 1750. See also Philip S. Foner and Ronald L. Lewis, eds., *The Black Worker: A Documentary History from Colonial Times to the Present*, vol. 1, *The Black Worker to 1869* (Philadelphia: Temple University Press, 1978), parts 3–7, esp. 152–54: the text of Ohio's 1804 "Act to Regulate Black and Mulatto Persons."

53. The Northwest Ordinance of 1784 was never put into effect, but the 1785 Ordinance was, and it recognized "military bounty" for veterans in the form of land grants. See Rudolf Freund, "Military Bounty Lands and the Origins of the Public Domain," in *The Public Lands: Studies in the History of the Public Domain*, ed. Vernon Carstensen (Madison: University of Wisconsin Press, 1963), 15–34; Ray Allen Billington, *Westward Expansion: A History of the American Frontier*, 2nd ed. (New York: MacMillan, 1960; 1949), 207–17; Benjamin Horace Hibbard, *A History of the Public Land Policies* (Madison: University of Wisconsin Press, 1965; 1924), 32–55; and *Northwest Ordinances of 1784–1787*, Library of Congress [online documents] available at http://www.thomas.loc.gov, Internet.

54. Allen, *White Race*, vol. 2, 357 n 23. With a shortage of soldiers, blacks were grudgingly recruited into the army after initially being refused entrance. See also Jordan, *White Over Black*, 302–4; and Benjamin Quarles, *The Negro in the American Revolution* (Chapel Hill: University of North Carolina Press, 1961).

55. Chilton Williamson, *American Suffrage: From Property to Democracy 1760–1860* (Princeton, NJ: Princeton University Press, 1960), 117; and Willi Paul Adams, *The First American Constitutions: Republican Ideology and the Making of the State Constitutions in the Revolutionary Era*, trans. by Rita Kimber and Robert Kimber (Chapel Hill: University of North Carolina Press, 1980; 1973), 216.

56. See Franklin and Moss, *From Slavery to Freedom*, 66–68. See also Sidney Kaplan, *American Studies in Black and White: Selected Essays 1949–1989*, ed. Allan D. Austin (Amherst: University Press of Massachusetts, 1991), 18–32.

57. Nikolai N. Bolkhovtinov, "The Declaration of Independence: A View from Russia," *Journal of American History* 85, no. 4 (March 1999): 1396–97.

58. *Dred Scott v. Sandford*, 60 U.S. 393 (1857). The litigation was the result of Scott claiming free status after Sandford had taken him into free territory. See also Don E. Fehrenbacher, *The Dred Scott Case: Its Significance in American Law and Politics* (New York: Oxford University Press, 1978). Fehrenbacher notes that this case "was the Supreme Court's first invalidation of a major federal law." That law was the 1820 Missouri Compromise that created a dividing line between free and slave states. See Franklin and Moss, *From Slavery to Freedom*, 178. Taney had been President Andrew Jackson's attorney general. Fehrenbacher, *The Dred Scott Case*, 340.

59. McPherson in *Battle Cry of Freedom*, 172–79. See also *Dred Scott* (1857). Free blacks did enjoy some tenuous citizenship privileges. As for the intent of the "Founding Fathers," while there is some truth in what Taney asserts, this is also an assumption that disregards ambiguous constitutional language that disguised the contradictions within Anglo-American racial attitudes. See Alfred Avins, ed., *The Reconstruction Amendments' Debates: The Legislative History and Contemporary Debates in Congress on the 13th, 14th, and 15th Amendments* (Richmond: Virginia Commission, 1967), for numerous debates over legislators' interpretation of their intent regarding future black citizenship.

60. *Dred Scott* (1857); and Allen, *White Race*, vol. 1, 185. Allen also points out here that "the United States Constitution implicitly made immigration a white-skin privilege, when in Article I, Section 9, Europeans were classed as migrants whilst Africans were classed as imports." After some experimenting, colonial Anglo-Americans finally reckoned free/slave and white/black status through descent through the mother of any given child. Ibid., vol. 2, 134.

61. *Dred Scott* (1857). See also Fehrenbacher, *The Dred Scott Case*, 343, where he makes the following point regarding this quote from Taney: "The gross inaccuracy of the final clause will be readily apparent. A large majority of American citizens—namely, women and children—were not members of the sovereign people in the sense of holding power and conducting the government through their representatives. . . . Citizenship and sovereign power were far from synonymous."

62. Fehrenbacher, esp. chapters 1, 2, 15, and 18. See also McPherson, *Battle Cry of Freedom*, 172–79. Citizenship includes civic responsibilities, constitutional guarantees of suffrage, office-holding, due process, right to a jury trial, and jury and military service.

63. See Derrick A. Bell Jr., *And We Are Not Saved: The Elusive Quest for Racial Justice* (New York: Basic, 1987), 34 n–35 n, where he cites historian William Wiecek's tally of eight accommodations to slavery made in the Constitution, beginning with the most notorious one (Article I, Section 2) that apportioned representatives in the House among the states based on population: all free persons and three-fifths of the slaves. See also Jack N. Rakove, *Original Meanings: Politics and Ideas in the Making of the Constitution* (New York: Vintage, 1997), esp. chapter 4, 336–37. Rakove found that delegates from the Northern states expressed more procedural than moral objections to slavery being accommodated in the Constitution, and they were unhappy with the prospect of counting slaves as property for taxation purposes and as people for white voting purposes. But they accepted compromise over slavery as "the price of union," fearing that the delegates from the Southern slaveholding states would walk out on the convention and the union if slavery was not safeguarded (Ibid., 75.). See also Ibid., 93, where Rakove notes that the South possibly gained more leverage with the constitutional provision that each state, regardless of population, was entitled to two seats in the Senate (which later passed the Compromises of 1820 and 1850 that solidified slavery's power) than they did with the "three-fifths" compromise.

64. Adams, *The First American Constitutions*, 176. See also Higginbotham, *In the Matter of Color*.

65. Higginbotham, *In the Matter of Color*, 89. See also Wesley, "Negro Suffrage."

66. *Proceedings and Debates of the Convention of North Carolina Called to Amend the Constitution of the State, which Assembled at Raleigh June 4, 1835* (Raleigh: Joseph Gales, 1836), 61–139. See also Stephen B. Oates, *The Fires of Jubilee: Nat Turner's Fierce Rebellion* (New York: Mentor, 1975).

67. *Proceedings*, 61–139.

68. Ibid. See the incredulous query made by Bryan: "Is a free negro a citizen?" (63).

69. *Proceedings*, 62. Mr. Gaston of Craven County (also in eastern North Carolina) invoked the federal Constitution in observing the "anomalous class" status of slaves as both persons and property (Ibid., 136). In predicting the westward expansion of slavery in mining and manufacture Gaston also cited a popular expression of the time: "[F]or it was a law of Nature that men would not work when they could get others to work for them" (Ibid., 139). A variation of that expression also appears in Thomas Jefferson's *Notes on the State of Virginia* (Chapel Hill: University of North Carolina Press, 1954; 1785), 163. While it is one of Jefferson's least-cited quotations today, it actually best sums up popular notions during that period of white entitlement and even appears in the same passage as his famous "I tremble for my country when I reflect that God is just" declaration. See chapter 7, note 12, of this book.

70. Jefferson, *Notes on the State of Virginia*, 61, 73.

71. Wesley, "Negro Suffrage," 145.

72. Ibid., 154.

73. Douglass, *The Life and Writings*, 163.

74. Wesley, "Negro Suffrage," 154.

75. Fields, "Slavery, Race and Ideology," 99.

76. David R. Roediger, *Towards the Abolition of Whiteness: Essays on Race, Politics, and Working Class History* (London: Verso, 1994), 181. See also Ian F. Haney López, *White By Law: The Legal Construction of Race* (New York: New York University Press, 1996). The omission of the precise term "slavery" from the Constitution represented a Southern concession to "Northern members' pronounced aversion to allowing the word *slavery* in the Constitution." Rakove, *Original Meanings*, 91.

77. Du Bois, *Black Reconstruction*, 7.

78. Edward Conrad Smith, ed., *The Constitution of the United States*, 11th ed. (New York: Barnes and Noble, 1979; 1936), 33. The Articles of Confederation were proposed by Congress 15 November 1777 and ratified 1 March 1781. The 1792 Militia Law also contained the "white" restriction. See Wesley, "Negro Suffrage," 152.

79. Smith, *The Constitution*, 29.

80. Ibid., 37. The Constitution was proposed by convention on 17 September 1787 and effective 4 March 1789.

81. Ibid., 42.

82. Ibid., 41.

83. Ibid., 29.

84. Ibid., 46–47. See also Abbot Emerson Smith, *Colonists in Bondage: White Servitude and Convict Labor in America 1607–1776* (New York: W. W. Norton, 1971).

85. See, for example, the advertisement seeking a Welsh indentured servant runaway in the *Cape Fear Mercury* of 11 November 1769 from Wilmington, NC, *Eighteenth-Century North Carolina Newspapers* (Raleigh: North Carolina Divisions of Archives and History, 1961), Edenton, reel 5, text-fiche; Franklin and Moss, *From Slavery to Freedom*; and Freddie L. Parker, *Running for Freedom: Slave Runaways in North Carolina 1775–1840* (New York: Garland, 1993).

86. See Kaplan, *American Studies*, 27; and Rakove, *Original Meanings*, 336–37. The 1787 Constitutional Convention debated setting property qualifications for suffrage but in the end decided to leave the making of election laws to the states (Rakove, *Original Meanings*, 224–25). See also Wesley, "Negro Suffrage," esp. 146–49, where he notes the limited citizenship privileges available to free blacks, one of those being suffrage in some states but often with property or special qualifications. There was disagreement among lawmakers as to whether free blacks in one state could enjoy those citizenship privileges in all other states or whether they should even continue to enjoy them in their home state. The New Jersey Constitution of 1776 made no suffrage restrictions based on race or sex, but in 1807 an act was passed that limited the franchise to white males. During the debate over the Pennsylvania Constitution of 1790 the word "white" was stricken from the suffrage requirements, only to keep reemerging as an issue for the next several decades until in 1838 a state constitutional convention limited the franchise to whites, despite a petition signed by 40,000 African Americans in protest. Ibid., 160–65.

87. Alexander Hamilton, James Madison, and John Jay, *The Federalist Papers*, ed. Clinton Rossiter (New York: Mentor, 1961; 1787), 337. Italics added. See also *Federalist Paper* No. 43, where Madison notes that slaves during "calm" times are "sunk below the level of men." He goes on to warn that during an insurrection they "may emerge into the human character." Ibid. 277.

88. Taney in *Dred Scott* (1857). Italics added.

89. See Du Bois, *Black Reconstruction*, 6–8. See also Ira Berlin, *Slaves without Masters: The Free Negro in the Antebellum South* (New York: Pantheon, 1974); and John Hope Franklin, *The Free Negro in North Carolina 1790–1860* (New York: W. W. Norton, 1971; 1943).

90. Du Bois, *Black Reconstruction*, 6.

91. Franklin and Moss, *From Slavery to Freedom*, 136–57.

92. See Harris, "Whiteness as Property," 1719; Walter Johnson, "The Slave Trader, the White Slave, and the Politics of Racial Determination in the 1850s," *Journal of American History* 87, no. 1 (June 2000): 13–38; and Pauli Murray, *Proud Shoes: The Story of an American Family* (New York: Harper and Row, 1984; 1956).

93. Charles Lenox Remond, "The Rights of Colored Citizens in Traveling," in Foner and Branham, *Lift Every Voice*, 193. This statement was made during a successful struggle to desegregate Massachusetts railroads.

94. See Noel Ignatiev, *How the Irish Became White* (New York: Routledge, 1995), esp. 1–3; and Matthew Frye Jacobson, *Whiteness of a Different Color: European Immigrants and the Alchemy of Race* (Cambridge: Harvard University Press, 1998), 15–90. Referring to the 1790 Naturalization Act, Jacobson notes that Irish and Germans were "well outside the deliberate intent of the 'free white persons' clause of 1790" (46–47).

95. Dorothy Sterling, *Ahead of Her Time: Abby Kelly and the Politics of Anti-Slavery* (New York: W. W. Norton, 1991), 191.

96. See Higginbotham, *In the Matter of Color*, part one (introduction), part two (colonial America, focusing on Virginia, Massachusetts, New York, South Carolina, Georgia, and Pennsylvania), and part four (the American Revolution). See also Fields, "Slavery"; and Allen, *White Race*, vol. 1 and vol. 2.

97. David R. Roediger, *The Wages of Whiteness: Race and the Making of the American Working Class* (London: Verso, 1991), 67. See also Aptheker, *American Negro Slave Revolts*; Benjamin Quarles, *Black Abolitionists* (New York: Da Capo, 1969); and Aileen S. Kraditor, *Means and Ends in American Abolitionism: Garrison and His Critics on Strategy and Tactics, 1834–1850* (Chicago: Ivan R. Dee, 1989; 1969).

98. See Paul Goodman, *Of One Blood: Abolitionism and the Origins of Racial Equality* (Berkeley: University of California Press, 1998), esp. chapters 12 and 13; Franklin and Moss, *From Slavery to Freedom*, 154–57; and Sterling, *Ahead of Her Time*. Black nationalist leader Martin Delany in 1852 had criticized three abolitionist newspapers—the *Liberator*, the *Standard*, and the *Freeman*—for hiring only one African American in each office, protesting that "the legitimate persons to fill any and every position about an anti-slavery establishment are colored persons. Nor will it do to argue in extenuation, that white men are as justly entitled to them as colored men; because white men do not from *necessity* become anti-slavery men in order to get situations; they being white men, may occupy any position they are capable of filling—in a word, their chances are endless, every avenue in the country being opened to them." Foner and Lewis, *The Black Worker*, vol. 1, 161–63 [From Martin Robison Delany, *The Condition, Elevation, Emigration, and Destiny of the Colored People of the United States* (Philadelphia, 1852), 26–30].

99. Goodman, *Of One Blood*, 186.

100. Franklin, *The Free Negro*, 143.

101. Ibid., 137.

102. Ibid., 138.

103. Ibid.

104. For example, see *Proceedings*, 61; Foner and Branham, *Lift Every Voice*, 78–287; Louis Filler, *Crusade against Slavery: Friends, Foes, and Reforms 1820–1860* (Algonac, MI: Reference, 1986); and Mark Andrew Huddle, ed., "North Carolina's Forgotten Abolitionist: The American Missionary Associa-

tion Correspondence of Daniel Wilson," *North Carolina Historical Review* 72, no. 4 (October 1995): 416–55.

105. See the Kentucky case *Beall v. Joseph (a negro)*, Hardin 51, May 1806 in Catterall, *Judicial Cases*, 281.

106. *Isaac v. Johnson*, 5 Munford 95, February 1816, in Ibid., 126–27.

107. See Foner and Branham, *Lift Every Voice*, 104–287.

108. Ibid. See, for example, Austin Steward (4 July 1827), "Termination of Slavery," 104–9; Frederick Douglass, "What to the Slave?," 246–68; William Wells Brown (27 September 1849), "I Have No Constitution, and No Country," 213–16; Sara G. Stanley (16–18 January 1856), "What, to the Toiling Millions There, Is This Boasted Liberty?," 284–87; and Peter Osborne (5 July 1832), "It Is Time for Us to Be Up and Doing," 123–24; and David Walker and Henry Highland Garnet, *Walker's Appeal and Garnet's Address to the Slaves of the United States of America* (Nashville: James C. Winston, 1994; 1848), 85: "Compare your own language above, extracted from your Declaration of Independence, with your cruelties and murders inflicted by your cruel and unmerciful fathers on ourselves. . . ." See also Sidney Kaplan and Emma Nogrady Kaplan, *The Black Presence in the Era of the American Revolution*, rev. ed. (Amherst: University of Massachusetts Press, 1991).

109. Absalom Jones (1 January 1808), "A Thanksgiving Sermon," in Foner and Branham, *Lift Every Voice*, 78.

110. Frederick Douglass, "What to the Slave?," 257. Two years earlier, during the week of the Fourth of July, Frederick Douglass was chosen as one of the vice presidents of the newly formed American League of Colored Laborers to promote black mechanic unity and business enterprise against hostile white labor and business interests. See Foner and Lewis, *The Black Worker*, vol. 1, 244–45.

111. Samuel H. Davis (15–19 August 1843), "We Must Assert Our Rightful Claims and Plead Our Own Cause," in Foner and Branham, *Lift Every Voice*, 194–98.

112. Quoted in Walker and Garnet, *Walker's Appeal*, 81: "But Americans, I declare to you, while you keep us and our children in bondage, and treat us like brutes, to make us support you and your families, we cannot be your friends."

113. See, for example, Suzanne Lebsock, *The Free Women of Petersburg: Status and Culture in a Southern Town, 1784–1860* (New York: W. W. Norton, 1985); and Catherine Clinton, *The Plantation Mistress: Women's World in the Old South* (New York: Pantheon, 1982).

114. See Sally Roesch Wagner, "The Iroquois Influence on Women's Rights," in Sakolsky and Koehnline, *Gone to Croatan*, 225–50.

115. Marylynn Salmon, *Women and the Law of Property in Early America* (Chapel Hill: University of North Carolina Press, 1986), 189–90.

116. Ibid., 141–42. See also Caterrall, *Judicial Cases*; and Bertie County Slave Papers, 1744–1815 (Raleigh: North Carolina Division of Archives). For example: "On November 3, 1773, Philip Watson gives to his [apparently married grown daughter] Penelopy War . . . one negro Gall named Venus about twelve years of age . . ." and William Merideth on 10 May 1779, "in consideration of love goodwill and affection which I have towards my loving Daughter Maryan Billops Have Given. . . . One Negro girl Name Lettice, one white Horse, womans Saddle and Bridle. . . ." Both these eastern North Carolina slaveholding men, incidentally, signed these legal documents with an "X" instead of their names, suggesting illiteracy and possibly poor backgrounds—including indentured servitude.

117. Elizabeth Fox-Genovese, *Within the Plantation Household: Black and White Women of the Old South*

(Chapel Hill: University of North Carolina Press, 1988), 35. See also Harriet Jacobs, *Incidents in the Life of a Slave Girl*, in *The Classic Slave Narratives*, ed. Henry Louis Gates Jr. (New York: Mentor, 1987), 333–515.

118. Franklin and Moss, *From Slavery to Freedom*, 113. See, for example, *Population Schedules of the Eighth Census of the United States: 1860 Slave Schedules. North Carolina*, microfilm, roll 925, vol. 3, 265–74, (Washington, D.C.: GSA, 1967); and *Agriculture of the United States in 1860: Compiled from the Original Returns of the Eighth Census*, vol. 17 (New York: Norman Ross, 1990; 1864), esp. 236. One sees quantitative diversity among white slaveowners as well as a significant number of women slaveowners when examining census records for each state. For example, North Carolina's New Hanover County (containing the port city of Wilmington) in 1860 counted 37 women out of 938 slaveholders (just under 4 percent). The majority of these women owned fewer than 10 slaves, while over a third owned more than 10 slaves; one woman, Ann Fennell, owned 44 slaves. See also microfilm census records (1830–60) for slaveholders in Virginia, Georgia, Kentucky, Louisiana, Tennessee, and Washington, D.C., at Perkins Library, Duke University. In 1822 in Charleston, South Carolina, there were 7 women out of 28 slaveholders who were listed as owners of the 34 slaves executed along with free black Denmark Vesey in his famous slave rebellion conspiracy, and women accounted for 12 of the 81 slaveholders of those slaves arrested and either found guilty or not guilty but not executed. See John Killens, ed., *The Trial Record of Denmark Vesey* (Boston: Beacon, 1970), 140–46. Vesey himself had bought his freedom in 1799 for $600 from a white female slaveholder, Mary Clodner, which he paid out of the $1,500 he won on a lottery ticket. See Douglas R. Egerton, *He Shall Go Out Free: The Lives of Denmark Vesey* (Madison, WI: Madison House, 1999), 73–74.

119. See Alice Kessler-Harris, *Out to Work: A History of Wage-Earning Women in the United States* (New York: Oxford University Press, 1982), chapters 1–3, esp. 68–69.

120. Ibid., 22.

121. Ibid., 29. See also *Abstracts of the Statistics of Manufacturers According to the Returns of the Seventh Census*, vol. 13 (New York: Norman Ross, 1990; 1850), ix, for 1850 census figures showing women workers nationally far outnumbering male workers in the textile industries.

122. Wesley, "Negro Suffrage," 157.

123. See Arthur M. Schlesinger Jr., *The Age of Jackson* (Boston: Little, Brown, 1947); and Robert V. Remini, ed., *The Age of Jackson* (Columbia: University of South Carolina Press, 1972).

124. Alexander Saxton, *The Rise and Fall of the White Republic: Class Politics and Mass Culture in Nineteenth-Century America* (London: Verso, 1996; 1990), 136. See also Chilton Williamson, *American Suffrage: From Property to Democracy, 1760–1860* (Princeton, NJ: Princeton University Press, 1960).

125. Richard E. Ellis, *The Union at Risk: Jacksonian Democracy, States' Rights, and the Nullification Crisis* (New York: Oxford University Press, 1987), 188–89. See also Schlesinger, *The Age of Jackson*; and Remini, *The Age of Jackson*.

126. Williamson, *American Suffrage*, vii.

127. Ibid., 3. Based on the original English categorization, the 1705 Virginia legal definition of "freeholder" was "every person who hath an estate real for his own life or the life of another or any estate of any greater dignity." Cited in John Gilman Kolp, *Gentlemen and Freeholders: Electoral Politics in Colonial Virginia* (Baltimore: Johns Hopkins University Press, 1998), 40.

128. Williamson, *American Suffrage*, 24–29. I have inserted "white" in parentheses: Williamson for some reason left African Americans and Native Americans out of "the adult male population" without so indicating.

129. Ibid., 80.

130. Ibid., 50. This practice, common throughout the colonies, was referred to as "fagot votes," possibly in reference to the old English word for kindling, indicating that after the votes were cast those "deeds" went up in smoke.

131. Ibid., 35–36.

132. Ibid., 35.

133. Ibid., 33

134. Ibid., 184–85, 229.

135. Ibid., 189. See also Wesley, "Negro Suffrage," 162: "Connecticut was the only New England state to forbid suffrage to Negroes. This was accomplished when the Convention of 1818 adopted an article granting the privilege of voting to white male citizens only. . . ."

136. Williamson, *American Suffrage*, 180.

137. Ibid. 208.

138. Ibid., 231–32.

139. Du Bois, *Black Reconstruction*, 7–8. Du Bois may have meant 1818 rather than 1814 for Connecticut. See also Williamson, *American Suffrage*, 278: "By 1858 the suffrage was denied to free Negroes in an overwhelming majority of the northern states." Native Americans were also deemed by whites as unfit to vote. By 1860 the property qualification for white males was almost totally eliminated.

140. See Noel Ignatiev, "The White Worker and the Labor Movement in Nineteenth-Century America," *Race Traitor: journal of the new abolitionism* 3 (spring 1994), 99–107. See also Sterling, *Ahead of Her Time*, 139–44, for an account of Abby Kelley's and Frederick Douglass's opposition to the Suffrage Association after unsuccessfully arguing to strike "white" from the proposed constitution. Free blacks and abolitionists walked out of the convention after initially supporting the suffragists. In the seven pages devoted to this revolt contained in *The Age of Jackson*—still considered by many to be one of the leading works on Jacksonian democracy—Arthur M. Schlesinger Jr. makes no mention of the attempted disfranchisement of blacks by the Dorr faction. Schlesinger, *The Age of Jackson*, 411–17.

141. Ignatiev, "The White Worker," 99–107; and Ignatiev, *How the Irish Became White*, 68–69, 74, 85.

142. Schlesinger, *The Age of Jackson*, 311; and Joseph Blau, ed., *Social Theories of Jacksonian Democracy: Representative Writings of the Period 1825–1850* (New York: Hafner, 1947), xiii.

143. Andrew Jackson, "A Political Test," from *Farewell Address of Andrew Jackson to the People of the United States and the Inaugural Address of Martin Van Buren, President of the United States* (Washington, 1837), 3–16, cited in Blau, *Social Theories*, 17.

144. Theophilus Fisk, "Capital Against Labor," an "address delivered at Julien Hall before the mechanics of Boston on Wednesday evening, May 30, 1835" (in the *New York Evening Post*, 6 August 1835, 2), in Ibid., 203; and Roediger, *The Wages of Whiteness*, 74–75. See also Ibid., 69, and chapter 4, passim, for how women textile mill strikers similarly distanced themselves from black slaves in Dover, New Hampshire, in 1828; Manayunk, Pennsylvania, in 1833; and Lowell, Massachusetts, in 1834 and 1836.

145. Allen, *White Race*, vol. 1, 186.

146. Ellis, *The Union at Risk*, 16; Remini, *The Age of Jackson*, 44, where Jackson is quoted as making this unwittingly ironic declaration in an 8 December 1829 speech: "In a country whose offices are created solely for the benefit of the people no one man has any more intrinsic right to official station than another."

147. Remini, *The Age of Jackson*, 17. Originally found in Gaillard Hurt, ed., *The First Forty Years of Washington Society Portrayed by the Family Letters of Mrs. Samuel Harrison Smith* . . . (New York: n.p., 1906), 290–97. On slave labor in the nation's Capitol, see "Slaves Built D.C.'s Freedom Symbols," *Raleigh News and Observer*, 23 July 2000, 5A.

148. The Beastie Boys, "Fight for Your Right to Party," *Licensed to Ill*, Def Jam, 1986, compact disc.

149. Robert V. Remini, ed., *The Jacksonian Era*, 2nd ed. (Wheeling, IL: Harlan Davidson, 1997; 1989), 21, 32.

150. Mary Hershberger, "Mobilizing Women, Anticipating Abolition: The Struggle against Indian Removal in the 1830s," *Journal of American History* 86, no. 1 (June 1999): 15–40.

151. Cited in *Morton v. Mancari*, 417 U.S. 535 (1974). See *Statutes at Large* 4, 737 (1834).

152. Remini, *The Jacksonian Era*, 46–47, 49–50.

153. *Proceedings*, 64.

154. Ibid., 61–62. See also Allen, *White Race*, vol. 2, especially chapter 9.

155. See Section 4.1 to 4.3, amendments to the state constitution in *Proceedings*, 421. It was not deemed necessary otherwise to liberalize the overall voting requirements: besides a one-year county residency requirement, one must simply be a "freeholder" to vote in elections for the state House of Commons but a freeholder owning at least 50 acres to vote in elections for the state Senate.

156. Ibid., 417.

157. See the Homestead Act of 1862 (limited to "free citizens") in *Statutes at Large*, vol. 12, (1862), 392–93. The Morrill Land Grant Act passed in July 1862 subsidized the building and maintenance of at least one agricultural and mechanical college per state on public land (Ibid., 503–5). See also Allen, *White Race*, vol. 1, 141, 152–55; Marian L. Smith, "Review of INS History," at http://www.ins.usdoj.gov, Internet; and Marian L. Smith, " 'Any Woman Who Is Now or May Hereafter Be Married': Women and Naturalization, ca. 1802–1940," *Prologue: Quarterly of the National Archives and Records Administration* 30 no. 2 (summer 1998). [Online document.] Until the Chinese Exclusion Act of 1882, immigration to the United States in the nineteenth century was unrestricted and even encouraged, but naturalization, still governed by the laws of 1790, 1795, and 1802, was limited to "free white persons."

158. Abraham Lincoln, *Life and Public Services of Hon. Abraham Lincoln*, ed. David V. Bartlett (Freeport, NY: Books for Libraries Press, 1969; 1860), 246.

159. Douglass quoted in Du Bois, *Black Reconstruction*, 61.

160. Ibid.

161. See López, *White By Law*.

162. See Franklin and Moss, *From Slavery to Freedom*, 177–78. *Uncle Tom's Cabin* sold more than 300,000 copies in one year and was also dramatized in theaters.

163. See Leonard P. Curry, *The Free Black in Urban America 1800–1854: The Shadow of the Dream* (Chicago: University of Chicago Press, 1981), especially chapter 6, "Race Riot: Prejudice Explodes."

164. Ibid., 96. See also Goodman, *Of One Blood*, 162,

165. Ignatiev, *How the Irish Became White*, 132. Note the irony in Grund's invocation of common law in white mob action in what could be called an early republican form of "white-affirmative action."

166. Ibid.

167. Aptheker, *American Negro Slave Revolts*, 264.

168. See Eric Lott, *Love and Theft: Blackface Minstrelsy and the American Working Class* (New York:

Oxford University Press, 1993), especially 211–33. Soon after its first appearance in book form, *Uncle Tom's Cabin* was adapted to the minstrel stage (there were no copyright laws then), with many different variations that both mocked the slaves and the slaveholders.

169. *Ibid.*, 35, 95–96, 148–49, and passim.

170. Sterling D. Spero and Abram L. Harris, "The Slave Regime: Competition Between Negro and White Labor," in *The Other Slaves: Mechanics, Artisans, and Craftsmen*, ed. James E. Newton and Ronald L. Lewis (Boston: G. K. Hall, 1978), 47.

171. Curry, *The Free Black*, 96–111.

172. See Ignatiev, *How the Irish Became White*; Anthony Gronowicz, *Race and Class Politics in New York City before the Civil War* (Boston: Northeastern University, 1998); and Iver Bernstein, *The New York City Draft Riots: Their Significance for American Society and Politics in the Age of the Civil War* (New York: Oxford University Press, 1990).

173. Hershberger, "Mobilizing Women," 15.

174. Howard Zinn, *A People's History of the United States* (New York: Harper, 1990; 1980), 150–66.

175. See Rodolfo F. Acuña, *Occupied America: A History of Chicanos*, 4th ed. (New York: Longman, 2000), esp. chapters 2–6; Dan W. Dickey, "Mexican Americans, Violence Toward," in *Encyclopedia of Southern Culture*, ed. Charles Reagan Wilson and William Ferris (Chapel Hill: University of North Carolina Press, 1988), 1488–89; Matt S. Meier and Feliciano Rivera, *The Chicanos: A History of Mexican-Americans* (New York: Hill and Wang, 1972) 70–133; and David G. Gutiérrez, "Migration, Emergent Ethnicity, and the 'Third Space': The Shifting Politics of Nationalism in Greater Mexico," *Journal of American History* 86, no. 2 (September 1991): 485–91.

176. Space does not permit a full treatment of the Mexican experience in the United States with regards to issues of labor and race. See Richard Delgado, *When Equality Ends: Stories About Race and Resistance* (Boulder, CO: Westview Press, 1999), 15–25; López, *White By Law*, 37–42, 204; and the previous note.

177. Mitchell Goodman, ed., *The Movement toward a New America: The Beginnings of a Long Revolution* (Philadelphia: Pilgrim Press, 1970), 230–42; and Richard A. Garcia, ed., *The Chicanos in America 1540–1974: A Chronology and Fact Book* (Dobbs Ferry, NY: Oceana, 1977).

178. See, for example, the 1972 Small Business Act cited in *Adarand v. Peña*, 115 U.S. 2097 (1995), referring to "Black Americans, Hispanic Americans, Native Americans, Asian Pacific Americans, and other minorities. . . ." This format was far from random, however. It reflected a popular conception of a hierarchy of oppression and resistance.

179. Gutiérrez, "Migration," 481–517.

180. Douglass quoted in Ignatiev, *How the Irish Became White*, 111. Taken from Frederick Douglass, *The Life and Times of Frederick Douglass; Written By Himself* (London: Collier, 1962), 298–99. For the Du Bois quote, see W. E. B. Du Bois, *W. E. B. Du Bois: A Reader*, ed. David Levering Lewis (New York: Henry Holt, 1995), 542 (from "Marxism and the Negro Problem," *Crisis*, May 1933).

181. Du Bois, *Black Reconstruction*, chapter 3; James W. Loewen, *Lies My Teacher Told Me: Everything Your American History Textbook Got Wrong* (New York: Touchstone, 1995), 190–91; and McPherson, *Battle Cry of Freedom*, chapters 7–8. McPherson argues that, despite Confederate language of counter-revolution, in this case "secession fit the model of a pre-emptive counter-revolution developed by historian Arno Mayer. Rather than trying to restore the old order, a pre-emptive counter-revolution strikes first to protect the status quo before the revolutionary threat can materialize" (245). See Ibid., chapters 1–7; and Du Bois, *Black Reconstruction*, chapter 3, for discussion of the long line of "compromises" (like the Missouri Compromise of 1820, the Compromise of 1850, and the 1854

Kansas-Nebraska Act) that nonetheless left slaveholders in the driver's seat with regards to federal and state power. Even before secession, the proposed slave empire of the Southern slaveholders included Cuba and Latin America. See also *Constitution of the Confederate States of America*, reprinted in *Encyclopedia of the Confederacy*, ed. Richard Nelson Current (New York: Simon and Schuster, 1993), Appendix 3, esp. 1781. For Southern white anti-Confederate resistance see Loewen, "Lies"; George Lee Tatum, *Disloyalty in the Confederacy* (Chapel Hill: University of North Carolina Press, 1934); Richard Nelson Current, *Lincoln's Loyalists: Union Soldiers in the Confederacy* (Boston: Northeastern University Press, 1992); William T. Auman and David D. Scarboro, "The Heroes of Civil War North Carolina," *North Carolina Historical Review* 58, no. 4 (October 1981): 327–63; and Philip F. Rubio, "Civil War Reenactments and Other Myths," in *Race Traitor*, ed. Noel Ignatiev and John Garvey (New York: Routledge, 1996), 182–94.

182. Current, *Confederacy*, esp. 1774–81. On the "Slave Power" reference, see, for example, Quarles, *Black Abolitionists*, 246.

183. Du Bois, *Black Reconstruction*, 49. The seven lower Southern states of South Carolina, Texas, Alabama, Mississippi, Georgia, Louisiana, and Florida, which also had the largest slave populations and white support, were the first to secede. The four upper Southern states of Arkansas, Tennessee, Virginia, and North Carolina, all of which initially voted down secession, voted to secede after South Carolina Confederate forces fired on Fort Sumter on 12 April 1861 and President Lincoln called for all states to provide militia to help crush the insurrection. See McPherson, *Battle Cry of Freedom*, chapters 8–9.

184. Du Bois, *Black Reconstruction*, 50. See also James M. McPherson, *For Cause and Comrades: Why Men Fought in the Civil War* (New York: Oxford University Press, 1997), esp. 110, where he notes that while only "20 percent of the sample of 429 Southern soldiers explicitly voiced proslavery convictions in their letters or diaries" (and a much higher percentage among slaveholding families), none dissented from that view, and the majority felt no need to discuss a "right" they took for granted.

Chapter 2

1. *Regents of the University of California v. Bakke*, 438 U.S. 265 (1978). See also Cheryl I. Harris, "Whiteness as Property," *Harvard Law Review* 106 (1993): 1709–91; and Kimberlé Crenshaw, "Black Women's Book Fair" lecture, Duke University, Durham, North Carolina, 25 March 1999.

2. The *Bakke* decision allowed for race to be used a factor in college admissions but determined that spaces for minorities may not be reserved. Marshall voted with the majority on the former but dissented on the latter. See chapter 6 of this book for a more detailed discussion of *Bakke*.

3. See Edward Conrad Smith, ed., *The Constitution of the United States with Case Summaries*, 11th ed. (New York: Barnes and Noble, 1979; 1936), 52–53; Alfred Avins, ed., *The Reconstruction Amendments' Debates: The Legislative History and Contemporary Debates in Congress on the 13th, 14th, and 15th Amendments* (Richmond: Virginia Commission on Constitutional Government, 1967), 200–268, 335–417; and W. E. B. Du Bois, *Black Reconstruction in America 1860–1880* (Cleveland: Meridian, 1968; 1935), chapters 8–9, for text, debate, and discussion of the Fourteenth and Fifteenth Amendments. Additionally, Section 1 of the Fourteenth Amendment significantly "contained the first use of the phrase 'equal protection' in a proposed constitutional provision." See Bernard Schwartz, ed., *Statutory History of the United States: Civil Rights Part 1* (New York: Chelsea House, 1970), 185. For modern critics of affirmative action who cite the Fourteenth and Fifteenth Amendments as racially neutral or color-

blind, see, for example, Paul D. Moreno, "Racial Classifications and Reconstruction Legislation," *Journal of Southern History* 61, no. 2 (1995): 271–304; and plaintiff's attorney Robinson Everett cited in *Shaw v. Reno*, 113 U.S. 2816 (1993); and *Shaw v. Hunt* 517 U.S. 899 (1995). On slavery and white supremacy as the cornerstone of Confederate secession, see Du Bois, *Black Reconstruction*, 48–53, and chapter 1, note 181 of this book.

    4. John David Skrentny, *The Ironies of Affirmative Action: Politics, Culture and Justice in America* (Chicago: University of Chicago Press, 1996), 6.

    5. Schwartz, *Civil Rights Part 1*, 619 (42nd Cong., 1st sess., 28 March–6 April 1871).

    6. Ibid. Italics added.

    7. Ibid. It is possible but very unlikely that Coburn coined the term, given the popularity of the legal use of the word "affirmative." Examples of Reconstruction debates utilizing the word "affirmative" for protecting black civil rights include: Rep. Benjamin Butler (R-Massachusetts) maintained that "affirmative declarations" and "affirmative guarantees" were useless without enforcement (Ibid., 613), while Sen. George F. Edmunds (R-Vermont) called for "affirmative assistance in protecting the lives and property of . . . fellow citizens . . ." (Ibid., 653). The word "affirm" shows up in many legal and political declarations during this period, such as abolitionist speeches and Supreme Court opinions. See also Smith, *The Constitution*, 51–53, for a new feature of constitutional amendments beginning with Reconstruction: the addition of an article declaring that "the Congress shall have power to enforce, by appropriate legislation, the provisions of this article." Such an assertive stance lent itself to subsequent "affirmative" declarations. See also Du Bois, *Black Reconstruction*, 619; Walter Clark, ed., *The State Records of North Carolina*, vol. 23, *Laws 1715–1776* (Goldsboro: Nash, 1904); and *Proceedings and Debates of the Convention of North Carolina Called to Amend the Constitution of the State, which Assembled at Raleigh June 4, 1835* (Raleigh: Joseph Gales, 1836).

    8. James M. McPherson, *The Abolitionist Legacy: From Reconstruction to the NAACP* (Princeton, NJ: Princeton University Press, 1975), chapter 1.

    9. Ibid. See also *Reconstruction Acts of 1867, Statutes at Large* 14 and 15 (1867); David S. Cecelski, "Abraham H. Galloway: Wilmington's Lost Prophet and the Rise of Black Radicalism in the American South," in *Democracy Betrayed: The Wilmington Race Riot of 1898 and Its Legacy*, ed. David S. Cecelski and Timothy B. Tyson (Chapel Hill: University of North Carolina Press, 1998), 59: "The 1867 Reconstruction Acts restored federal military authority in the South and required states in the former Confederacy to pass a constitution that guaranteed universal male suffrage before they could be readmitted to the Union. The acts also opened the polls to black voters while banning from political life any antebellum officeholder who had taken an oath to uphold the U.S. Constitution but sided with the Confederacy." In addition see Robert J. Kaczorowski, "To Begin the Nation Anew: Congress, Citizenship, and Civil Rights after the Civil War," *American Historical Review* 92, issue 1, supplement to vol. 92 (February 1987): 45–68, on how the Reconstruction amendments were "constitutionally revolutionary (67)" and represented the framers' "adoption of the most radical abolitionist theory of constitutionalism before the Civil War (49)." In fact, he adds: "The essential reason that Radical Republicans criticized the Fourteenth Amendment as too moderate was its failure to provide the same protection for voting rights as for civil rights." See also Du Bois, *Black Reconstruction*, 264–70, for a discussion of Thaddeus Stevens and the Committee of Fifteen's revolutionary programs of constitutional change—with half their proposals affecting the freedpeople. The Committee of Fifteen, according to Du Bois, was a postwar bipartisan, bicameral body, which was based on the English parliamentary model, that set out to increase popular representation as well as the power of the legislative branch.

10. See *Civil Rights Cases*, 109 U.S. 3 (1883); Du Bois, *Black Reconstruction*, 690–91; and Smith, *The Constitution*, 52–53. Section 1 of the Fourteenth Amendment, the section most cited today, reads: "All persons born or naturalized in the United States, and subject to the jurisdiction thereof, are citizens of the United States and of the State wherein they reside. No State shall make or enforce any law which shall abridge the privileges or immunities of citizens of the United States; nor shall any State deprive any person of life, liberty, or property, without due process of law; nor deny to any person within its jurisdiction the equal protection of the laws." Section 2 apportioned representatives in Congress based on total population and proportionally penalized states that disfranchised male voters. Section 3 blocked any former civilian or military official at any level in the United States who had taken part in secession and rebellion from holding office unless over-ruled by a vote of Congress. Section 4 repudiated the Confederate debt. Section 5 gave Congress the power to enforce the article as a whole.

11. McPherson, *The Abolitionist Legacy*, 3.

12. Ibid.

13. Ibid., 79.

14. Ibid.; see also Lydia Marie Child, *Lydia Maria Child Selected Letters, 1817–1880*, ed. Milton Meltzer and Patricia G. Holland (Amherst: University of Massachusetts, 1982), 439–78; and Doro-thy Sterling, *Ahead of Her Time: Abby Kelley and the Politics of Antislavery* (New York: W. W. Norton, 1991). The Freedmen's Bureau provided land, work, schools, and medical care to the freedpeople and refugees between 1865 and 1870. See Du Bois, *Black Reconstruction*, esp. 220–30, 647–67; *Freed-men's Bureau Act of 1865*, Statutes at Large 13 (1865), 507–9; and amended *Freedmen's Bureau Act of 1866*, Statutes at Large 14 (1866), 173–77.

15. See Cecelski, "Abraham H. Galloway," 43–73. Galloway was a runaway slave in eastern North Carolina who became a major recruiter for black soldiers in the Union army, as well as a soldier himself. During Reconstruction he became a leading figure in statewide Republican politics. See also Pauli Murray, *Proud Shoes: The Story of an American Family* (New York: Harper and Row, 1984; 1956), for the story of her grandfather, Robert G. Fitzgerald, and her great-uncle, Richard B. Fitz-gerald. A Pennsylvania transplant and the son of a former slave and abolitionist, Robert had served in the Union army and navy before coming to North Carolina after the war. He taught school in Goldsboro and Hillsborough and was a Republican Party activist, while his brother, Richard, who had driven wagons for the Union army, became a successful entrepreneur with the establishment of his brick-making business in Durham.

16. Frederick Douglass, *The Life and Writings of Frederick Douglass*, ed. Philip S. Foner, vol. 4, *Reconstruction and After* (New York: International Publishers, 1955), 40–45, 231–39; and Robert L. Allen, *Reluctant Reformers: Racism and Social Reform Movements in the United States* (Washington, D.C.: Howard University Press, 1983), 139–48. Allen points out that Douglass, Harriet Tubman, and Sojourner Truth (who did not oppose the amendments despite her dislike of the compromise) all continued to campaign for female suffrage and equality after these debates.

17. Commonly remembered as Ida B. Wells today, Wells took the name Ida B. Wells-Barnett after her marriage to prominent Chicago attorney Ferdinand Lee Barnett in 1895. (A more detailed discussion of her contribution to this struggle follows in chapter 3.) See Ida B. Wells, *Crusade for Justice: The Autobiography of Ida B. Wells*, ed. Alfreda M. Duster (Chicago: University of Chicago Press, 1972); Gerda Lerner, ed., *Black Women in White America: A Documentary History* (New York: Vintage, 1973), 198; and Rosalyn Terborg-Penn, *African-American Women in the Struggle for the Vote, 1850–1920* (Bloomington: Indiana University Press, 1998), 111 and passim. The Fifteenth Amendment consists of two sections. Section 1 reads: "The right of citizens of the United States to vote shall not be

denied or abridged by the United States or by any State on account of race, color, or previous condition of servitude." Section 2 gives Congress the power to enforce this article. See Smith, *The Constitution*, 53.

18. Deborah K. King, "Black Feminist Ideology," in *Black Women's History: Theory and Practice*, vol. 1, ed. Darlene Clark Hine (Brooklyn: Carlson, 1990), 332.

19. Wendell Phillips, *Wendell Phillips On Civil Rights and Freedom*, ed. Louis Filler, 2nd ed. (Washington, D.C.: University Press of America, 1982; 1965), 189. Charles Sumner, on the other hand, opposed legislation for the eight-hour workday. See Timothy Messer-Kruse, *The Yankee International: Marxism and the American Reform Tradition, 1848–1876* (Chapel Hill: University of North Carolina Press, 1998), 7.

20. See Douglass, *The Life and Writings*.

21. McPherson, *The Abolitionist Legacy*, 70–72.

22. Douglass, *The Life and Writings*, 164.

23. Ibid., 228.

24. Ibid., 33–35, 204–6.

25. Ibid., 101; Du Bois, *Black Reconstruction*, 691–92; and McPherson, *The Abolitionist Legacy*, 92–93.

26. Douglass, *The Life and Writings*, 31–32.

27. Ibid., 31.

28. Ibid., 388. After the bank failed, Douglass called for reimbursement by Congress to its black depositors because Congress had chartered and promoted the bank without legislative oversight. See also Claude F. Oubre, *Forty Acres and a Mule* (Baton Rouge: Louisiana State University Press, 1978); Marland E. Buckner Jr., "Liberty and Economy in Lowcountry South Carolina: The Case of the Freedmen's Bank," in *Keep Your Head to the Sky: Interpreting African American Home Ground*, ed. Grey Gundaker (Charlottesville: University Press of Virginia, 1998), 211–26; and McPherson, *The Abolitionist Legacy*, 75, on the exaggeration of the "extent and consequences of that failure" of the bank.

29. See, for example, Moreno, "Racial Classifications," 271–304. A similar attempt at "de-colorizing" and de-contextualizing the words of Martin Luther King Jr. has been made in recent years. See Michael Eric Dyson, *I May Not Get There with You: The True Martin Luther King, Jr.* (New York: Free Press, 2000), 11–29, 282–306.

30. Douglass, *The Life and Writings*, 164. See Moreno, "Racial Classifications," 299, for his assertion that this speech demonstrated Douglass's opposition to (black) "race-based preferential treatment." See also Paul D. Moreno, *From Direct Action to Affirmative Action: Fair Employment Policy in America, 1933–1972* (Baton Rouge: Louisiana State University Press, 1997), 8, for his dismissal of what he calls Thurgood Marshall's "untenable" though "novel interpretation" of Reconstruction as an early precedent for "racial quotas in higher education admissions" in the 1978 *Bakke* case. Moreno maintains that black preferential treatment in Reconstruction was never Republican policy but solely an example of Democratic race-baiting. Actually, Douglass's beliefs were shared by black Reconstruction activists who desired both protection and egalitarianism. Modern historians should more carefully consider the context and listen more closely to words such as these spoken at the South Carolina Colored People's Convention of November 1865: "We ask for no special privileges or peculiar favors. We ask only for even-handed Justice, or for the removal of such *positive obstructions* as past, and recent Legislatures have seen fit to throw in our way and heap upon us." See Thomas Holt, *Black Over White: Negro Political Leadership in South Carolina during Reconstruction* (Urbana: Univer-

sity of Illinois Press, 1977), 19. Italics added. For another example of black "color blindness" opposing white privilege, see Du Bois, *Black Reconstruction*, 296–300, for an account of the famous 7 February 1866 White House confrontation between President Andrew Johnson and a black delegation led by Frederick Douglass, in which George T. Downing told Johnson: "We are Americans, native-born Americans; we are citizens. . . . We see no recognition of color or race in the organic law of the land." Ibid., 297.

31. Douglass, *The Life and Writings*, 276–81. Delany had been commissioned as a major in an all-black regiment at the very end of the Civil War. During Reconstruction Delany accepted an appointment as a Freedmen's Bureau official in South Carolina. See John Hope Franklin and Alfred A. Moss Jr., *From Slavery to Freedom: A History of Negro Americans*, 6th ed. (New York: McGraw-Hill, 1988; 1947), 196; and Oubre, *Forty Acres*, 69.

32. Douglass, *The Life and Writings*, 281. Note Douglass's reference to Irish and Germans as distinct from "whites," reflecting a still-popular notion at that time that these two immigrant groups were in transition from foreigners or ethnic minorities to full-fledged "white people." But see infra note 89 for an 1864 congressional committee minority report that defines Irish and Dutch people as being also "Caucasians." Compare also the overall content of that quote with this one and their relevance to today's affirmative action debate. The reductionist tone of the latter and the optimistic tone of the former can be seen, respectively, in today's incredulous affirmative action opponents and ambivalent black proponents.

33. Ibid., 279. Delany's support for minimum black representative quotas and his insistence on elected black leadership is a matter of record. See Holt, *Black Over White*, 106: "Delany then [during an 1867 Southern lecture tour] outlined a specific formula for the equitable distribution of offices based roughly on population ratios; it entailed demands for the lieutenant governorship, two congressmen, one senator, and the appropriate quota of state and county offices."

34. Douglass, *The Life and Writings*, 228, from *New National Era*, 6 October 1870. Moreno missed or ignored the many black protections (or "preferences") that defined this era (like the Freedmen's Bureau and the Enforcement Acts), as well as the white race-based preferences (such as in hiring, suffrage, education, and public accommodations) that Douglass and other abolitionists opposed.

35. "Forget that I'm black—but don't forget that I'm black" is one popular expression of that paradox today.

36. Douglass, *The Life and Writings*, 280. See also Douglass in Ibid., 520 (from his 1884 pamphlet "Why Is the Negro Lynched?"): "Let the white people of the North and South conquer their prejudices" was his response to the question of how to solve America's "national" problem—which he said the United States actually had, as opposed to what was commonly called a "Negro problem."

37. Ibid., 279.

38. Ibid., 377 (from "Address to the People of the United States," Louisville, Kentucky, 24 September 1883). Citizenship, Douglass argued, should not be based on color, but while black conventions were based on unity against oppression, white conventions maintained oppression: "In point of fact, however, white men are already in convention against us in various ways and at many important points. The practical construction of American life is a convention against us. Human law may know no distinction among men in respect of rights, but human practice may. . . ."

39. Ibid., 58–60.

40. Ibid., 354–70 (from "The United States Cannot Remain Half-Slave and Half-Free," Washington, D.C., April 1863) and 388–89 (from "Address to the People").

41. Ibid., 218–20 (from "My Son, Lewis Douglass," speech in Rochester, New York, August

1869). Douglass was bitter over his son being denied a printing job in Rochester, which undoubtedly brought back memories of white dockworker attacks on blacks in Baltimore in his own younger days in that city.

42. Ibid., 357. See supra note 40.

43. Ibid. In the *National Standard*, 15 October 1870, Douglass wrote, "It is, therefore, not the Negro's color that makes him distasteful, but the assumption of equal manhood." Ibid., 230.

44. Ibid., 357. In the *New National Era*, 6 October 1870, Douglass wrote that still "the Negro is not abolished as a degraded caste" (Ibid., 228). He might have therefore been sympathetic to the notion of abolishing "the white" as an elevated caste. Douglass's idea of eventually abolishing race as a determinant was especially aimed at whites, but to this day there is no mainstream acceptance by white people of the notion of "color blindness" involving the abolition of whiteness.

45. Du Bois, *Black Reconstruction*, 283. Johnson's veto was overridden by Congress, which then encased the essence of the Civil Rights Act within the Fourteenth Amendment to make it veto-proof.

46. Ibid., 282–83.

47. Ibid., 136.

48. According to McPherson in *The Abolitionist Legacy*, 5, those activists and elected officials who fought slavery both before and during the Civil War and continued to fight for equality during Reconstruction still called themselves "abolitionists." See also Du Bois, who referred to the forces of "abolition-democracy" in *Black Reconstruction*, 184–85.

49. McPherson, *The Abolitionist Legacy*, 5. See also Avins, *Debates*, 402 (40th Cong., 3rd sess., 17 February 1869, S.p. 1309), for Sen. George H. Williams's (Union Republican-Oregon) contention that three-fourths of white Americans would oppose the Fifteenth Amendment if put to a vote, citing the recent Michigan referendum opposing striking the word "white" from their state constitution. Sen. John Sherman (R-Ohio) noted that the constitutions of "at least thirty states" including his own would now have the "white" qualification deleted. Ibid., 387, 9 February 1869, S.p. 1039.

50. See Avins, *Debates*. See also Du Bois, *Black Reconstruction*, 298; and Douglass, *The Life and Writings*, 182–91, for President Johnson's assertion of poor white victimhood in the 1866 "interview" with eleven black delegates at the White House referred to in supra note 30. See also Philip S. Foner and Ronald L. Lewis, eds., *The Black Worker: A Documentary History from Colonial Times to the Present*, vol. 1, *The Black Worker to 1869* (Philadelphia: Temple University Press, 1978), parts 9–10.

51. David R. Roediger, *The Wages of Whiteness: Race and the Making of the American Working Class* (London: Verso, 1991), 167–84.

52. Foner and Lewis, *The Black Worker*, vol. 1, parts 9–10, esp. 370–74. The *Advocate* was the national organ of the National Labor Union. See infra note 142.

53. Foner and Lewis, *The Black Worker*, vol. 1, parts 9–10, esp. 390–91, 402–3. Here are two remarkable samples from the *Voice*: (1) An article dated 5 October 1865, called "Justice," challenged white Baltimore laborers who refused to work with blacks and concluded: "To elevate a class only is to do nothing. We have to establish a principle—the principle of justice—if we would have a secure foundation for our work." (2) A reply dated 17 November 1866 to an attack by another labor paper—the *Detroit Daily Union*—on the *Voice's* support for black Massachusetts state legislative candidates: "They reveal a clear case of *color-phobia*," they said of the *Union*, employing a popular term that they had earlier defined as follows: *"This peculiar disease, confined entirely to the white race, is of quite modern origin, nothing being recorded of it in history."* Italics added.

54. Sen. Charles Sumner (R-Massachusetts), the most radical of the Republicans, later posi-

tioned himself with the Liberals out of his personal and political opposition to President Ulysses S. Grant, although without changing his own radical pro-equality politics. See Allen, *Reluctant Reformers*, 47.

55. They were also formerly known as "War Democrats" for their opposition to the war, abolition, or both. McPherson, *Battle Cry of Freedom*, 505.

56. Alexander H. Stephens (D-Georgia), the former vice president of the Confederacy and author of the infamous 1861 speech lauding white supremacy as the basis for the Confederacy, served in the Reconstruction Congress from 1873 to 1882. See Du Bois, *Black Reconstruction*, 49–50 and passim.

57. Ibid., 627. See also Richard Valelly, "Voting Rights in Jeopardy," *American Prospect* 46 (September–October 1999), 49: "From 1867 to 1877 about 2000 blacks served as federal, state, and local office holders in the ex-Confederate states subject to congressional Reconstruction. They were almost all strongly Republican in their policy views, and concentrated in the Deep South states with majority black or significantly black populations: South Carolina, Mississippi, Louisiana, North Carolina, Alabama, and Georgia, in that order. Between 1868 and 1876 an average of 268 black men served during the legislative sessions of the state legislatures in 10 southern states."

58. Du Bois, *Black Reconstruction*, 690–92.

59. Frederick Douglass raised this as a motive. See Douglass, *The Life and Writings*, 61; and Allen, *Reluctant Reformers*, 45.

60. See James M. McPherson, *Abraham Lincoln and the Second American Revolution* (New York: Oxford University Press, 1990), 40. Abandoning his United States Senate seat for the presidency of Confederate States of America, Jefferson Davis took with him the white supremacist mantle of Chief Justice Taney when he declared that the South was leaving the Union "to save ourselves from a revolution" that would make "property in slaves so insecure as to be comparatively worthless. . . . Our struggle is for inherited rights." Quoted in Ibid., 27.

61. See Du Bois, *Black Reconstruction*, 84–127, 670–71. See also Thomas W. Higginson, *Army Life in a Black Regiment* (Lansing: Michigan State University Press, 1960; 1870); and Roediger, *The Wages of Whiteness*, 168–69, where Roediger also cites Marx's contemporary observation to that effect.

62. Du Bois, *Black Reconstruction*, 293, 319, 374. Du Bois points out how many congressional opponents of black suffrage, not daring to directly oppose it because of growing popular support, called for letting the states decide, thus taking their chances on the fact that many states still limited suffrage to naturalized white males and would presumably oppose it.

63. Avins, *Debates*, 83 (38th Cong., 2nd sess., 9, 10, 11 January 1865, H.p. 214).

64. Richard Hofstadter, *The American Political Tradition and the Men Who Made It* (New York: Knopf, 1959), 132. Passed by Congress 31 January 1865, the Thirteenth Amendment was ratified by the states 6 December 1865. The Fourteenth Amendment was passed by Congress 13 June 1866 and ratified 9 July 1868. The Fifteenth Amendment was passed 26 February 1869 and ratified 3 February 1870. Smith, *The Constitution*, 51–53.

65. Avins, *Debates*, 81 (38th Cong., 2nd sess., 5, 6, 7 January 1865, H.p. 155). Two strong motivating factors for abolition for white Northern Republicans, Avins points out were winning the war and punishing the South. Ibid., v.

66. Du Bois, *Black Reconstruction*, 374. The "Ku Klux Act" was the actual name given to this law: the nineteenth-century Ku Klux Klan was also known as the "Ku Klux." See Albion W. Tourgée, *A Fool's Errand: By One of the Fools* (Cambridge, MA: Belknap, 1966; 1879), 193.

67. See Sen. Edgar Cowan (R-Pennsylvania) in Avins, *Debates*, 70 (38th Cong., 1st sess., 6 May 1864, S.p. 2140).

68. See Allen, *Reluctant Reformers*, 32–37; Bernard Schwartz, *Statutory History of the United States: Civil Rights Part* 2 (New York: Chelsea House, 1970).

69. McPherson, *The Abolitionist Legacy*, 180. Operating here were not just sexual stereotypes but a fear of "diluting whiteness" by mass intermarriage with mulatto offspring: the property interest in white mothers "safeguarding whiteness."

70. Avins, *Debates*, 621–22, 626–27, 662, 675, 683, 695, 732–35.

71. Ibid; see also 698 (Sen. William T. Hamilton [D-Maryland], 43rd Cong., 1st sess., 22 May 1874, S.p. app. 362). Opponents knew that enshrining the Civil Rights Act in the Constitution made it almost invincible. Most civil rights provisions were in fact later weakened in the federal statute revision of 1873. See Schwartz, *Civil Rights Part 1*, 803.

72. Avins, *Debates*, 212–13 (39th Cong., 1st sess., 8 May 1866, S.p. 2459–60).

73. Ibid., 675–76 (43rd Cong., 1st sess., 30 April, 4 May 1874, S.p. 236–44). Rep. Thomas M. Norwood (D-Georgia) anticipated today's affirmative action opponents by calling whites "victims" of "forced association," and he ridiculed an imagined "preferences and quotas" system of exactly equal racialized seating arrangements, table service, and menu items at hotels and inns.

74. Lynch's remarks underscored Theodore Allen's definition of racial oppression's "hallmark": the refusal of the oppressor to recognize social distinctions among the oppressed. See Allen, *White Race*, vol. 1, 32.

75. Avins, *Debates*, 715 (43rd Cong., 2nd sess., 3 February 1875, H.p. 944).

76. Ibid., 721. Rep. Thomas Whitehead (Conservative-Virginia) characterized this as problack discrimination by the "northern republican" sleeping-car magnate George Pullman. This kind of reasoning drove Sen. Oliver H. P. T. Morton (Union Republican-Indiana) to muse in an 1868 debate: "It is a little remarkable, Mr. President, that whenever any allusion is made to placing the negro upon a political equality with the white man, they call it placing him over the white man . . ." Ibid., 329.

77. Philip S. Foner and Robert James Branham, eds., *Lift Every Voice: African American Oratory, 1787–1900* (Tuscaloosa: University of Alabama Press, 1998), 563 [*Congressional Record*, 43 Cong., 2nd sess., vol. 2, part 1, 565–67]. Italics added. Note Rapier's reference to "uncommon law of the most positive character" as positing Reconstruction legislation within Anglo-American legal tradition as well as being something radically new, with "positive" being synonymous with "affirmative." See infra note 133 for similar remarks by Thaddeus Stevens. See also Richard Zuczek's appraisal in his *State of Rebellion: Reconstruction in South Carolina* (Columbia: University of South Carolina Press, 1996), 39: that with the Reconstruction Acts coercion had replaced cajoling as a federal strategy.

78. Hiram R. Revels, "Abolish Separate Schools," in Foner and Branham, *Lift Every Voice*, 509, (*Congressional Globe*, 41st Cong., 3rd sess., part 2, 1054). Revels had taken the seat previously held by former Confederate President Jefferson Davis. See also Du Bois, *Black Reconstruction*, 449–50. See Avins, *Debates*, xxi, on Sumner's advocacy during this debate of integrated schools to eradicate "prejudice," which for abolitionists meant white supremacy.

79. Derrick A. Bell Jr., *Race, Racism, and American Law*, 2nd ed. (Boston: Little Brown, 1980), 32 n 7. See also Avins, *Debates*, xi–xiii.

80. Avins, *Debates*, 428 (41st Cong., 2nd sess., 23, 24 February 1870, S.p. 1513).

81. Du Bois, *Black Reconstruction*, 266.

82. Avins, *Debates*, 426–32 (17–24 February 1870, S.p. 1510–66).

83. Ibid., 426 (S.p. 1510). In a strange twist, Sen. John Sherman (R-Ohio) argued that the light-skinned Revels (born to free parents in North Carolina) was "undoubtedly" a citizen because he had voted more than twenty years before in Ohio—a state whose 1802 constitution defined a "white male citizen" as "one who was nearer white than black." During this debate, an argument was also made in general terms that blacks could not make informed votes or serve as public officials because they could not meet white standards—a charge that abolitionists disputed vehemently.

84. Marshall in *Bakke* (1978).

85. Ibid. See supra note 1.

86. See *Freedmen's Bureau Act of 1865; Freedmen's Bureau Act of 1866;* Ira Berlin et al., eds., *Free at Last: A Documentary History of Slavery, Freedom, and the Civil War* (New York: New, 1992), xxxiii; and Du Bois, *Black Reconstruction*, 220–21.

87. See *Freedmen's Bureau Act of 1865;* and *Freedmen's Bureau Act of 1866.*

88. Congress, House, Rep. Nathaniel G. Taylor (Unionist-Tennessee) speaking, *Congressional Globe*, 39th Cong., 1st sess., 30 January 1866, text-fiche, vol. 36, card 10, roll 4171. Taylor also concluded that "refugee" protection for homeless whites had lost meaning because they had "all gone home." Therefore this legislation was "solely for the freedmen . . . [and] class legislation [for] . . . blacks to the exclusion of all whites. . . ." Sen. James A. McDougall (D-California) declared that it "undertakes to make the negro in some respects . . . superior, . . . and gives them favors that the poor white boy in the North cannot get" (remarks of Sen. McDougall cited by Marshall in *Bakke* [1978]). Rep. Charles E. Phelps (Unionist-Maryland) complained: "The very discrimination it makes between 'destitute and suffering' negroes and destitute and suffering white paupers proceeds upon the distinction that, in the omitted case, civil rights and immunities are already sufficiently protected by the possession of political power, the absence of which in the case provided for necessitates governmental protection." Cited by Marshall in *Bakke* (1978).

89. Avins, *Debates*, 55. The report comes from Rep. Martin Kalbfleish (D-New York) and Rep. Anthony L. Knapp (D-Illinois), minority, Select Committee on Emancipation, 20 January 1864.

90. While historians universally agree that most of this free land (available with a nominal filing fee) was gobbled up by speculators and the railroads while Congress did little to help average farmers, some also argue that the act was one that nevertheless advertised and opened the West to millions of white settlers in the coming decades. This would come to be a West of cheap land for whites (subsidized by the federal government) after the Native Americans were removed by the U.S. Army—suggesting a vast social network of whiteness linking European American settlers that contradicts the still popular "frontier individualism" mythology of historian Frederick Jackson Turner. See Franklin and Moss, *From Slavery to Freedom*, 97. See also Ray Allen Billington, *Westward Expansion: A History of the American Frontier*, 2nd ed. (New York: MacMillan, 1960; 1949), 698–705; Benjamin Horace Hibbard, *A History of the Public Land Policies* (Madison: University of Wisconsin Press, 1965; 1924), 347–85; Fred A. Shannon, "The Homestead Act and the Labor Surplus," 297–313, and Paul Wallace Gates, "The Homestead Law in an Incongruous Land System," in *The Public Lands: Studies in the History of the Public Domain*, ed. Vernon Carstensen (Madison: University of Wisconsin Press, 1963), 315–48. See the *Homestead Act of 1862, Statutes at Large* 12 (1862); and *Morrill Land Grant Act of 1862, Statutes at Large* 12 (1862). Both these acts made women as well as men eligible for their benefits. See also Gil Kujovich, "Public Black Colleges: The Long History of Unequal Instruction," *Journal of Blacks in Higher Education* 3 (spring 1994): 65–76; and R. B. Atwood, "The Future of the Negro Land-Grant College," *Journal of Negro Education* 27, no. 3 (summer 1958): 384. On the 1866 Southern Homestead Act see Melvin L. Oliver and Thomas M. Shapiro, *Black Wealth/*

White Wealth: A New Perspective on Racial Inequality (New York: Routledge), 14–15. Ex-Confederates had been barred from the 1862 Homestead Act—but now all they had to do was swear that they had not taken up arms against the Union. Blacks also faced massive discrimination in applying for homesteads. For another view of the Southern Homestead Act see Franklin and Moss, *From Slavery to Freedom*, 214, stating that many freedpeople were still able to take advantage of the Southern Homestead Act grants of 80 acres per family. They cite Florida, for example, where freedpeople secured homesteads covering 160,960 acres, and Arkansas, where freedpeople claimed 116 out of 243 homesteads. But this does not contradict the act's primary success as one favoring whites, especially the more affluent. See also Allen, *White Race*, vol. 1, 140–41, 152–53, on the 1876 repeal of this act in favor of timber and mining interests (which had already gobbled up much of the land while the act was in effect) and the debt and foreclosure encountered by many western homesteaders.

91. See Oubre, *Forty Acres*, 87–90, 186–90; and infra note 131.

92. Du Bois, *Black Reconstruction*, 311. Du Bois shows how during his presidential tenure Johnson had a habit of changing political positions from support to opposition on any matter that upon further reflection he feared would benefit black people in any way, despite the fact that such opposition would in turn retard progress for white people as well (Ibid., 280–81). Examples included basing representation on the number of voters, confiscation of ex-slaveholders' land and penalizing their wealth, and universal male suffrage.

93. Avins, *Debates*, 714. The 1866 law had mandated a $1,000 maximum fine.

94. Ibid.

95. Charles Sumner, *Charles Sumner: His Complete Works*, ed. George Frisbie Hoar, vol. 15 (Boston: Lee and Shepard, 1900 (1874), 308. Three years earlier he had tried unsuccessfully to have the term "white" deleted from naturalization laws (see Sumner, *Charles Sumner*, vol. 14, 238–39).

96. Ibid., vol. 15, 8. See Avins, *Debates*, xxvi, for an example of Sumner's method in congressional debate of reading letters from African Americans calling for passage of his proposed 1871 civil rights amendment, complaining of discrimination, and threatening the Republican Party with loss of votes unless that legislation was passed. See also Zuczek, *State of Rebellion*, 50, on the collapse of the Freedmen's Bureau at the end of 1868.

97. Schwartz, *Civil Rights Part 1*, 737–38 (43rd Cong., 2nd sess., 3–4 February 1875, House).

98. Ibid., 564 (41st Cong., 3rd sess., 15 February 1871, House). See also remarks of Sen. Willard Warner (R-Alabama) opposing Sumner's proposed amendment to the Fifteenth Amendment banning all forms of discrimination: "I hope the Congress of this country will not single out one race for protection; but that we shall go at once to the broad, grand, affirmative proposition which shall secure . . . the citizens of this country their rights." Ibid., 406.

99. Avins, *Debates*, 400–417 (40th Cong., 3rd sess., 1 February–3 March 1869). There are many today who still argue that the Fourteenth Amendment was never designed specifically to protect the rights of blacks. On the contrary, during the 1874 debate on the Civil Rights Bill, Sen. Frederick Frelinghuysen (R-New Jersey) declared approvingly (and not untypically for a Republican) that "the majority of the Supreme Court in the Slaughter-house case . . . giving construction to the thirteenth, fourteenth, and fifteenth amendments in the light of the history which called them into being, make them apply especially, though not exclusively . . . to the enfranchisement of the colored race" (Schwartz, *Civil Rights Part 1*, 665, 43rd Cong., 1st sess., 27 April–22 May 1874, Senate). See also McPherson, *The Abolitionist Legacy*, chapter 1; infra note 144; and Marshall, *Bakke* (1978).

100. Avins, *Debates*, 107–49.

101. Ibid., and 212–13. Lydia Maria Child wrote to Rep. George W. Julian (R-Indiana) on 27 March 1864 praising his bill (which passed the House but was then dropped by Republican leadership) to extend the 1862 Homestead Act to forfeited and confiscated Confederate lands—giving them to the black and white poor. See Child, *Child*, 439–40.

102. See Internet website of the National Coalition of Blacks for Reparations in America (N'COBRA), found at http://www.ncobra.org, where they discuss not only this black folk wisdom but also Reconstruction-era black reparations societies: "One such group, the National Ex-Slave, Mutual Relief, Bounty and Pension Association (NEMRB and PA) attracted hundreds of thousands of dues-paying members from the late 1800s to about 1915." See also Horace Mann Bond, "Forty Acres and a Mule," *Opportunity* 13, no. 5 (May 1935): 140–41, 151, writing during the Great Depression on the irony of desperately poor white Arkansas sharecroppers demanding forty acres and a mule at the same time that white historians of Reconstruction were still using that phrase to ridicule blacks' alleged childlike faith in the coming Jubilee.

103. W. E. B. Du Bois, *The Souls of Black Folk* (New York: Penguin, 1989; 1903), 25. Italics added.

104. Oubre, *Forty Acres*, 31: "The Freedmen's Bureau never controlled more than two-tenths of one percent of the land of the land in the South and President Johnson's amnesty proclamation forced restoration of most of that land." See also Julie Saville, *The Work of Reconstruction: From Slave to Wage Laborer in South Carolina, 1860–1870* (Cambridge: Cambridge University Press, 1994), 86: "Virtually all former slaves expected the possession of land to be the material basis of their emancipation."

105. Buckner, "Freedmen's Bank," 215–16; and Moreno, "Racial Classifications," 293.

106. Oubre, *Forty Acres*, 73. That proposal was made by Carl Schurz and John W. Sprague. Their notion was that the federal government could transport freedpeople voluntarily to Union Pacific land in order to settle the land and protect it from American Indians and to remove what they considered the surplus black population from the South and thereby raise the labor value of those left behind.

107. Ibid., 104. See also Franklin and Moss, *From Slavery to Freedom*, 196, for an account of the black soldiers and white officers of the Fifty-fourth Massachusetts Regiment serving a year without pay rather than accept discriminatory pay under the 1862 Enlistment Act, which provided white privates with $13 a month but gave black privates only $7 a month.

108. See, for example, Berlin et al., *Free at Last*; Willie Lee Rose, *Rehearsal for Reconstruction: The Port Royal Experiment* (New York: Vintage, 1964); and B. A. Botkin, ed., *Lay My Burden Down: A Folk History of Slavery* (Chicago: University of Chicago Press, 1969; 1945).

109. The Port Royal Experiment provided land in 1862 to freedpeople in liberated coastal South Carolina. See Rose, *Rehearsal for Reconstruction*. See also Lerone Bennett Jr., *The Shaping of Black America* (New York: Penguin, 1993; 1975), 187–89, for excerpts and an analysis of Gen. Sherman's famous Special Field Order Number 15 that he issued 15 January 1865 after meeting with black ministers and church officials and Secretary of War Edwin Stanton. Among other things the order allocated forty acres for each black family along the coast and on the Sea Islands from South Carolina to Florida. It mandated that "in the settlements hereafter to be established, no white person, unless military officers and soldiers, detailed for duty, will be permitted to reside. . ." (Ibid., 188). See also Andrew Billingsley, *Mighty Like a River: The Black Church and Social Reform* (New York: Oxford University Press, 1999), 24–34, for a more detailed account of that historic meeting.

110. Jacqueline Jones, *Labor of Love, Labor of Sorrow: Black Women, Work and the Family, From Slavery to the Present* (New York: Vintage, 1986), 62.

111. Kevin K. Gaines, *Uplifting the Race: Black Leadership, Politics, and Culture in the Twentieth Century* (Chapel Hill: University of North Carolina Press, 1998), 23.

112. Ibid.: "Senator W. B. Roberts pointed to Bolivar County in his home state of Mississippi, where black voters held a sixteen-to-one majority over whites as an example of the effectiveness of fusion politics. There, fusion allowed 'the Negroes to have some of the offices, and the whites of course [to have] the best ones.' Even this state of affairs proved intolerable to whites, as Democratic 'redeemers' throughout the South made good on their promises to displace blacks, particularly black Republicans from preferred jobs." See also Gerald David Jaynes, *Branches without Roots: Genesis of the Black Working Class in the South, 1862–1882* (New York: Oxford University Press, 1986).

113. For examples and refutation see Allen, *White Race*, vol. 1, 192–97; Avins, *Debates*, 30–31.

114. Berlin et al., *Free at Last*, 41.

115. "Religio-racial" is Theodore Allen's term for English oppression of the Irish. See Allen, *White Race*, vol. 1., 47–48. See also Ibid., 109, for how Ireland itself had just seen something of an "affirmative action" plan in the Catholic Emancipation Act of 1829 that eased some restrictions on the general Catholic population while promoting a buffer clerical class.

116. See Noel Ignatiev, *How the Irish Became White* (New York: Routledge, 1995); Allen, *White Race*, vol. 1; Roediger, *The Wages of Whiteness*; and Iver Bernstein, *The New York City Draft Riots: Their Significance for American Society and Politics in the Age of the Civil War* (New York: Oxford University Press, 1990), 113, where he points out that while commitment to whiteness was prevalent among New York Irish, many were also loyal Unionists, some fighting for the Irish Sixty-ninth Regiment in the Union army.

117. See Bernstein, *Draft Riots*; Paul A. Gilje, *Rioting in America* (Bloomington: University of Indiana Press, 1996), 91–92; and McPherson, *Battle Cry of Freedom*, 609–11.

118. Sterling D. Spero and Abram L. Harris, *The Black Worker: The Negro and the Labor Movement* (New York: Atheneum, 1969; 1931), 3–15.

119. Karl Marx and Frederick Engels, "Manifesto of the Communist Party," in *Selected Works in One Volume* (New York: International Publishers, 1968), 45–46: "The essential condition for the existence, and for the sway of the bourgeois class, is the formation and augmentation of capital; the condition for capital is wage-labour. Wage-labour rests exclusively on competition between the labourers."

120. See Allen, *White Race*, vol. 1, 193, where he reveals that 15,000 European immigrants were coming into New York City *each year* by 1855, while the African-American population there was only approximately 12,500.

121. Bernstein, *Draft Riots*, 29. On mass scapegoating rites and their antidote, see Theophus H. Smith, *Conjuring Culture: Biblical Formations of Black America* (New York: Oxford University Press, 1994), 98–99; and Orlando Patterson, *Rituals of Blood: Consequences of Slavery in Two American Centuries* (Washington, D.C.: Civitas Counterpoint, 1998), 169–232.

122. See Bernstein, *Draft Riots*; and Ignatiev, *How the Irish Became White*.

123. See, for example, Herbert Hill, *Black Labor and the American Legal System: Race, Work, and the Law* (Madison: University of Wisconsin Press, 1985; 1977); and John Hope Franklin, *The Free Negro in North Carolina, 1790–1860* (New York: W. W. Norton, 1971; 1943), 136–43.

124. See Bernstein, *Draft Riots*, 9–10, 41, where he points out that, although Democratic demagogues got poor immigrants to believe their warning that emancipated blacks would soon come North to compete for jobs with them, the riot itself was actually "primarily the doing of wage earners accustomed to considerable control over the conduct of their jobs. Judging from the aggres-

sive tone and wide-ranging scope of the riots, these workers also had a sense of their own political importance." See also Du Bois, *Black Reconstruction*, 701, whose observation here of the postbellum South in many ways also describes 1863 New York City: "White labor saw in every advance of Negroes a threat to their racial prerogatives, so that in many districts Negroes were afraid to build decent homes or dress well, or own carriages, bicycles or automobiles, because of possible retaliation on the part of the whites." Two years later Boston's *Voice* made this prediction: "Look at it a moment. There are now four million of the negro race about to enter the field of free labor. If we take them upon equal ground with ourselves in the contest for the elevation of labor, they become an ally; but if we reject them—say we will not work in the shop with them, what is the result? The black man's interests and ours are severed." "Justice," in Foner and Lewis, *The Black Worker*, vol. 1, 391.

125. Du Bois, *Black Reconstruction*, 377–79, 708.

126. McPherson, *The Abolitionist Legacy*, 71.

127. Ibid., 71–72.

128. Ibid., 53–80.

129. Ibid., 39.

130. Ibid., 114.

131. *Civil Rights Cases* (1883). White legislators, labor leaders, and suffragists echoed this theme. See Allen, *Reluctant Reformers*. See also Marshall in *Bakke* (1978); and Allen, *White Race*, vol. 1, 140–41, on the significance of land redistribution in countering racial oppression and promoting "social equality." Impeachment proceedings against Johnson were instituted by Republicans suspecting a coup after his 3 December 1867 annual message to Congress, where he warned of the threat to white rule in congressional attempts to "Africanize the half of our country." See Du Bois, *Black Reconstruction*, 342.

132. Schwartz, *Civil Rights Part 1*, 547.

133. Avins, *Debates*, 212. Some might call this section a "preference and quota" section if brought to a vote today. Said Stevens: "The second section I consider the most important in the article. It fixes the basis of representation in Congress." Anticipating the Fifteenth Amendment guarantee of universal male suffrage two years later, the second section as passed proportionally penalized states that disfranchised male voters: "Representatives shall be apportioned among the several States according to their respective numbers, counting the whole number of persons in each State, excluding Indians not taxed. But when the right to vote at any election for the choice of Electors for President and Vice-President of the United States, Representatives in Congress, the executive and judicial officers of a State, or the members of the legislators thereof, is denied to any of the male inhabitants being twenty-one years of age, and citizens of the United States, or in any way abridged except for participation in rebellion or other crime, the basis for representation therein shall be reduced in the proportion which the number of such male citizens shall bear to the whole number of male citizens twenty-one years of age in such State." See Smith, *The Constitution*, 52. Du Bois points out in *Black Reconstruction*, 294, that it was actually Sumner who stopped Stevens and other Republicans from initially being willing to compromise on the vital issue of black enfranchisement.

134. See Smith, *The Constitution*, 52; and Du Bois, *Black Reconstruction*, especially the Reconstruction-era constitutional conventions in Mississippi (438) and North Carolina (544) for debates over disfranchisement and the significant representation of former slaves as delegates and eventually legislators.

135. See Reid Mitchell, *Civil War Soldiers* (New York: Viking, 1988), 179; William T. Auman and

David D. Scarboro, "The Heroes of America in Civil War North Carolina," *North Carolina Historical Review* 58, no. 4 (October 1981): 327–63; Richard Nelson Current, *Lincoln's Loyalists: Union Soldiers from the Confederacy* (Boston: Northeastern University Press, 1992); Georgia Lee Tatum, *Disloyalty in the Confederacy* (Chapel Hill: University of North Carolina Press, 1934); and Philip F. Rubio, "Civil War Reenactments and Other Myths," in *Race Traitor*, ed. Noel Ignatiev and John Garvey (New York: Routledge, 1996), 182–94.

136. See Du Bois, *Black Reconstruction*; McPherson, *The Abolitionist Legacy*; and Zuczek, *State of Rebellion*.

137. See supra note 136.

138. See supra note 136.

139. Du Bois, *Black Reconstruction*, 167; and Eric Foner, *Nothing but Freedom: Emancipation and Its Legacy* (Baton Rouge: Louisiana State University Press, 1983), 29–73. For example, Foner cites Texas political leader and railroad promoter J. W. Throckmorton declaring in 1865: "But I do believe we will be enabled to adopt a coercive system of labor." A New Orleans newspaper also during that time maintained that slavery must be replaced with a new labor system "prescribed and enforced by the state." Ibid., 49.

140. Foner, *Nothing but Freedom*, 48–49. The Mississippi code required blacks to have written proof of employment, and any white could arrest any black person who walked off the job.

141. Ibid. "With Redemption, the state again stepped forward as an instrument of labor control. . . . Georgia's Redeemer Governor James M. Smith was quite candid about the intention: 'We may hold inviolate every law of the United States, and still so legislate upon our labor system as to retain our old plantation system' " (Ibid., 53). The Hayes-Tilden compromise that withdrew federal troops from the South and ended Reconstruction in exchange for Rutherford B. Hayes's presidential victory in a contested election was formulated in 1876 and implemented in 1877. See Du Bois, *Black Reconstruction*, 691–92.

142. Du Bois, *Black Reconstruction*, 354–60. The first of these, the National Labor Union (NLU) formed in 1866, initially invited black workers on a "halting note" as Du Bois says: "Negroes were welcomed to the labor movement, not because they were laborers but because they might be competitors in the labor market . . ." (Ibid., 354). Black labor was forced to form its own organization (which they also called the National Labor Union) after that was requested by the white NLU. See also William H. Harris, *The Harder We Run: Black Workers since the Civil War* (New York: Oxford University Press, 1982), 25–27 and 194 n 40. According to Harris, the Knights of Labor (KOL), founded in 1869, attempted to organize integrated locals beginning in 1876 but later abandoned the effort upon encountering white resistance and folded in the 1880s largely because of white supremacy. The subsequent formation of the American Federation of Labor (AFL) in 1881 with its segregated, privileged, exclusive white locals solidified the hold of Jim Crow on the labor movement. Coincidentally, the white NUL, the KOL, and the AFL all embraced racial equality in their official pronouncements. See further discussion in chapter 3 of this book.

143. Foner, *Nothing but Freedom*, 54.

144. See *Slaughterhouse Cases*, 83 U.S. 36 (1873), where the majority opinion declared that the Fourteenth Amendment had overturned *Dred Scott v. Sandford*, 60 U.S. 393 (1857). See also Kaczorowski, "To Begin the Nation Anew," 65 n 78. During the 25 October 1996 "*Plessy v. Ferguson* 100 Years Later: A North Carolina Perspective" conference at North Carolina Central University in Durham, Robinson Everett, attorney for the five white plaintiffs in the *Shaw v. Reno* decision (113 U.S. 2816 [1993]) that was responsible for the elimination of North Carolina's two majority-minor-

ity congressional districts, claimed that the Fourteenth Amendment was never designed specifically to protect the rights of black people. He added that the plaintiffs' litigation (initiated because they believed that "segregated" districts violated their rights) never actually said that they were white. Since *DeFunis v. Odegaard*, 416 U.S. 312 (1974), legal challenges to affirmative action by white plaintiffs (including *Bakke* in 1978) have all argued for protections against racial discrimination under the Fourteenth Amendment as if that had really happened to them. See George E. Curry, ed., *The Affirmative Action Debate* (Reading, MA: Addison-Wesley, 1996).

145. Foner and Branham, *Lift Every Voice*, 521–36.

146. Ibid., 528.

147. Ibid., 529.

148. Ibid., 527.

149. Ibid., 521–36.

150. See Richard F. America, ed., *The Wealth of Races: The Present Value of Benefits from Past Injustices* (New York: Greenwood, 1990), for how much white wealth was based on black slavery. See also *Original Returns of the Eighth Census of the United States of America in 1860* (New York: Norman Ross, 1990; 1864), for tremendous white literacy and educational advantages over even free blacks, not to mention 4 million slaves.

151. Du Bois, *Black Reconstruction*, 700. The restoration of "white rights" in that period to counter any efforts at black compensation is similar to the protectionist undertone in today's white opposition to affirmative action.

152. Cheryl I. Harris, "Whiteness as Property," in *Critical Race Theory: The Key Writings That Formed the Movement*, ed. Kimberlé Crenshaw et al. (New York: New Press, 1995), 286.

153. Hill, *Black Labor*, 74–77. See also *U.S. v. Reese*, 92 U.S. 214 (1875); *U.S. v. Cruikshank*, 92 U.S. 542 (1875); *Civil Rights Cases*, 109 U.S. 3 (1883); *Plessy v. Ferguson*, 163 U.S. 527 (1896); and *Hodges v. U.S.*, 203 U.S. 1 (1906).

154. For a discussion of citizenship debates concerning women, Asians, Mexicans, and indigenous peoples and how they flowed (and differed) from debates over black civil rights, see Avins, *Debates*, xvi–xix, 335–417, passim; Allen, *Reluctant Reformers*, 121–63; and Dee Brown, *Bury My Heart at Wounded Knee* (New York: Holt, Reinhart and Winston, 1971).

155. Du Bois, *Black Reconstruction*, 708, 726.

Chapter 3

1. Rayford W. Logan, *The Negro in American Life and Thought: The Nadir 1877–1901* (New York: Dial, 1954), 52.

2. See C. Vann Woodward, *The Strange Career of Jim Crow*, 3rd rev. ed. (New York: Oxford University Press, 1974; 1955); Kevin K. Gaines, *Uplifting the Race: Black Leadership, Politics, and Culture in the Twentieth Century* (Chapel Hill: University of North Carolina Press, 1996); and Howard Zinn, *A People's History of the United States* (New York: Harper, 1990; 1980), chapters 11–13.

3. See Robert L. Allen, *Reluctant Reformers: Racism and Social Reform Movements in the United States* (Washington, D.C.: Howard University Press, 1983), chapters 3–4; H. Leon Prather Sr., *We Have Taken a City: Wilmington Racial Massacre and Coup of 1898* (Rutherford, NJ: Farleigh Dickson University Press, 1984); and Lerone Bennett Jr., *The Shaping of Black America* (New York: Penguin, 1993; 1975), 255–56.

4. Logan, *The Negro*; and Zinn, *People's History*, chapters 11–13. A monthly series in the *Postal*

Record, the monthly organ of the National Association of Letter Carriers (NALC), AFL-CIO, barely mentions these attacks on blacks or exclusion of black workers, yet the second installment is entitled "The Not-so-Gay Nineties: Workers Crushed by Bitter Defeats, Political Schisms." *Postal Record* 112, no. 2 (March 1999): 8.

5. Gaines, *Uplifting the Race*, 25.

6. Jacquelyn Dowd Hall, *Revolt against Chivalry: Jessie Daniel Ames and the Women's Campaign Against Lynching*, rev. ed. (New York: Columbia University Press, 1993), 133–34.

7. Wells-Barnett quoted in Allen, *Reluctant Reformers*, 157–58.

8. White quoted in Leon F. Litwack, *Trouble in Mind: Black Southerners in the Age of Jim Crow* (New York: Knopf, 1998), 20. See also John Hope Franklin and Alfred A. Moss Jr., *From Slavery to Freedom: A History of Negro Americans*, 6th ed. (McGraw-Hill, 1988; 1947), 319.

9. See Frank L. Auerbach, *The Immigration and Nationality Act: A Summary of Its Principal Provisions* (New York: Common Council for American Unity, 1952); and Matthew Frye Jacobson, *Whiteness of a Different Color: European Immigrants and the Alchemy of Race* (Cambridge: Harvard University Press, 1998).

10. See supra note 9.

11. See Noel Ignatiev, *How the Irish Became White* (New York: Routledge, 1995); and Jacobson, *Whiteness of a Different Color*.

12. See Richard Delgado, *The Coming Race War? And Other Apocalyptic Tales of America after Affirmative Action and Welfare* (New York: New York University Press, 1996), 92–95. See also Jacobson, *Whiteness of a Different Color*.

13. Logan, *The Negro*, 43–50.

14. Ibid.; and Philip S. Foner and Ronald L. Lewis, *The Black Worker: A Documentary History from Colonial Times to the Present*, vol. 5, *The Black Worker from 1900 to 1919* (Philadelphia: Temple University Press, 1980), 119–27. A notable Democratic exception was the administration of President Woodrow Wilson. See Kenneth O'Reilly, "The Jim Crow Policies of Woodrow Wilson," *Journal of Blacks in Higher Education* 17 (autumn 1997): 117–21.

15. Logan, *The Negro*, 52.

16. Ibid., 50.

17. W. E. B. Du Bois, *Black Reconstruction in America 1860–1880* (Cleveland: Meridian, 1968; 1935), 691. Between 1890 and 1910, 288 Fourteenth Amendment cases brought before the Supreme Court dealt with corporations and 19 with African Americans. See Logan, *The Negro*, 100. *Slaughterhouse Cases* 83 U.S. 36 (1873) recognized black civil rights but as federal, not state protections. By disallowing the application of the "privileges and immunities clause" to state laws, the Court left blacks defenseless against hostile state laws. See also Logan, *The Negro*, 98–101.

18. *Civil Rights Cases*, 109 U.S. 3 (1883). Italics added.

19. Ibid. Italics added. Remarkably, only two of the seven cases heard in the *Civil Rights Cases* originated in the South.

20. Ibid. Italics added.

21. Logan, *The Negro*, 109.

22. Derrick A. Bell Jr., *Race, Racism, and American Law*, 2nd ed. (Boston: Little, Brown, 1980), 35.

23. Ibid., 37.

24. Ibid., 91. See also Logan, *The Negro*, 109. For a compilation of Jim Crow laws state by state see Pauli Murray, *States' Laws on Race and Color* (Cincinnati: Women's Division of Christian Service, 1950). For a chronicle of the Jim Crow social rituals themselves see Stetson Kennedy, *The Jim Crow Guide: The Way It Was* (Boca Raton: Florida Atlantic University Press, 1990; 1959).

25. See Joseph Campbell with Bill Moyers, ed., and Betty Sue Flowers, *The Power of Myth* (New York: Doubleday, 1988), 31. In this sense mythology helps explain the *faith* or *belief* that individuals and groups use to hold on to particular ideologies that may not necessarily be well thought-out or even rational.

26. R. C. Lewontin, Steven Rose, and Leon J. Kamin, *Not in Our Genes: Biology, Ideology, and Human Nature* (New York: Pantheon, 1984), 26, 242. On the origins of the Civil Service and built-in inequality, its adoption by states and municipalities following the passing of the Pendleton Act, and the importance of the term "merit" to the act's passage, see Frances Gottfried, *The Merit System and Municipal Civil Service: A Fostering of Social Inequality* (New York: Greenwood, 1988), chapter 1, esp. 7.

27. Lewontin, Rose, and Kamin, *Not in Our Genes*, 26.

28. Andrew Carnegie, *The Gospel of Wealth and Other Timely Essays*, ed. Edward C. Kirkland (Cambridge, MA: Belknap, 1962); and Louis Harlan, *Booker T. Washington: The Wizard of Tuskegee 1901–1915* (New York: Oxford University Press, 1986; 1983), 134.

29. Herbert Gutman, *Work, Culture, and Society in Industrializing America* (New York: Knopf, 1976); and Warren B. Smith, *White Servitude in Colonial South Carolina* (Columbia: University of South Carolina Press, 1961). Horatio Alger was a popular nineteenth-century novelist who wrote inspirational "rags-to-riches" stories of "self-made men."

30. Alexander Saxton, *The Rise and Fall of the White Republic: Class Politics and Mass Culture in Nineteenth Century America* (London: Verso, 1996; 1990), 343, 370. See also Sean Wilentz, "Society, Politics, and the Market Revolution, 1815–1848," in *The New American History*, ed. Eric Foner (Philadelphia: Temple University Press, 1990), 66–68.

31. Logan, *The Negro*, 166. See also Richard Hofstadter, *Social Darwinism in American Thought, 1860–1915* (Philadelphia: University of Pennsylvania Press, 1944).

32. Logan, *The Negro*, 167.

33. Ibid.

34. Ibid., 168.

35. James McPherson, *The Abolitionist Legacy: From Reconstruction to the NAACP* (Princeton, NJ: Princeton University Press, 1975), 70–72.

36. Zinn, *People's History*, 314–49. See also Timothy Messer-Kruse, *The Yankee International: Marxism and the American Reform Tradition, 1848–1876* (Chapel Hill: University of North Carolina Press, 1998); and Philip S. Foner and Ronald L. Lewis, *The Black Worker: A Documentary History from Colonial Times to the Present*, vol. 3, *The Black Worker during the Era of the Knights of Labor* (Philadelphia: Temple University Press, 1978), which includes the reaction by black and white workers to support by the Knights of Labor in 1894 (as that organization was declining) for the wholesale deportation of African Americans (281–83). But before their downhill slide the Knights, in opening their doors to black labor, had been "a beacon of racial enlightenment in a dark sea," according to Leon Fink, *Workingmen's Democracy: The Knights of Labor and American Politics* (Urbana: University of Illinois Press, 1983), 169, who also notes that blacks "adopted" the Knights more than they were recruited. Allen states that at the Knights' peak during the great nationwide strike wave of 1886, the Knights "claimed to have between 60,000 and 95,000 black members out of a total membership of 700,000" (*Reluctant Reformers*, 190). Most black members were in the South, and most were in segregated locals. Violence from without and the withdrawal of the white trade unions hastened the Knights' eventual collapse (Ibid., 191). Allen also notes that Booker T. Washington in his youth had been a West Virginia coal miner and Knights of Labor member—and would later write that discrimination

made black workers "very willing strikebreakers" (Ibid., 200). Alice Kessler-Harris, *Out to Work: A History of Wage-Earning Women in the United States* (New York: Oxford University Press, 1982), 86, comments that the Knights advocated equal pay for women in 1878 and allowed women to join in 1879, and at its peak women made up about 10 percent of the national membership.

37. Zinn, *People's History*, 247–89, 346–49.

38. Thomas R. Brooks, *Toil and Trouble: A History of American Labor*, 2nd ed. (New York: Delta, 1971; 1964), 86–92; and Zinn, *People's History*, 270–71. These figures are not expressed in constant wages.

39. For example, see Brooks, *Toil and Trouble*; Zinn, *People's History*; chapter 7, note 23, of this book; Gutman, *Work, Culture, and Society*; Sean Wilentz, *Chants Democratic: New York City and the Rise of the American Working Class, 1788–1850*, (New York: Oxford University Press, 1984); and Fink, *Working-men's Democracy*. For a discussion of this tendency in both the "old" and "new" labor history see Ignatiev, *How the Irish Became White*, afterword; and David R. Roediger, *Towards the Abolition of Whiteness: Essays on Race, Politics, and Working Class History* (London: Verso, 1994), chapters 1 and 6.

40. Melvyn Dubofsky, *We Shall Be All: A History of the Industrial Workers of the World* (Chicago: Quadrangle, 1969), esp. 12, 86, 127. See also Allen, *Reluctant Reformers*, 190–91, on the Knights of Labor and 192–93 on the strengths and weaknesses of the IWW, which was perhaps 10 percent African American: "In their denunciation of Jim Crow, lynching, disfranchisement and the [Chinese] exclusion movement on the West Coast, they in effect challenged white supremacy. However, this challenge was weakened by their insistence that there was no 'race problems,' only the class struggle. Consequently, they lacked any concrete program to alleviate the racial oppression of nonwhites, and this limited their appeal. They did not, for example, actively support the black struggle for the vote."

41. Theodore W. Allen, *The Invention of the White Race*, vol. 1, *Racial Oppression and Social Control* (London: Verso: 1994), 155.

42. Ibid., 156–57.

43. Ibid., 157.

44. Manning Marable, *Black American Politics: From Washington Marches to Jesse Jackson* (London: Verso, 1985), 76–77. See also Du Bois, *Black Reconstruction*, 701, speaking of the postbellum South: "Mob violence and lynching were the inevitable result of the attitude of these two classes [rich and poor whites] and for a time were a sort of permissible Roman holiday for the entertainment of vicious whites." See also chapter 2, note 125, of this book.

45. Frederick Douglass, *The Life and Writings of Frederick Douglass*, vol. 4, *Reconstruction and After*, ed. Philip S. Foner (New York: International Publishers, 1955), 520.

46. Prather, *We Have Taken a City*, 166.

47. Ibid. See also Hall, *Revolt Against Chivalry*; and *The Black Press in America*. Produced and directed by Stanley Nelson. 1 hour. Half Nelson, 1998.

48. See the chapter entitled " 'Race,' Religion, and Human Sacrifice in the Postbellum South," in Orlando Patterson, *Rituals of Blood: Consequences of Slavery in Two American Centuries* (Washington, D.C.: Civitas Counterpoint, 1998), 169–232; and Franklin and Moss, *From Slavery to Freedom*, 310–18.

49. There was no official death toll, suggesting a cover-up, notes Prather. The lowest suggested figure of seven deaths has never been given much credibility, but the true figure will never be known. See Prather, *We Have Taken a City*, 173; and David S. Cecelski and Timothy B. Tyson, eds., *Democracy Betrayed: The Wilmington Race Riot of 1898 and Its Legacy* (Chapel Hill: University of North Carolina Press, 1998).

50. See Prather, *We Have Taken a City;* and Cecelski and Tyson, *Democracy Betrayed.*

51. Prather, *We Have Taken a City,* 166; Litwack, *Trouble in Mind,* 365–66.

52. Ibid., 35: "An often repeated claim was that there were at least a thousand Negro office-holders in the state after the complete Fusion victory in 1896."

53. Helen G. Edmonds, *The Negro and Fusion Politics in North Carolina 1894–1901* (New York: Russell and Russell, 1973; 1951), 218–22.

54. Allen, *Reluctant Reformers,* chapter 3. See also Lawrence C. Goodwyn, *Democratic Promise: The Populist Movement in America* (Oxford: Oxford University Press, 1976); and Lawrence C. Goodwyn, "Populist Dreams and Negro Rights: East Texas as a Case Study." *American Historical Review* 76, no. 5 (December 1971): 1435–56, for a critical examination of how white supremacy—both internal and external—contributed to that movement's downfall.

55. Thomas Holt, *Black Over White: Negro Political Leadership in South Carolina during Reconstruction* (Urbana: University of Illinois Press, 1977), 75, 176.

56. Ibid., 211.

57. Edmonds, *The Negro,* 218–22.

58. Ibid.; See also Prather, *We Have Taken a City,* 73; and LeeAnn White's, "Love, Hate, Rape, Lynching: Rebecca Latimer Felton and the Gender Politics of Racial Violence," in Cecelski and Tyson, *Democracy Betrayed,* 143–62.

59. Prather, *We Have Taken a City,* 24.

60. Ibid., 61.

61. Ibid., 146.

62. Ibid., 147.

63. Ibid., 26.

64. Ibid.; and David S. Cecelski and Timothy B. Tyson, "Introduction," in Cecelski and Tyson, *Democracy Betrayed,* 3–13.

65. See Gunnar Myrdal, *An American Dilemma: The Negro Problem and Modern Democracy* (New York: Harper, 1944), 569.

66. Myrdal quoted in Prather, *We Have Taken a City,* 173; Cripps quoted in Ibid., 166.

67. Ibid., 166–67.

68. Herbert Hill, "Black Labor and Affirmative Action: An Historical Perspective," in *The Question of Discrimination: Racial Inequality in the United States Labor Market,* ed. Steven Shulman and William Darity Jr. (Middletown, CT: Wesleyan University Press, 1989), 208.

69. James W. Loewen, *Lies My Teacher Told Me: Everything Your American History Textbook Got Wrong* (New York: Touchstone, 1995), 162. See also Robert Peterson, *Only the Ball Was White* (Englewood Cliffs, NJ: Prentice-Hall, 1970); and J. Peder Zane, "A Race of a Different Color," *Raleigh (NC) News and Observer,* 28 February 1999, 4G.

70. See Elliot Rudwick, *Race Riot at East St. Louis, July 2 1917* (Carbondale: Southern Illinois University Press, 1964); and Foner and Lewis, *The Black Worker,* vol. 5, 285–333. See also James R. Grossman, *Land of Hope: Chicago, Black Southerners, and the Great Migration* (Chicago: University of Chicago Press, 1989). See David Levering Lewis, *W. E. B. Du Bois: Biography of a Race 1868–1919* (New York: Henry Holt, 1993), 538, on AFL President Samuel Gompers's defense of the East St. Louis white mobs, which earned him the public rebuke of former President Theodore Roosevelt.

71. Hill, "Black Labor," 201. Hill also has argued with labor historian Herbert Gutman's sanguine appraisal of the United Mine Workers' (UMW) admission of black members and cited examples from the *United Mine Workers Journal* articles in 1903 and 1905 praising the racial basis for that

first "union label" campaign. See Herbert Hill, "Myth-Making as Labor History: Herbert Gutman and the United Mine Workers of America," *International Journal of Politics, Culture and Society* 2 (1988): 132–200; Herbert Gutman, "The Negro and the United Mine Workers of America" in *Work, Culture, and Society*, 121–208; and Ignatiev, *How the Irish Became White*, 180–82.

72. Hill, "Black Labor," 199–201. For Asian immigration, assimilation, and resistance as well as white labor opposition, see Alexander Saxton, *The Indispensable Enemy: Labor and the Anti-Chinese Movement in California* (Berkeley: University of California Press, 1971). For an account of resistance by Chinese working people, see Charles J. McClain, *In Search of Equality: the Chinese Struggle against Discrimination in Nineteenth-Century America* (Berkeley: University of California Press, 1994); and Su-cheng Chan, *Asian Americans: An Interpretive History* (Boston: Twayne, 1991), esp. chapter 2.

73. Hill, "Black Labor," 199–200. See also Samuel Gompers, *Seventy Years of Life and Labor: An Autobiography*, vol. 2 (New York: Dutton, 1925).

74. Hill, "Black Labor," 251.

75. Ibid., 203.

76. George B. Squires, "Editorial," *American Federationist* (June 1904): 507, in Foner and Lewis, *The Black Worker*, vol. 5, 124.

77. Hill, "Black Labor," 200.

78. Samuel Gompers speech in Foner and Lewis, *The Black Worker*, vol. 5, 124. Blumenbach's five-race concept in 1775 that called Europeans "Caucasians" because of their imagined origin in the Caucasus Mountains of Russia shows no more signs of disappearing now than it did in Gompers's time. This is especially ironic given that the dark-skinned people of the Caucasus region (including Dagestan, Chechnya, and Ingushetia) have in the past and since the breakup of the Soviet Union come under racist attack by prejudiced light-skinned Russians, who describe the Caucasians as "blacks." See Michael Gordon, "Moscow Bombings Expose Ethnic Tension," *Duke University Chronicle*, 15 September 1999, 2. On Blumenbach, see Winthrop D. Jordan, *White Over Black: American Attitudes Toward the Negro, 1550–1812* (Baltimore: Penguin, 1969), 222–23.

79. See Gaines, *Uplifting the Race*. See Franklin and Moss, *From Slavery to Freedom*, 287–90, on the 1910 founding of the NAACP by a group of concerned prominent white citizens (like Mary White Ovington and Oswald Garrison Villard, the grandson of William Lloyd Garrison) who were appalled at the 1908 Springfield, Illinois white race riots and lynchings (W. E. B. Du Bois was originally the only black NAACP officer); and the 1911 founding of the National League on Urban Conditions among Negroes (or National Urban League), which also had many white members. On the "new abolitionist" founding designation of the NAACP, see McPherson, *The Abolitionist Legacy*, 5. See also Allen Edward Burgess, "Tar Heel Blacks and the New South Dream: The Coleman Manufacturing Company, 1896–1904" (Ph.D. diss., Duke University, 1977), on how the black middle-class owners and promoters of the first black-owned cotton mill in the United States (located in Concord, North Carolina) combined self-help with activism and represented a "blending of the conflicting philosophies of Booker T. Washington and W. E. B. Du Bois" (Ibid., vi). Burgess contends that establishing a black cotton mill in the South was "deliberately made for its highly symbolic effect because Southern cotton mills" had been invariably all-white (Ibid., vii). Richard B. Fitzgerald, one of the mill's incorporators, first came south after Reconstruction (Ibid., 217). See chapter 2, note 15, of this book.

80. W. E. B. Du Bois, *The Philadelphia Negro: A Social Study* (Philadelphia: University of Pennsylvania Press, 1996; 1899), 351. The Talented Tenth theory of Du Bois also related to uplift and mediation, although years later he protested that he had really meant Talented Tenth to mean

Notes to pages 70–72

nothing more than black leadership and service rather than a black elite. See W. E. B. Du Bois, W. E. B. Du Bois: A Reader, ed. David Levering Lewis (New York: Henry Holt, 1995), 347–53. See also Nancy J. Weiss, The National Urban League, 1910–1940 (New York: Oxford University Press, 1974), 47, who argues that both the NAACP and the Urban League were "an authentic product of the Progressive Era" and that a distinction must be made between white supremacist Progressive-era politics and the "complex of social justice movements that paid some positive heed to the problems of blacks." See also Lewis, W. E. B. Du Bois, chapter 8, 422–23, 538, on left- and right-wing Progressives, Du Bois's uplift notions and debates with white Progressives, as well as analysis of the critique of white supremacy in chapter 16 of Du Bois's The Philadelphia Negro.

81. Darlene Clark Hine, "Black Women's History in Slavery and Freedom," in Black Women's History: Theory and Practice, ed. Darlene Clark Hine, vol. 1 (Brooklyn: Carlson, 1990; 1901), 250.

82. See Booker T. Washington, Up from Slavery (New York: Airmont, 1967; 1901).

83. Ibid., 144–45: "As a rule, I believe in universal, free suffrage but I believe that in the South we are confronted with peculiar conditions that justify the protection of the ballot in many of the states, for a while at least, either by an educational test, a property test, or by both combined; but whatever tests are required, they should be made to apply with equal and exact justice to both races." See also Louis R. Harlan, Booker T. Washington: The Making of a Black Leader 1856–1901 (London: Oxford University Press, 1972) 291; and Gaines, Uplifting the Race.

84. Gaines, Uplifting the Race, 28.

85. Logan, The Negro, 275–76; and Washington, Up from Slavery, 134–37.

86. Harlan, The Wizard of Tuskegee, viii. In The Making of a Black Leader, 3, Harlan points out: "Washington clandestinely financed and directed a number of court suits challenging the grandfather clause, denial of jury service to blacks, Jim Crow transportation, and peonage." But his public pronouncements, especially relating to lynching, were devastatingly accommodationist and represented a "conservative Social Darwinist proposal that whites everywhere readily accepted." Harlan, Wizard of Tuskegee, 33.

87. Washington, Up from Slavery, 134–37.

88. See Franklin and Moss, From Slavery to Freedom, 286–90; Zinn, People's History, 340–41; Philip S. Foner and Robert James Branham, eds., Lift Every Voice: African American Oratory, 1787–1900 (Tuscaloosa: University of Alabama Press, 1998), 714; and McPherson, The Abolitionist Legacy.

89. Logan, The Negro, 50.

90. Gil Kujovich, "Public Black Colleges: The Long History of Unequal Instruction," Journal of Blacks in Higher Education 3 (spring 1994): 65–76. See also Alexander Saxton, The Rise and Fall of the White Republic: Class Politics and Mass Culture in Nineteenth-Century America (London: Verso, 1996; 1990).

91. Kujovich, "Public Black Colleges." See also Rayford W. Logan, The Betrayal of the Negro: From Rutherford B. Hayes to Woodrow Wilson, enl. ed. (New York: Collier, 1965; 1954), 368, for a discussion of the Hatch Act of 1887 that supplemented the Morrill Act of 1862 and provided for the establishment of agricultural extension stations in connection with the land-grant colleges. This act did not provide for equitable fund distribution (white colleges outstripped black by $21.5 million to $3.8 million in total value). A 1914 amendment to remedy this inequity was defeated. Logan also notes: "At the end of World War I, none of the seventeen Negro land-grant colleges provided military training as required by the first Morrill Act of 1862" (394). The first black ROTC would not appear until 1942 at Prairie View A&M University in Texas.

92. See Kujovich, "Public Black Colleges," 65–76; Second Morrill Land Grant Act, Statutes at Large 26 (1890), 417–19; and Julian B. Roebuck and Komanduri S. Murty, Historically Black Colleges and

232

Universities: Their Place in American Higher Education (Westport, CT: Praeger, 1993), 27–28. Roebuck and Murty point out that Southern state governments established public historically black colleges (HBCUs) to collect federal funds for the development of white schools, to limit black education, and keep blacks out of white schools.

93. Kujovich, "Public Black Colleges," 70.

94. Ibid., 66.

95. David Hoard, vice chancellor for development at North Carolina Central University, quoted in Sara McGill, "Historically Black Schools Face Dropping Enrollment," *Duke University Chronicle*, 7.

96. Kujovich, "Public Black Colleges," 66. See also James D. Anderson, *The Education of Blacks in the South, 1860–1935* (Chapel Hill: University of North Carolina Press, 1988), esp. chapters 5–6, on the white supremacist ideology of the Hampton-Tuskegee model and the Rosenwald Fund. Anxious to reproduce a docile black labor force as well as avoid having blacks compete with white labor, Northern philanthropists and Southern reformers promoted the caste system in the curriculum in the private black colleges and in the black public primary schools in the South that they helped to fund. (African American parents and children increasingly resisted these indoctrination efforts.) The period 1880–1930 also saw the rise of the public high school in America that mostly left out blacks. African Americans, who had championed the universal public school during Reconstruction, were now "double taxed." They not only had to pay for the operation of white schools that they were not allowed to use, but they also had to supplement philanthropic donations to build and maintain separate black public primary schools with their own funds, labor, and land because state appropriations were so inadequate. In the 1920s Southern employers allowed whites on a mass scale to seize control of what had previously been considered "Negro jobs"—everything from mail handler to truck driver. The philanthropists then "found themselves in the peculiar position of advocating and implementing secondary industrial education to train black youth in certain occupations just at the time when black workers were being pushed out of those jobs and replaced by white workers." Ibid. 234.

97. Ibid., 70. See also Alabama State Archives website at http://www.archives.state.al.us, Internet.

98. Kujovich, "Public Black Colleges," 71.

99. Ibid., 75. Given this well-documented history of inequality in higher education, it is still amazing to hear many white people today deny that historically black colleges are underfunded and accept the standard white definition of them as "inefficient" and therefore deserving of whatever budget crisis they experience. Those crises are generally not experienced on nearly the same scale by traditionally white institutions (TWIs). Perhaps, then, the question is being put the wrong way. Instead of declaring that HBCUs are "underfunded," we could better say that TWIs are and have always been overfunded and furthermore can also better absorb whatever waste and poor planning are to be found in any given college administration. The parallels between the "inefficient black college" and the "lazy incompetent black worker" archetypes in white mythology are clear. They both are historically constructed self-serving arguments and also provide ammunition in the political war against affirmative action.

100. Du Bois, *A Reader*, 536.

101. Richard Krickus, *Pursuing the American Dream: White Ethnics and the New Populism* (Bloomington: Indiana University Press, 1976), 83–84.

102. Jacobson, *Whiteness of a Different Color*, 46–47. Jacobson notes that Irish and Germans were "well outside the deliberate intent of the 'free white persons' clause of 1790."

103. See Noel Ignatiev, " 'Whiteness' and American Character: An Essay," *Konch* 1, no. 1 (winter 1990): 136–39; and Ignatiev, *How the Irish Became White*. See also Jacobson, *Whiteness of a Different Color;* and Peter H. Wang, *Legislating Normalcy: The Immigration Act of 1924* (San Francisco: R. and E. Research, 1975), 124–25.

104. Hill, "Black Labor," 191.

105. James A. Dunlevy and Henry A. Gemery, "Economic Opportunity and the Responses of 'Old' and 'New' Migrants to the United States," *Journal of Economic History* 38, no. 4 (December 1978): 901.

106. See John J. Bukowczyk, *And My Children Did Not Know Me: A History of Polish Americans* (Bloomington: Indiana University Press, 1987), 10–29. As a personal note, my maternal grandparents were early-twentieth-century immigrants from Poland (1907) and Greece (1919). Their families and friends settled in rural central Illinois, working in the mines and factories in addition to starting their own businesses. Initially "Anglo-Saxon" natives of that locale often referred to the Poles as "hunkies," which came from the derogatory term for Hungarians, but within one generation were embracing the diversity of the newcomers' culture as the latter were also assimilating. (Telephone conversation with author's mother, Mary Kranos Rubio, 7 March 1999.)

107. Dunlevy and Gemery, "Economic Opportunity," 902.

108. Jacobson, *Whiteness of a Different Color*, 68.

109. 61st Cong., 3rd sess., *Reports of the Immigration Commission: A Dictionary of Races and Peoples* (Washington, D.C.: GPO, 1911). Prepared for the commission by Daniel Folmar and Elnora C. Folkmar, it utilized a number of "scholarly" sources, especially *The Races of Europe* by William Z. Ripley (1899).

110. *Reports of the Immigration Commission*, 2. On the 1940 preliminary naturalization petition form issued by the INS of the Department of Labor, applicants are asked to choose their "race and nationality" from a "partial list" of 52 choices: " 'race' is to be determined from the original stock or blood of your ancestors and the language you speak, as distinguished from 'nationality,' which means the country of which you are a citizen or subject." The list of "races or peoples" includes only one surviving member of Blumenbach's original list: "Negro." It makes no mention of "Caucasians," "Nordics," "Alpines," "Mediterraneans," "whites," or "Mongoloids" but offers options from all the way from "Albanian" to "West Indian (other than Cuban)." The new immigration priorities are suggested in the next phrase: "The term 'Cuban' refers to the Cuban people (not Negroes). . . . Any alien with admixture of blood of the African Negro will be classified as 'Negro.' " Given the popularity of "white" in the United States as a racial category (though not found in Poland), Elizabeth (Elizabieta) Migda Kranos, my maternal grandmother, logically wrote "white" on the line where it says "My race is," but crossed it out and wrote "Polish" after apparently noticing and directing her attention to the above racial classifications. The revised immigration forms in that same year (1940, when the INS was also transferred to the Department of Justice) shrank these categories to a handful, including "African or African descent," "Filipino," and, for the first time, "white." Quotations are taken from copies of forms belonging to Elizabeth Migda Kranos, in author's possession. (In 1940 Elizabeth had to reapply to regain her U.S. citizenship, which she had lost in 1919 by marrying my grandfather, Mark Kranos, whose status was at that time an "alien" from Greece. However, when my mother married my father, Carlos Manuel Rubio, whose father was Cuban, a distant Polish relative—herself a recent U.S. immigrant—complained that my mother had married a Cuban whom she presumed to therefore have African ancestry.) I am indebted to my mother for providing me with these forms, as well as INS senior historian Marian L. Smith, Washington, D.C.,

personal conversation with author, 6 December 1999, and electronic communication, 14 December 1999, that included an excerpt from her unpublished paper on the subject of race and immigration. See also Marian L. Smith, " 'Any Woman Who Is Now or May Hereafter Be Married . . .': Women and Naturalization, ca. 1802–1940," *Prologue: Quarterly of the National Archives and Records Administration* 30 no. 2 (summer 1998) [online document].

111. *Reports of the Immigration Commission*, 104.

112. See also David J. Hellwig, "Black Leaders and United States Immigration Policy, 1917–1929," *Journal of Negro History* 66, no. 2 (1981): 110–27, for black leaders and newspapers who supported, if ambivalently, some of the restrictive immigration legislation. This was, argues Hellwig, primarily out of fear of blacks being displaced by immigrants, but many blacks during this era also subscribed to popular stereotypes and scapegoating of the southern and eastern European.

113. *Reports of the Immigration Commission*, 79–81.

114. Thomas Archdeacon, *Becoming American: An Ethnic History* (New York: Free Press, 1983), 146. In some cases this was done voluntarily by the immigrants themselves, although my maternal grandfather, Markos Kraniotakis, from the Greek island of Crete, probably had his name shortened to "Mark Kranos" by customs officials. My Polish ancestors with the last names of Migda and Sledz kept their last names intact, as did many Poles and other European immigrants, even if they did Anglicize their first names. Not atypically, the ocean passage for the Poles was "probably paid for by the coal company" they were to work for. Mary Kranos Rubio, telephone conversation with author, 7 March 1999.

115. "Eugenics" was invented by Sir Francis Galton and Kurt Pearson of Britain at the end of the nineteenth century. It represented a campaign for selective breeding, believing that "differences in ability could be quantified and partitioned," and developed statistical techniques that "proved" biological determinism and white superiority. See Lewontin, Rose, and Kamin, *Not in Our Genes*, 26.

116. Kitty Calavita, *U.S. Immigration Law and the Control of Labor 1820–1924* (London: Academic Press, 1984), 108.

117. Ibid.

118. Delgado, *The Coming Race War?*, 92–94.

119. Carl Campbell Brigham, *A Study of American Intelligence* (Princeton, NJ: Princeton University Press, 1923), 183. Brigham concluded: "At one extreme we have the distribution of the Nordic race group. At the other extreme we have the American negro. Between the Nordic and the negro, but closer to the negro than to the Nordic, we find the Alpine and Mediterranean types." Ibid., 183.

120. Delgado, *The Coming Race War?*, 92. See Madison Grant, *The Passing of the Great Race, or the Racial Basis of European history* (New York: Charles Scribner's Sons, 1918). See also today's recycling of these old arguments in Richard J. Herrnstein and Charles Murray, *The Bell Curve: Intelligence and Class Structure in American Life* (New York: Free Press, 1994).

121. Leland Ware cited in Cheryl I. Harris, "Whiteness as Property," *Harvard Law Review* 106 (1993): 1771.

122. Lewontin, Rose, and Kamin, *Not in Our Genes*, 83–90; and Wang, *Legislating Normalcy*, 60.

123. Calavita, *U.S. Immigration Law*, 109.

124. Wang, *Legislating Normalcy*, 61, House Committee on Immigration, "Europe as an Emigrant-Exporting Continent and the United States as an Immigrant-Receiving Nation: Hearings," 68th Cong., 1st sess., 1924, 1276. See also Ibid., 68 n 26, House Committee on Immigration and Naturalization, "Biological Aspects of Immigration: Hearings," 66th Cong., 2nd sess., 1920, 22; and U.S. Cong. House, Committee on Immigration and Naturalization, "Analysis of America's Melting Pot: Hearings," 67th Cong., 3rd sess., 1923, 757.

125. Lewontin, Rose, and Kamin, *Not in Our Genes*, 105–6.

126. Ignatiev, *How the Irish Became White*, 65. The quotation comes from a 1797 speech during the congressional debate by Federalist Congressman Harrison Gray Otis of Boston.

127. Wang, *Legislating Normalcy*, especially 107, for quoting the *New York Times* (5 April 1924 and 19 April 1924) in praise of the act: "The emphasis is thus placed on the American side of the hyphen."

128. Ibid., 70 n 43, Hon. Salvatore A. Cotillo, "Memorandum in opposition to the Johnson Bill, H.R. 101" (New York: Grand Court Sons of Italy of the State of N.Y., n.d.)

129. Jacobson, *Whiteness of a Different Color*, 85–86; See *Cong. Record*, 68th Cong., 1st sess., vol. 65. Among the entries, note the petitions in support (carpenters and joiners from Superior, Arizona, 6687), those opposed (New Jersey legislature, 3669, or orthodox Rabbis, 2754), and the joint statement of 28 March 1924 by Samuel Gompers and American Legion National Commander John R. Quinn (5120–21) railing against expected opposition from "racial groups in the United States," and urging immigration prohibition (but accepting restriction). Supporters also warned of the "menace to American institutions" from the expected immigrant "flood" from "South Europe" (including Greece and the "Near East") that "seethes with revolutionary doctrines" and was used to the "low European standard of living." Note also the chilling declaration (6687) by the immigration bill's cosponsor Rep. Albert Johnson (R-Washington) to the Daughters of the American Revolution on 18 April 1924: "We are about to require examination of immigrants overseas. . . . Our right to say who shall live among us and be of us has been challenged, and our nation has been threatened with 'grave consequences.' "

130. Jacobson, *Whiteness of a Different Color*, 9.

131. See Frank Zappa with Peter Occhiogrosso, *The Real Frank Zappa Book* (New York: Poseidon, 1989).

132. Roediger, *Towards the Abolition of Whiteness*, 186. On the other hand, antiblack diatribes were starting to appear during Red Summer (1919) in Chicago's *Naród Polski* (Polish Nation). See Bukow-czyk, *And My Children*, 99. See also David Levering Lewis, *When Harlem Was in Vogue* (New York: Penguin, 1997; 1981), 19–20, 46–47, on black resistance in the 1919 Chicago race riot that in its aftermath saw 23 blacks and 15 whites dead, 537 people injured, and more than 1,000 left homeless.

133. There were only seventy opposed votes in the House and six in the Senate. Wang, *Legislating Normalcy*, 124–25.

134. Jacobson, *Whiteness of a Different Color*, 90.

135. Ibid., 78.

136. Auerbach, *The Immigration and Nationality Act*, 19–27; and *Immigration Act of 1924*, Statutes at Large 43 (1924), 153–69. National origins immigration quotas were eliminated in 1965. Smith, INS senior historian, personal conversation, 6 December 1999. See also INS website, available at http://www.ins.doj.gov, Internet.

137. Within this archetype, of course, there are some regional variations. There is some similarity here to how the mental image of "American citizen" still conjures for many a ponytailed Revolutionary-era Bostonian Minuteman. See "On Whiteness: Readers Respond to HMR's Questionnaire," *Hungry Mind Review* 47 (fall 1998), 22–24; and David R. Roediger, *Towards the Abolition of Whiteness: Essays on Race, Politics, and Working Class History* (London: Verso, 1994), 181–98.

138. Lothrop Stoddard, "The Permanent Menace from Europe," in *The Alien in Our Midst: or "Selling Our Birthright for a Mess of Pottage,"* ed. Madison Grant and Charles Steward Davison (New York: Galton, 1930), 68–69. Physical appearance has long been a marker for race but has also varied

over the years as we have seen—yet its convoluted history of social and historical construction leaves us with popular as well as official confusion of skin color with racial identity (especially where whiteness as the superior and default caste is concerned). The 2000 U.S. Bureau of the Census Form D-1, for example, asked U.S. residents to mark the box or boxes for the "race" and "ethnicity" that "this person considers himself/herself to be." Question number 5 is for those of "Spanish/Hispanic/Latino" ethnic descent, followed by question number 6 concerning race, beginning with "White," followed by "Black/African American," "American Indian," eleven choices under "Asian," and "Some Other Race" (which can include multiracial or biracial, but they want you to "be specific").

139. Ibid., 227.

140. Madison Grant, "Closing the Flood-Gates," in Ibid , 15; and Grant and Davis, *Passing of the Great Race*, 80, where they conflate immigrants as "the weak, the broken, and the mentally crippled of all races drawn from the lowest stratum of the Mediterranean basin and the Balkans, together with the hordes of the wretched, submerged populations of the Polish ghettoes." "The Melting Pot" was the name of a popular melodrama of the day. Written by Israel Zangwill, it opened on Broadway in 1908. It featured a talented young male musician protagonist from a Russian Jewish immigrant family who "seizes the opportunity that America gives him, writes his American symphony, marries the gentile girl of his dreams, and becomes a proud American." See Gary Gerstle, "Theodore Roosevelt and the Divided Character of American Nationalism," *Journal of American History* 86, no. 3 (December 1999): 1298.

141. Ignatiev, " 'Whiteness' and American Character," 136.

142. Thomas Göbel, "Becoming American: Ethnic Workers and the Rise of the CIO," *Labor History* 29, no. 2 (spring 1988): 173.

143. Ibid., 174–76.

144. Jacobson, *Whiteness of a Different Color*, 14.

145. Harris, "Whiteness as Property," 1746.

146. See *Plessy v. Ferguson* (1896); Gaines, *Uplifting the Race*, 28–30; Jessica Foy, "Plessy v. Ferguson," in *Encyclopedia of Southern Culture*, ed. Charles Wilson Reagan and William Ferris (Chapel Hill: University of North Carolina Press, 1988), 828–29; and Charles A. Lofgren, *The Plessy Case: A Legal-Historical Interpretation* (New York: Oxford University Press, 1987).

147. Harris, "Whiteness as Property," 1747.

148. Ibid., 1748.

149. Ibid., 1749.

150. Harlan dissent in *Plessy v. Ferguson* (1896).

151. Ibid.; and Harlan dissent in *Civil Rights Cases* (1883).

152. Harlan dissent in *Plessy v. Ferguson* (1896).

153. Harlan dissent in *Civil Rights Cases* (1883).

154. Harlan dissent in *Plessy v. Ferguson* (1896).

155. Ibid. See also Anderson, *The Education of Blacks*, 188, 192–93, on Harlan's opinion in *Cumming v. School Board of Richmond County, Georgia*. That 1899 decision, which upheld the school board's right to close a black high school (one of perhaps four in the South) significantly impeded Southern public black education—in fact, black Southerners in general did not obtain public high schools until after World War II. Disregarding *Plessy's* separate but equal principle, Harlan, according to Anderson, "concluded that the black plaintiffs' demand for substantially equal facilities would damage white children without assisting blacks" and that the plaintiffs had failed to establish that the board's action was racially motivated. Ibid., 192.

156. Prather, *We Have Taken a City*, 161; and Gaines, *Uplifting the Race*, 228.

157. Gaines, *Uplifting the Race*, 25.

158. O'Reilly, "Woodrow Wilson"; and Allen, *Reluctant Reformers*, 97. During this time the Civil Service Commission began taking photographs of job prospects to screen out black applicants.

159. "Reading from the Crisis," *New Crisis* 107, no. 4 (July/August 2000): 60.

160. Ibid., 56.

161. Ibid., 58. The article also notes that many black and white speakers in the United States condemned Washington's remarks at the time.

162. Prather, *We Have Taken a City*, 167.

163. See James Baldwin, *The Price of the Ticket: Collected Nonfiction, 1948–1985* (New York: St. Martin's, 1985).

164. Allen, *Reluctant Reformers*, 121–63; Rosalyn Terborg-Penn, *African-American Women in the Struggle for the Vote, 1850–1920* (Bloomington: Indiana University Press, 1998); and Louise Michele Newman, *White Women's Rights: The Racial Origins of Feminism in the United States* (New York: Oxford University Press, 1999).

165. Terborg-Penn, *African-American Women*, 166.

166. W. E. B. Du Bois, *W. E. B. Du Bois: A Reader*, ed. David Levering Lewis (New York: Henry Holt, 1995), 542 (from "Marxism and the Negro Problem," *Crisis*, May 1933).

167. Zinn, *People's History*, 373: "There was some truth to the standard picture of the twenties as a time of prosperity. . . . Unemployment was down, from 4,270,000 in 1921 to a little over 2 million in 1927. The general level of wages for workers rose. . . . But prosperity was concentrated at the top. . . . Six million families (42 percent of the total) made less than $1,000 a year [half the income of the average working-class family]." See also Franklin and Moss, *From Slavery to Freedom*, 311–13.

168. Wyn Craig Wade, *The Fiery Cross: The Ku Klux Klan in America* (New York: Simon and Schuster, 1987), 139.

169. See David M. Chalmers, *Hooded Americanism: The First Century of the Ku Klux Klan* (Garden City, NY: Doubleday, 1965), 28–38.

170. Ibid.; and Wade, *The Fiery Cross*, 117–254. Denver's Stapleton International Airport (replaced in the 1990s by Denver International Airport) was named for Benjamin F. Stapleton, a Klansman who was elected governor of Colorado in 1923 but who broke with the Klan two years later. See Chalmers, *Hooded Americanism*, 127, 132; and Robert Alan Goldberg, *Hooded Empire: The Ku Klux Klan in Colorado* (Urbana: University of Illinois Press, 1981), 29–35, 107. See also Timothy Messer-Kruse, "Memories of the Ku Klux Klan Honorary Society at the University of Wisconsin," *Journal of Blacks in Higher Education* 23 (spring 1999): 83–93, for an account of the Klan-inspired student group at the University of Wisconsin being one of the most popular on campus, as well as counting among its members the school's leading undergraduate scholars, and whose activities included frequently parading in blackface.

171. Franklin and Moss, *From Slavery to Freedom*, 310–18.

172. Chalmers, *Hooded Americanism*, 296–99.

173. Wang, *Legislating Normalcy*, 124–25.

174. Goldberg, *Hooded Empire*, vii.

175. See Chalmers, *Hooded Americanism*; and Wade, *The Fiery Cross*, esp. 419–34 for 1920 Klan official documents such as their "Kloran" that calls for "the eternal maintenance of white supremacy," and wording similar in their constitution or "Kreed."

176. See supra note 175.

177. August Meier and Elliot Rudwick, *Black Detroit and the Rise of the UAW* (Oxford, England: Oxford University Press, 1981), especially 178 n, where they quote a government investigator from the Office of War Information in 1942 who told of how blacks and Poles lived amicably together in Hamtramck "on the same streets and in the same house." There was no fear of "depreciating property values" until real estate agents and Ku Klux Klan demagogues used the new Sojourner Truth Housing Project as a racist mobilization target. The investigator reports: "The second generation Poles were the first to take up the battle cry for segregation and discrimination. Like others of foreign descent in Detroit, they were beginning to fear the competition of young and status-conscious Negroes in jobs. The younger Poles are now inducing anti-Negro attitudes among the older generation and the Negroes are being forced out of Hamtramck." Originally in "The Social Dynamics of Detroit," report prepared for Bureau of Intelligence, Office of War Information, 3 December 1942, NA RG 44, Box 1814.

178. Chalmers, *Hooded Americanism*, 196.

179. Logan, *The Betrayal of the Negro*, 11–12. John Hope Franklin, he says, picks the year 1923, while Du Bois sees the "first part of the twentieth century" as the end of the nadir.

180. Ibid., and 393.

181. Nathan Irvin Huggins, ed., "Introduction," in *Voices From The Harlem Renaissance* (New York: Oxford University Press, 1995), 4. See also Lewis, *When Harlem Was in Vogue*, esp. preface. For a discussion of white participation in the Harlem Renaissance, see Ibid., 98–103; and Ann Douglas, *Terrible Honesty: Mongrel Manhattan in the 1920s* (New York: Farrar, 1995).

182. See *Messenger*, vols. 1–10 (1917–1921) (New York: Negro Universities Press, 1969); Franklin and Moss, *From Slavery to Freedom*, 308; and Lewis, *When Harlem Was in Vogue*.

183. Hill, *Black Labor*, 238.

184. Ibid.

185. Ruth O'Brien, *Worker's Paradox: The Republican Origins of New Deal Labor Policy, 1886–1935* (Chapel Hill: University of North Carolina Press, 1998), 17.

186. Ibid., 72.

187. Ibid., 22.

188. Ibid., 13.

189. Ibid., 17.

190. Ibid., 137.

191. Herbert Hill, *Black Labor and the American Legal System: Race, Work, and the Law* (Madison: University of Wisconsin Press, 1985; 1977), 341. O'Brien says nothing at all in *Worker's Paradox* about the features of the act or the union tactics that Hill cites.

192. *Davis-Bacon Act, Statutes at Large* 46 (1931), 1494. The act was expanded in 1935 to include construction contracts of $2,000 or more. In 1938 the *Fair Labor Standards Act* (FLSA) became an extension of this act. More worker benefits were added to the Davis-Bacon Act in 1964. See O'Brien, *Workers' Paradox*, 33–40.

193. Armand J. Thieblot Jr., *Prevailing Wage Legislation: The Davis-Bacon Act, State "Little Davis-Bacon" Acts, the Walsh-Healey Act, and the Service Contract Act* (Philadelphia: University of Pennsylvania Press, 1986), 120.

194. Ibid., 30.

195. David Bernstein, "The Davis-Bacon Act: Let's Bring Jim Crow to an End," *Cato Briefing Paper* no. 17, 18 January 1993; available at http://www.cato.org/pubs/briefs/bp-017es.html, Internet.

Chapter 4

1. Harold Preece, "Confession of an Ex-Nordic: The Depression Not an Unmixed Evil," *Opportunity* 13, no. 8 (August 1935): 232–33.

2. Ibid., 233.

3. Ibid. See also Jacquelyn Dowd Hall, *Revolt against Chivalry: Jessie Daniels Ames and the Women's Campaign against Lynching*, rev. ed. (New York: Columbia University Press, 1993); Patricia Sullivan, *Days of Hope: Race and Democracy in the New Deal Era* (Chapel Hill: University of North Carolina Press, 1996), 73, 87–89; and John Hope Franklin and Alfred A. Moss Jr., *From Slavery to Freedom: A History of Negro Americans*, 6th ed. (New York: McGraw-Hill, 1988; 1947), 345, on the 1931 Scottsboro Boys case. Nine young black men were charged with raping two white women near Scottsboro, Alabama, and sentenced to death. Their eventual release was secured by the efforts of the International Labor Defense, the Communist Party, and the NAACP, in a case that saw the Supreme Court overturning the conviction because of inadequate counsel and one of the women admitting that they had invented the story of their rape. See also chapter 3, note 40, in this book.

4. Howard Zinn, *A People's History of the United States* (New York: Harper, 1990; 1980), 386–88.

5. Christopher Lawrence Tomlins, *The State and the Unions: Federal Labor Relations Policy and the Organized Labor Movement in America, 1935–55* (Ann Arbor, MI: University Microfilms, 1984).

6. See Jervis Anderson, *A. Philip Randolph: A Biographical Portrait* (New York: Harcourt, 1973), 247–61.

7. *National Labor Relations Act of 1935*, Statutes at Large 49 (1935), 454. Italics added. The NLRA also excluded from its protection agricultural and domestic workers.

8. Ibid., 452.

9. Herbert Hill, *Black Labor and the American Legal System: Race, Work, and the Law* (Madison: University of Wisconsin Press, 1985; 1977), 101, italics added; and *National Labor Relations Act*, 453.

10. Hill, *Black Labor*, 93–169. For the majority labor history view that the Wagner Act was an overall good, see, for example, Leon Fink, "American Labor History," in *The New American History*, ed. Eric Foner (Philadelphia: Temple University Press, 1990), 246; and Thomas R. Brooks, *Toil and Trouble: A History of American Labor* (New York: Dell, 1971; 1964).

11. Hill, *Black Labor*, 93–169. See also Herbert Garfinkel, *When Negroes March: The March on Washington Movement in the Organizational Politics for FEPC* (New York: Atheneum, 1969; 1959).

12. See Hill, *Black Labor*, chapter 2, esp. 74–86; Bernard Schwartz, ed., *Statutory History of the United States: Civil Rights Part 2* (New York: Chelsea House, 1970), 1018–19; and Derrick A. Bell Jr., *Race, Racism, and American Law*, 2nd ed. (Boston: Little, Brown, 1980). For her theory that the 1935 Wagner Act had its origins in the labor policies of the previous Republican administrations, see Ruth O'Brien, *Workers' Paradox: The Republican Origins of New Deal Labor Policy, 1886–1935* (Chapel Hill: University of North Carolina, 1998), 2–9. For a rebuttal of that view, see Howell John Harris, review of *Workers' Paradox: The Republican Origins of New Deal Labor Policy, 1886–1935*, by Ruth O'Brien, *Journal of American History* 86, no. 2 (December 1999): 1372–73.

13. Hill, *Black Labor*, 105.

14. Ibid., 106.

15. See William H. Harris, *The Harder We Run: Black Workers since the Civil War* (New York: Oxford University Press, 1982), 137, 163; *Labor Management Relations Act*, Statutes at Large 61 (1947), 136; and Benjamin J. Taylor and Fred Witney, eds., *Labor Relations Law* (Englewood Cliffs, NJ: Prentice-Hall, 1971), 192–224, 589–617. The Labor Management Relations Act is more commonly known as the Taft-Hartley Act. Among other things, it banned the closed shop where employees at a unionized

workplace had to join the union, although a 1951 act legalized the union shop whereby a worker, after a short time (usually their employer's "probationary" period), could be compelled to join a union. Union dues that were formerly collected personally could now be simply "checked off" or automatically deducted from a worker's paycheck. But Harris points out how the closed shop was actually still in operation among the construction trade unions until President Johnson banned hiring hall discrimination in 1965.

16. David Montgomery, *Workers Control in America: Studies in the History of Work, Technology, and Labor Struggles* (Cambridge: Cambridge University Press, 1986; 1979), 165.

17. See, for example, Harvard Sitkoff, *A New Deal for Blacks: The Emergence of Civil Rights as a National Issue*, vol. 1, *The Depression Decade* (New York: Oxford University Press, 1978), 331.

18. See, for example, Zinn, *People's History*, 394.

19. See, for example, George Lipsitz, "The Possessive Investment in Whiteness: Racialized Social Democracy and the 'White' Problem in American Studies," *American Quarterly* 47, no. 3 (September 1995): 369–87.

20. See Sitkoff, *A New Deal for Blacks*, esp. chapter 7.

21. See August Meier and Elliot Rudwick, *Black Detroit and the Rise of the UAW* (New York: Oxford University Press, 1981), 125–34; and Alfred M. Rubio, former labor organizer (and my paternal uncle), unpublished oral history by author, Somerville, Massachusetts, 19 October 1996. Mr. Rubio was a United Auto Workers (UAW) shop steward and committeeman at the General Motors Electromotive Plant in Chicago from 1942 to 1943. He also recalled how management would manipulate the seniority system to favor whites and would "instigate known prejudiced white workers" to harass black workers or improperly instruct black apprentices. UAW officials responded with shop floor meetings to deal with white prejudice. See also an analysis of the 1944 Philadelphia transit strike in Hill, *Black Labor*, 245, 274–308.

22. Meier and Rudwick, *Black Detroit*, 125–34.

23. Steve Fraser and Gary Gerstle, eds., *The Rise and Fall of the New Deal Order, 1930–1980* (Princeton, NJ: Princeton University Press, 1989); Thomas A. Webster, "Employers, Unions and Negro Workers," *Opportunity* 19 (October 1941): 295–97; Beth Tompkins Bates, "A New Crowd Challenges the Agenda of the Old Guardian NAACP, 1933–1941," *American Historical Review* 102, no. 2 (April 1997): 340–77; and Kevin Gaines, "Rethinking Race and Class in African-American Struggles for Equality, 1885–1941," *American Historical Review* 102, no. 2 (April 1997): 378–87.

24. Anderson, *Randolph*, chapter 16.

25. See Franklin and Moss, *From Slavery to Freedom*, 339–59; Zinn, *People's History*, 386; Jill Quadagno, *The Color of Welfare: How Racism Undermined the War on Poverty* (New York: Oxford University Press, 1994), 20–24; and John David Skrentny, *The Ironies of Affirmative Action: Politics, Culture, and Justice in America* (Chicago: University of Chicago Press, 1996), 28–29.

26. See esp. Ed Gillespie and Bob Schellhas, *Contract with America: The Bold Plan by Rep. Newt Gingrich, Rep. Dick Armey and the House Republicans to Change the Nation* (New York: Times Books, 1994), 66–69; and Barbara Ransby, "US: The Black Poor and the Politics of Expendability," *Race and Class: A Journal for Black and Third World Liberation* 38, no. 2 (October–December 1996): 1–12. See also Frances Fox Piven and Richard A. Cloward, *Regulating the Poor: The Functions of Public Welfare* (New York: Pantheon, 1971), xv, for this observation: "As for relief programs themselves, the historical pattern is clearly not one of progressive liberalization; it is rather a record of periodically expanding and contracting relief rolls as the system performs its two main functions: maintaining civil order and enforcing work."

27. On the New Deal legacy see Melvin L. Oliver and Thomas M. Shapiro, *Black Wealth/White Wealth: A New Perspective on Racial Equality* (New York: Routledge, 1997), 17–18; and Douglas S. Massey and Nancy A. Denton, *American Apartheid: Segregation and the Making of the Underclass* (Cambridge: Harvard University Press, 1993), 53–55.

28. On the other hand, some agencies like the Works Project Administration (WPA) with its Federal Writers Project (FWP), the Federal Theater Project (FTP), and the Federal Art Project (FAP) that have provided a model for today's public arts support also did much to subsidize African American artists. On the WPA and the CCC see Zinn, *People's History*, 394; Franklin and Moss, *From Slavery to Freedom*, 353–54; and Sitkoff, *A New Deal for Blacks*, 51, 74–75. According to Sitkoff, despite an unemployment rate twice that of whites, blacks made up no more than 6 percent of the more than 2 million CCC enrollees from 1933 to 1936, after which the number rose to a high of 11 percent by its end in 1942. This rise was due in part to civil rights groups' protests against CCC discrimination and segregation.

29. Mink and Quadagno cited in Oliver and Shapiro, *Black Wealth/White Wealth*, 38. "Furthermore, since more black women are single, divorced, or separated, they cannot look forward to sharing a spouse's benefit." As Quadagno, *The Color of Welfare*, notes, again, the tax contributions of black working women "subsidize the benefits of white housewives" (162).

30. *The Concise Columbia Encyclopedia*, 2nd ed. (New York: Columbia University Press, 1998), s.v. "new deal," 575. The National Recovery Act, which established the National Recovery Administration, was ruled unconstitutional in 1935 by the United States Supreme Court, which held that it gave too much power to the executive branch. See Zinn, *People's History*, 383.

31. William C. Berman, *The Politics of Civil Rights in the Truman Administration* (Columbus: Ohio State University Press, 1970).

32. *The Concise Columbia Encyclopedia*, 2nd ed. (New York: Columbia University Press, 1998), s.v. "great depression," 334. A depression is "characterized by falling prices, restriction of credit, reduced production, numerous bankruptcies, and high unemployment." Ibid., s.v. "depression," 219. See also Zinn, *People's History*, 383.

33. James A. Hodges, "New Deal," in *Encyclopedia of Southern Culture*, ed. Charles Reagan Wilson and William Ferris (Chapel Hill: University of North Carolina Press, 1988), 649.

34. Thomas Ferguson, "Industrial Conflict and the Coming of the New Deal: The Triumph of Multinational Liberalism in America," in Fraser and Gerstle, *The Rise and Fall*, 4, 16.

35. Nancy J. Weiss, *Farewell to the Party of Lincoln: Black Politics in the Age of FDR* (Princeton, NJ: Princeton University Press, 1983), 174–79, 210–11; and Robert C. Weaver, *Negro Labor: A National Problem* (New York: Harcourt, 1946), 15.

36. Weiss, *Farewell*, 286. Also see the *Wade in the Water* radio series (Bernice Johnson Reagon, creator, National Public Radio, 1996) for music of African Americans that reflected trust and hope in Franklin and Eleanor Roosevelt. Du Bois was generally supportive of Roosevelt's policies. See W. E. B. Du Bois, *W. E. B. Du Bois: A Reader*, ed. David Levering Lewis (New York: Henry Holt, 1995), 480–81.

37. W. E. B. Du Bois, *Against Racism: Unpublished Essays, Papers, Addresses, 1887–1961 by W. E. B. Du Bois*, ed. Herbert Aptheker (Amherst: University of Massachusetts Press, 1985), 103–58.

38. Charles Abrams, *Forbidden Neighbors: A Study of Prejudice in Housing* (New York: Harper, 1955), 227.

39. See supra note 27; and Abrams, *Forbidden Neighbors*.

40. Abrams, *Forbidden Neighbors*, 229–30.

41. Ibid.

42. Paul K. Conklin, The New Deal (New York: Crowell, 1969) 76–77, 98–99; and Zinn, People's History, 381–97.

43. Franklin and Moss, From Slavery to Freedom, 352–56. See also George E. Paulsen, A Living Wage for the Forgotten Man: The Quest for Fair Labor Standards, 1933–1941 (Selinsgrove, PA: Susquehanna University Press, 1996). President Roosevelt, says Paulsen, called the FLSA "the second most important New Deal reform after the Social Security Act." Ibid., 7.

44. Quadagno, Color of Welfare, 20. See also Frank Freidel, F.D.R. and the South (Baton Rouge: Louisiana State University Press, 1965); and Franklin and Moss, From Slavery to Freedom, 352–53.

45. Harris, The Harder We Run, 99–102; and Philip S. Foner and Ronald L. Lewis, eds., The Black Worker: A Documentary History from Colonial Times to the Present, vol. 7, The Black Worker from the Founding of the CIO to the AFL-CIO Merger, 1936–1955 (Philadelphia: Temple University Press, 1983), 170. See also Nicholas Lemann, The Promised Land: The Great Migration and How It Changed America (New York: Knopf, 1991).

46. See supra note 45. See also Sitkoff, A New Deal for Blacks, 53.

47. Foner and Lewis, The Black Worker, vol. 7, 170–208.

48. Letter from J. R. Butler to STFU Executive Council, 18 July 1938, in Ibid., 180–81.

49. Ibid., 170.

50. Letter from E. B. McKinney to J. R. Butler, 31 August 1938, in Ibid., 185; and E. B. McKinney's Pledge of Allegiance, 5 December 1938, in Ibid., 186.

51. Harris, The Harder We Run, 100–101. In 1910, 75 percent of white farmers owned their land, while the number of black farmers had dropped to 25 percent. Ibid., 31–32.

52. Paul D. Moreno, From Direct Action to Affirmative Action: Fair Employment Policy in America, 1933–1972 (Baton Rouge: Louisiana State University Press, 1997), 42.

53. B. D. Amis, "National Recovery Act in U.S.A. Means Negro Repressive Act," The Negro Worker 4 (April–May 1934): 17–18, in Foner and Lewis, The Black Worker, vol. 7, 115.

54. Ira De A. Reid, "Black Wages for Black Men," in Opportunity 12 (March 1934): 73–76, in Ibid., 99–103.

55. Robert C. Weaver, "A Wage Differential Based on Race," Crisis 41 (August 1934): 236, 238, in Ibid., 99.

56. John P. Davis, "NRA Codifies Wage Slavery," Crisis 41 (October 1934): 298–99, 304, in Ibid., 111. In the same article, Davis cautioned against too much optimism being invested in the federal construction contract black quotas (discussed later in this chapter) as being "far too few to make an effective in the unemployment conditions of Negro construction industry workers" (117). Davis cofounded, along with Robert Weaver, the advocacy group Negro Industrial League in 1933, which itself spawned the 1935 coalition of twenty-two black organizations called the Joint Committee on National Recovery. Davis also was organizer-secretary for the National Negro Congress, founded in 1935. See Ibid., 585.

57. Harris, The Harder We Run, 106; and Amis, "National Recovery Act," 114–15.

58. Amis, "National Recovery Act." 115.

59. Du Bois, A Reader, 541 ("Marxism and the Negro Problem" from Crisis, 1933). Italics added. See also Du Bois's quote from the Crisis (December 1933): 292 (quoted in Hill, Black Labor, 102): "The American Federation of Labor is not a labor movement. It is a monopoly of skilled laborers, who joined the capitalists in exploiting the masses of labor, whenever and wherever they can. . . ." Yet see Gerald Horne, Black and Red: W. E. B. Du Bois and the Afro-American Response to the Cold War, 1944–1963 (Albany: State University of New York Press, 1986), 50, for an account of how during the 1946 strike wave "Du Bois went so far as to back the railway workers' strike even though they abjectly barred Black workers from their ranks."

60. Herbert Hill, "The Racial Practices of Organized Labor—In the Age of Gompers and After" (New York: NAACP, 1965), reprint, *New Politics* 9.

61. Joseph E. Holloway, ed., *Africanisms in American Culture* (Bloomington: Indiana University Press, 1991), ix–xxi, 1–18. Among the early English indentured servants those skills were in short supply.

62. Hill, "Racial Practices," 7–11. Of the early labor organizations in the late nineteenth and early twentieth centuries, only the Industrial Workers of the World (IWW) refused to organize segregated locals. See also Harris, *The Harder We Run*, 48–50.

63. Mitchell quoted in Hill, "Racial Practices," 11.

64. Ibid., 7–11.

65. Hill, *Black Labor*, 334–72 and passim on segregated seniority systems; and Quadagno, *Color of Welfare*, 21. In *Negro Labor*, Robert C. Weaver offers two contrasting views on the seniority system: (1) "Were there no union seniority agreements hundreds of thousands of Negroes would be displaced from their wartime jobs during the reconversion" (Ibid., 282); and (2) "While it seemed that no appreciable relaxations in seniority can or will be made by unions during reconversion, it is possible that some relaxations may ultimately be required by events." Ibid., 305.

66. Montgomery, *Workers' Control in America*, 140.

67. Ibid., 140–49.

68. Hill, *Black Labor*, 336–37. Hill also notes here how prior to emancipation the Houston and Texas Central Railroad Company, as well as its white employees, owned slaves.

69. Ibid., 347.

70. Herbert Hill, "Black Labor and Affirmative Action: An Historical Perspective," in *The Question of Discrimination: Racial Inequality in the United States Labor Market*, ed. Steven Shulman and William Darity (Middletown, CT: Wesleyan University Press, 1989), 195.

71. Richard W. Steele, " 'No Racials': Discrimination against Ethnics in American Defense Industry, 1940–1942," *Labor History* 32, no. 1 (winter 1991): 66–90. See also Franklin and Moss, *From Slavery to Freedom*, 351, on the Civil Service Commission no longer requiring applicants to indicate race or provide photographs during this period of rising black employment in government. But after an interview, officials could use the "rule of three" to pick a second- or third-ranked white over a first-ranked black applicant.

72. Meier and Rudwick, *Black Detroit*, 34–38.

73. Willard Townsend, "Citizen CIO," in *Crisis* 50 (October 1943): 299–300, 312, in Foner and Lewis, *The Black Worker*, vol. 7, 372. The AFL expelled the CIO in 1937. Ibid., 2.

74. Hill, *Black Labor*, 23.

75. Bruce Nelson, "CIO Symposium: Robert H. Zieger, *The CIO, 1935–1955* (Chapel Hill: University of North Carolina Press, 1995)" in *Labor History* 37, no. 2 (spring, 1996): 157.

76. Earl Lewis in Ibid., 173.

77. Ibid.

78. Meier and Rudwick, *Black Detroit*, 209.

79. Arnold B. Walker, "St. Louis' Employers, Unions and Negro Workers," *Opportunity* 19, no. 11 (November 1941): 337.

80. Ibid., 337. See also Hill, *Black Labor*, 241–43, on this government order to enforce federal government construction contract policy.

81. See Nancy L. Grant, *TVA and Black Americans: Planning for the Status Quo* (Philadelphia: Temple University Press, 1990); John P. Davis, "A Black Inventory of the New Deal," *Crisis* 42 (May 1935):

141–42, 154–55, in Foner and Lewis, eds., *The Black Worker*, vol. 7, 117–18; and Richard Lowitt, "Tennessee Valley Authority (TVA)," in Wilson and Ferris, *Encyclopedia of Southern Culture*, 365–67.

82. W. E. B. Du Bois, *Black Reconstruction in America 1860–1880* (Cleveland: Meridian, 1968; 1935), 694.

83. Meier and Rudwick, *Black Detroit*, 30–44, 62–66; and Hill, *Black Labor*, 260–73. For the successful proportional hiring demands of the Packinghouse Workers Organizing Committee (PWOC) at Swift and Company in Chicago, see Sitkoff, *A New Deal for Blacks*, 184.

84. Herbert Hill, "Black Workers, Organized Labor, and Title VII of the 1964 Civil Rights Act: Legislative History and Litigation Record," in *Race in America: The Struggle for Equality*, ed. Herbert Hill and James E. Jones Jr. (Madison: University of Wisconsin Press, 1993), 263–341; and Hill, *Black Labor*, 267–70. For a more favorable view of the CIO see Robert H. Zieger, *The CIO: 1935–1955* (Chapel Hill: University of North Carolina Press, 1995). But Zieger notes the more principled stands on equality taken by the CIO left-wing unions compared with the "moderation" of the CIO's leaders (Ibid., 375), or most CIO affiliates, as he comments: "However, most CIO unions downplayed the race card and subsumed concern for black workers under class appeals that ignored or evaded confrontations with racist forces in the community and on the shop floor" (374). See also Steve Rosswurm, ed., *The CIO's Left-Led Unions* (New Brunswick, NJ: Rutgers University Press, 1992); Bruce Nelson, "Organized Labor and the Struggle for Black Equality in Mobile during World War II," *Journal of American History* 80, no. 3 (December 1993): 952–88; and Robert Korstad and Nelson Lichtenstein, "Opportunities Found and Lost: Labor, Radicals, and the Early Civil Rights Movement," *Journal of American History* 75, no. 3 (December 1988): 786–811.

85. Moreno, *Direct Action*, 30–65. For problems with CIO unions see Weaver, *Negro Labor*, 219–22.

86. Moreno, *Direct Action*, 30–65; and Foner and Lewis, *The Black Worker*, vol. 7, 119–24.

87. *New Negro Alliance v. Sanitary Grocery Co.*, 303 U.S. 552 (1938).

88. Harris, *The Harder We Run*, 108.

89. Meier and Rudwick, *Black Detroit*, 20–23.

90. Vere E. Johns, "To Boycott—Or Not to Boycott: We Must Have Jobs," *Crisis* 41 (September 1934): 256–60, 274, in Foner and Lewis, *The Black Worker*, vol. 7, 119–21.

91. Ibid., 120.

92. George Schuyler, "To Boycott—Or Not to Boycott: A Deadly Boomerang," in *Crisis* 41 (September 1934): 256–60, 274, in Foner and Lewis, *The Black Worker*, vol. 7, 121–24.

93. Ibid., 121.

94. Ibid., 122.

95. Moreno, *Direct Action*, 30–65.

96. Ibid.; Mark W. Kruman, "Quotas for Blacks: The Public Works Administration and the Black Construction Worker," *Labor History* 16, no. 1 (winter 1975): 37–51; and Clarence R. Johnson, "Negro Labor in Public Housing," *Crisis* 48, no. 2 (February 1941): 44–45. Moreno sees these examples as aberrations in the "color-blind" Depression-era civil rights movement that set a precedent that was later adopted by the 1960s civil rights movement. But contrary to what Moreno suggests, no such thing as a "color-blind" civil rights movement ever existed. There was in both eras an *antiwhite supremacist* movement that was mainly led by middle-class African Americans trying to stay ahead of insurgent black workers, both mollify and modify recalcitrant white labor, and maintain a moral and egalitarian high ground against opponents who claimed the same with their "neutral" seniority system. See Manning Marable, "Staying on the Path to Racial Equality," in *The*

Affirmative Action Debate, ed. George E. Curry (Reading, MA: Addison-Wesley, 1996), 5–6, where he notes how the stated "color-blind" goals of civil rights leaders like Walter White, Roy Wilkens, Bayard Rustin, and Kenneth G. Clark confused inclusion with pluralism and culture with race.

97. Mark Solomon, *The Cry Was Unity: Communists and African Americans, 1917–1936* (Jackson: University Press of Mississippi, 1998), xix.

98. Ibid., 152. Solomon also notes how a CP-led coalition induced the WPA to adopt "a policy of inclusive hiring and promotion on public works projects." Ibid., 274.

99. Moreno, *Direct Action*, 30–65. See also Ibid., 57, where Weaver justified black proportionalism in 1936: "It was humanly impossible to define discrimination in a situation where a borrower, a contractor, and a labor union were involved." Mary McLeod Bethune, who also supported black quotas in her agency, was Director of Negro Affairs of the NYA and part of President Roosevelt's "Black Cabinet." See Weiss, *Farewell*, 136–56.

100. Hill, *Black Labor*, 96.

101. Du Bois, *Against Racism*, 134. Hugh S. Johnson was director of the NRA.

102. Randolph resigned from the NNLC in 1940 because of what he considered heavy Communist influence. See Harris, *The Harder We Run*, 112, 116.

103. Anderson, *Randolph*, 251.

104. Ibid., 257. This is based on Randolph's and others' account of the exchange, including NAACP executive secretary Walter White.

105. Ibid.

106. Franklin and Moss, *From Slavery to Freedom*, 533.

107. Specifically, that would take the form of a 22 March 1948 confrontation with President Harry S. Truman. Truman's Executive Order 9981 of 26 July 1948 banning segregation in the military was the result of that confrontation and stemmed from Randolph's threat in early April that he would encourage black and white youths to resist the draft until segregation was abolished. See Anderson, *Randolph*, 276–80.

108. Hill, *Black Labor*, 376; and Harris, *The Harder We Run*, 116.

109. Harris, *The Harder We Run*, 117.

110. Manning Marable, "Staying on the Path to Racial Equality," 4. But in her essay "Affirmative Action: Why We Need It, Why It Is Under Attack," Mary Frances Berry disagrees (in Curry, *Debate*). Writing on the FEPC, Berry says that "little progress resulted for African-Americans. The federal compliance programs were routinely understaffed and underfunded, and they lacked enforcement authority. The ten million workers on the payrolls of the one hundred largest defense contractors included few blacks in 1960." Ibid., 301.

111. Hugh Davis Graham, *The Civil Rights Era: Origins and Development of National Policy 1960–1972* (New York: Oxford University Press, 1990), 134. State FEPCs survived the New Deal in about half the country—mostly the North—as late as 1963.

112. Garfinkel, *When Negroes March*, 154–62; and Graham, *The Civil Rights Era*, 12: the FEPC track record was about a third of 14,000 complaints resolved, though only about a fifth of the complaints in the South were resolved. See Hill, *Black Labor*, 377, for this excerpt from the FEPC final report of June 28, 1946: "The minority groups most frequently subjected to discrimination during the war, as recorded by charges filed with the FEPC, were Negroes, Jews, Mexican-Americans, and a scattering of religious creeds, as well as Nisei, aliens and citizens of recent origin. . . . Negroes, comprising the largest group, filed 80 percent of FEPC complaints. . . . However, the seniority of colored workers is less than that of white workers in those industries which have continued into the postwar

period because Negro workers entered war production very late. . . . They were unable, because of racial barriers, to transfer to other employment. And their low seniority, in those industries in which they are still employed, subjects them to the risk of further displacement by returning veterans. . . ."

113. Louis Ruchames, *Race, Jobs, and Politics: The Story of the FEPC* (New York: Columbia University Press, 1953), 156–57.

114. Louis C. Kesselman, "The Fair Employment Practice Commission Movement in Perspective," *Journal of Negro History* 31, no. 1 (January, 1941): 35–36.

115. Harris, *The Harder We Run*, 118. See also Kesselman, "The Fair Employment Practice Commission," 30–46.

116. Robin D. G. Kelley, *Race Rebels: Culture, Politics, and the Black Working Class* (New York: Free Press, 1994), 184.

117. Reprinted from *Survey Graphic* 31 (November 1942): 488–89, in Foner and Lewis, *The Black Worker*, vol. 7, 252.

118. A. Philip Randolph, "Why Should We March?" in *A Documentary History of the Negro People in the United States 1933–1945*, ed. Herbert Aptheker (Secaucus, NJ: Citadel, 1974), 418–21.

119. Steven F. Lawson, *Running for Freedom: Civil Rights and Black Politics in America since 1941* (New York: McGraw-Hill, 1991), 5, 11–12; Hill, *Black Labor*; and Foner and Lewis, *The Black Worker*, vol. 7.

120. Lawson, *Running for Freedom*, 1–30.

121. See, for example, C .L. R. James et al., eds., *Fighting Racism in World War II* (New York: Monad Press, 1980).

122. Robert E. Desroches, " 'Not Fade Away': The Narrative of Venture Smith, an African American in the Early Republic," *Journal of American History* 84, no. 1 (June 1997): 40–66.

123. See Foner and Lewis, *The Black Worker*, vol. 7, 239–50. With seven of every ten black women workers in service work (mostly domestic), their labor helped facilitate white women's entrance to the factory. But between 1940 and 1944, black women left farm labor—from 16 percent to 8 percent—and entered blue and white collar jobs (from 1.5 million in 1940 to 2.1 million in 1944). In metal, chemical, and rubber factories their numbers rose from 3,000 to 150,000 over this same period. See also Sherna Berger Gluck, *Rosie the Riveter Revisited: Women, the War, and Social Change* (Boston: Twayne, 1987), 24: "The expansion of jobs in the defense industries, coupled with Roosevelt's executive order prohibiting discrimination in hiring, helped black women get out of white women's kitchens. In Los Angeles, for instance, in 1940, over 55 percent of nonwhite women workers were in private household service. Ten years later, this figure was down 15 percent."

124. Weaver, *Negro Labor*, 18. See Franklin and Moss, *From Slavery to Freedom*, 442, where they note that Weaver was named head of the Housing and Home Finance Agency by President John F. Kennedy in 1961, and after the agency was elevated to Cabinet rank in 1965, he was appointed by President Lyndon B. Johnson as secretary of the new Department of Housing and Urban Development (HUD), making him the first African American to hold a Cabinet office.

125. Steele, " 'No Racials,' " 77–78.

126. Real income grew 50 percent during the war, and from 1930 to 1945 organized labor grew from 3 million to 15 million members thanks in large part to the Wagner Act. See William H. Chafe, "America since 1945," in *The New American History*, ed. Eric Foner (Philadelphia: Temple University Press, 1990), 145.

127. See supra note 15. The 1947 Taft-Hartley Act in addition to enlarging the NLRB also (1)

mandated that unions and employers must inform the other party and a government mediation service before terminating a collective-bargaining agreement, (2) denied protection to workers on wildcat strikes, (3) provided the government with the power to invoke an eighty-day injunction against any strike that was deemed a peril to national health or safety, and (4) required any union wishing to avail itself of the NLRB facilities to file reports and affidavits with the U.S. Department of Labor certifying that its officers were not Communists.

Chapter 5

1. See William L. Patterson, ed., *We Charge Genocide: The Historic Petition to the United Nations for Relief from a Crime of the United States Government against the Negro People* (New York: International Publishers, 1970; 1951); and Charles Abrams, *Forbidden Neighbors: A Study of Prejudice in Housing* (New York: Harper, 1955). See also Howard Zinn, *A People's History of the United States* (New York: Harper, 1990; 1980), 416–34.

2. See Philip S. Foner and Ronald L. Lewis, eds., *The Black Worker: A Documentary History from Colonial Times to the Present,* vol. 7, *The Black Worker from the Founding of the CIO to the AFL–CIO Merger, 1936–1955* (Philadelphia: Temple University Press, 1983); and Sanford Wexler, *The Civil Rights Movement: An Eyewitness History* (New York: Facts on File, 1993).

3. See Patterson, *We Charge Genocide.*

4. Derrick A. Bell Jr., *Race, Racism, and American Law,* 2nd ed. (Boston: Little, Brown, 1980), 364–473.

5. See Andrew Wiese, "The Other Suburbanites: African American Suburbanization in the North before 1950," *Journal of American History* 85, no. 4 (March 1999): 1495–524.

6. See Richard Sennett and Jonathon Cobb, *The Hidden Injuries of Class* (New York: Vintage, 1973), 48.

7. See Douglas S. Massey and Nancy A. Denton, *American Apartheid: Segregation and the Making of the Underclass* (Cambridge: Harvard University Press, 1993), chapter 2; Abrams, *Forbidden Neighbors;* and Kenneth T. Jackson, *Crabgrass Frontier: The Suburbanization of the United States* (New York: Oxford University Press, 1985); as well as the discussion in chapter 1 of this book.

8. See Keith W. Olson, *The GI Bill, the Veterans, and the Colleges* (Lexington: University of Kentucky Press, 1974); and Davis R. B. Ross, *Preparing for Ulysses: Politics and Veterans during World War II* (New York: Columbia University Press, 1969).

9. Theodore Spaulding, "Philadelphia Hate Strike," *Crisis* 51, no. 9 (September 1944): 281.

10. Foner and Lewis, *The Black Worker,* vol. 7, 265–301.

11. Ross, *Preparing for Ulysses,* 34–35.

12. Olson, *The G.I. Bill,* 20.

13. Ibid., 21.

14. Hilary Herbold, "Never a Level Playing Field: Blacks and the GI Bill," *Journal of Blacks in Higher Education* 5 (winter 1994/95): 104. See also Harold M. Hyman, *American Singularity: The 1787 Northwest Ordinance, the 1862 Homestead and Morrill Acts, and the 1944 G.I. Bill* (Athens: University of Georgia Press, 1986), 71; and *Servicemen's Readjustment Act of 1944, Statutes at Large* 58 (1944), 284–94.

15. Ross, *Preparing for Ulysses,* 277–87.

16. See *Servicemen's Readjustment Act of 1944,* 58 (1944), 284–301; and *Veterans' Preference Act of 1944, Statutes at Large* 58 (1944), 387–91.

17. Ross, *Preparing for Ulysses,* 150–57; See Congress, Senate, Committee on Military Affairs,

Notes to pages 118–20

Superseniority Rights of Veterans: Hearing before a Subcommittee of the Committee on Military Affairs, 79th Cong., 2nd sess., 12 July 1946, for manufacturers' support for "superseniority," a discussion of *Fishgold's* unanswered questions, and ambivalent opposition by labor representatives (they opposed the policy but carefully supported many of its features). See also Robert C. Weaver, *Negro Labor: A National Problem* (New York: Harcourt, 1946), 282–88, where he points out organized labor's quandary but actual support for (white) veterans' preferences that contradicted the seniority system's avowed "impartiality."

18. Weaver, *Negro Labor*, 287.

19. *Superseniority Rights of Veterans*, 29.

20. Herbold, "Never a Level Playing Field," 105. See also *Servicemen's Readjustment Act of 1944*; Hyman, *American Singularity*; and John David Skrentny, *The Ironies of Affirmative Action: Politics, Culture, and Justice in America* (Chicago: University of Chicago Press, 1996). Note also electronic communication, 8 April 1999, from Carlos M. Rubio, an army veteran and my father, on the "52–20 Club." The popular term referred to all veterans eligible to collect the weekly "readjustment allowance of $20 (a not insignificant amount in 1946) for fifty-two weeks upon presenting a check-off card. To receive the allowance veterans were expected to demonstrate that they had not worked the previous week and also that they had sought work and would continue to do so. It was administered by state branches of the United States Employment Service and could be collected in any state by a veteran from any other state. See also Timothy B. Tyson, *Radio Free Dixie: Robert F. Williams and the Roots of Black Power* (Chapel Hill: University of North Carolina Press, 1999), 54–55, for a recollection by Robert F. Williams (who would go on to become a prominent civil rights and Black Power leader) of the resentment and harassment black workers faced at the hands of white employees at the employment office in his hometown of Monroe, North Carolina—including demands that they accept work for less than $20 a week. This pattern was repeated throughout the South and elsewhere in the United States. See also August Meier and John Bracey Jr., eds., *Papers of the NAACP, Part 9, Discrimination in the United States Armed Forces 1918–1955, Series C, Veterans Affairs Committee, 1940–1950* (Bethesda, MD: University Publications of America, 1989) reels 6, 7, 8, 12.

21. Herbert Hill, *Black Labor and the American Legal System: Race, Work, and the Law* (Madison: University of Wisconsin Press, 1985; 1977), 378. Most veterans and three-fourths of black veterans wanted new jobs, says Hill, citing the 1946 *Final Report of the FEPC*.

22. Ronald Roach, "From Combat to Campus: GI Bill Gave a Generation of African Americans an Opportunity to Pursue the American Dream," *Black Issues in Higher Education* 14, no. 13 (21 August 1998): 26–27.

23. Ibid., 27.

24. Stephanie Coontz, *The Way We Never Were: American Families and the Nostalgia Trap* (New York: Basic Books, 1992), 161.

25. Syracuse University Archives and Records Management, "Remembering the GI Bulge: The Servicemen's Readjustment Act of 1944," [online document] available at http://sumweb.syr.edu/archives/giserve.htm, Internet.

26. Hyman, *American Singularity*, 71.

27. Herbold, "Never a Level Playing Field," 104–8.

28. John Hope Franklin and Alfred A. Moss Jr., *From Slavery to Freedom: A History of Negro Americans*, 6th ed. (New York: McGraw-Hill, 1988; 1947), 412.

29. *Pittsburgh Courier* (Pittsburgh: Pittsburgh Courier Publishing, 1910–1950), microfilm, 1946, reel 35. Perkins Library Collection, Duke University. This nationally recognized black newspaper also carried articles that year on the campaign for a black officer to be appointed to deal with racial

discrimination in benefits administration. See also Meier and Bracey, *Papers of the NAACP, Veterans Affairs Committee*, reel 7.

30. Steven F. Lawson, *Running for Freedom: Civil Rights and Black Politics in America since 1941* (New York: McGraw-Hill, 1991), 34–39. See also William C. Berman, *The Politics of Civil Rights in the Truman Administration* (Columbus: Ohio State University Press, 1970).

31. Massey and Denton, *American Apartheid*, 44. Massey and Denton statistically track the process of the suburb/city white/black color line: for example, between 1930 and 1970 "the average level of black spatial isolation" went from 32 percent to nearly 74 percent in Northern cities and about the same in the South. Ibid., 48.

32. Abrams, *Forbidden Neighbors*, 140.

33. *Miracle on 34th Street*, prod. by William Perlberg, dir. by George Seaton, 1 hour 37 min., Twentieth Century–Fox, 1947. The previous year, Frank Capra's Christmas classic *It's a Wonderful Life* featured the now-archetypal George Bailey (Jimmy Stewart) taking over the family-owned "Building and Loan," an upstart savings and loan corporation that functions more as a home-buying cooperative with the slogan "Own Your Own Home." The B&L's nemesis is local banker/developer/ slumlord Henry Potter (Lionel Barrymore). The triumphant conclusion shows all the B&L's working-class investors repaying Stewart and honoring his personal sacrifice. African Americans are also practically invisible in this film, but two black women and a black man appear in this final scene (one being the elder Baileys' maid), possibly as investors—although no blacks appeared in the "bank run" scene earlier in the film. The inaugural residents of Bailey's new working-class subdivision are "the Martini family"—with heavy Italian accents to emphasize ethnic background, recent immigration, and a contrast marking their road from discrimination to assimilation. *It's a Wonderful Life*, prod. and dir., Frank Capra, 2 hours 9 minutes, RKO Radio, 1946.

34. Abrams, *Forbidden Neighbors*, 146. This particular reference from the September 1950 issue of *House Beautiful* actually frames the "American house of today" as the product of the "aspirations and ideals [of] . . . 1776."

35. Hoover quoted in Ibid., 147. Originally cited in Nelson L. North, *Real Estate Selling and Leasing* (New York: Prentice-Hall, 1938), 139. Italics added. If "race" were not such a loaded term in United States history and especially during this period, we could give Hoover the benefit of the doubt and suppose that he possibly meant the entire human race or even some kind of multicultural united American *raza*.

36. Coontz, *Never Were*, 77. Italics added.

37. U.S. President's Committee on Civil Rights, *To Secure These Rights: The Report of the President's Committee on Civil Rights* (New York: Simon and Schuster, 1947), 68. This committee listed specific measures for the government to help eliminate segregation in all aspects of social life.

38. Lawson, *Running for Freedom*, 20–30; Roach, "From Combat to Campus," 26–28. Famous African Americans who were GI Bill beneficiaries include Robert L. Carter, Jackie Robinson, and Harry Belafonte.

39. The latter phrase and many like it were actually used in the 1935 FHA manual, quoted in Abrams, *Forbidden Neighbors*, 230, while "homogeneous" (see, for example, Ibid., 143) became a twentieth-century euphemism for "white," especially White Anglo-Saxon Protestant (or WASP).

40. Massey and Denton, *American Apartheid*, 53. A 1942 poll found 84 percent of white American respondents agreeing that "there should be separate sections in towns and cities for Negroes to live in" (Ibid., 49).

41. "Across the country, smug white communities show a poverty of awareness, a poverty of

humanity, indeed, a poverty of ability to act in a civilized manner toward non-Anglo human beings. The white middle-class suburbs need 'freedom schools' as badly as the black communities. Anglo-conformity is a dead weight on their necks too. All this is an educative role crying to be performed by those whites so inclined." Stokely Carmichael (Kwame Ture) and Charles V. Hamilton, *Black Power: The Politics of Liberation in America* (New York: Vintage, 1967), 82.

42. Abrams, *Forbidden Neighbors*, 102, 172, 182. Fairless Hills was another all-white subdivision near Levittown and was actually financed by the U.S. Steel Corporation. For "Little Boxes" recording ("Little boxes / on the hillside / little boxes / made of ticky-tacky. . . ."), see folksinger/activist Pete Seeger, *Pete Seeger's Greatest Hits*, Columbia, ca. 1970, LP. Seeger's liner notes read: "California songwriter Malvina Reynolds was driving through suburbs of San Francisco on the way to a booking, when she saw the endless rows of identical houses 'Take the wheel, Bud,' she said to her husband, 'I feel a song coming on.' When they arrived where she was supposed to sing, she performed *Little Boxes*."

43. See also Iver Bernstein, *The New York City Draft Riots: Their Significance for American Society and Politics in the Age of the Civil War* (New York: Oxford University Press, 1990); Abrams, *Forbidden Neighbors*, 91–136; and Glenn T. Eskew, " 'Bombingham': Black Protest in Postwar Birmingham, Alabama," *American Historical Review* 102, no. 2 (April 1997): 371–90.

44. Abrams, *Forbidden Neighbors*, 236. Italics added. See also Jean Reynolds, "South of White Phoenix," *New Abolitionist* 2, no. 5 (September–October 1999): 4–5, which traces that metropolitan area's segregated neighborhoods to HOLC and FHA defining "South Phoenix" as "not a fixed geographical area" south of the Salt River but representing a line that "Negroes" and "Latin Americans" could not cross. Houses north of Van Buren Street were reserved for those who could finance these "better" homes on the basis of a down payment and white skin.

45. August Meier Jr. and John Bracey, eds., *Papers of the NAACP, Part 1, Supplement, 1951–1955* (Frederick, MD: University Publications of America, 1987), microfilm, reel 8. Perkins Library Collection, Duke University.

46. Abrams, *Forbidden Neighbors*, 217–43. The racial covenant has its roots in early neighborhood attempts to exclude businesses deemed noxious (like brothels and glue factories) before the advent of zoning laws, according to Abrams. They were first invoked against people in the late nineteenth century with the West Coast influx of Chinese workers. Homeowners and home builders enjoyed legal protection from 1918 on for these devices, which reserved most vacant land in some cities (80 percent in Chicago and Los Angeles, for example). Over 7 million homes were built in the 1920s, but only a small fraction were for blacks. Of the 9 million new homes built between 1935 and 1950, less than 1 percent were available to blacks. By 1952 only some 50,000 units out of almost 3 million FHA–insured houses were available to those not considered white.

47. Ibid., 220. Abrams here points out: "Intervention was prompted by a freshened national sensitiveness to racial oppression in Germany and by the responsibilities assumed by the nation under the United Nations Charter and the Report of the President's Committee on Civil Rights."

48. Ibid., 224–43. The FHA ruled in 1949 that it would no longer insure mortgages on properties having covenants placed on them after February 1950 but would insure those that did have them before that date. However, building, realty, and neighborhood groups found ways to exploit "the part of the [1948 Supreme Court] decision which held restrictions valid between parties." Ibid., 224.

49. Robert Frederick Burk, *The Eisenhower Administration and Black Civil Rights* (Knoxville: University of Tennessee Press, 1984), 117. *Shelley v. Kraemer* 334 U.S. 1 (1948), in contrast to today's

Supreme Court rulings, explicitly pointed to the Fourteenth Amendment as having been enacted to protect black civil rights. .

50. Burk, *The Eisenhower Administration*, 101. The CGCC was also a product of pressure from black civil rights and labor groups. It "urged the Bureau of Employment Security to 'act positively and affirmatively to implement the policy of nondiscrimination in its functions of placement counseling, occupational analysis and industrial services, labor market information, and community participation in employment services.' " See Manning Marable, "Staying on the Path to Racial Equality," in *The Affirmative Action Debate*, ed. George E. Curry (Reading, MA: Addison-Wesley, 1996), 4–5.

51. Massey and Denton, *American Apartheid*, 5. The refugee image and terminology are still commonly invoked today, sometimes conflated with "natural" disasters. See, for example, Laurent Belsie, "Immigrant Flood Chases City Dwellers to White Enclaves," *Washington Times*, 7–13 June 1999, 1, reprinted from *Christian Science Monitor*.

52. Abrams, *Forbidden Neighbors*, 150–90.

53. Lawson, *Running for Freedom*, 20–30; and *Pittsburgh Courier*, microfilm, 1946. See supra note 29.

54. See Nicholas Lemann, *The Promised Land: The Great Black Migration and How It Changed America* (New York: Knopf, 1991).

55. Lawson, *Running for Freedom*, 20–30.

56. Testifying before the House Committee on Foreign Affairs in 1949, W. E. B. Du Bois declared: "We invent witch hunts. If in 1850 an American disliked slavery, the word of exorcism was 'abolitionist.' He was a 'nigger lover.' He believed in free love and murder of kind slave masters. He ought to be lynched and mobbed. Today the word is 'Communist.' Never mind its meaning in a man's mind." See W. E. B. Du Bois, *W. E. B. Du Bois: A Reader*, ed. David Levering Lewis (New York: Henry Holt, 1995), 759.

57. Meier and Bracey, *Papers of the NAACP, Part 1, Supplement*, microfilm, 1951–1955, reel 8. See supra note 45.

58. Pauli Murray, *Proud Shoes: The Story of an American Family* (New York: Harper and Row 1984; 1956), vii–viii.

59. E. Franklin Frazier, *Black Bourgeoisie: The Rise of a New Middle Class in the United States* (London: Collier, 1969; 1957), 90–91; and Robert L. Allen, *Reluctant Reformers: Racism and Social Reform Movements in the United States* (Washington, D.C.: Howard University Press, 1983), 207–45.

60. Meier and Bracey, *Papers of the NAACP, Part 1, Supplement*, microfilm, 1951–1955, reel 8. Italics added. This is also yet another example that counters the mythology of "affirmative action" being a civil rights expression invented by President John F. Kennedy in 1961.

61. Foner and Lewis, *The Black Worker*, vol. 7, 566. Tavenner was committee counsel. Coleman Young invoked the Fifth Amendment in response to committee questions of his involvement with "communist organizations."

62. Aldon D. Morris, *The Origins of the Civil Rights Movement: Black Communities Organizing for Change* (New York: Free Press, 1984), 30–35.

63. Samuel A. Stouffer, *Communism, Conformity, and Civil Liberties: A Cross-Section of the Nation Speaks Its Mind* (New York: Doubleday, 1953), 230–31.

64. Foner and Lewis, *The Black Worker*, vol. 7, 164.

65. Mark Ellis, "J. Edgar Hoover and the 'Red Summer' of 1919," *Journal of American Studies* 28, no. 1 (April 1994): 39–59.

66. See Athan G. Theoharis and John Stuart Cox, *The Boss: J. Edgar Hoover and the Great American Inquisition* (Philadelphia: Temple University Press, 1988), 10–11 n; and Kenneth O'Reilly, "*Racial*

Matters": *The FBI's Secret File on Black America 1960—1972* (New York: Free Press, 1989), for a full look at Hoover's sympathy for segregation, opposition to hiring black agents and police officers, and surveillance of civil rights groups, including Rosa Parks's Montgomery Improvement Association in 1956. Hoover also harassed black activist-artist Paul Robeson (see Lewis, *Du Bois*, 798—800).

67. Stouffer, *Civil Liberties*, 172—78. This is even taking into consideration the less sophisticated early polling techniques than those of today.

68. Weaver, *Negro Labor*, ix.

69. Berman, *The Politics of Civil Rights*, 97—99.

70. Zinn, *People's History*, 419—30; Stouffer, *Civil Liberties*, 174; and Anna Hass Morgan, former Communist Party activist and my paternal grandmother, unpublished first draft autobiography, 1990, 567—625.

71. See, for example, the decision by the NAACP board to fire Du Bois in 1947 after Arthur Schlesinger Jr. wrote in *Life* magazine that the NAACP had been infiltrated by Communists. Lewis in *Du Bois*, 9.

72. Manning Marable, *Black American Politics: From Washington Marches to Jesse Jackson* (London: Verso, 1985), 99. Marable also notes that the NAACP brief saw all racial distinction as "a badge of inferiority," and with *Brown* black civil rights leaders became more tied to the "color-blind" strategy. Testifying in 1963 before Congress on the Civil Rights Bill, NAACP President Roy Wilkins attacked employment quotas as "evil."

73. See *Brown v. Board of Education*, 347 U.S. 483 (1954).

74. See, for example, Todd S. Welch, "The Supreme Court Ruled Correctly in *Adarand*," in Curry, *Debate*, 157—64; and Harlan in *Civil Rights Cases*, 109 U.S. 3 (1883).

75. J. Harvie Wilkinson III, *From Brown to Bakke: The Supreme Court and School Integration: 1954—1978* (Oxford: Oxford University Press, 1979), 95—127. See also Wexler, *Civil Rights Movement*, 33—35.

76. See, for example, Richard O. Boyer and Herbert M. Morais, *Labor's Untold Story* (New York: UE, 1972; 1955), 370; and Thomas R. Brooks, *Toil and Trouble: A History of American Labor*, 2nd ed. (New York: Dell, 1971; 1964), 230.

77. Foner and Lewis, *The Black Worker*, vol. 7, 613—14. In the following years AFL—CIO unions had to be sued many times for discriminating against black workers, who felt compelled in 1959 to organize the Negro American Labor Council (NALC)—a black labor advocacy organization led by A. Philip Randolph; William H. Harris, *The Harder We Run: Black Workers since the Civil War* (New York: Oxford University Press, 1982), 140—41. See also Hill, *Black Labor*.

78. Herbert Hill, "The Racial Practices of Organized Labor: The Contemporary Record," in *The Negro and the American Labor Movement*, ed. Julius Jacobson (Garden City, NY: Anchor, 1968), 287.

79. Harris, *The Harder We Run*, 138. Curiously, the CIO allowed one leftist labor union to stay: the United Packinghouse Workers union, which became a positive model for "race relations" studies and affirmative action policies in trade unions.

80. Morgan, Unpublished autobiography, 585—92.

81. Ibid., 585. Besides suffering police harassment as retribution for her strike support, Morgan believed that that support was the reason that she was called before the Ohio General Assembly's Un-American Activities Commission in 1952. (Telephone conversation with author, 11 September 1994.) Morgan was found guilty of contempt for refusing to answer their questions—a conviction that was later overturned in 1959 by the United States Supreme Court. See *Raley v. State of Ohio*, 360 U.S. 423 (1959); and Nora Sayre, *Previous Convictions: A Journey through the 1950s* (New Brunswick, NJ: Rutgers University Press, 1995), 400—5. Anna later moved with her second husband, Richard

M. Morgan (a noted anthropologist and archaeologist, himself fired from his job as museum curator at Ohio State University on trumped-up charges that Anna believed had to do with his civil rights activities) to Chicago's diverse southside Hyde Park neighborhood. This neighborhood (see Abrams, *Forbidden Neighbors*, 182) had seen numerous house bombings attributed to the Hyde Park Property Owners Association immediately following World War I. I remember visiting their home on South Greenwood Avenue in the 1960s—just a few doors down from a Nation of Islam mosque.

82. Robin D. G. Kelley, *Hammer and Hoe: Alabama Communists during the Great Depression* (Chapel Hill: University of North Carolina Press, 1990), 118–19, 148, 227–28. See also Mark Solomon, *The Cry Was Unity: Communists and African Americans, 1917–1936* (Jackson: University Press of Mississippi, 1998), 255: "Social consciousness and a social agenda were hallmarks of the Mine, Mill and Smelter Workers, which defined its role in far broader terms than wages and hours. The union became a civil rights movement, embracing the struggle for black and (in the Southwest) Mexican-American equality."

83. Kelley, *Hammer and Hoe*, 112–13, 134–37; "The NAACP and the Communists," Editorial, *Crisis* 56, no. 3 (March 1949): 72; Herbert Hill, "Communist Party—Enemy of Negro Equality," *Crisis* 58, no. 6 (June–July 1951): 365–71; Walter White, "The Negro and the Communists," *Crisis* 57, no. 8 (August–September 1950): 502–6. The issues provoking such distrust and disillusionment included the change in the Comintern (Communist International) line that dogmatically called for an independent black nation in the South.

84. See, for example, *Pittsburgh Courier*, microfilm, for a 22 June 1946 article on a threatened work stoppage by AFL Construction, Maintenance, and General Laborers Union on a Davis Dam project on the Colorado River in Phoenix, Arizona, against race bias in hiring: "Warns Contractors for $77,000,000 Project to End Discrimination." See also John Egerton, *Speak Now against the Day: The Generation Before the Civil Rights Movement in the South* (New York: Knopf, 1994); and William H. Chafe, *Civilities and Civil Rights: Greensboro, North Carolina and the Black Struggle for Freedom* (New York: Oxford University Press, 1980).

85. Paul D. Moreno, *From Direct Action to Affirmative Action: Fair Employment Policy in America, 1933–1972* (Baton Rouge: Louisiana State University Press, 1997), 82.

86. David Montgomery, *Workers' Control in America: Studies in the History of Work, Technology, and Labor Struggles* (Cambridge: Cambridge University Press, 1986; 1979), 142–52.

87. Ibid., 142. See chapter 6 of this book,,notes 30–31.

88. Hill, *Black Labor*, 127.

89. *Pittsburgh Courier*, 22 June 1946, 1, microfilm. Three months later, at their national convention, the National Association of Letter Carriers (NALC) rejected resolutions that supported the maintenance of the FEPC and opposed lynching. See *Pittsburgh Courier* 14 September 1946: 5, "Letter Carriers Reject Resolution for FEPC: Liberals Out-Voted," microfilm.

90. *Pittsburgh Courier*, 4 April 1947, 5, "Tunstall Case Retrial: Seeks Job Protection from Rail Brotherhood," microfilm. See also Hill, *Black Labor*, 112–13, for an analysis of the United States Supreme Court 1949 decision *Graham v. Brotherhood of Locomotive Firemen and Enginemen* and the 1952 *Brotherhood of Railroad Trainmen v. Howard* as reaffirming and broadening their 1944 *Steele* decision. *Steele* had outlawed the "50% Negro quota" (see Harris, *The Harder We Run*, 118) and declared that "because the union derived its authority as bargaining agent from a federal statute, and was therefore the beneficiary of a federal grant of power, it could not abuse its position by depriving Negro workers of their rights." Hill, *Black Labor*, 112.

91. Hill, *Black Labor*, 25, 59, 86. The primary purpose of lynchings, as Manning Marable has

pointed out, was to blunt black protest against Jim Crow and check any upward aspirations among African Americans. See Marable, *Black American Politics*, 76–77. H. Leon Prather Sr. has shown in *We Have Taken a City: Wilmington Racial Massacre and Coup of 1898* (Rutherford, NJ: Farleigh Dickinson University Press, 1984) how that white race riot in Wilmington, North Carolina, resulted in massive transfer of jobs and property from blacks to whites.

92. *Hughes v. Superior Court of California*, 339 U.S. 460 (1950).

93. *New Negro Alliance v. Sanitary Grocery Co.*, 303 U.S. 552 (1938).

94. Chafe, *Civilities and Civil Rights*, 45–50, 150–54, 211. For an account of the standard red-baiting of the civil rights movement after the *Brown* decisions by groups like the White Citizens' Council, see Francis M. Wilhoit, *The Politics of Massive Resistance* (New York: G. Baziller, 1973); and Morris, *Origins*, 30–35.

95. See, for example, the oral history of Ella Turner Surry in John Langston Gwaltney, *Drylongso: A Self-Portrait of Black America* (New York: Random House, 1980), 241–42. See also Bernadette Gross, "Tokens and Traitors: On Stigma and Self-Hate," in *We Won't Go Back: Making the Case for Affirmative Action*, ed. Charles R. Lawrence III and Mari J. Matsuda (Boston: Houghton Mifflin, 1997), 132: "It is revealing that Black parents admonish their children to prove their worth by outshining their white peers."

96. Gerald Horne, *Black and Red: W. E. B. Du Bois and the Afro-American Response to the Cold War, 1944–1963* (Albany: State University of New York Press, 1986), 62.

97. *Brown v. Board of Education* [II], 349 U.S. 294 (1955).

98. Lewis M. Steel quoted in Derrick A. Bell Jr., *And We Are Not Saved: The Elusive Quest for Racial Justice* (New York: Basic Books, 1987), 60. The article originally appeared in the *New York Times Magazine* 13 October 1956. In response to Steel's firing, NAACP General Counsel Robert Carter and his entire staff resigned. The NAACP responded to the incident months later by explaining that Steel had been fired not for criticizing the Court but for charging that the NAACP's court victories "have been merely symbolic and not substantive." See Bell's account and NAACP quote in Ibid., 61.

99. Du Bois quoted in Ibid., 62.

100. Ibid.; Robert L. Allen, *Reluctant Reformers: Racism and Social Reform Movements in the United States* (Washington, D.C.: Howard University Press, 1983), 314–15. See also Richard Delgado, *The Coming Race War? And Other Apocalyptic Tales of Affirmative Action and Welfare* (New York: New York University Press, 1996), 56–57, for a summation of Derrick Bell's and Mary Dudziak's research and analysis that included findings of support for the NAACP Legal Defense Fund from the State Department and the U.S. Attorney General.

101. I use the term "historically white institutions" to refer to the white origins, identity, and predominance in those institutions, not to suggest that all of their members where white.

102. For a study of how this process took place in one large Southern city (Charlotte, North Carolina), see Thomas W. Hanchett, *Sorting Out the New South City: Race, Class, and Urban Development in Charlotte, 1875–1975* (Chapel Hill: University of North Carolina Press, 1998).

Chapter 6

1. Aldon D. Morris, *The Origins of the Civil Rights Movement: Black Communities Organizing for Change* (New York: Free Press, 1984); Robin D. G. Kelley, *Race Rebels: Culture, Politics, and the Black Working Class* (New York: Free Press, 1994), 77–100; and Robert L. Allen, *Reluctant Reformers: Racism*

and Social Reform Movements in the United States (Washington, D.C.: Howard University Press, 1981), postscript.

2. Manning Marable, *Race, Reform, and Rebellion: The Second Reconstruction in Black America, 1945–1982* (Jackson: University Press of Mississippi, 1984), 129.

3. Morris, *Origins*, xii, 54–55.

4. Ibid., 1–3. Morris refers to the social, economic, and personal oppression of Jim Crow as "the tripartite system of racial domination" that "protected the privileges of white society and generated tremendous black suffering" (Ibid., 1). Furthermore, black church and community protest helped blur class distinctions within the movement. Morris also makes the point that most black professionals could drive and at least avoid the ritual humiliation of city bus segregation. See also Harvard Sitkoff, *The Struggle for Black Equality 1954–1992*, rev. ed. (New York: Hill and Wang, 1993; 1981), 233. For critical assessments of affirmative action's benefit almost wholly to the black middle-class, see essays by William Bradford Reynolds, Todd Welch, and Glen Loury in *The Affirmative Action Debate*, ed. George E. Curry (Reading, MA: Addison-Wesley, 1996).

5. The predominantly white Students for a Democratic Society (SDS) was inspired by the originally integrated Student Nonviolent Coordinating Committee (SNCC), which in the 1960s asked whites to leave SNCC and concentrate on organizing in white communities against white supremacy (white activists would then split on support for Black Power). See Morris, *Origins*, 221–23; Allen, *Reluctant Reformers*, 317, 328–35; Kirkpatrick Sale, *SDS* (New York: Vintage, 1974); and Stokely Carmichael (Kwame Ture) and Charles V. Hamilton, *Black Power: The Politics of Liberation in America* (New York: Vintage, 1967), chapter 3.

6. Morris, *Origins*, 3.

7. Ibid., 41.

8. See Kelly, *Race Rebels*; Morris, *Origins*; and E. Franklin Frazier, *Black Bourgeoisie: The Rise of a New Middle Class in the United States* (New York: Collier, 1969; 1957).

9. Morris, *Origins*, 3.

10. Ibid., 1: "In a typical Southern city during the 1950s at least 75 percent of black men in the labor force were employed in unskilled jobs. . . . By contrast only about 25 percent of white males were employed in these menial occupations. . . . [A]pproximately 50 percent of black women in the labor force were domestics, while slightly less than 1 percent of white women were employed as domestics. . . . [N]onwhite families earned nationally only 54 percent of the median income of white families."

11. Ibid., 27.

12. See Derrick A. Bell Jr., *Race, Racism, and American Law*, 2nd ed. (Boston: Little, Brown, 1980), 454–55.

13. See John David Skrentny, *The Ironies of Affirmative Action: Politics, Culture, and Justice in America* (Chicago: University of Chicago Press, 1996), 6–7. Skrentny asserts that the "color-blind" model that "preceded" affirmative action was taken for granted by the civil rights movement. Then, in a dramatic shift, somehow movement leaders and government officials (with surprisingly little opposition from the corporate world) launched an aggressive campaign by government as well as private corporations to remove barriers to employment and enrollment of African Americans following the urban rebellions of the 1960s, after which the Kerner Commission report played a large role in a shift in government policy. Skrentny's pragmatic model sounds more benign than Paul Moreno's opportunist civil rights movement model (see infra note 14). Both, however, miss the mark given the evidence of affirmative action's historical roots. See also Robert J. Weiss, *"We Want Jobs": A*

History of Affirmative Action (New York: Garland, 1997), on the origins of affirmative action in post–World War II black protest against job discrimination.

14. Skrentny, The Ironies of Affirmative Action, 6–7, 28–33, 72–127. See also Paul D. Moreno, From Direct Action to Affirmative Action: Fair Employment Law and Policy in America, 1933–1972 (Baton Rouge: Louisiana State University, 1997).

15. Hugh Davis Graham, The Civil Rights Era: Origins and Development of National Policy, 1960–1972 (New York: Oxford University Press, 1990), 197–201. That particular euphemism came from California FEPC panelist Charles Wilson during a hearing on Bank of America hiring negotiations (Ibid., 197–98). In 1964, the Illinois FEPC's ordering of Motorola to hire a black worker who had failed a company test became a "quota" issue during the Civil Rights Bill debate (Ibid., 149–50). In 1965, racial record-keeping was reintroduced into federal records for the first time in ten years—although this time it would be designated by the applicants themselves. Ibid., 199–201.

16. Ibid., 100–21; and Morris, Origins. From 1960 to 1962 some four hundred black ministers in Philadelphia initiated boycotts against firms like Pepsi, Esso, Gulf, and Sun Oil that resulted in hiring goals. The tactic was copied in Boston, Detroit, and New York, where in 1963 Sealtest Milk "pledged to give Negroes and Puerto Ricans 'exclusive exposure' for at least a week when hiring their next fifty employees." Gordon Carey, CORE national program director, explained to the Denver chapter in 1963 how their "line" had changed from "merit employment" to " 'compensatory' hiring" because "employers . . . have a responsibility and obligation to make up for past [exclusionary] sins" (Graham, The Civil Rights Era, 105). See also Carmichael and Hamilton, Black Power, especially the suggestion for "new forms of political representation" as an antidote to Southern white voting district gerrymandering practices (176).

17. Graham, The Civil Rights Era, 111–13.

18. Marable, Race, Reform, and Rebellion, 59–60; and Robert L. Allen, "Past Due: The African American Quest for Reparations," Black Scholar 28, no. 2 (summer 1998): 2–17. Allen includes in his history of reparations demands Sojourner Truth's post–Civil War petition campaign for free public lands for former slaves, Callie House's lawsuits and petitions to Congress in the 1890s for reparations, as well as public demands by Bishop Henry McNeal Turner and Marcus Garvey for payment due to both slave descendants and Africa itself.

19. Taken from King's famous "I Have a Dream" speech at the 28 August 1963 March on Washington. See Martin Luther King Jr., A Testament of Hope: The Essential Writings of Martin Luther King, Jr., ed. James Melvin Washington (San Francisco: Harper and Row, 1986), 217–20.

20. Original 1966 Black Panther Party program reprinted in Mitchell Goodman, ed., The Movement toward a New America: The Beginnings of a Long Revolution (Philadelphia: Pilgrim Press, 1970), 211.

21. Reprinted in E. Franklin Frazier and C. Eric Lincoln, The Black Church since Frazier (New York: Schocken Books, 1974), 179–90.

22. See Boris I. Bittker, The Case for Black Reparations (New York: Random House, 1973), 79–80.

23. See Report of the National Advisory Commission on Civil Disorders (New York: Bantam, 1968); the commission is also known as the Kerner Commission.

24. Eyes on the Prize, prod. and dir. Henry Hampton. 6 hours. Blackside, Alexandria, VA, 1986. See also Howell Raines, My Soul is Rested: Movement Days in the Deep South Remembered (New York: G. P. Putnam's Sons, 1977), 40–51.

25. Herbert Shapiro, White Violence and Black Response: From Reconstruction to Montgomery (Amherst: University of Massachusetts Press, 1988), 434.

26. Mary Fair Burks, "Trailblazers: Women in the Montgomery Bus Boycott" in Black Women in

United States History, series ed. Darlene Clark Hine, vol. 16, *Women in the Civil Rights Movement: Trailblazers and Torchbearers, 1941–1965*, ed. Vicki L. Crawford, Jacqueline Anne Rouse, and Barbara Woods (Brooklyn: Carlson, 1990), 83.

27. Taylor Branch, *Parting the Waters: America in the King Years 1954–63* (New York: Touchstone, 1988), 144–47. King later amended this demand for black bus drivers for routes in black neighborhoods to a request that "the company accept applications from qualified Negroes, with the intention of hiring them when job positions became available." His widow, Coretta Scott King, later said that those initial tentative steps changed to a full frontal assault on segregation when their demands were rejected. See *Eyes on the Prize*.

28. Branch, *Parting the Waters*, 144–47.

29. Marable, *Race, Reform and Rebellion*, 42. The *Brown* decision itself was conceived in large part as a result of some of the justices having been influenced by the works of black sociologists about the negative effects of segregation on black schoolchildren.

30. Rosa Parks interview by Gloster Current, NAACP Director of Branches, 31 July 1963, in August Meier and John H. Bracey Jr., eds., *Papers of the NAACP, Part 21: NAACP Relations with the Modern Civil Rights Movement* (Bethesda, MD: University Publications of America, 1994), microfilm, reel 20. Perkins Library Collection, Duke University.

31. Philip S. Foner, Ronald L. Lewis, and Robert Cvornyek, eds., *The Black Worker: A Documentary History from Colonial Times to the Present*, vol. 8, *The Black Worker since the AFL–CIO Merger, 1955–1980* (Philadelphia: Temple University Press, 1994), 326.

32. Ibid., 328–29.

33. King, *A Testament of Hope*, 367. Similar arguments were made in a speech given by National Urban League president Whitney M. Young Jr. to the Third Annual Convention of the Negro American Labor Council, 9 November 1962, reprinted in Foner, Lewis, and Cvornyek, *The Black Worker*, vol. 8, 314–17. See also Martin Luther King Jr., *Why We Can't Wait* (New York: Mentor, 1968; 1964), for his arguments in favor of "compensatory or preferential treatment for the Negro" (134) and for his candid rebuttal to those who feared that voting rights legislation would lead to "bloc voting": "by forming a bloc a minority makes its voice heard" (150).

34. Quoted in Mike Davis, "LA: The Fire This Time," *Covert Action Information Bulletin* 41 (summer 1992): 12. For a detailed analysis of the Watts uprising, see Gerald Horne, *Fire This Time: The Watts Uprising and the 1960s* (Charlottesville: University Press of Virginia, 1995).

35. See Martin Luther King Jr., "Black Power Defined," in *A Testament of Hope*, 303–12 (originally appeared in *New York Times Magazine*, 11 June 1967). The very meaning of the term "Black Power," like "affirmative action" today, was consistently being defined, debated, and redefined: Was it "fair"? Was it threatening to white people? See also Michael Eric Dyson, *I May Not Get There With You: The True Martin Luther King, Jr.* (New York: Free Press, 2000), chapter 5, entitled " 'We Did Engage in a Black Power Move': An Integrationist Embraces Enlightened Black Nationalism."

36. Gene Roberts, "Dr. King Planning Large Protests to 'Dislocate' Large Cities," *New York Times*, 16 August 1967, reproduced in Goodman, *The Movement*, 137.

37. Malcolm X, *Malcolm X Speaks: Selected Speeches and Statements*, ed. George Breitman (New York: Grove Press, 1965), 14. See also Steven F. Lawson, *Running for Freedom: Civil Rights and Black Politics in America since 1941* (New York: McGraw-Hill, 1991), 99.

38. *Papers of the NAACP, Civil Rights Movement*, microfilm, reel 20. Pauli Murray was also among a number of women's rights advocates who successfully blocked Sen. Dirksen's (R-Illinois) filibuster against the inclusion of a sex discrimination clause in Title VII of the 1964 Civil Rights Act.

39. Malcolm X, *Malcolm X Speaks*, 15. It would take Lyndon B. Johnson to engineer the passage of the Civil Rights Act of 1964, however.

40. See James Boggs, *Racism and the Class Struggle: Further Pages from a Black Worker's Notebook* (New York: Monthly Review, 1970), 12; and *Eyes on the Prize*.

41. *Eyes on the Prize*; and Morris, *Origins*, 257–74.

42. *Eyes on the Prize*.

43. See Kelley, *Race Rebels*, 84. For more on the legacy of the black middle class from early in the twentieth century, see Kevin K. Gaines, *Uplifting the Race: Black Leadership, Politics, and Culture in the Twentieth Century* (Chapel Hill: University of North Carolina Press, 1996).

44. Graham, *The Civil Rights Era*, 164.

45. Ibid., 165.

46. Ibid. See also Lawson, *Running for Freedom*, 113.

47. Graham, *The Civil Rights Era*, 174; See also Bell, *Race, Racism, and American Law*, for his analysis (148–50) and quotation (149) of Chief Justice Earl Warren's opinion upholding the Voting Rights Act in *South Carolina v. Katzenbach*, 383 U.S. 301 (1966): "The heart of the Act is a complex scheme of stringent remedies aimed at areas where voting discrimination has been most flagrant. . . ." These included the striking down of literacy tests and new voting regulations, plus the addition of federal examiners, poll watchers, and provisions for those denied access to balloting. The title of President Lyndon B. Johnson's speech, "To Fulfill These Rights" (in Curry, *Debate*, 16–24), is reminiscent of the title of President Truman's commission's report in 1948, "To Secure These Rights." The Johnson passage most quoted in today's affirmative action debate reads: "You do not take a person who, for years, has been hobbled by chains and liberate him, bring him to the starting line of a race and then say, 'You are free to compete with all the others,' and still justly believe that you have been completely fair." Calling his legislation just a "beginning," Johnson drew on "Kennedy liberals" Bill Moyers and Daniel Patrick Moynihan to write his speech, which he had Martin Luther King Jr., Roy Wilkins, and Whitney Young review. See Graham, *Civil Rights Era*, 174–76, 510–11. The result (which received an enthusiastic response from the audience at that historically black college's commencement) includes these sometimes-jarring juxtapositions: "equal opportunity is essential, but not enough. . . . Ability is stretched or stunted by the family you live with, and the neighborhood you live in, by the school you go to and the poverty or the richness of your surroundings" (Ibid., 18); "For Negro poverty is not white poverty" (Ibid., 20); "Perhaps most important . . . is the breakdown of the Negro family structure. For this, most of all, white America must accept responsibility." Ibid., 21.

48. Manning Marable, "Staying on the Path," in Curry, *Debate*, 5.

49. William H. Chafe, "America since 1945," in *The New American History*, ed. Eric Foner (Philadelphia: Temple University Press, 1990), 143–60.

50. Linda Faye Williams, "Tracing the Politics of Affirmative Action," in Curry, *Debate*, 244.

51. Mary Frances Berry, "Why We Need It: Why It is Under Attack," in Ibid., 302; and John Hope Franklin and Alfred A. Moss Jr., *From Slavery to Freedom: A History of Negro Americans*, 6th ed. (New York: McGraw-Hill, 1988; 1947), 449. Title VII applied to firms with twenty-five or more employees. Its 1972 revision changed that to fifteen or more employees. Title VII and the rest of the Civil Rights Bill had to overcome a stiff Southern filibuster, which was accomplished by liberal Democrats acceding to conservative Republican opposition to "racial quotas." See Graham, *The Civil Rights Era*, 125–76. See Susan D. Clayton and Faye J. Crosby, *Justice, Gender, and Affirmative Action* (Ann Arbor: University of Michigan Press, 1992), on affirmative action in Title VII (13), on the

proactive executive orders of President Johnson (13–14), and for a discussion (18–19) of the 1978 "Uniform Guidelines on Employee Selection Procedures" developed as a joint effort by the Departments of Labor and Justice, the EEOC, and the Civil Service Commission (now the Office of Personnel Management). The two-step "Guidelines" process calls for first determining whether the percentages of race, sex, and ethnic groups in various job classifications match qualified labor pool percentages. If not, the reasons for that inequality are investigated, and the second step then requires affirmative action to correct it, including reinstatement with or without back pay, more aggressive recruitment, training, or advancement. See also Title VII of the *Civil Rights Act of 1964*, *U.S. Code* 42, secs. 2000(e)–2000(e-17) (1999).

52. See Charles W. Whalen Jr. and Barbara Whalen, *The Longest Debate: A Legislative History of the 1964 Civil Rights Act* (Cabin John, MD: Seven Locks Press, 1985), 18. See also Graham, *The Civil Rights Era*; and Bernard Schwartz, ed., *Statutory History of the United States: Civil Rights Part 2* (New York: Chelsea House, 1970).

53. Schwartz, *Civil Rights Part 2*, 1178, U.S. Senate, 88th Cong., 2nd sess., 17 February–19 June 1964. See, for example, this exchange between Sen. Joseph Clark (D-Pennsylvania) and Sen. Sam Ervin (D-North Carolina):

Sen. Clark: Does the Senator believe that in the modern world, in the light of the agitation which has gone on for some years for equal justice under the law for our Negro citizens, it is the right of an employer to deny a job to a man solely because of his race or color?

Sen. Ervin: I say that a man should be permitted.

54. Ibid., 1178.

55. Ibid., 1201; see also 1018–19 for a summary of how civil rights proponents had to argue mainly on the basis of the interstate commerce clause of the Constitution (Article I, Section 8), because of the judicial handicap that had been attached to the Fourteenth Amendment by *Civil Rights Cases* (1883). That decision had specifically thrown out Title II's ancestor—the public accommodations section of the 1875 Civil Rights Act—a fact that opponents were not shy about bringing out in 1964. See also Bell, *Race, Racism, and American Law*, 91, for his trenchant observation of the lasting effects and limitations of *Civil Rights Cases* (1883): "It should be noted that the requirement in the Civil Rights Cases that the state must be involved in discriminatory behavior to evoke the Fourteenth Amendment has been expanded but never overturned, even though discrimination in many private areas of activity has been rendered illegal by contemporary civil rights laws."

56. Schwartz, *Civil Rights Part 2*, 1123.

57. See *United Steelworkers v. Weber*, 443 U.S. 193 (1979), including n 29 (Sen. Norris Cotton [R-New Hampshire] and Sen. Carl Curtis [R-Nebraska]). Italics added. The quote from *Civil Rights Cases* was obviously no accident.

58. Ibid., n 29. See also Schwartz, *Civil Rights Part 2*.

59. Schwartz, *Civil Rights Part 2*, 1038. The section prohibits employment discrimination on the basis of an "individual's race, color, religion, sex, or national origin." This provision is repeatedly used throughout the section.

60. See Pauli Murray, *Autobiography of a Black Activist, Feminist, Lawyer, Priest, and Poet* (Knoxville: University of Tennessee Press, 1990), 355; and Theodore Spaulding, "Philadelphia Hate Strike," *Crisis* 51, no. 9 (September 1944): 283.

61. Graham, *The Civil Rights Era*, 137.

62. Ibid., 134–39; and Murray, *Autobiography*, 355.

63. Murray, *Autobiography*, 355. Strangely, nowhere in her account does Murray, a cofounder of the National Organization for Women (NOW) and a scrupulous legal scholar and historian, discuss the NWP's role in the passage of this clause.

64. Ibid. Rep. Green opposed the sex discrimination clause, arguing: "It will clutter up the bill and it may later . . . be used to help destroy this section of the bill by some of the very people who today support it." Pauli Murray also served with Green on the Committee on Civil and Political Rights, a study group formed by the PCSW to assist the president in formulating policy on women's issues. Ibid., 347–48.

65. Graham, *The Civil Rights Era*, 138.

66. Ibid., 205–32.

67. Ibid., 228.

68. Ibid., 229. "In subsequent years the women's share of EEO complaints would settle at a level of one-quarter" (Ibid., 520 n 90). President Johnson's 1968 Executive Order 11375 "forbade federal contractors from discriminating against women and . . . required them to file affirmative action programs." See Alice Kessler-Harris, *Out to Work: A History of Wage-Earning Women in the United States* (New York: Oxford University Press, 1982), 315. This order was extended by President Nixon's Executive Order 11478 in 1969, which covered federal government employees, and goals and timetables were added in 1971. Ibid., 387 n 40.

69. Schwartz, *Civil Rights Part 2*, 1128.

70. Ibid., 1152.

71. Ibid., 1318.

72. Ibid.

73. Ibid., 1209.

74. Lawson, *Running for Freedom*, 112–15; and Skrentny, *The Ironies of Affirmative Action*, 81.

75. Dwight D. Eisenhower, *Public Papers of the Presidents of the United States:* (Washington, D.C.: Office of the *Federal Register*, National Archives and Records Service, 1958), 1957, 690–94.

76. *Papers of the NAACP, Civil Rights Movement*, microfilm, reel 20. See also Marable, *Race, Reform, and Rebellion*, 79.

77. Morris, *Origins*, 270–74.

78. Herbert Hill, "The AFL–CIO and the Black Worker: Twenty-five Years after the Merger," *Journal of Intergroup Relations* 10, no. 1 (spring 1982): 58 (reprint); and Alan Draper, "*Brown v. Board of Education* and Organized Labor in the South," *Historian* 57, no. 1 (autumn 1994): 75–88.

79. See Ronald P. Formisano, *Boston against Busing: Race, Class, and Ethnicity in the 1960s and 1970s* (Chapel Hill: University of North Carolina Press, 1991); and Hill, "The AFL–CIO," 43.

80. Franklin and Moss, *From Slavery to Freedom*, 436–70.

81. Lawson, *Running for Freedom*, 131–33.

82. See Charles A. Kothe, ed., *A Tale of 22 Cities: Report on Title VII of the Civil Rights Act of 1964 Compiled from NAM Seminars* (New York: National Association of Manufacturers, 1965). The editor was also vice president, Industrial Relations Division of NAM: "It is important," he declared optimistically, "that we recognize at the outset that the law imposes no great or unusual burden on the employer. As a matter of fact, the level of its requirements is far below most of the self-imposed standards of most enlightened employers. The law requires no affirmative action as such" (7).

83. See *Report of the National Advisory Commission*, 127, on what it called the valuable service performed by black middle-class "white helmet counter-rioters'" in de-fusing riots.

84. See Industrial Research Unit, Department of Industry, Wharton School of Finance and

Commerce, University of Pennsylvania, *The Racial Policies of American Industry: Report* (Philadelphia: University of Pennsylvania Press, 1968). I still remember being hired in the fall of 1969 at the Chrysler plant in Belvidere, Illinois, and being taken (along with other white new-hires) to my job in the clean Trim Department—walking past the dirtier, noisier Body Shop that was almost all black (male and female). This was a common report at auto plants throughout the country at that time. See also Herbert Hill, "Black Workers, Organized Labor, and Title VII of the 1964 Civil Rights Act: Legislative History and Litigation Record," in *Race in America: The Struggle for Equality*, ed. Herbert Hill and James E. Jones Jr. (Madison: University of Wisconsin Press, 1993), 286–91, for an account of nationwide nonviolent NAACP protests in 1964 to advance black hiring and promotion in the auto industry—acceded to by General Motors but resisted by the UAW.

85. See Franklin and Moss, *From Slavery to Freedom*, 459. See also *Report of the National Advisory Commission*.

86. See Margery Austin Turner, Michael Fix, and Raymond J. Struyk, eds., *Opportunities Denied, Opportunities Diminished: Racial Discrimination in Hiring* (Washington, D.C.: Urban Institute Press, 1991); and Harry Cross, et al., eds., *Employer Hiring Practices: Differential Treatment of Hispanic and Anglo Job Seekers* (Washington, D.C.: Urban Institute Press, 1990).

87. *Inner City Voice*, (Detroit: n.p., 1969), microfilm, reel 19. Perkins Library Collection, Duke University.

88. *DeFunis*, a precursor to *Bakke*, involved a white law student who claimed he was denied admission to the University of Washington Law School "because of his race." See Herbert Hill, "Affirmative Action and the Constitution," Rosenberg/Humphrey Lecture, City College of New York, 27 April 1988, 5; *DeFunis v. Odegaard*, 416 U.S. 312 (1974); and Linda Greene, "Race in the Twenty-first Century: Equality Through Law?" in *Critical Race Theory: The Key Writings That Formed the Movement*, ed. Kimberlé Crenshaw et al. (New York: New Press, 1995), 299. The case was moot since he had already been accepted by the law school and had almost finished by the time the Supreme Court heard the case.

89. Eric Williams, *Capitalism and Slavery* (New York: Russell and Russell, 1944), 19.

90. Interview with John Watson, cofounder of LRBW, *Radical America* July 1968, reproduced in Goodman, *The Movement*, 185.

91. See Dan Georgakas and Marvin Surkin, *Detroit: I Do Mind Dying: A Study in Urban Revolution* (New York: St. Martin's Press, 1975); Midnight Notes Collective, eds., *Midnight Oil: Work, Energy, War 1973–1992* (Brooklyn: Autonomedia, 1992), 143–68; and James Boggs, *Racism and the Class Struggle: Further Pages from a Black Worker's Notebook* (New York: Monthly Review, 1970).

92. Jeremy Rifkin, *The End of Work: The Decline of the Global Labor Force and the Dawn of the Post-Market Era* (New York: Jeremy P. Tarcher, 1995), chapter 5, "Technology and the African-American Experience." For example, Rifkin notes: "Despite the fact that the [River Rouge] complex had plenty of room for expansion, Ford management made the decision in the late 1950s to move much of the production away from the site to new automated plants in the suburbs." During this time, he adds, Ford, GM, and Chrysler together constructed twenty-five automated plants in Detroit (Ibid., 74). The River Rouge plant, Rifkin points out, had been home to the UAW's most militant locals. Over 30 percent black, Local 600 was so powerful "that it could cripple Ford's entire operation with a single strike action" (Ibid.). See also Timothy B. Tyson, *Radio Free Dixie: Robert F. Williams and the Roots of Black Power* (Chapel Hill: University of North Carolina Press, 1999), 62, for his discussion of one of Local 600's most famous members in the late 1940s, black nationalist leader Robert F. Williams.

93. Hill, "The AFL–CIO," 53.

94. David L. Perlman, "High Court Decision Backs Affirmative Action On Jobs," *AFL–CIO News*, 30 June 1979, reproduced in Foner, Lewis, and Cvornyek, *The Black Worker*, vol. 8, 34–35. In *Weber* (1979), Brian Weber, a white United Steelworker shop steward, sued after not being accepted into a black-advantage apprenticeship program that had been crafted between his union and Kaiser Aluminum and Chemical Corporation in Gramercy, Louisiana, in response to black workers' legal action against the lack of training programs and opportunities for blacks—who occupied only 1.83 percent of skilled jobs. The program, which reserved 50 percent of the openings for blacks, was considered remedial and "temporary" and otherwise left the historically white-advantage seniority system intact. Just three years earlier in a 1976 case the AFL–CIO "went out of its way" to attack compensatory justice for race and gender discrimination in a Seventh District federal court case. See also Hill, "The AFL–CIO," 54.

95. *Firefighters v. Stotts*, 467 U.S. 561 (1984).

96. In fact, all unions have some kind of equal employment opportunity, affirmative action, or "cultural diversity" committee, whether assertive or tokenistic. See the AFL–CIO website at http://www.aflcio.org, Internet.

97. Graham, *The Civil Rights Era*, 285. These highly paid construction jobs included "electrical and sheet-metal workers, plumbers, roofers, structural ironworkers, [and] steamfitters. . . ." Ibid., 288.

98. Ibid., 278.

99. Lincoln, *The Black Church since Frazier*, 120–23.

100. Leon H. Sullivan, *Build, Brother, Build* (Philadelphia: Macrae Smith, 1969), 74.

101. Ibid., 79.

102. Graham, *The Civil Rights Era*, 278–87.

103. Ibid., 287–88.

104. Ibid., 288–89. The plan would take into account local demographics as well: Philadelphia at the time was about 30 percent black. The findings embarrassed the unions, who wanted to maintain a progressive image.

105. Ibid., 290–97.

106. Ibid., 326–27, 324–35; and Arthur A. Fletcher, "A Personal Note in History," in Curry, *Debate*, 25–30.

107. "The unions in these trades still have only about 1.6% minority group membership," Fletcher declared in 1969. "If you didn't have that type of name ['Polish or Italian or Irish'], you didn't participate. In essence, public taxes were being used to take care of a family clan called a union." Fletcher, "Personal Note," 27–28.

108. Ibid.; See also Graham, *The Civil Rights Era*, 326–27.

109. Fletcher, "Personal Note," 26. From his account it appears that Fletcher believed that he was going to be able to thus use institutionalized white supremacy against itself. See also Arthur A. Fletcher, *The Silent Sell-Out: Government Betrayal of Blacks to the Craft Unions* (New York: The Third Press, 1974).

110. Graham, *The Civil Rights Era*, 334–45. In doing so they echoed the proportional representation logic employed in President Roosevelt's FEPC. See also Skrentny, *The Ironies of Affirmative Action*, 200–1.

111. Skrentny, *The Ironies of Affirmative Action*, 201.

112. Graham, *The Civil Rights Era*, 335.

113. See Lawson, *Running for Freedom*, 130–43. Wallace also did well among white voters nationally in the 1964 and 1972 Democratic primaries. See also Dan T. Carter, *From George Wallace to Newt Gingrich: Race in the Conservative Counterrevolution, 1963–1994* (Baton Rouge: Louisiana State University Press, 1996).

114. Lawson, *Running for Freedom*, 138; and Robin D. G. Kelley, *Into the Fire: African Americans since 1970* (New York: Oxford University Press, 1996), 65–68. While busing was opposed by many black parents as well, the NAACP with general black community support fought in the courts for busing plans primarily as a way to force better-equipped predominantly white schools to share resources with black students. White resentment of the disruption of the neighborhood school (seldom a concern when it was blacks who had been bused out of their communities) was secondary to the fear of "black invasion" of white communities and the diminishing of the caste status of white schools and "white education." Most antibusing struggles were in the North.

115. See Carter, *From George Wallace;* and Dan T. Carter, *The Politics of Rage: George Wallace, the Origins of the New Conservatism, and the Transformation of American Politics* (New York: Simon and Schuster, 1995).

116. Carter, *From George Wallace*, 18.

117. Ibid., 19.

118. Ibid., 20.

119. It is also possible that some of the same white working-class fans of George Wallace became receptive to and even voted for black civil rights leader Rev. Jesse Jackson in the 1988 Democratic presidential primaries, where Jackson did astonishingly well in every region, including among alienated white workers. But Jackson's success lay in not in pulling whites across the color line but "crossing over" himself. To do so meant "toning down" his 1984 campaign Rainbow Coalition rhetoric that had once heavily emphasized both economic and civil rights issues—especially with its promotion of Voting Rights Act enforcement: "Speaking in the language, minus the racism, of white populists of the past," relates Steven F. Lawson, "Jackson attacked the 'economic violence' that wealthy corporations and their representatives in Washington had perpetrated on the economically disadvantaged." Lawson, *Running for Freedom*, 249. Self-described populist activist and columnist Jim Hightower of Texas felt moved to proclaim of Jackson: "He is transcending the fact that he is a black candidate. . . ." Ibid., 250.

120. Graham, *The Civil Rights Era*, 340–41.

121. Ibid., 427–76. "Pattern-or-practice" lawsuits, as the name suggests, are filed in response to institutional patterns or practices of discrimination (including statistical evidence of such) rather than solely being based upon the testimony of a single plaintiff. See Hill, *Black Labor*, 53, 257.

122. Hill, "The AFL–CIO," 52; and Skrentny, *The Ironies of Affirmative Action*, 221. Skrentny is accurate in pointing out that both Roy Wilkins and Whitney Young, because of their revulsion for Nixon's anti–civil rights policies, had to be coaxed into supporting the Philadelphia Plan. But when he declares that two years after the plan was revived "some civil rights groups were still booing loudly," the only example he cites is Bayard Rustin. In fact, civil rights groups and black activists generally wanted tougher plans, not weaker ones or no plans at all.

123. Paul Good, "The Bricks and Mortar of Racism," *New York Times Magazine* (21 May 1972), in Foner and Lewis, *The Black Worker*, vol. 8., 458.

124. Ibid., 464.

125. Ibid.

126. Ibid. In 1972, Peter Brennan was appointed secretary of labor by President Nixon.

127. Ibid., 466.

128. Ibid., 467. Italics added. Black and Latino joint campaigns were common during this period, and not just against construction unions. See, for example, Herbert Hill, "Black-Jewish Conflict in the Labor Context: Race, Jobs, and Institutional Power," *Race Traitor: Journal of the new abolitionism* 5 (winter 1996): 85, on the successful 1963 NAACP discrimination lawsuit in New York City against the International Ladies Garment Workers Union (ILGWU): "After the Holmes case, a black woman and a Puerto Rican man were added to the union's General Executive Board, some black and Latino workers were moved into better paying, more skilled jobs, and several were employed in previously all-white positions within the union."

129. Weiss, "*We Want Jobs*," 179–85. Cosponsoring the complaint petition, adds Weiss, were the NAACP, NOW, the American Civil Liberties Union (ACLU), and the Mexican-American Legal Defense Fund. The NAACP was now officially supporting superseniority, which the chief AT&T unions—the Communications Workers of America and the International Brotherhood of Electrical Workers—nevertheless challenged.

130. Robert Gooding-Williams, ed., *Reading Rodney King/Reading Urban Uprising* (New York: Routledge, 1993), 68. The Kerner Commission, an eleven-member panel headed by Illinois Governor Otto Kerner, was created by President Johnson in 1967 to examine the causes and suggest remedies for the widespread rioting in many of the nation's urban black ghettos that summer. See *Report of the National Advisory Commission;* and supra note 23.

131. See Carmichael and Hamilton, *Black Power;* Breitman, *Malcolm X Speaks;* Nixon quoted in Marable, *Race, Reform, and Rebellion,* 108–9; and Skrentny, *The Ironies of Affirmative Action,* 101.

132. Clayborne Carson, *In Struggle: SNCC and the Black Awakening of the 1960s* (Cambridge: Harvard University Press, 1981,) 215–28; and Morris, *Origins,* 105–6.

133. See Philip S. Foner, ed., *The Black Panthers Speak* (Philadelphia: J. P. Lippincott, 1970), 70–73.

134. Nikhil Pal Singh, "The Black Panther Party and the 'Undeveloped Country' of the Left," in *The Black Panther Party Reconsidered,* ed. Charles E. Jones (Baltimore: Black Classic Press, 1998), 86.

135. *Mr. Muhammad Speaks* (New York: n.p., 1960), microfilm, reel 1; and *Muhammad Speaks* (Chicago: Muhammad Mosque No. 2, 1961–75), microfilm, passim. Perkins Library Collection, Duke University.

136. The letter has "Important" handwritten at the top, presumably by either King or his secretary. See August Meier and John H. Bracey Jr., eds., *Records of the SCLC, 1954–1970, Part 1: Records of the President's Office* (Baltimore: University Publications of America, 1995), microfilm, reel 2. Perkins Library Collection, Duke University.

137. See *At the River I Stand,* prod. and dir. David Applebee, Allison Graham, and Steven John Ross. 1 hour. Memphis State University, Memphis, 1993; and Foner, Lewis, and Cvornyek, *The Black Worker,* vol. 8, 403–7.

138. See supra note 137.

139. Lyndon Johnson, *Public Papers of the Presidents of the United States* (Washington, D.C.: Office of the Federal Register, National Archives and Records Service, 1968), 1967, 326.

140. Henry Hampton and Sarah Flynn Fayer, eds., *Voices of Freedom: An Oral History of the Civil Rights Movement from the 1950's through the 1980s* (New York: Bantam, 1990), 400.

141. Formisano, *Boston against Busing,* 28.

142. *Report of the National Advisory Commission,* 36.

143. See Nathan Wright Jr., *Ready to Riot* (New York: Holt, 1968).

144. See, for example, longtime leftist labor activists and authors James Boggs and Grace Lee Boggs quoted in Singh, "The Black Panther," 77.

145. David O. Sears and John B. McConahay, *The Politics of Violence: The New Urban Blacks and the Watts Riot* (Boston: Houghton Mifflin, 1973), 23.

146. Hill, "The AFL–CIO," 77.

147. Foner, Lewis, and Cvornyek, *The Black Worker*, vol. 8, 364–65. Besides the legacy of the BSCP, see other black-led "dual unions" like the NAPFE. Founded in 1913, the NAPFE calls itself "the only surviving, predominantly African American Trade Union." See Paul Nehru Tennassee, "NAPFE: A Legacy of Resistance and Contributions 1913–1999," *National Alliance* 55, no. 10 (October 1999): 12. Information also comes from telephone conversation between the author and Jacqueline Moore, *National Alliance* monthly magazine editor in Washington, D.C., 21 April 1997, regarding NAPFE's function as what this author would call an advocacy dual union that files EEO complaints for postal workers.

148. Georgakas and Surkin, *Detroit*; and Carson, *In Struggle*, 294–95. Forman would later complain that while the campaign did obtain substantial funds from white churches, very little went to the BEDC.

149. Bittker, *The Case for Black Reparations*, 79–80.

150. "The Allen Building Takeover: Thirty Years Later," *Duke University Chronicle* (supplement) 12 February 1999, 1–8.

151. Ibid., 6.

152. See "The Thirteen Demands and Response," *Beloit College (WI) Round Table*, 17 February 1969, 10 (originally printed in the *University of Wisconsin Daily Cardinal*). See Bill Gansner, "Blacks Demand Change, 'On Strike, Shut it Down,' " in Ibid., 11. See also coverage of student strikes at Columbia University (1968) and San Francisco State University (1969) in Goodman, *The Movement*, 25–32, 525–28; and William L. Van Deburg, *New Day in Babylon: The Black Power Movement and American Culture, 1965–1975* (Chicago: University of Chicago Press, 1992), 64–82. 153. Gansner, "Blacks Demand Change," 11.

154. Goodman, *The Movement*, 123–262. On the Chicano movement in particular see Rodolfo F. Acuña, *Occupied America: A History of Chicanos*, 4th ed. (New York: Longman, 2000; 1972), chapter 12; Matt S. Meier and Feliciano Rivera, *The Chicanos: A History of Mexican Americans* (New York: Hill and Wang, 1972), 236–80; and Richard A. Garcia, ed., *The Chicanos in America 1540–1974: A Chronology and Fact Book* (Dobbs Ferry, NY: Oceana, 1977). On the Native American movement in particular see Ward Churchill and Jim Vander Wall, *Agents of Repression: The FBI's Secret Wars against the Black Panther Party and the American Indian Movement* (Boston: South End Press, 1990), esp. 119–22; and Howard Zinn, *A People's History of the United States* (New York: Harper, 1990; 1980), 513–26.

155. Powell in *Bakke* (1978).

156. Blackmun in Ibid.

157. Brennan in Ibid. Brennan states that there were two blacks and one Chicano medical students at UC–Davis during 1968 and 1969. Brennan also points out that black doctors only made up 2.2 percent of all physicians nationwide from 1950 to 1970.

158. Ibid., including n 58. Italics added.

159. *Bakke* (1978).

160. Derrick Bell Jr., "Racial Realism," in Crenshaw, *Critical Race Theory*, 304. See also Bernard Schwartz, *Behind Bakke: Affirmative Action and the Supreme Court* (New York: New York University Press, 1988).

161. Cheryl I. Harris, "Whiteness as Property," *Harvard Law Review* 106 (1993): 1769–73; George Lipsitz, *The Possessive Investment in Whiteness: How White People Profit from Identity Politics* (Philadelphia:

Temple University Press, 1998), 36–37; and *Bakke* (1978). Lipsitz also mentions Bakke himself being the beneficiary of the "illegally segregated Dade County, Florida school district." See also Joel Dreyfuss and Charles Lawrence III, *The Bakke Case: The Politics of Inequality* (New York: Harcourt Brace Jovanovich, 1979). For Sen. Sumner's 1870 Senate speech, see chapter 2, n 96.

162. Hampton and Frayer, *Voices of Freedom*, 654.

163. Ibid., 648–57; and Marable, *Race, Reform, and Rebellion*, 187. Authorities were shocked later to find that of those arrested during the riot, only a third had prior arrest records compared with over 70 percent in the Watts and Newark riots. See Bruce D. Porter, *The Miami Riots of 1980* (Lexington, MA: Lexington Books, 1984), 113.

164. Franklin and Moss, *From Slavery to Freedom*, 471; and Lawson, *Running for Freedom*, 135.

165. Williams, "Tracing the Politics," 249–56.

166. See, for example, Lawson, *Running for Freedom*, 184–89. Lawson points out how Ford, while continuing Nixon's attack on school busing, supported the extension of black voting rights in the South. His brief term also marked a transition that a civil rights coalition was able to use in strengthening certain affirmative action initiatives in federal agencies. See also Hugh Davis Graham, "Civil Rights Policy in the Carter Presidency," in *The Carter Presidency: Policy Choices in the Post–New Deal Era*, ed. Gary M. Fink and Hugh Davis Graham (Lawrence: University Press of Kansas, 1998), 202–7.

167. Lawson, *Running for Freedom*, 138–39. See also Elaine R. Jones, "Race and the Supreme Court's 1994–1995 Term," in Curry, *Debate*, 152: "The Voting Rights Act effectively neutralized the continued refusal of white voters to vote for black candidates." Hugh Davis Graham cites these results: "Between 1962 and 1970, black voters in the South increased from 1.5 million to 3.3 million. . . . The number of black elected officials in the South followed suit, increasing from approximately seventy in 1965 to 700 in 1970, and to 1,600 in 1975" (*The Civil Rights Era*, 452–53). Nationwide, from 1968 to 1988 elected black officials "increased six times over, to a total of nearly 7,000" (Ibid., 563 n. 14). See also Peter Skerry, *Mexican-Americans: The Ambivalent Minority* (New York: Free Press, 1993), 330–33, for his highly critical treatment of the 1975 amendment of the 1965 Voting Rights Act that designated Asians and "persons of Spanish heritage" as "language minorities" subject to the same protection as African Americans (Latino civil rights groups were instrumental in this process) and the Reagan administration Justice Department, in attempting to ingratiate themselves with Latino voters in the election years of 1986 and 1988, successfully suing the Los Angeles city and county governments, respectively, for inadequately representing Latinos in both those governments' redistricting plans.

168. Weiss, "*We Want Jobs*," 207–11. Founded in 1965, the OFCC added "Programs" to its title in 1971 and became part of the Employment Standards Administration (ESA). In 1979, all government contract compliance came under the OFCCP of the Department of Labor (DOL). See DOL website at http://www/dol.gov, Internet.

169. Marable, *Race, Reform, and Rebellion*, 183.

170. Ibid., 185–86. See also Lawson, *Running for Freedom*, 193–204; and Fink and Graham, *The Carter Presidency*. While Carter streamlined civil rights enforcement (Graham, "Civil Rights Policy," in Ibid., 202–23) and backed minority set-asides in contracting, his administration failed to push housing and school desegregation. He also supported and maintained "large-scale federal subsidies that encouraged suburbanization" (Thomas J. Sugrue, "Carter's Urban Policy Crisis," in Fink and Graham, *The Carter Presidency*, 150). In both a preview of Reaganism and as a response to white conservative pressure, Carter proposed $3 billion in social service spending cuts in 1979 (William E. Leuchtenburg, "Jimmy Carter and the Post–New Deal Presidency," in Ibid., 13). "Faced with a

choice between full employment and a balanced budget, Carter decided that having more men and women out of work was an acceptable price to pay for stability." Ibid., 12.

171. Jimmy Carter, *The Public Papers of the Presidents of the United States* (Washington, D.C.: Office of the *Federal Register*, National Archives and Records Service, 1982), 1980, 1492. Both Democratic and Republican presidents, it could be said, have responded to as well as shaped a majority-white constituency that has resisted attacks on its relative privileges. See also Miles Corwin, "L.A. Copying Miami's Failures at Rebuilding after Riots," (Massachusetts Institute of Technology) *Tech*, 13 April 1993, 2.

172. Williams, "Tracing the Politics," 249.

173. Ibid., 250. Williams (251) notes that the cases in which EEOC found "no cause" jumped from approximately 30 percent to 60 percent between 1981 and 1991, direct beneficiaries of EEOC enforcement dropped from 38,114 to 29,429 during this period, and class action settlements fell from 45 percent to 9 percent.

174. Lawson, *Running for Freedom*, chapters 7–8.

175. See Hill, "The AFL–CIO," 53.

176. Williams, "Tracing the Politics," 250–51. For a sympathetic as well as revealing portrait of Reagan's efforts, see Nicholas Laham, *The Reagan Presidency and the Politics of Race: In Pursuit of Colorblind Justice and Limited Government* (Westport, CT: Praeger, 1998). Laham argues that Reagan's major focus was to curtail enforcement of civil rights laws in addition to outlawing quotas. He notes that NAM president Alexander Trowbridge in 1985 opposed Reagan's efforts, declaring: "NAM believes that the current executive order [11246] provides the framework for an effective affirmative action policy. Since it was signed into law, dramatic progress has been achieved in incorporating tolerated minorities and women into our workforce" (98). See James C. Harvey, "The Reagan Administration and Affirmative Action (Part Two)," *Thurgood Marshall Law Review* 10, no. 2 (spring 1985): 353–64, for a discussion of the Reagan administration's attempt to destroy affirmative action in the New Orleans police and Memphis firefighters cases. In the latter it opposed measures protecting newly hired blacks against layoffs in 1981, while in the former it ordered the EEOC to withdraw support for proposed target quotas of 50 percent black new-hires in 1983. With echoes of *Plessy* the Supreme Court declared that in the Memphis case (*Firefighters v. Stotts* [1984]) white firefighters "had been deprived of their property rights of seniority."

177. Lawson, *Running for Freedom*, 198. See also Weiss, "*We Want Jobs*"; and Robert J. Weiss, " 'We Want Jobs': The History of Affirmative Action" (Ph.D. diss., New York University, 1985).

178. Marshall in *Bakke* (1978).

179. Just as Reconstruction not only improved the social position of African Americans but also provided social progress for the whole United States, an item deserving research and discussion today is the issue of how modern white families have been shielded much more than people of color from the worst effects of the overall drop in real wages since 1973 (as well as subsequent economic downturns and layoffs), in large part because of the fact that white women have become the prime beneficiaries of affirmative action in attaining better-paying jobs and greater choice in jobs—notwithstanding the persistence of the gender wage differential. For white pro-black activity in the 1960s, both spontaneous and organized, see Goodman, *The Movement*, esp. sections 1–2; Morris, *Origins*, 221–23; Zinn, *People's History*, 444–47; and Todd Gitlin, *The Sixties: Years of Hope, Days of Rage* (New York: Bantam, 1987). See also supra note 5.

180. Marshall in *Bakke* (1978).

Chapter 7

1. Herbert Hill, "Race, Affirmative Action and the Constitution," Rosenberg/Humphrey Lecture, City College of New York, 27 April 1988, 8: "Affirmative action without numbers, whether in the form of quotas, goals, or timetables, is meaningless; there must be some benchmark, some tangible measure of change." See also Christopher Edley Jr., *Not All Black and White: Affirmative Action and American Values* (New York: Hill and Wang, 1996), 18, for this leading affirmative action proponent's emphatic declaration: *"Affirmative action does not mean quotas; quotas are illegal."*

2. The Civil War was the ultimate form of coercion needed to abolish slavery, with federal troops also used to enforce Reconstruction. See W. E. B. Du Bois, *Black Reconstruction in America 1860–1880* (Cleveland: Meridian, 1968; 1935).

3. John David Skrentny, *The Ironies of Affirmative Action: Politics, Culture, and Justice in America* (Chicago: University of Chicago Press, 1996), 196. For recent scholarship on the affirmative action struggle see, for example, Jody Dunlap, "A Study of the Conflict Between Seniority Rights and the Anti-Discrimination Goals of Title VII and Affirmative Action" (Ph.D. diss., Pepperdine University, 1986); John Hinshaw, "Dialectic of Division: Race and Power among Western Pennsylvania Steelworkers, 1937–1975" (Ph.D. diss., Carnegie-Mellon University, 1994); and Ronnie Bernard Tucker, "Affirmative Action, the Supreme Court, and Political Power in the Old Confederacy: An Impact Assessment, 1964–1995" (Ph.D. diss., Mississippi State University, 1998).

4. See Nancy Stein, "Affirmative Action and the Persistence of Racism," *Social Justice* 22, no. 3 (fall 1995): 28–45; and Martha S. West, "History Lessons," *Women's Review of Books* 13, no. 5 (February 1996), 19.

5. Roger Wilkins, "The Case for Affirmative Action: Racism Has Its Privileges," *Nation* 260, no. 12 (27 March 1995): 415.

6. Louis Harris, "The Future of Affirmative Action," in *The Affirmative Action Debate*, ed. George E. Curry (Reading, MA: Addison-Wesley, 1996), 326–36. Another popular argument holds that there was widespread white support for affirmative action until the American economy went into a tailspin beginning in the 1970s, followed by the Reagan-Bush era transfer of wealth, layoffs, and demagoguery against people of color. See Linda Faye Williams, "Tracing the Politics of Affirmative Action," in Ibid., 241–57).

7. W. Richard Merriman and Edward G. Carmines quoted in W. Avon Drake and Robert D. Holsworth, *Affirmative Action and the Stalled Quest for Black Progress* (Urbana: University of Illinois Press, 1996), 117.

8. According to one study, these programs "seemingly have had no significant impact on aggregate minority employment: Their enforcement apparently redistributes minorities across categories of employers." See Farrell Bloch, *Antidiscrimination Law and Minority Employment: Recruitment Practices and Regulatory Restraints* (Chicago: University of Chicago Press, 1994), 117.

9. See Herbert Hill on Title VII as an effective weapon against workplace discrimination in "Black Workers, Organized Labor, and Title VII of the 1964 Civil Rights Act: Legislative History and Litigation Record," in *Race in America: The Struggle for Equality*, ed. Herbert Hill and James E. Jones Jr. (Madison: University of Wisconsin Press, 1993), 263–344; and Jean Zorn and Stephen Zorn, review of *Lift Every Voice: Turning a Civil Rights Setback into a New Vision of Social Justice*, by Lani Guinier, *Nation* 266, no. 17 (11 May 1998), 34–36. The Zorns point out that the Voting Rights Act of 1965, a response to Southern black protests, was then interpreted in quota terms by the courts. Voting districts were judged in compliance if blacks were elected in approximately proportional numbers to their demographics.

Notes to pages 169–70

10. See Bloch, *Antidiscrimination Law*, 9–13; and Rene Sanchez, "Berkeley, UCLA Cut Minority Admission," *Raleigh News and Observer*, 1 April 1998, 1A, for a discussion on how California and Texas public universities no longer rely on race as an admissions factor. This has lead to a drastic drop in black admissions. While most of the nation's public universities still rely on the 1978 *Bakke* case and use race as one consideration in admissions, educators have eyed those states closely as well as looming test cases in the courts. See also "Fewer Minorities Studying Medicine," *Raleigh News and Observer*, 2 November 1997, 13A, on a study by the American Association of Medical Colleges showing an 11 percent drop in people of color applying to medical schools, with 6.8 percent fewer accepted in 1997 than in 1996 (with that drop being directly attributed to school administrators' reactions to California's Proposition 209 and the Texas *Hopwood* decision—see infra notes 72–81). See also the Florida Board of Regents ignoring "protests from students and black leaders" and endorsing "Gov. Jeb Bush's plan to end affirmative action in admissions at the state's 10 public universities," in "Regents Endorse End to Affirmative Action," *Raleigh News and Observer*, 20 November 1999, 9A. On voting rights issues see "Court Makes It Harder to Create Districts Favoring Minority Vote," *Raleigh News and Observer*, 13 May 1997, 2A, on the Court's setting aside a Louisiana court's mandate to a local school board to reconsider establishing majority-black districts; *Shaw v. Reno* 113 U.S. 2816 (1993) and *Shaw v. Hunt* 517 U.S. 899 (1996); and Richard Valelly, "Voting Rights in Jeopardy," *American Prospect* 46 (September–October 1999), 43–49, on minority office-holding in jurisdictions covered by the 1965 Voting Rights Act being dependent on past federal intervention and the Supreme Court's steady erosion of that act even if Congress renews it in 2007.

11. See Steven F. Lawson, *Running for Freedom: Civil Rights and Black Politics in America since 1941* (New York: McGraw-Hill, 1991), 211, where he points out that "by the mid-1980s, the number of black households with incomes under $10,000 comprised 30.3 percent of the total, a leap of 11 percent."

12. Thomas Jefferson, *Notes on the State of Virginia* (Chapel Hill: University of North Carolina Press, 1954; 1785), 163. Writing over a century before psychology pioneers Sigmund Freud and Carl Jung first discussed "collective memory," Jefferson added this contribution to the American race war apocalypse discourse: "Deep rooted prejudices entertained by the whites; ten thousand recollections, by the blacks, of the injuries they have sustained; new provocations; the real distinctions which nature has made; and many other circumstances, will divide us into parties, and produce convulsions which will probably never end but in the extermination of the one or the other race" (138). Such declarations were common among both the slaveholding and nonslaveholding elite in Jefferson's day. See, for example, Sidney Kaplan, *American Studies in Black and White: Selected Essays 1949–1989*, ed. Allan D. Austin (Amherst: University of Massachusetts Press, 1991), 18–32.

13. David W. Bartlett, *The Life and Public Service of Abraham Lincoln* (Freeport, NY: Books for Libraries Press, 1969; 1860), 199.

14. Abraham Lincoln, *Abraham Lincoln: An Autobiography*, ed. Nathaniel Wright Stephenson (Indianapolis: Bobbs-Merrill, 1926), 308–9.

15. Reprinted in Mark E. Neely, ed., *The Abraham Lincoln Encyclopedia* (New York: McGraw-Hill, 1982), 271–72. Contemporary documents during the slavery era show that the apocalyptic fears and fantasies of Jefferson and Lincoln were not uncommon—especially in the South—and reveal the insecure, guilty underside of popular white callousness. On Lincoln and black soldiers see Du Bois, *Black Reconstruction*, 98–100.

16. "We would, in a word," predicted Calhoun, "change conditions with them—a degradation

greater than has ever yet fallen to the lot of a free and enlightened people. . . ." Quoted in John L. Thomas, ed., *John C. Calhoun: A Profile* (New York: Hill and Wang, 1968), xv. Calhoun's ideological descendants might have mournfully considered his words in this anecdote in James M. McPherson, *Battle Cry of Freedom: The Civil War Era* (New York: Ballantine, 1989), 862: "In 1865 a black soldier who recognized his former master among a group of Confederate prisoners he was guarding called out a greeting: 'Hello, massa: bottom rail on top dis time!' "

17. Indicative of the pathological white fear of black success were the 1910 nationwide white riots after black heavyweight boxer Jack Johnson defeated Jim Jeffries, tagged the "Great White Hope." The *Chicago Tribune* had earlier published white fears of general black "insubordination" should Jeffries lose. See Lerone Bennett Jr., *Before the Mayflower: A History of Black America*, 5th ed. (New York: Penguin, 1984; 1962), 341–42.

18. See W. E. B. Du Bois, *W. E. B. Du Bois: A Reader*, ed. David Levering Lewis (New York: Henry Holt, 1995), 453–65 (originally published in *Darkwater: Voices from Within the Veil*). Malcolm X also made this cogent observation concerning whites and their attempted denial of guilt when he would often tell black audiences: "Do you know why the white man really hates you? It's because every time he sees your face, he sees a mirror of his crime—and his guilty conscience can't bear to face it." Quoted in Stephen Steinberg, *Turning Back: The Retreat from Racial Justice in American Thought and Policy* (Boston: Beacon, 1995), 158.

19. An integral part of American law is the phrase "to be made whole," which evokes the English common law concept of equity. In the context of labor law, the phrase expresses the desire of a plaintiff pleading before the National Labor Relations Board (NLRB), for example, to have job, seniority, and back pay restored by the employer. The NLRB's "layman's guide" to labor law, for instance, contains this passage: "[T]he National Labor Relations Act is not a criminal statute. It is entirely remedial. It is intended to prevent and remedy unfair labor practices, not to punish the person responsible for them. The Board is authorized by Section 10 (c) not only to issue a cease-and-desist order, but 'to take such affirmative action including reinstatement of employees with or without back pay, as will effectuate the policies of this Act.' " See National Labor Relations Board, *A Layman's Guide to Basic Law Under the National Labor Relations Act* (Washington, D.C.: GPO, 1971), 52.

20. W. E. B. Du Bois, *The Souls of Black Folk* (New York: Penguin, 1989; 1903), 5.

21. Tracy L. Robinson, "The Intersections of Dominant Discourses Across Race, Gender, and Other Identities," *Journal of Counseling and Development* 77, no. 1 (winter 1999): 76.

22. An example of the former would be the popular expression that still has currency, "second-class citizens," which of course implies that someone else (white people) has "first-class citizenship." For the latter, we have the already cited examples of Frederick Douglass and W. E. B. Du Bois, as well as George Schuyler's essay "The Caucasian Problem" in *What the Negro Wants*, ed. Rayford W. Logan (Chapel Hill: University of North Carolina Press, 1944), 281–97.

23. Many leftist and labor historians have trouble marking white workers as beneficiaries of white supremacy and accepting only the "capitalist ruling class" as such an active agent. These historians wind up unintentionally blaming the victim—in this case black workers. See, for example, Howard Zinn, *A People's History of the United States* (New York: Harper, 1990; 1980), 230–31, for the standard assessment of black workers in 1863 New York City being used as strikebreakers and thus in a sense provoking the white race riot against them. Based in large part on the work of Du Bois and Malcolm X as well as the considerable historical evidence, labor historian Eric Arnesen dismisses the insights and analyses concerning the labor movements' "white" problem by Herbert Hill, Noel Ignatiev, and David Roediger as mere "psychohistory" and "metaphor." What Arnesen offers

by way of rebuttal can be summed up as follows: white workers are not all bad and black workers have been able to take care of themselves when dealing with discrimination. He also lists historical examples of "racial unity" in union struggles (which do not, however, erase predominant white supremacist labor practices nor imply a level playing field). See Eric Arnesen, "Up from Exclusion: Black and White Workers, Race, and the State of Labor History," *Reviews in American History* 26, no. 1 (March 1998): 146–74. See also Peter Erickson, "Seeing White," *Transition* 67: 166–85, on his proposal for "living with whiteness."

24. See Henry Louis Gates Jr. *The Signifying Monkey: A Theory of African-American Literary Criticism* (New York: Oxford University Press, 1988); and David Walker and Henry Highland Garnet, *Walker's Appeal and Garnet's Address to the Slaves of the United States of America* (Nashville: James C. Winston, 1994; 1848), 20–26, 39.

25. See Robert Farris Thompson, *Flash of the Spirit: African and Afro-American Art and Philosophy* (New York: Vintage Books, 1984); and John Michael Spencer, *The Rhythms of Black Folk: Race, Religion, and Pan-Africanism* (Trenton: Africa World Press, 1995).

26. Theophus H. Smith, *Conjuring Culture: Biblical Formations of Black America* (New York: Oxford University Press, 1994), 212.

27. *The Holy Bible*, KJV (New York: American Bible Society, 1990; 1611), 840. It is not far-fetched to also suggest that there is a connection from that parable to affirmative action through common law's origins in medieval Christian Britain. Matthew is also a biblical book with a long history of popularity in the black church. See Smith, *Conjuring Culture*, 7–8; and an 18 September 1787 speech by Cyrus Bustill, "I Speak to Those Who Are in Slavery," in *Lift Every Voice: African American Oratory, 1787–1900*, ed. Philip S. Foner and Robert James Branham (Tuscaloosa: University of Alabama Press, 1998), 20–26. Bustill, a former slave and abolitionist, cites that biblical passage in the context of temperance: "Given by our Lord and master . . . how he Received them that Came in at the Eleventh hour of the Day, how he, Gave them waggens [wages] Equil with them that (had) Born the Burden and the heat of Day . . ." (24). See also Frederick Douglass's 1865 speech "What the Black Man Wants," in Frederick Douglass, *The Life and Writings of Frederick Douglass*, vol. 4, *Reconstruction and After*, ed. Philip S. Foner (New York: International Publishers, 1955), 162, where he quotes Matthew 16:24: "I put it to the American sense of honor. The honor of a nation is an important thing. It is said in the Scriptures, 'What doth it profit a man if he gain the whole world, and lose his own soul?' It may be said, also, What doth it profit a nation if it gain the whole world, but lose its honor?"

28. Nat Turner, "Confession," 1 November 1831, in *The Confessions of Nat Turner and Related Documents*, ed. Kenneth S. Greenberg (Boston: Bedford, 1996) 47–48. Italics added. It is an open question as to what horrified whites more—Turner's military insurrection or his postcapture invocation of an apocalypse that would penalize them for holding blacks in bondage.

29. See, for example, Kimberlé Crenshaw et al., eds., *Critical Race Theory: The Key Writings That Formed the Movement* (New York: New Press, 1995), especially essays by Cheryl I. Harris, Mari Matsuda, Derrick A. Bell Jr., and Duncan Kennedy; and the *Race Traitor* (4–5) editorials as well as Herbert Hill, "Black-Jewish Conflict in the Labor Context: Race, Jobs, and Institutional Power," *Race Traitor: journal of the new abolitionism* 5 (winter 1996): 96.

30. See, for example, the website of Americans United for Affirmative Action (AUAA), cofounded by Martin Luther King III, at http://www.auaa.org, Internet. For a discussion of the power as well as the limitations of a movement that has won impressive monetary and hiring concessions from such corporate giants as Texaco, Avis, and Denny's in the mid-1990s see "Lead Story" news-

cast, Black Entertainment Television, 17 November 1996. See also Louis Gray, "Anger Voiced Over Admissions: Students Take to the Streets in Protest of 209," in *University of California–Berkeley Daily Californian*, 3 April 1998; and Daniel Hernandez, "Hundreds Join in Walkout: Teach-ins Held to Address Issues." Ibid., 23 October 1998. See also Rob Hotakainen, "Jackson Tells Bush to Ax Admissions Plan in Fla.," *Raleigh News and Observer*, 8 March 2000, 4A, for a march of 10,000 mostly black protesters in Tallahassee "calling on Florida Gov. Jeb Bush to scrap his plan to end race-based college admissions." Similar to the plan in Texas, Bush's plan would "eliminate racial 'set-asides and preferences' [Bush's words] in favor of a new system that would guarantee college admission to the top 20 percent of students in every Florida high school senior class. . . ." Dubbed "the largest demonstration in Florida's history" by organizers, news reports indicated that affirmative action based on compensation and reparations—not diversity—was the underlying theme expressed by marchers and speakers. See, for example, Mary Frances Berry, "Snake Oil: Jeb Bush's Higher Education Initiative Is No Substitute for Affirmative Action," *Emerge* 11, no. 7 (May 2000): 56–59. See also the Black Radical Congress 1999 "Freedom Agenda" that includes demands for both affirmative action and reparations at their Internet website, http://www.blackradicalcongress.org.; and "The Black Radical Congress: A Black Freedom Agenda for the Twenty-first Century," *Black Scholar* 28, no. 1 (spring 1998): 71–73.

31. See Crenshaw, "Black Women."

32. Thomas C. Holt, "African-American History," in *The New American History*, ed. Eric Foner (Philadelphia: Temple University Press, 1990), 223.

33. For example, legal scholar Richard Delgado has suggested in his book *The Coming Race War? And Other Apocalyptic Tales of America after Affirmative Action and Welfare* (New York: New York University Press, 1996), 120–21, that the campaign to end affirmative action as well as federal welfare programs can also be read as a dare for black communities to rebel—and be subsequently suppressed.

34. William Bradford Reynolds, "An Experiment Gone Awry," in Curry, *Debate*, 130. How ironic that Reynolds should compare affirmative action to President Andrew Jackson's "spoils system." See also chapter 1, note 145, of this book on Theodore Allen's characterization of Jackson's spoils system as a white system. See also Theodore W. Allen, *The Invention of the White Race*, vol. 1, *Racial Oppression and Social Control* (London: Verso, 1994), 136–37, for how white racial quotas had already been a part of Anglo-American colonial law, whereby one white was to be employed for every so many blacks: one to four in 1750 Georgia, for example.

35. Delgado, *The Coming Race War?*, 73. As Frederick Douglass observed in 1865: "The story of our inferiority is an old dodge, as I have said; for wherever men oppress their fellows, wherever they enslave them, they will endeavor to find the needed apology for such enslavement and oppression in the character of the people oppressed and enslaved." In Douglass, *The Life and Writings*, 161 (see supra note 27).

36. When one "looks white" in this country, as most European Americans do, there is literally no end to the truly astonishing, revealing, and often contradictory daily anecdotes to be heard from those who either actively or passively consider themselves "white" as an identity: whether in all-white or integrated settings. For example, a white coworker of mine some years ago at a Durham, North Carolina, post office spoke out angrily on the shop floor about the unfairness of his teenage son receiving a suspension from his high school for an infraction when "certain ones" (everybody knew he meant black students) were routinely not suspended because of "favoritism" on account of the principal being black. Yet within an hour's time that same coworker was excitedly confiding to me how, even if his son did not go to college, he had been recently informed by a general contrac-

tor friend that "a white brickmason" could expect to earn between $75,000 and $100,000 a year. (In fact, 61 percent of all out-of-school suspensions in Durham public schools are served by black males, with only 7 percent being issued to white males. See Damien Jackson, "Illuminating Suspension: Does Color Play a Role in Durham Schools' Discipline Procedures," Durham [NC] *Independent*, 8 March 2000, 15.) Incidentally, this was not someone who would describe himself, nor would his black coworkers describe him, as "a racist." See also "Plan to Name School after MLK Opposed," *Raleigh News and Observer*, 5 January 1998, 4A, regarding a group of white parents in Riverside, California, "fighting a plan to name a new school after Martin Luther King, Jr., claiming it would be branded as a black school, hurting graduates' college chances. . . . The school is scheduled to open in September 1999. It would be about two-thirds white." The school did in fact open then under that name.

37. Hill, "Race," 6: "But it is *the removal of the preferential treatment traditionally enjoyed by white workers at the expense of black as a class* that is at issue in the affirmative action controversy." See also Derrick A. Bell Jr., *Race, Racism, and American Law*, 2nd ed. (Boston: Little, Brown, 1980), 454: "Rather, working-class whites fear that remedial assistance to blacks may threaten the traditional status relationships between the two groups, with blacks on the bottom. . . ." In the whiteness-equals-merit formulation we are also seeing the residual effects of centuries' old white supremacist ideology that defined white as intellectually superior to black.

38. See, for example, Benjamin P. Bowser and Raymond G. Hunt, eds., *Impacts of Racism on White Americans* (Ann Arbor, MI: Books on Demand, 1998; 1981); Joe L. Kincheloe et al., eds., *White Reign: Deploying Whiteness in America* (New York: St. Martin's Press, 1998); and David T. Wellman, *Portraits of White Racism*, 2nd ed. (Cambridge, England: Cambridge University Press, 1993; 1977). See also Geralda Miller, "Study: Racial Prejudice Reason for Affirmative Action Opposition," *Durham (NC) Carolina Times*, 19 February 2000, 1, for a report on the 1995 study by the Michigan Institute for Social Research that surveyed 1,139 adult white residents of metropolitan Detroit:

The study found that whites who subscribed to statements reflecting a less blatant, more subtle brand of racial prejudice, agreeing, for example, that blacks should work their way up, that blacks blame whites too much for their problems, and that blacks have gotten more than they deserve, were also more likely to oppose affirmative action.

The researchers found that whites who admitted to some forms of traditional racial prejudice, such as believing that some groups are dominant over others and that their own race was inherently superior, tended to support government help for blacks and favor affirmative action.

39. See, for example, Andrew Hacker, *Two Nations: Black and White, Separate, Hostile, Unequal* (New York: Ballantine, 1995; 1992). See Orlando Patterson, *Rituals of Blood: Consequences of Slavery in Two American Centuries* (Washington, D.C.: Civitas Counterpoint, 1998), 238–65 for a discussion of the trial, verdict, and popular reaction to this case. Simpson, a former pro football star, television commentator, and movie actor, was acquitted in 1995 of murdering his ex-wife Nicole Brown Simpson and her friend Ronald Goldman. Many said Simpson won this controversial case because he could afford a high-priced defense against the damaging evidence against him. Race was the centerpiece, however, in the national discussion that contained an undercurrent of the historically familiar brute black rapist image. Many whites nationwide also expressed intense anger out of a belief that Simpson was acquitted because the jury was mostly black and therefore biased in Simpson's favor, as well as being somehow guilty of reverse racism and therefore not having properly discharged their civic responsibilities nor demonstrated fitness for citizenship. Some even called for changes in how juries are selected, clearly implying the elimination of potential black jurors. The ghost of Justice Roger Taney did indeed seem to walk the earth in the aftermath of that verdict. See David Broder, "Jury verdicts aren't the problem," *Raleigh News and Observer*, 12 October 1995, A21.

40. "Reverse discrimination" is a widespread white anecdotal rather than evidential phenomenon: "White men averaged only 1.7% of discrimination charges filed at the Equal Employment Opportunity Commission in the fiscal years between 1987 and 1994," writes Eleanor Holmes Norton ("Affirmative Action in the Workplace," in Curry, *Debate*, 44–45). "This is certainly not because of a reluctance to file; white men file the lion's share of age discrimination complaints at the EEOC." But lawsuits like *Shaw v. Reno* (1993) and *Shaw v. Hunt* (1996) have become part of what could be called a "white class action suit" phenomenon in popular culture, contrary to the declaration by Justice Stevens (joined by Chief Justices Burger, Stewart, and Rehnquist) in *Bakke* (1978): "This is not a class action suit."

41. Hill, *Black Labor*, esp. introduction. White denial typically does not merely deny the existence of white privilege and black discrimination but also shunts black grievances into other categories (for example, class) or invokes "reasonable" apologia like "blacks don't test well because their homes don't value education" or "blacks commit more crimes and therefore merit greater police scrutiny." As a reflex mechanism, white denial counters what ultimately can flow from identifying with black grievances: the necessity to take action to end white supremacy. See Dinesh D'Souza, *The End of Racism: Principles for a Multiracial Society* (New York: Free Press, 1995), for that author's white denial justification.

42. Hacker, *Two Nations*, 31–32.

43. George Lipsitz, *The Possessive Investment in Whiteness: How White People Profit from Identity Politics* (Philadelphia: Temple University Press, 1998), 36.

44. Orfield quoted in Ibid., taken from Gary Orfield, "School Desegregation After Two Generations: Race, Schools, and Opportunity in Urban Society," in Hill and Jones, *Race in America*, 245.

45. New York Times/CBS poll in "Views of Affirmative Action," *New York Times*, 14 December 1997.

46. See George E. Curry and Trevor W. Coleman, "The Verdict on Judge Thomas: Clarence Thomas five years later," *Emerge* 8, no. 2 (November 1996): 38. They quote Anne Sulton, a Denver lawyer, who said of the 1995 *Adarand* decision: " 'In fact, it has provided the basis for a generalized attack on affirmative action in higher education in Colorado and in other areas that are related to employment.' She said that a group of Republicans in her state tried to get an initiative on the November 5 ballot that would have ended all state affirmative action programs based on race, but not programs for women." Ibid., 4.

47. The court in *Missouri* "limited the remedial relief [increased teacher salaries and program funding] available to minority students by striking down district court efforts to improve student achievement and to attract white students back into the public schools." See Frank R. Parker, "The Damaging Consequences of the Rehnquist Court's Commitment to Color-Blindness versus Racial Justice," *American University Law Review* 45, no. 3 (February 1996) [online journal] available at http://www.wcl.american.edu/pub/journals/lawrev/parker.htm, Internet. See also *Missouri v. Jenkins*, 515 U.S. 70 (1995); *Swann v. Mecklenburg*, 402 U.S. 1 (1971); and *Milliken v. Bradley*, 433 U.S. 267 (1977).

48. *Shaw v. Reno* (1993); *Shaw v. Hunt* (1996); Elaine R. Jones, "Race and the Supreme Court's 1994–1995 Term," in Curry, *Debate*, 153; and J. Morgan Kousser, *Colorblind Injustice: Minority Voting Rights and the Undoing of the Second Reconstruction* (Chapel Hill: University of North Carolina Press, 1999), 6–7, 366–455. Kousser recounts the astonishing claims by *Shaw* plaintiffs' attorney (and Duke University law professor) Robinson Everett that white voters in North Carolina had suffered an "impression of injustice," and that a black representative would be beholden to black voters (380). Kousser also notes that Justice O'Connor's majority opinion never mentions that those dis-

tricts were only 57 percent—not 100 percent—black (384–85). See also another *Shaw* plaintiff (and also a Duke law professor) Melvin B. Shimm, Letter to the editor, *Raleigh News and Observer*, 11 April 2000, 12A: "But conferring political advantage on these same [black] citizens primarily on the basis of their race similarly offends the fundamental democratic precept that all persons must be treated equally under the law." See also Derrick A. Bell Jr., *And We Are Not Saved: The Elusive Quest for Racial Justice* (New York: Basic, 1987). While in "Groups, Representation, and Race-Conscious Districting: A Case of the Emperor's Clothes," in Crenshaw et al., *Critical Race Theory*, 205–34, Lana Guinier cautions that the black legislator per se should not be romanticized, she also notes that critics' "dissatisfaction with racial group representation ignores the essentially group nature of political participation" (205).

49. See *Richmond v. J. A. Croson Co.*, 488 U.S. 469 (1989); *Adarand v. Peña*, 115 U.S. 2097 (1995); *Fullilove v. Klutznick*, 448 U.S. 448 (1980); *Metro Broadcasting v. FCC*, 497 U.S. 547 (1990); and Parker, "Damaging Consequences."

50. *Wards Cove v. Antonio*, 109 U.S. 2115 (1989); *Griggs v. Duke Power*, 401 U.S. 424 (1971); Linda Greene, "Race in the Twentieth Century: Equality Through Law?" in Crenshaw et al., *Critical Race Theory*, 293–94, argues that *Wards Cove* left Title VII "an empty shell." For a different view—that the 1991 Civil Rights Act overrode *Wards Cove* (with the latter's burden on the plaintiff to show discrimination)—see Carl E. Brody Jr., "A Historical Review of Affirmative Action and the Interpretation of Its Legislative Intent by the Supreme Court," [online journal article], available at http://www.uakron.edu/lawrev/brody.html, Internet.

51. *Wygant v. Jackson*, 476 U.S. 267 (1986). The original agreement came about in response to black protests. See also *Firefighters v. Stotts*, 467 U.S. 561 (1984).

52. "Race, Law and Justice: The Rehnquist Court and the American Dilemma," Conference at American University (AU), Washington, D.C., 21 September 1995, *American University Law Review* 45, no. 3 (February 1996), [online journal] available at http://www.wcl.american.edu/pub/journals/lawrev/45–3.htm, Internet. See especially the remarks of Nell Jessup Newton. See also *Morton v. Mancari*, 417 U.S. 535 (1974); *Rosebud Sioux Tribe v. Kneip*, 430 U.S. 584 (1977); and *Oliphant v. Suquamish Tribe*, 435 U.S. 191 (1978). *Morton v. Mancari* held that "employment preference for American Indians by Bureau of Indian Affairs [BIA] was not racial classification, but rather political action to further Indian self-government" (see "Race, Law and Justice," n 112). Ironically, *Morton* was decided the same year as *DeFunis*, at which time Newton relates: "Indian tribes refused to join in *DeFunis* . . . and the Bakke debate, on the advice of [white] attorneys who represented them. . . . These attorneys advised them: 'You don't need affirmative action. You don't need to get involved with that. You already get to have affirmative action because magically you're not a racial group. You're a political group.'" Another irony was the fact that joining the "non-Indians" suing the BIA for employment discrimination against "non-Indians" in amicus briefs were the Montana Inter-Tribal Policy Board and the Mexican American Legal Defense and Education Fund. By contrast, *Oliphant* and *Rosebud*, according to Newton, were "basically saying that Indian tribes can't govern non-Indians" by the government either removing non-Indians from tribal jurisdiction or unilaterally moving the reservation boundaries. See also *Rice v. Cayetano*, 98 U.S. 818 (2000). Invoking the Fifteenth Amendment, a white Hawaiian successfully caused to be overturned the Office of Hawaiian Affairs (OHA) practice of limiting suffrage for its board of trustees elections to "Native Hawaiians." The OHA, according to state statute, advocates and disburses funds for those "of Hawaiian ancestry" and serves "as a receptacle for reparations."

53. Harry P. Pachon, "Invisible Latinos: Excluded from Discussions of Inclusion," in Curry,

Debate, 184. Pachon makes mention of the 1995 Glass Ceiling Commission representing progress for Latino inclusion. Ibid., 184–90.

54. Ibid., 186.

55. David G. Gutiérrez, "Migration, Emergent Ethnicity, and the 'Third Space': The Shifting Politics of Nationalism in Greater Mexico," *Journal of American History* 86, no. 2 (September 1999): 497. See also Rodolfo F. Acuña, *Occupied Mexico: A History of Chicanos*, 4th ed. (New York: Longman, 2000), chapter 8, esp. 192–94.

56. Gutiérrez, "Migration," 497.

57. William Javier Nelson, "Latinos: The Indian Escape Hatch," *Race Traitor: journal of the new abolitionism* 6 (summer 1996): 47. On the African roots of Latin American settlement see Thompson, *Flash of the Spirit*; and John Hope Franklin and Alfred A. Moss Jr., *From Slavery to Freedom: A History of Negro Americans*, 6th ed. (New York: McGraw-Hill, 1988; 1947), 46–52. See also Mirta Ojito, "Living Worlds Apart in a New Land: Pair Find It Hard to Cross U.S. Racial Divide," *Portland Oregonian*, 22 June 2000, A12, A13, for an account of racial segregation in Miami's Cuban American community. Few Latino populations in the U.S. have done as well as the Cubans, who are not only entitled by federal law to political asylum upon reaching U.S. soil (reflecting official U.S. hostility to Cuba's Communist government) but also qualify for affirmative action programs as well. One way of reading the anger expressed by so many Miami Cuban Americans at the federal government's seizing of Elián Gonzalez, the six-year-old Cuban shipwreck survivor who was held by his Miami relatives, was as an infringement on its privileged immigrant, political interest group, and white status. See also Anita Snow, "Havana Welcomes Boy," *Raleigh News and Observer*, 29 June 2000, A1, A16, including "Chronology" and "Reactions to Departure"; Thomas D. Boswell and James R. Curtis, *The Cuban-American Experience: Culture, Images, and Perspectives* (Totowa, NJ: Rowman and Allanheld, 1983), chapter 6; and *U.S. Bureau of the Census Statistical Abstract of the United States: 1999*, 119th ed. (Washington, D.C.: GPO, 1999), 54, showing Cuban Americans in 1998 with the highest percentage rate of college education, family income, and homeownership and the lowest rate of unemployment, domicile renting, and persons and families living below the poverty level compared to other Hispanics.

58. Scalia opinion in *Adarand v. Peña* (1995). Scalia's statement, similar to the majority opinion written by Justice O'Connor, was aimed ostensibly at all nonwhite "races" (in this conception) while framing itself within the historical context of black-originated litigation and civil rights protest.

59. Souter dissent in Ibid. Italics added. Compare this quote with that of Du Bois at the very end of this chapter.

60. Theodore Hsien Wang and Frank H. Wu, "Beyond the Model Minority Myth," in Curry, *Debate*, 195.

61. Charlotte Brooks, "In the Twilight Zone between Black and White: Japanese American Resettlement and Community in Chicago, 1942–1945," *Journal of American History* 86, no. 4 (March 2000): 1655–87.

62. *Bakke* (1978).

63. Wang and Wu, "Beyond the Model Minority Myth," 195. See also former California Governor Pete Wilson, "The Minority-Majority Society," in Curry, *Debate*, 167–74, in which he claims that Hispanics and Asians as well as whites are "victims of reverse discrimination" (presumably at the hands of African Americans) in jobs and higher education.

64. Frank Wu in "Race, Law and Justice"; and Robert S. Chang, *Disoriented: Asian-Americans, Law, and the Nation-State* (New York: New York University Press, 1999), 114–17.

65. David T. Wellman with Howard Pinderhughes, *Portraits of White Racism*, 2nd ed. (Cambridge: Cambridge University Press, 1993; 1977), 235. Pinderhughes's study also focused on the predominantly Italian American working-class neighborhood of Bensonhurst in Brooklyn, New York, where "turf" and privilege notions revolved mainly around race. See also Michael A. Fletcher, "Asian Americans Coping with Success: Achievements Mask Challenges, Report Says," *Washington Post*, 4 March 2000, A3.

66. Wellman, *Portraits*, 235–36.

67. The 1995 Glass Ceiling Commission of the U.S. Department of Labor included in their "glossary of terms" this definition of "white American": "[T]he U.S. Bureau of the Census definition includes persons who indicated their race as 'white' or reported themselves as Canadian, German, Italian, Lebanese, Near Easterner, Arab, or Polish." See Glass Ceiling Commission, *Good for Business: Making Full Use of the Nation's Human Capital. The Environmental Scan: A Fact-Finding Report of the Federal Glass Ceiling Commission* (Washington, D.C.: Department of Labor, 1995), 170.

68. See press releases, articles, and discussions relating to Arab discrimination and assimilation in the online edition of Arab-American Anti Discrimination Committee (ADC) *Chronicle*, available at http://www.adc.org, Internet; and the Arab American online English edition of *Al-Hewar*, available at http://www.alhewar.com, Internet. See also John Garvey, "Taxi Driver (Not the Movie)," *New Abolitionist* 3, no. 1 (January/February 2000): 5, where Garvey, himself a former New York City cab driver, draws a parallel between nineteenth-century Irish Americans who adopted black antipathy as the price of becoming "white" with the much publicized reluctance and even refusal today by many New York City cab drivers (many of whom are foreign born, dark skinned, and Arab American) to pick up black customers.

69. Bill Clinton, "Mend It, Don't End It," in *ADC Chronicle*, 258–76. See also Eun Kyung Kim, "Clinton Administration Changes Approach to Racial Preferences," *Durham (NC) Carolina Times*, 10 May 1997, 1, on Clinton's cautious approach to race-based preferences in awarding $200 billion in annual federal contracts. Without administration support and with the Supreme Court's antagonism to affirmative action, civil rights leaders were taking no chances with the case of a white female teacher from Piscataway, New Jersey, about to come before the Supreme Court. In a form of "reverse reparations," they raised over $300,000 to settle the case out of court and keep it from becoming another anti-affirmative action precedent. The white teacher had sued the school district after being threatened with a layoff in favor of a black teacher with the same seniority, and the district court had denied her plea based in part on *Weber*. See Joan Biskupic, "Rights Groups Pay to Settle Bias Case," *Washington Post*, 22 November 1997, A01.

70. See Equal Employment Opportunity Commission (EEOC) Reports from EEOC website, available at http://www.eeoc.gov/stats, Internet. These reports also reveal that in fiscal year 1992 race-based charges made up 40.9 percent of all claims, while sex-based charges comprised 30.1 percent; by 1998 they were 36.2 percent and 307 percent, respectively. The "no reasonable cause" sex-based charges dismissed during that six-year period went from 53.8 percent to 55.0 percent, with the "reasonable cause" findings increasing from 3.4 percent to 5.2 percent, compared to 1.8 percent to 2.9 percent for race over that same period.

71. "Texaco Tapes Show Bias in Workplace Far from Gone," Editorial, *USA Today*, 14 November 1996, 14A. See also "Civil Rights Lawsuits Increase in 1990s," *Raleigh News and Observer*, 17 January 2000, 5A, on the U.S. Justice Department's statistics showing that "job bias statistics filed in U.S. District Courts soared from 6,936 in 1990 to 21, 540 in 1998. . . . Civil rights complaints of all varieties more than doubled from 1990 to 1998, from 18,793 to 42,354."

72. Mary Frances Berry, "Affirmative Action: Why We Need It, Why It Is Under Attack," in Curry, *Debate*, 311–12, on a 1991 Urban Institute study of job hunting. See also Harry Cross et al., eds., *Employer Hiring Practices: Differential Treatment of Hispanic and Anglo Job Seekers* (Washington, D.C.: Urban Institute Press, 1990).

73. See Manning Marable, "Staying on the Path to Racial Equality," in Curry, *Debate*, 3–15. Marable cites, among other things: (1) a 1995 *USA Today*/CNN/Gallup poll that shows only 8 percent of white women believed their qualifications were questioned because of affirmative action, and 40 percent described job discrimination as not being a problem for them (Ibid., 9); and (2) the 1990 census figures that show white women holding 40 percent of all middle management positions and gaining greater ground than black or Latino men in real earnings; see also Heidi Hartmann, "Who Has Benefited from Affirmative Action," in Ibid., 77–96, where she states that 1994 statistics "suggest that African-American women have not shared in the gains in the most desirable occupations to the same extent as white women" (81). See Acuña, *Occupied Mexico*, 452, where he notes that 66 percent of white males and 58 percent of white females voted for Proposition 209. See the Internet website of the National Organization for Women (NOW), available at http://www.now.org, for speeches, legislative updates, calls to action, and articles in the *National Now Times*, with affirmative action listed as one of NOW's "key issues."

74. Curry, *Debate*, 97–98.

75. Ibid. Even with Proposition 209 calling for the abolition of gender as well as (black) "racial preferences," 1996 Republican presidential candidate Robert Dole declared affirmative action a failure as a *race*, not a *gender* program. The preservation of "white rights" of the "white Christian native-born woman" is now an unspoken subtext. See James Rosen, "Affirmative Action Draws Dole's fire," *Raleigh News and Observer*, 29 October 1996, 1A.

76. In early 1998, conservative activist Clint Bolick launched a project (ironically dubbed "Project for All Deliberate Speed") to pressure all fifty state attorneys general to eliminate race preferences. See "Foes of Affirmative Action Pressure Legal Officers," *Raleigh News and Observer*, 12 March 1998, 5A.

77. Andrew Hacker, *Dissent* 42 (fall 1995): 466.

78. Manning Marable, *Beyond Black and White: Transforming African-American Politics* (London: Verso, 1995), 86–87. Marable notes that the 1990 census showed mean on-the-job earnings for all American adults totaling $15,105. See also Peter Skerry, "Borders and Quotas: Immigration and the Affirmative Action State," *Public Interest* 96 (1989): 86–102.

79. See, for example, Kimberlé Crenshaw, keynote speaker on Critical Race Theory, "Black Women's Book Fair," Duke University, Durham, NC, 25 March 1999, for remarks on Proposition 209; and George Derek Musgrove, "Good at the Game of Tricknology: Proposition 209 and the Struggle for the Historical Memory of the Civil Rights Movement," *Souls: A Critical Journal of Black Politics, Culture, and Society* 1, no. 3 (summer 1999): 7–24.

80. See Earl Ofari Hutchinson, "Why Do So Many Blacks Oppose Affirmative Action?," Durham [NC] *Carolina Times*, 21 December 1996, 10. Black businessman Ward Connerly's leading role in the campaign for Proposition 209, after he had benefited from affirmative action contracts, is an example of this traditional conservatism combined with middle-class uplift ideology, assimilationism, and hypocrisy. See Paul Rockwell, "Angry White Guys for Affirmative Action," [online article], available at http://www.dnai.com/~awgfaa, Internet; and Lipsitz, *The Possessive Investment*, 224–28, on Connerly and other regents "hooking up" the admission of family and friends, as well as the Proposition 209 campaign manager Joe C. Gelman's acknowledgment that organizers used Connerly as a

shield against accusations of racism. See also Drake and Holsworth, *Black Progress*, 35, on Harold Cruse's black "nationalist objections to affirmative action"; and Stephen L. Carter, *Reflections of an Affirmative Action Baby* (New York: Basic, 1991).

81. Drake and Holsworth, *Black Progress*, 92–93, and supra note 48. See also "Atlanta's Mayor Firm on Preferences," *Raleigh News and Observer*, 16 July 1999, 7A, on Atlanta Mayor Bill Campbell's defiance of a lawsuit against that city's affirmative action program, begun in 1975 by Atlanta's first black mayor, Maynard Jackson, and which has sustained criticism by "both white and minority business people [that it] . . . amounts to a patronage system." See also Adolph Reed Jr., *Stirrings in the Jug: Black Politics in the Post-Segregation Era* (Minneapolis: University of Minnesota Press, 1999), 5, 95, 142, for Reed's account of Jackson's breaking the 1977 sanitation workers' strike in Atlanta: 2,000 workers (almost all black) were fired while Jackson portrayed it as a racial attack on his administration by the white-led AFSCME. Reed further critiques the Atlanta "set-aside" model of affirmative action as too limited and "developmentalist." Ibid., 70, 77, 106, 112, 174.

82. See María E. Enchautegui et al., *Do Minority-Owned Businesses Get a Fair Share of Government Contracts?* (Washington, D.C.: Urban Institute, 1997). The report is based on fifty-eight surveys of eighteen states and Washington, D.C., and a "variety of governmental units" (Ibid., 27). See also Ibid., viii, for how affirmative action in this arena includes both factoring race in awards and assistance in the areas of lending, bonding, technical help, and expanded notice.

83. See Ibid., 2, where the authors note that, although an important issue, contracting is the "least prominent" of the three primary affirmative action debate arenas that include employment and higher education; and Ibid., vii, where they state: "In 1990, procurement at all levels of government represented $450 billion, or almost 10 percent of GNP. State and local government spending accounted for more than half of all procurement—approximately $250 billion." The authors add that government contracting is likely to rise and government employment to fall with government downsizing.

84. Ibid., 49: "Opinion polls indicate that young African Americans are more likely than white Americans to want to form their own businesses." Eighty-three percent of black firms (which take in only 1 percent of all receipts) had no employees, compared with 74 percent of all firms. See Ibid., 3. See also Ibid., 33: "While minorities account for 21 percent of the population, they own only 12 percent of businesses and receive only 6 percent of all receipts."

85. Ibid., viii, on barriers to minority contracting; Ibid., 37: "Fifty percent of white business owners had close relatives who owned a business. A quarter worked for close relatives who owned a business"; and Ibid., 42–43, on (1) black contractors (most of whom have to compete as subcontractors with white subcontractors for a white prime contractor's project) seeing their bids dropped, excluded, or ignored, or even finding their work and equipment sabotaged, and (2) white markup of construction supplies and manipulation of the bid process (white prime contractors do this by not publicizing contracts or may even reveal minority subcontractor bids to white competitors, permitting the latter to then underbid the former).

86. Ibid., x. The authors continue: "That is, minority-owned businesses received fewer government contracting dollars than would be expected otherwise based on their availability. Minority-owned businesses as a group received only 57 cents on each dollar they would be expected to receive based on the percentage of all 'ready, willing, and able' firms that are minority-owned."

87. Ibid., 22. See Ibid., 44–48, for goals and sanctions of federal affirmative action programs in contracting.

88. *U.S. Bureau of the Census Statistical Abstract of the United States: 1994*, 114th ed. (Washington,

D.C.: GPO, 1994), 157, 418; and Julianne Malveux, "The Future of Work and Who Will Get It," in *The State of Black America 1998*, ed. Lee A. Daniels (Washington, D.C.: National Urban League, 1998), 54. See also Victoria Valle, "Sitting In for Diversity," in Curry, *Debate*, 213: enrollment in the University of California system by black residents was already stalled at 4.3 percent from 1978 to 1994.

89. See "Flood of Applications Makes College Admission Tougher than Ever," *Raleigh News and Observer*, 12 June 1999, 7A, for statistics revealing that 67 percent (up from 50 percent in 1977) of high school seniors are expected to attend college, where record numbers (14.8 million) currently attend, with "suburban schools sending 70 to 80 percent of their students to college," according to Robert Zemsky, director of the Institute for Research on Higher Education at the University of Pennsylvania, who adds: "Other routes into the work force are withering. Vocational education has been cut in half. This is the wave accompanying globalization of the economy."

90. See Parker, "Damaging Consequences." The Supreme Court's refusal to rule against Cheryl Hopwood's successful 1996 suit against the University of Texas law school for not admitting her because she was white (in *Hopwood v. Texas*) led to Texas and Louisiana abolishing race as a consideration in college admissions. Jennifer Gratz's case (*Gratz v. University of Michigan*) was taken up by the Center for Individual Rights eager to find a white woman plaintiff. Gratz, who comes from a working-class background and who applied only to the University of Michigan because she assumed she would get in, claims to be a victim of preferences given to "unqualified black and Hispanic students," although there seems to be no such category as "unqualified whites." See Lisa Belkin, "She Says She Was Rejected by a College for Being White. Is She Paranoid, Racist, or Right?" in *Glamour*, November 1998, 278–81. Besides interviewing Gratz, Belkin talked with Michigan undergraduate Andrea Guzman, a Latina from a poor background, who makes an observation common in minority student experience: "Some white students will tell you to your face that they don't think you should be here." Ibid., 281.

91. Allen S. Hammond IV, "Standing at the Edge of the Digital Divide," in Daniels, *The State of Black America*, 205.

92. See Andrew Hacker, "Malign Neglect: The Crackdown on African-Americans," *Nation* 261, no. 2 (10 July 1995): 45–49; Robert Gooding-Williams, ed., *Reading Rodney King/Reading Urban Uprising* (New York: Routledge, 1993); Haki Madhubuti, ed., *Why L.A. Happened: Implications of the '92 Los Angeles Rebellion* (Chicago: Third World Press, 1993); Midnight Notes Collective, eds., *Midnight Oil: Work, Energy, War 1973–1992* (Brooklyn: Autonomedia, 1992); Ellis Cose, *The Rage of a Privileged Class* (New York: Harper, 1993). See also Derrick A. Bell Jr.'s nightmare fantasy of whites today selling blacks to alien "Space Traders" in *Faces at the Bottom of the Well: The Permanence of Racism* (New York: Basic, 1992), 158–94; and the sequel in *Gospel Choirs: Psalms of Survival for an Alien Land Called Home* (New York: Basic, 1996), 17–28.

93. Hacker, "Malign Neglect"; Eric Foner, *Nothing but Freedom: Emancipation and Its Legacy* (Baton Rouge: Louisiana State University Press, 1983), 39–73; and Joe Davidson, "Crime Pays Big Time: Warehousing Blacks Means More Profits for the Prison Industry," *Emerge* 9, no. 1 (October 1997): 36–46.

94. Mumia Abu-Jamal, *Live from Death Row* (Reading, MA: Addison-Wesley, 1995), 128. California prison guards now earn more than $10,000 more annually than schoolteachers, and the number of prison guards has doubled in at least sixteen states. See Joe Davidson, "Caged Cargo: African-Americans Are Grist for the Fast-growing Prison Industry's Money Mill," *Emerge* 9, no. 1 (October 1997), 46.

95. James Boggs, *Racism and the Class Struggle: Further Pages from a Black Worker's Notebook* (New York: Monthly Review, 1970), 13.

96. See, for example, Gail Williams O'Brien, *The Color of the Law: Race, Violence, and Justice in the Post–World War II South* (Chapel Hill: University of North Carolina Press, 1999).

97. Davidson, "Caged Cargo," 36–46. Private prison space has grown from 350 beds to 80,000 beds since the early 1980s and is still growing (Ibid., 37). See "A Look at the New Slave Labor System," in a newsletter and direct mailing circulated in the fall of 1999 by IFCO/Pastors for Peace (Interreligious Foundation for Community Organization, founded in New York City in the wake of the 1970 reparations campaign against white churches discussed in chapter 6),which noted, among other things: "The 13th Amendment to the US Constitution abolished slavery everywhere except in prisons. In the 1970's Chief Justice Warren Burger called for turning prisons into factories with fences"; A Department of Justice publication makes it clear: "Inmates represent a readily available and dependable source of entry-level labor that is cost-effective alternative to work forces found in Mexico, the Caribbean Basin, Southeast Asia, and the Pacific Rim countries"; and "US prisoners are being paid as little as 11 cents per hour—in some cases no wages at all—to manufacture goods for corporations such as McDonald's, TWA, and Starbucks. These same multinational corporations, also including General Electric, American Express, AT&T, Sprint, MCI, and Chevron earn an estimated $40 billion a year from prison labor in the United States." See also Daniel Burton-Rose, ed., *The Ceiling of America: An Inside Look at the U.S. Prison Industry* (Monroe, ME: Common Courage, 1998), esp. 102–6, 114–21.

98. Sue Sturgis, "Working for the Gov," (*Durham (NC) Independent*, 9 April 1997, 16–17.

99. Barbara Ransby, "US: The Black Poor and the Politics of Expendability," *Race and Class: A Journal for Black and Third World Liberation* 38, no. 2 (October–December 1996): 6. The United States "now has the largest incarcerated population in the world." See also Nicholas Confessore, "Prisoner Proliferation," *American Prospect* 46 (September–October 1999), 69.

100. Davidson, "Caged Cargo," 37.

101. Ransby, "US," 6.

102. Abu-Jamal, *Live*, 129. In a related item, President Clinton was told by an angry audience at Riverside Church in New York City "that as a result of [welfare reform] law, students on public assistance have been forced to drop out of college in order to meet city work requirements." See Adam Nagourney, "A Surprise as President Is Assailed Over Welfare," *New York Times*, 19 February 1997, B6.

103. Ransby, "US," 8. See also "13% of Black Men Barred from Voting," *Raleigh News and Observer*, 23 October 1998, 7A: "A total of 1.4 million African-American men nationwide—13 percent of all black men—will not be able to vote in the election next month because they were once convicted of a felony. . . . The percentage of black men disenfranchised from the system is seven times the national average . . . according to the study conducted jointly by the Sentencing Project and Human Rights Watch." For another view that acknowledges a history of racism in the American legal system but objects to "diversity" measures like race-based jury selection or discussion of the "drug war," see Randall Kennedy, *Race, Crime, and the Law* (New York: Pantheon Books, 1997).

104. Sturgis, "Working for the Gov"; and the website of AFSCME Corrections United (ACU), the largest organization of unionized prison guards in the U.S. and a division of American Federation of State, County, and Municipal Employees (AFSCME). Available at http://www.afscme.org, Internet. See also Gordon Lafer, "Captive Labor: America's Prisoners As Corporate Workforce," *American Prospect* 46 (September–October 1999): 66–70.

105. "Veterans' Preference Bill Introduced in Senate," *APWU News Service* [American Postal Workers Union monthly bulletin] 27, no. 14 (1 August 1997). Beginning with the *Veterans' Preference Act of 1944, Statutes at Large* 58 (1944), 387–91, veterans, their spouses, and their unmarried widows or widowers could receive five extra points (ten if they have a disability) upon taking the civil service examination. Veterans could also apply military service time toward their government service.

106. See *Veterans' Preference Acts, U.S. Code*, vol. 5, secs. 3301–63, 3501–4 (1999); and *Veterans' Benefits Acts, U.S. Code*, vol. 38, secs. 3001–7001 (1958). Numerous references are made between them to direct loans, housing assistance, preferential government hiring, contracts, and training programs for veterans. One typical reference is this one in *Veterans' Benefits*, vol. 38, sec. 4212, entitled "Veterans' Employment Emphasis Under Federal Contracts": "In addition to requiring affirmative action to employ such veterans [disabled and Vietnam] under such contracts and subcontracts and in order to promote the implementation of such requirements, the President shall implement the provisions of this section by promulgating regulations which shall require that . . . each such local [employment] office shall give such veterans priority in referral to such employment openings." The secretary of labor is charged with responding to any incidence of discrimination. In 1974 the wording "affirmative action" was substituted for the words "special emphasis" that previously appeared in this passage.

107. Ibid.

108. See U.S. Congress, House, Subcommittee on Civil Service of the Committee on Government Reform and Oversight, *H.R. 240, Veterans' Employment Opportunities Act of 1997*, 105th Cong., 1st sess., 26 February 1997, 76.

109. Ibid., 7

110. See Congress, House, Committee on Post Office and Civil Service, *Appointment and Promotion of Veterans of World War II*, 81st Cong., 1st sess., 3 June 1946, 5.

111. Ibid., 4. Italics added.

112. See "Letter Carriers' Victory Shines Amid Economic Trauma of the Seventies," *Postal Record* 112, no. 10 (November 1999), 10–15; M. Brady Mikusko, *Carriers in a Common Cause: A History of Letter Carriers and the NALC* (Washington, D.C.: National Association of Letter Carriers, 1989), 64 ; Leon H. Sullivan, *Build, Brother, Build* (Philadelphia: Macrae Smith, 1969), 66; and Hacker, *Two Nations*, 116–17, 121, on how blacks, as 10.2 percent of the workforce, make up almost 20 percent of the U.S. Postal Service, including 26.8 percent of postal clerks. See also the line uttered more than once ("There's always work at the Post Office!") by comedian-actor Robert Townsend's character's mother in his film *Hollywood Shuffle* (prod. and dir. Robert Townsend, 82 min., Samuel Goldwyn, 1987). Her suggestion was proposed as an honest, blue-collar alternative to his frustrated actor character trying out for stereotyped black film and television roles in Hollywood.

113. See the collected essays in Richard F. America, ed., *The Wealth of Races: The Present Value of Benefits from Past Injustices* (New York: Greenwood, 1990).

114. Lori Robinson, "The Big Pay Back: White Backlash Stirs Reparations Movement," *Emerge* 8, no. 4 (February 1997), 42–51; Crenshaw et al., *Critical Race Theory*; Angela Hagerty, "Examining Equality: The Fair Employment Act (NI) 1989 and Its Review," reprinted from *Web Journal of Current Legal Issues*, [online journal] available at http://ncl.ac.uk/~nlawww/articles2/hegarty2.html, Internet; M. M. Litman, "Affirmative Action Addresses Inequalities," *Duke University Chronicle*, 25 November 1997, 12; and Kenneth J. Cooper, "Where Quotas Work: Some Nations Mandate Affirmative Action," *Emerge* 9, no. 7 (May 1998): 62–66.

115. See, for example, James P. Shenton, "Ethnicity and Immigration," in Foner, *The New American History*, 265–66.

116. See Malik Shabazz, "Reparations for African-Americans and Africa," *Crisis* 101, no. 1 (January 1994): 20–22, 27; and Michael D'Orso, *Like Judgement Day: The Ruin and Redemption of a Town Called Rosewood* (New York: Boulevard Books, 1996), 204–8. The attorney for the Rosewood families, Steve Hanlon, used the 1988 Japanese-American Reparation Act (which awarded $20,000 and an apology to each family) in their legislative campaign for compensation. The final settlement of $1.5 million included $150,000 to each survivor and college scholarship money for minority students. D'Orso offers this account of the process: "The language of the bill was no small matter. The distinction, for example, between the terms *compensation* and *reparation* was enormously important. Compensation, as Hanlon make painstakingly clear to every reporter he faced, is a strictly judicial term, involving payments for specific losses or damages identified and measured through legal procedure. Compensation is what is paid each time a lawsuit is won in court or a claims bill is passed by a legislature. Reparation, on the other hand, is a much broader 'extra-judicial' concept, extending beyond the strict boundaries of the law. Reparations involves payments to make amends for more general wrongs and injuries, such as the devastation done during a war or the suffering inflicted by a system such as slavery. The Rosewood bill sought compensation, not reparation. But that distinction was already becoming lost in the clamor of alarm . . . that this claim would open for every group with a historical grievance against the government" (Ibid., 206). See also N'COBRA website, ttp://www.ncobra.org, Internet; and the *Alaska Native Claims Settlement Act, Statutes at Large* 85 (1971): 688–92, 702–3. See also a report on an Oklahoma state commission recommending reparations be paid to the survivors and descendants of a 1921 white riot in Tulsa that killed almost 300 people, most of them African Americans, in Renee Ruble, "Oklahoma Weighs Reparations for Riot Survivors," *Raleigh News and Observer*, 5 February 2000, 5A.

117. Bittker, *Black Reparations*, 31.

118. America, "Overview and Summary," in America, *Wealth*, 11.

119. Stanley H. Masters, "The Social Debt to Blacks: A Case for Affirmative Action," in Ibid., 179–90. For more on affirmative action and reparations, see Crenshaw et al., *Critical Race Theory*. See, for example, Mari Matsuda, "Looking to the Bottom: Critical Legal Studies and Reparations," in Ibid., 63–79.

120. David H. Swinton quoted in William Darity Jr., "Forty Acres and a Mule: Placing a Price Tag on Oppression," in America, *Wealth*, 10. See also Llena Jackson-Leslie, "Race, Sex and Meritocracy," *Black Scholar* 25, no. 3 (summer 1995): 24–29; and James E. Jones Jr., "The Rise and Fall of Affirmative Action," in Hill and Jones, *Race in America*, 345–69.

121. David Swinton, "Racial Equality and Reparations," in America, *Wealth*, 161.

122. See supra note 57; and Charles Fried, "Uneasy Preferences: Affirmative Action, in Retrospect," *American Prospect* 46 (September–October 1999): 53. An intriguing piece of modern white folklore heard in casual conversation as well as observed routinely in letters columns to newspapers in North Carolina has claimed that the deaths of white soldiers during the Civil War should somehow constitute sufficient blood payment or legal tender to black people for the sins of slavery. See also Randall Robinson, *The Debt: What America Owes to Blacks* (New York: Dutton, 2000); and "Aetna—Not Glad We Met Ya," *Nation* 270, no. 13 (3 April 2000): 7, on that mammoth insurance corporation's "acknowledgment that it is considering how to make amends for having sold life insurance policies on slaves in the 1850s."

123. Swinton quoted in *Berkeley Working Paper #1*, "An Illustrative Estimate: The Present Value of the Benefits from Racial Discrimination, 1929–1969," in America, *Wealth*, 163.

124. Ibid.

125. Darity, "Forty Acres and a Mule," 11. Figures originated with the director of research for the Equal Opportunity Commission, Melvin Humphrey.

126. Swinton, "Racial Equality and Reparations," 161.

127. Robert S. Browne, "Achieving Parity through Reparations," in America, Wealth, 200. In an interesting irony, the demand for reparations was dropped by the Housekeepers Association (HA, now affiliated with UE Local 150) during labor negotiations with the University of North Carolina–Chapel Hill after an outcry led by Republican state legislators. The housekeepers then realized that not only could reparations as a political demand not be awarded in a legal settlement, but it would have amounted to only $1 million—$19 million less than they were asking for in back pay. Alan McSurely (HA attorney), telephone interview by author, 11 November 1996.

128. Melvin L. Oliver and Thomas M. Shapiro, Black Wealth/White Wealth: A New Perspective on Racial Equality (New York: Routledge, 1997), 43 and passim. Discriminatory real estate practices "cost the black community approximately $83 billion" (Ibid., 185). White alumni of traditionally white colleges pass on a kind of inheritance to their children with the admissions preference called a "legacy," similar to white construction workers or police officers obtaining positions for their children. See Hill, "Race."

129. Oliver and Shapiro, Black Wealth, 103.

130. Ibid., 109. Home ownership is the basis of home equity, an important source of wealth to the middle class, not to mention the government subsidy that is the home mortgage interest tax deduction. Mortgage rate discrimination by banks, or "the price of being black," is projected to be "about $21.5 billion for the next generation of black homeowners." Ibid., 147.

131. Ibid.

132. See Robin D. G. Kelley, Into the Fire: African Americans since 1970 (New York: Oxford University Press, 1996) for these relevant statistics: "In 1970, 15.7 percent of black families had incomes over $35,000; by 1986 the percentage had grown to 21.2 percent. Likewise, black families earning more than $50,000 almost doubled, increasing from 4.7 percent in 1970 to 8.8 percent in 1986 . . ." (58). By 1970 "28 percent of all employed African Americans held government jobs, and approximately 60 percent of all black professional workers were employed by governmental bodies . . . [while] in 1970 African Americans held only 1 percent of the managerial and administrative jobs in manufacturing" (Ibid., 60). Also, from 1972 to 1977, "the number of black-owned firms and their proportion of total industry revenue declined for the most part. . . . A recent survey of 500 black entrepreneurs with an annual revenue of $100,000 or more revealed that 90 percent had been turned down by banks when they applied for business loans." Ibid., 61.

133. Oliver and Shapiro, Black Wealth, 162. Italics added. Oliver and Shapiro define "net worth" as "the straightforward value of all assets less any debts," while "net financial assets" "excludes equity accrued in a home or vehicle from the calculation of a households available resources." Ibid., 58.

134. "Until It Hurts," 3–5.

135. W. E. B. Du Bois, Black Reconstruction in America 1860–1880 (Cleveland: Meridian, 1968; 1935). As unlikely as these arguments seem to many, it is relevant to point out that a minority of people in this country on both the eve of the Civil War and again on the eve of the civil rights era thought the end was near for slavery and Jim Crow, respectively.

136. David Levering Lewis, "Du Bois and the Challenge of the Black Press," New Crisis 104, no. 1 (July 1997): 43–44. Lewis relates how Southern congressmen used Du Bois's editorials on separate black economic development as justification for racial wage differentials under the New Deal's National Industrial Recovery Act.

137. See David G. Savage, "Justices Let Stand Affirmative Action Ban," *Raleigh News and Observer*, 4 November 1997, 1A. The same article disclosed congressional Republicans' division on affirmative action repeal and fears of a black voter backlash; Sam Howe Verhovek, "After Debate, Houston Votes to Maintain Affirmative Action Policy," *Duke University Chronicle*, 6 November 1997, 6; Anthony S. Platt, "U.S. Race Relations at the Crossroads in California," *Monthly Review* 48, no. 5 (October 1966): 29; and Robert Staples, "Black Deprivation–White Privilege: The Assault on Affirmative Action," *Black Scholar* 25, no. 3 (summer 1995): 2–6.

138. Contributing to this paradoxical image is the voluntary nature of those programs. See Hartmann, "Who Has Benefited," in Curry, *Debate*, 86, who concurs with researcher Barbara Bergmann that "virtually all affirmative action is actually voluntary," if for no other reason than government compliance monitoring is very limited.

139. Stephanie M. Wildman, "Privilege in the Workplace: The Missing Element in Antidiscrimination Law," in *Privilege Revealed: How Invisible Preference Undermines America*, ed. Stephanie M. Wildman, (New York: New York University Press, 1996), 28.

140. Cheryl I. Harris, "Whiteness as Property," in Crenshaw et al., *Critical Race Theory*, 289–90.

141. Ibid., 289.

142. Skrentny, *The Ironies of Affirmative Action*, 127.

143. Oliver and Shapiro, *Black Wealth*, 177.

144. Tim Simmons and Irwin Spencer, "Busing for Balance Halted: Ruling in Charlotte Case Probably Will Influence Triangle Policies," *Raleigh News and Observer*, 11 September 1999, 1A, 16A. A related article also notes that Wake County (which contains the state capital of Raleigh) already relies upon income level in determining magnet school admissions. See T. Keung Hui, "Wake, Durham Have Eye on Other Cases," in Ibid., 16A. See also Thomas W. Hanchett, *Sorting Out the New South City: Race, Class, and Urban Development in Charlotte, 1875–1975* (Chapel Hill: University of North Carolina Press, 1998), 252–53. NCCU Chancellor Julius Chambers had been the plaintiff's attorney in *Swann*, where he had "focused relentlessly on the role government played in promoting residential segregation" (Ibid., 253). Busing in this case amounted to what might be called a "white flight tax."

145. Paul Nowell, "Lawsuit Challenges Desegregation Policy," *Raleigh News and Observer*, 18 April 1999, 3B. The article notes that his daughter "is half white and half Hispanic" and "fell into the 'nonblack' category that the school system uses to allot magnet seats." The NAACP and many black parents supported the school district. But see also the editorial "An Abysmal Failure to Many" from the *Carolinian*, a Raleigh, North Carolina, African American weekly newspaper, which reacted to the judge's decision by noting how black students had made most of the bus trips, endured "outsider" status at their new schools, found themselves "tracked" in an internal Jim Crow system, lost black teachers as role models, and saw achievement decline with morale. "Many black parents and others in the African-American community," concluded the *Carolinian*, "are responding, 'Good riddance [to busing]!' " Reprinted in *Raleigh News and Observer*, 26 September 1999, 32A.

146. Mark Z. Barabak, "GOP Senator to Focus on Women, Minorities," *Los Angeles Times*, 9 May 1999, A22.

147. See "Message from the Chairman" Secretary of Labor Robert B. Reich in Glass Ceiling Commission, *Good for Business*, iii. Reich also notes that Elizabeth Dole's husband, Sen. Robert Dole (R-Kansas), introduced the 1991 Glass Ceiling Act based on the original *Report on the Glass Ceiling Initiative* of that same year. The act was made law as Title II of the Civil Rights Act of 1991, establishing the bipartisan Glass Ceiling Commission.

148. In the writings on HBCUs, there is a curious variance in the total numbers of HBCUs—anywhere from 102 to 118. See Julian B. Roebuck and Komanduri S. Murty, *Historically Black Colleges and Universities: Their Place in Higher Education* (Westport, CT: Praeger, 1993), 97, who base their figure of 109 upon official government figures that include United States territories as well as states.

149. Ernie Suggs, "Fighting to Survive," *Durham Herald-Sun*, series, fall 1997.

150. Roebuck and Murty, *Historically Black Colleges*. See also R. B. Atwood, "The Future of the Negro Land-Grant College," *Journal of Negro Education* 27, no. 3 (summer, 1958): 381–91.

151. Suggs, "Fighting to Survive."

152. *U.S. v. Fordice*, 505 U.S. 717 (1992); and Gloria A. Mixon et al., "Historically Black Colleges and Universities: A Future in the Balance," [online document, originally appearing in *Academe*, January/February 1995], available at http://eric-web.tc.columbia.edu/hbcu/report.html, Internet.

153. See Alexandra Phanor, "The Bleaching of Bluefield: Why Is This Historically Black College 92 Percent White?," *Source* (August 1999): 83.

154. Tim Chavez, "Diversity Mistaken for Racism," *Nashville Tennessean*, 15 October 1998; and Monique Fields, "White Fraternity May Be Headed to TSU," *Nashville Tennessean*, 22 January 1999.

155. See Wellman, *Portraits*, 223–47. See also William G. Bowen and Derek Bok, *The Shape of the River: Long-term Consequences of Considering Race in College and University Admissions* (Princeton, NJ: Princeton University Press, 1998). Some TWIs now feature a popular curriculum called "whiteness studies," which is intended to make white students feel better about themselves in the diversity mix. For an account of the debate over and confrontation with one of the most egregious examples of this phenomenon at Arizona State University, see Joel Olson, "Inventing White Roots: Bogus 'White Culture' Class Is Liberal Attempt to Save the White Race," *New Abolitionist* 3, no. 1 (January/February 2000): 1, 4.

156. See Theodore Cross and Robert Bruce Slater, "The Financial Footings of the Black Colleges," *Journal of Blacks in Higher Education* 5 (winter 1994/1995): 76–79.

157. See *AFL–CIO News* [online document], available at http://www.aflcio.org/publ/newsonline/, Internet, for the following articles: "AFL–CIO Action Opens Early" (95oct6/fullpart.html); "Clinton Stand on Affirmative Action Praised by Labor" (95jul31/affirm.html); James B. Parks, "Labor to Fight for Affirmative Action" (96March8/affirm.html); James B. Parks, "Unions Renew King's Cry for Justice" (96jan19/march.html); Sharolyn Rosier, " 'Little Davis-Bacon' Under Siege: Prevailing Wage Merits Ignored in Statehouses" (95aug11/davba.html); and Sharolyn Rosier, "UAW Writers Win Top ILCA Awards," (96sep20.ilca.htm). The latter is in reference to Andy Neather and Dave Elsila, "Putting Together the Affirmative Action Puzzle," *Solidarity* (May 1995): 7–9, 11. This award-winning article argues, among other things, that "the nation has been working on the ['equality and opportunity'] puzzle for over 200 years" (7). See also speech by AFL–CIO Secretary-Treasurer Tom Donahue, "The Black-Labor Alliance: Strengthening the Partnership for Economic Justice," A. Philip Randolph Institute Conference, Chicago, 30 June 1995, [online document], available at http://www.aflcio.org/publ/speech95/sp06302.htm, Internet. See also the account of the speech by AFSCME President Gerald W. McEntee at the 2000 Florida pro-affirmative action march by assistant editor Lynne Scott in "Let's Hear It for Affirmative Action," *AFSCME Public Employee* 65, no. 3 (May/June 2000), back page: "McEntee reminded the crowd that organized labor was responsible for including affirmative action in the historic Civil Rights Act of 1964."

158. See Glass Ceiling Commission, *Good for Business*, where, for example, it states: "Du Pont's mentoring program is tied to other initiatives to develop and advance high potential minorities and women"; that Exxon recruits "female and minority high school students" by providing them with

"professional-level mentors"; and that JC Penney Company maintains workshops "to create an awareness of cultural differences, to develop an understanding of how these diverse cultures benefit the workplace . . ." (183). See also Equal Employment Opportunity Commission, *"Best" Equal Employment Opportunity Policies, Programs, and Practices in the Private Sector: Task Force Report* (Washington, D.C.: GPO, 1998), 7; and Peter Schrag, "The Diversity Defense," *American Prospect* 46 (September–October 1999): 57–70.

159. See Jeremy Rifkin, *The End of Work: The Decline of the Global Labor Force and the Dawn of the Post-Market Era* (New York: Jeremy P. Tarcher, 1995), especially 3–14, 165–80; and George Caffentzis, *From Capitalist Crisis to Proletarian Slavery: An Introduction to Class Struggle in the U.S. 1973–1998* (Jamaica Plain, MA: Midnight Notes, 1998), esp. 22: "NAFTA [the 1994 North American Free Trade Agreement between the U.S., Canada, and Mexico, which phased out tariffs over fifteen years, allowing the free flow of capital across their national boundaries] has definitely been successful for US capital. Since 1994 real wages both in Mexico and the US have fallen while trade, capital flow, and profits have increased dramatically in the US." Overall since 1974, Caffentzis points out, "the real wage, hours of work, security of employment, share of the total social product, capacity to strike, average level of employment have constantly and, at times, dramatically deteriorated" (2). See also David Thelen, "Rethinking History and the Nation-State: Mexico and the United States"; and "Chronology: Some Events in the History of Mexico and the Border," *Journal of American History* 86, no. 2 (September 1999): 439–55.

160. Derrick A. Bell Jr., "Remembrances of Racism Past: Getting Beyond the Civil Rights Decline," in Hill and Jones, *Race in America*, 81.

161. W. E. B. Du Bois, *John Brown: A Biography* (Armonk, NY: M. E. Sharpe, 1997; 1909), 195. Italics added.

BIBLIOGRAPHY

ARTICLES

"An Abysmal Failure to Many." Editorial reprinted from *Raleigh (NC) Carolinian* in *Raleigh News and Observer*, 26 September 1999, 32A.

"Aetna—Not Glad We Met Ya." *Nation* 270, no. 13 (3 April 2000): 7.

"AFL-CIO Action Opens Early." *AFL-CIO News*, 6 October 1995. [Online document.] Available at http://www.aflcio.org/newsonline/publ/95oct6/fullpart.html. Internet.

Allen, Robert L. "Past Due: The African American Quest for Reparations." *Black Scholar* 28, no. 2 (summer 1998): 2–17.

"The Allen Building Takeover: Thirty Years Later." *Duke University Chronicle* (supplement) 12 February 1999, 1–8.

Arnesen, Eric. "Up from Exclusion: Black and White Workers, Race, and the State of Labor History." *Reviews in American History* 26, no. 1 (March 1998): 146–74.

"Atlanta's Mayor Firm on Preferences." *Raleigh News and Observer*, 16 July 1999, 7A.

Atwood, R. B. "The Future of the Negro Land-Grant College." *Journal of Negro Education* 27, no. 3 (summer 1958): 381–91.

Auman, William T., and David D. Scarboro. "The Heroes of America in Civil War North Carolina." *North Carolina Historical Review* 58, no. 4 (October 1981): 327–63.

Barabak, Mark Z. "GOP Senator to Focus on Women, Minorities." *Los Angeles Times*, 9 May 1999, A22.

Bates, Beth Tompkins. "A New Crowd Challenges the Agenda of the Old Guardian NAACP, 1933–1941." *American Historical Review* 102, no. 2 (April 1997): 340–77.

Belkin, Lisa. "She Says She Was Rejected by a College for Being White. Is She Paranoid, Racist, or Right?" *Glamour*, November 1998, 278–81.

Belsie, Laurent. "Immigrant Flood Chases City Dwellers to White Enclaves." *Washington (D.C.) Times*, 7–13 June 1999, 1. Reprinted from *Christian Science Monitor*.

Bernstein, David. "The Davis-Bacon Act: Let's Bring Jim Crow to an End." *Cato Briefing Paper*, no. 17. 18 January 1993. [Online document.] Available at http://www.cato.org/pubs/briefs/bp-017es.html. Internet.

Bibliography

Berry, Mary Frances. "Snake Oil: Jeb Bush's Higher Education Initiative Is No Substitute for Affirmative Action." *Emerge* 11, no. 7 (May 2000): 56–59.

Biskupic, Joan. "Rights Groups Pay to Settle Bias Case." *Washington Post*, 22 November 1997.

"The Black Radical Congress: A Black Freedom Agenda for the Twenty-first Century." *Black Scholar* 28, no. 1 (spring 1998): 71–73.

Bolkhovtinov, Nikolai N. "The Declaration of Independence: A View from Russia." *Journal of American History* 85, no. 4 (March 1999): 1396–97.

Bond, Horace Mann. "Forty Acres and a Mule." *Opportunity* 13, no. 5 (May 1935): 140–41, 151.

Broder, David. "Jury Verdicts Aren't the Problem." *Raleigh News and Observer*, 12 October 1995, 21A.

Brody, Carl E., Jr. "A Historical Review of Affirmative Action and the Interpretation of Its Legislative Intent by the Supreme Court." [Online document.] Available at http://wwwuakron.edu/law rev/brody.html. Internet.

"Broken Promise: *Brown v. Board of Education* Forty Years Later." *Nation* 258, no. 20 (23 May 1994).

Brooks, Charlotte. "In the Twilight Zone between Black and White: Japanese American Resettlement and Community in Chicago, 1942–1945." *Journal of American History* 85, no. 4 (March 2000): 1655–87.

Cawley, Alexa Silver. "A Passionate Affair: The Master-Servant Relationship in Seventeenth-Century Maryland." *Historian* 61, no. 4 (summer 1999): 751–63.

Chavez, Tim. "Diversity Mistaken for Racism." *Nashville Tennessean*, 15 October 1998.

Chicago Surrealist Group. "Three Days that Shook the New World Order: The Los Angeles Rebellion of 1992." *Race Traitor: journal of the new abolitionism* 2 (summer 1993): 1–17.

"Civil Rights Lawsuits Increase in the 1990s." *Raleigh News and Observer*, 1 January 2000, 5A.

Clayton, Dewey. "Black Congressional Representation in the South: Making the Case for Majority Black Districts." *Black Scholar* 28, no. 2 (summer 1998): 36–46.

"Clinton Stand on Affirmative Action Praised by Labor." *AFL-CIO News*, 31 July 1995. [Online document.] Available at http://www.aflcio.org/newsonline/publ/95jul31/affirm.html. Internet.

Confessore, Nicholas. "Prisoner Proliferation." *American Prospect* 46 (September–October 1999): 69.

Cooper, Kenneth J. "Where Quotas Work: Some Nations Mandate Affirmative Action." *Emerge* 9, no. 7 (May 1998): 62–66.

Corwin, Miles. "L.A. Copying Miami's Failures at Rebuilding after Riots." (Massachusetts Institute of Technology) *Tech*, 13 April 1993, 2.

Court Makes It Harder to Create Districts Favoring Minority Voters." *Raleigh News and Observer*, 13 May 1997, 2A.

Cross, Theodore, and Robert Bruce Slater. "The Financial Footings of the Black Colleges." *Journal of Blacks in Higher Education* 5 (winter 1994/1995): 76–79.

Curry, George E., and Trevor W. Coleman. "The Verdict on Judge Thomas: Clarence Thomas Five Years Later." *Emerge* 8, no. 2 (November 1996): 38–48.

Davidson, Joe. "Caged Cargo: African-Americans Are Grist for the Fast-growing Prison Industry's Money Mill." *Emerge* 9, no. 1 (October 1997): 36–46.

———. "Crime Pays Big Time: Warehousing Blacks Means More Profits for the Prison Industry." *Emerge* 9, no. 1 (October 1997): 36–46.

Davis, Mike. "LA: The Fire This Time." *Covert Action Information Bulletin* 41 (summer 1992): 12–21.

———. "A Prison-Industrial Complex: Hell Factories in the Field." *Nation* 260, no. 7 (20 February 1995): 229–33.

Desroches, Robert E. " 'Not Fade Away': The Narrative of Venture Smith, an African American in the Early Republic." *Journal of American History* 84, no. 1 (June 1997): 40–66.

Bibliography

Draper, Alan. "*Brown v. Board of Education* and Organized Labor in the South." *Historian* 57, no. 1 (autumn 1994).

Dunlevy, James A., and Henry A. Gemery. "Economic Opportunity and the Responses of 'Old' and 'New' Migrants to the United States." *Journal of Economic History* 38, no. 4 (December 1978).

Ellis, Mark. "J. Edgar Hoover and the 'Red Summer' of 1919." *Journal of American Studies* 28, no. 1 (April 1994): 39–59.

Epperson, Terrence. "Whiteness in Early Virginia." *Race Traitor: journal of the new abolitionism* 7 (winter 1997): 9–20.

Erickson, Peter. "Seeing White." *Transition* 67: 166–85.

Eskew, Glenn T. " 'Bombingham': Black Protest in Postwar Birmingham, Alabama." *American Historical Review* 102, no. 2 (April 1997): 371–90.

"Fewer Minorities Studying Medicine." *Raleigh News and Observer*, 2 November 1997, 13A.

Fields, Barbara Jeanne. "Slavery, Race and Ideology in the United States of America." *New Left Review* 181 (May–June 1990): 95–118.

Fields, Monique. "White Fraternity May Be Headed to TSU." *Nashville Tennessean*, 22 January 1999.

Fletcher, Michael A. "Asian Americans Coping with Success: Achievements Mask Challenges, Report Says." *Washington Post*, 4 March 2000, A3.

"Flood of Applications Makes College Admission Tougher than Ever." *Raleigh News and Observer*, 12 June 1999, 7A.

"Foes of Affirmative Action Pressure Legal Officers." *Raleigh News and Observer*, 12 March 1998, 5A.

Fried, Charles. "Uneasy Preferences: Affirmative Action, in Retrospect." *American Prospect* 46 (September–October 1999): 50–59.

Gaines, Kevin K. "Rethinking Race and Class in African-American Struggles for Equality, 1885–1941." *American Historical Review* 102, no. 2 (April 1997): 378–87.

Gansner, Bill. "Blacks Demand Change, 'On Strike, Shut it Down.' " *Beloit (WI) College Round Table*, 16 February 1969, 11.

Garvey, John. "Taxi Driver (Not the Movie)." *New Abolitionist* 3, no. 1 (January/February 2000): 5.

Gerstle, Gary. "Theodore Roosevelt and the Divided Character of American Nationalism." *Journal of American History* 86, no. 3 (December 1999): 1280–307.

Göbel, Thomas. "Becoming American: Ethnic Workers and the Rise of the CIO." *Labor History* 29, no. 2 (spring 1988): 173–98.

Goodwyn, Lawrence C. "Populist Dreams and Negro Rights: East Texas as a Case Study." *American Historical Review* 76, no. 5 (December 1971): 1435–56.

Gordon, Michael. "Moscow Bombings Expose Ethnic Tension." *Duke University Chronicle*, 15 September 1999, 2.

Gray, Louis. "Anger Voiced Over Admissions: Students Take to the Streets in Protest of 209." *University of California-Berkeley Daily Californian*, 3 April 1998.

Gutiérrez, David G. "Migration, Emergent Ethnicity, and the 'Third Space': The Shifting Politics of Nationalism in Greater Mexico." *Journal of American History* 86, no. 2 (September 1999): 481–517.

Hacker, Andrew. *Dissent* 42 (fall 1995): 465–67.

———. "Malign Neglect: The Crackdown on African-Americans." *Nation* 261, no. 2 (10 July 1995): 45–49.

Hagerty, Angela. "Examining Equality: The Fair Employment Act (NI) 1989 and Its Review." *Web Journal of Current Legal Issues*. [Online journal.] Available at http://ncl.ac.uk/nlawww.articles2/hegarty2.html. Internet.

Bibliography

Harris, Cheryl I. "Whiteness as Property." *Harvard Law Review* 106 (1993): 1709–91.

Harris, Howell John. Review of *Workers' Paradox: The Republican Origins of New Deal Labor Policy, 1886–1935*, by Ruth O'Brien. *Journal of American History* 86, no. 2 (December 1999): 1372–73.

Hellwig, David J. "Black Leaders and United States Immigration Policy, 1917–1929." *Journal of Negro History* 66, no. 2 (1981): 110–27.

Herbold, Hilary. "Never a Level Playing Field: Blacks and the GI Bill." *Journal of Blacks in Higher Education* 5 (winter 1994/1995): 104–8.

Hernandez, Daniel. "Hundreds Join in Walkout: Teach-ins Held to Address Issues." *University of California-Berkeley Daily Californian*, 23 October 1998.

Hershberger, Mary. "Mobilizing Women, Anticipating Abolition: The Struggle Against Indian Removal in the 1830s." *Journal of American History* 86, no. 1 (June 1999): 15–40.

Hill, Herbert. "The AFL-CIO and the Black Worker: Twenty-five Years after the Merger." *Journal of Intergroup Relations* 10, no. 1 (spring 1982). Reprint.

———. "Black-Jewish Conflict in the Labor Context: Race, Jobs, and Institutional Power." *Race Traitor: journal of the new abolitionism* 5 (winter 1996): 72–103.

———. "Communist Party—Enemy of Negro Equality." *Crisis* 58, no. 6 (June–July 1951): 365–71.

———."Myth-Making as Labor History: Herbert Gutman and the United Mine Workers of America." *International Journal of Politics, Culture and Society* 2 (1988): 132–200.

———. "NAACP and the Communists." Editorial. *Crisis* 56, no. 3 (March 1949): 72.

———. "The Racial Practices of Organized Labor—In the Age of Gompers and After." New York: NAACP, 1965.

Hotakainen, Rob. "Jackson Tells Bush to Ax Admissions Plan in Fla." *Raleigh News and Observer*, 8 March 2000, 4A.

Huddle, Mark Andrew, ed. "North Carolina's Forgotten Abolitionist: The American Missionary Association Correspondence of Daniel Wilson." *North Carolina Historical Review* 72, no. 4 (October 1995): 416–55.

Hui, T. Keung. "Wake, Durham Have Eye on Other Cases." *Raleigh News and Observer*, 11 September 1999, 1A, 16A.

Humphrey, Norman Daymond. "The Growing Crisis in American Caste." *Crisis* 51, no. 7 (July 1944): 224–25.

Hutchinson, Earl Ofari. "Why Do So Many Blacks Oppose Affirmative Action?" Durham [NC] *Carolina Times*, 21 December 1996, 10.

IFCO/Pastors for Peace (Interreligious Foundation for Community Organization). "A Look at the New Slave Labor System." Fall 1999 newsletter and direct mailing.

Ignatiev, Noel. " 'Whiteness' and American Character: An Essay." *Konch* 1, no. 1 (winter 1990): 136–39.

———. "The White Worker and the Labor Movement in Nineteenth-Century America." *Race Traitor: journal of the new abolitionism* 3 (spring 1994): 99–107.

Jackson, Damien. "Illuminating Suspension: Does Color Play a Role in Durham Schools' Discipline Procedures?" *Durham (NC) Independent*, 8 March 2000, 15.

Jackson-Leslie, Llena. "Race, Sex and Meritocracy." *Black Scholar* 25 no. 3 (summer 1995): 24–29.

Johnson, Clarence R. "Negro Labor in Public Housing." *Crisis* 48, no. 2 (February 1941): 44–45.

Johnson, Walter. "The Slave Trader, the White Slave, and the Politics of Racial Determination in the 1850s." *Journal of American History* 87, no. 1 (June 2000): 13–38.

Kaczorowski, Robert J. "To Begin the Nation Anew: Congress, Citizenship, and Civil Rights after

Bibliography

the Civil War." *American Historical Review* 92, Issue 1, supplement to Vol. 92 (February 1987): 45–68.

Kay, Marvin L. Michael. Review of *The Invention of the White Race*, Vol. 2, *The Origin of Racial Oppression in Anglo-America*, by Theodore W. Allen. *Journal of American History* 86, no. 3 (December 1999): 1326–27.

Kesselman, Louis C. "The Fair Employment Practice Commission Movement in Perspective." *Journal of Negro History* 31, no. 1 (January 1941): 31–46.

Kim, Eun-Kyung. "Clinton Administration Changes Approach to Racial Preferences." *Durham (NC) Carolina Times*, 10 May 1997, 1.

Korstad, Robert, and Nelson Lichtenstein. "Opportunities Found and Lost: Labor, Radicals, and the Early Civil Rights Movement." *Journal of American History* 75, no. 3 (December 1988): 786–811.

Kruman, Mark W. "Quotas for Blacks: The Public Works Administration and the Black Construction Worker." *Labor History* 16, no. 1 (winter 1975): 37–51.

Kujovich, Gil. "Public Black Colleges: The Long History of Unequal Instruction." *Journal of Blacks in Higher Education* 3 (spring 1994): 65–76.

Lafer, Gordon. "Captive Labor: America's Prisoners as Corporate Workforce." *American Prospect* 46 (September–October 1999): 66–70.

"Letter Carriers' Victory Shines Amid Economic Trauma of the Seventies." *Postal Record* 112, no. 10 (November 1999): 10–15.

Lewis, David Levering. "Du Bois and the Challenge of the Black Press." *New Crisis* 104, no. 1 (July 1997): 43–44.

Lewis, Earl. "CIO Symposium: Robert H. Zieger, *The CIO, 1935–1955* (Chapel Hill, University of North Carolina Press, 1995)." *Labor History* 37, no. 2 (spring 1996): 171–77.

Lipsitz, George. "The Possessive Investment in Whiteness: Racialized Social Democracy and the 'White' Problem in American Studies." *American Quarterly* 47, no. 3 (September 1995): 369–87.

Litman, M. M. "Affirmative Action Addresses Inequalities." *Duke University Chronicle*, 25 November 1997, 12.

Loewen, James W. "Lies across the South." *Southern Exposure* nos. 1 and 2 (spring/summer 2000): 33–48.

Main, Jackson Turner. "The Distribution of Property in Post-Revolutionary Virginia." *Mississippi Valley Historical Review* 41 (1954–55): 241–58.

McGill, Sara. "Historically Black Schools Face Dropping Enrollment." *Duke University Chronicle*, 18 February 1999, 7.

Messer-Kruse, Timothy. "Memories of the Ku Klux Klan Honorary Society at the University of Wisconsin." *Journal of Blacks in Higher Education* 23 (spring 1999): 83–93.

Miller, Geralda. "Study: Racial Prejudice Reason for Affirmative Action Opposition." Durham [NC] *Carolina Times*, 19 February 2000, 1.

Minter, John. "Racism Benefits Whites: Franklin." *Charlotte (NC) Post* 30 October 1997, 1.

Mixon, Gloria A., John Quincy Adams, Taft Broome, Barbara Curry, Belinda Peters, Kenneth S. Tollett Sr., and Helen D. Irvin. "Historically Black Colleges: A Future in the Balance." [Online document, originally in *Academe*, January/February, 1995]. Available at http://eric-web.tc.colum bia.edu/hbcu/report.html. Internet.

Moreno, Paul D. "Racial Classifications and Reconstruction Legislation." *Journal of Southern History* 61, no. 2 (1995): 271–304.

Musgrove, George Derek. "Good at the Game of Tricknology: Proposition 209 and the Struggle for the Historical Memory of the Civil Rights Movement." *Souls: A Critical Journal of Black Politics, Culture, and Society* 1, no. 3 (summer 1999): 7–24.

Nagourney, Adam. "A Surprise as President Is Assailed Over Welfare." *New York Times,* 19 February 1997, B6.

Neather, Andy, and David Elsila. "Putting Together the Affirmative Action Puzzle." *Solidarity* (May 1995): 7–9, 11.

Nelson, Bruce. "CIO Symposium: Robert H. Zieger, *The CIO, 1935–1995* (Chapel Hill: University of North Carolina Press, 1995)." *Labor History* 37, no. 2 (spring 1996): 157–61.

———. "Organized Labor and the Struggle for Black Equality in Mobile during World War II." *Journal of American History* 80, no. 3 (December 1993): 952–88.

Nelson, William Javier. "Latinos: The Indian Escape Hatch." *Race Traitor: journal of the new abolitionism* 6 (summer 1996): 43–50.

Ngai, Mae M. "The Architecture of Race in American Immigration Law: A Reexamination of the Immigration Act of 1924." *Journal of American History* 86, no. 1 (June 1999): 67–92.

Nowell, Paul. "Lawsuit Challenges Desegregation Policy." *Raleigh News and Observer,* 18 April 1999, 3B.

Ojito, Mirta. "Living Worlds Apart in a New Land: Pair Find It Hard to Cross U.S. Racial Divide." *Portland Oregonian,* 22 June 2000, A12, A13.

Olson, Joel. "Inventing White Roots: Bogus 'White Culture' Class Is Liberal Attempt to Save the White Race." *New Abolitionist* 3, no. 1 (January/February 2000): 1, 4.

O'Reilly, Kenneth. "The Jim Crow Policies of Woodrow Wilson." *Journal of Blacks in Higher Education* 17 (autumn 1997): 117–21.

Parker, Frank R. "The Damaging Consequences of the Rehnquist Court's Commitment to Color-Blindness versus Racial Justice." *American University Law Review* 45, no. 3. [Online journal.] Available at http://www.wcl.american.edu/pub/journals/lawrev/parker.htm. Internet.

Parks, James B. "Labor to Fight for Affirmative Action." *AFL-CIO News,* 8 March 1996. [Online document.] Available at http://www.aflcio.org/newsonline/publ/96mar8/affirm.html. Internet.

———. "Unions Renew King's Cry for Justice." *AFL-CIO News,* 19 January 1996. [Online document.] Available at http://www.aflcio.org/newsonline/publ/96jan19/march.html. Internet.

Phanor, Alexandra. "The Bleaching of Bluefield: Why Is This Historically Black College 92% White?" *Source* (August 1999): 83.

"Plan to Name School After MLK Opposed." *Raleigh News and Observer,* 5 January 1998, 4A.

Platt, Anthony S. "U.S. Race Relations at the Crossroads in California." *Monthly Review* 48, no. 5 (October 1996): 29

Preece, Harold. "Confession of an Ex-Nordic: The Depression Not an Unmixed Evil." *Opportunity* 13, no. 8 (August 1935): 232–33.

Ransby, Barbara. "US: The Black Poor and the Politics of Expendability." *Race and Class: A Journal for Black and Third World Liberation* 38, no. 2 (October–December 1996): 1–12.

"Readings from the *Crisis:* "Appeal to Europe" and "Commentary." *New Crisis* 107, no. 4 (July/August 2000): 56–69.

"Regents Endorse End to Affirmative Action." *Raleigh News and Observer,* 20 November 1999, 9A.

Reynolds, Jean. "South of White Phoenix: The Geography of Whiteness." *New Abolitionist* 2, no. 5 (September–October 1999): 4–5.

Roach, Ronald. "From Combat to Campus: GI Bill Gave a Generation of African Americans an Opportunity to Pursue the American Dream." *Black Issues in Higher Education* 14, no. 13 (21 August 1997): 26–28.

Bibliography

Robinson, Lori. "The Big Pay Back: White Backlash Stirs Reparations Movement." *Emerge* 8, no. 4 (February 1997): 42–51.

Robinson, Tracy L. "The Intersections of Dominant Discourses across Race, Gender, and Other Identities." *Journal of Counseling and Development* 77, no. 1 (winter 1999): 73–79.

Rockwell, Paul. "Angry White Guys for Affirmative Action." [Online article.] Available at http://www.dnai.com/awgfaa. Internet.

Rosen, James. "Affirmative Action Draws Dole's Fire." *Raleigh News and Observer*, 29 October 1996, 1A.

Rosier, Sharolyn A. " 'Little Davis-Bacon' Under Siege: Prevailing Wage Merits Ignored in State-houses." *AFL-CIO News*, 11 August 1999. [Online document.] Available at http://www.aflcio.org/newsonline/publ/95aug11/davba.html. Internet.

Ruble, Renee. "Oklahoma Weighs Reparations for Riot Survivors." *Raleigh News and Observer*, 5 February 2000, 5A.

Sanchez, Rene. "Berkeley, UCLA Cut Minority Admission," *Raleigh News and Observer*, 1 April 1998, 1A.

Savage, David G. "Justices Let Stand Affirmative Action Ban." *Raleigh News and Observer*, 4 November 1997, 1A.

Schrag, Peter. "The Diversity Defense." *American Prospect* 46 (September–October 1999): 57–70.

Scott, Lynne. "Let's Hear It for Affirmative Action." *AFSCME Public Employee* 65, no. 3 (May/June 2000), back page.

Shabazz, Malik. "Reparations for African-Americans and Africa." *Crisis* 101, no. 1 (January 1994): 20–22, 27.

Shimm, Melvin G. Letter to the editor. *Raleigh News and Observer*, 11 April 2000, 12A.

Simmons, Tim, and Irwin Speizer. "Busing for Balance Halted: Ruling in Charlotte Case Probably Will Influence Triangle Policies." *Raleigh News and Observer*, 11 September 1999, 1A, 16A.

Skerry, Peter. "Borders and Quotas: Immigration and the Affirmative Action State." *Public Interest* 96 (1989): 86–102.

"Slaves Built D.C.'s Freedom Symbols." *Raleigh News and Observer*, 23 July 2000, 5A.

Smith, Marian L. " 'Any Woman Who Is Now or May Hereafter Be Married': Women and Natural-ization, ca. 1802–1940." *Prologue: Quarterly of the National Archives and Records Administration* 30 no. 2 (summer 1998). [Online document.]

———. "Review of INS History." [Online document.] Available at http://www.ins.usdoj.gov; Internet.

Snow, Anita. "Havana Welcomes Boy." *Raleigh News and Observer*, 29 June 2000, A1, A16.

Spaulding, Theodore. "Philadelphia Hate Strike." *Crisis* 51, no. 9 (September 1944): 281–83, 301.

Staples, Robert. "Black Deprivation-White Privilege: The Assault on Affirmative Action." *Black Scholar* 25, no. 3 (summer 1995): 2–6.

Steele, Richard W. " 'No Racials': Discrimination against Ethnics in American Defense Industry, 1940–1942." *Labor History* 32, no. 1 (winter 1991): 66–90.

Stein, Nancy. "Affirmative Action and the Persistence of Racism." *Social Justice* 22, no. 3 (fall 1995): 28–45.

Sturgis, Sue. "Working for the Gov." Durham [NC] *Independent*, 9 April 1997, 16–17.

Suggs, Ernie. "Fighting to Survive." *Durham [NC] Herald-Sun*, series, fall 1997.

Syracuse University Archives and Records Management. "Remembering the GI Bulge: The Service-men's Readjustment Act of 1944." [Online document.] Available at http://sumweb.syr.edu/archives/giserve.html. Internet.

Bibliography

Tennassee, Paul Nehru. "NAPFE: A Legacy of Resistance and Contributions 1913–1999." *National Alliance* 55, no. 10 (October 1999): 12–15.

"Texaco Tapes Show Bias in Workplace Far from Gone." Editorial. *USA Today*, 14 November 1996, 14A.

Thelen, David. "Rethinking History and the Nation-State: Mexico and the United States"; and "Chronology: Some Events in the History of Mexico and the Border." *Journal of American History* 86, no. 2 (September 1999): 439–55.

"The Thirteen Demands and Response." *Beloit (WI) College Round Table*, 17 February 1969, 10.

"13% of Black Men Barred from Voting." *Raleigh News and Observer*, 23 October, 1998, 7A.

"Until It Hurts." Editorial. *Race Traitor: journal of the new abolitionism* 5 (winter 1996): 3–5.

Valelly, Richard. "Voting Rights in Jeopardy." *American Prospect* 46 (September–October 1999): 43–49.

Verhovek, Sam Howe. "After Debate, Houston Votes to Maintain Affirmative Action Policy." *Duke University Chronicle*, 6 November 1997, 6.

"Veterans' Preference Bill Introduced in Senate." *APWU News Service* [American Postal Workers Union monthly bulletin] 27, no. 14 (1 August 1997).

"Views of Affirmative Action." New York Times/CBS poll. *New York Times*, 14 December 1997.

Walker, Arnold B. "St. Louis' Employers, Unions and Negro Workers." *Opportunity* 19, no. 11 (November 1941): 337.

Webster, Thomas A. "Employers, Unions and Negro Workers." *Opportunity* 19 (October 1941): 295–97.

Wesley, Charles H. "Negro Suffrage in the Period of Constitution-Making 1787–1865." *Journal of Negro History* 32 (April 1947): 143–68.

West, Martha S. "History Lessons." *Women's Review of Books* 13, no. 5 (February 1996), 19.

White, Walter. "The Negro and the Communists." *Crisis* 57, no. 8 (August–September 1950): 502–6.

Wiese, Andrew. "The Other Suburbanites: African American Suburbanization in the North before 1950." *Journal of American History* 85, no. 4 (March 1999): 1495–524.

Wilkins, Roger. "The Case for Affirmative Action: Racism Has Its Privileges." *Nation* 260, no.12 (27 March 1995): 409–15.

Zane, J. Peder. "A Race of a Different Color." *Raleigh News and Observer*, 28 February 1999, 4G.

Zorn, Jean, and Stephen Zorn. "Review of *Lift Every Voice: Turning a Civil Rights Setback into a New Vision of Social Justice*, by Lani Guinier." *Nation* 266, no. 17 (11 May 1998): 34–36.

BOOKS

Abrams, Charles. *Forbidden Neighbors: A Study of Prejudice in Housing*. New York: Harper, 1955.

Abu-Jamal, Mumia. *Live from Death Row*. Reading, MA: Addison-Wesley, 1995.

Acuña, Rodolfo F. *Occupied America: A History of Chicanos*. 4th ed. New York: Longman, 2000; 1972.

Adams, Willi Paul. *The First American Constitutions: Republican Ideology and the Making of the State Constitutions in the Revolutionary Era*. Translated by Rita Kimber and Robert Kimber. Chapel Hill: University of North Carolina Press, 1980; 1973.

Allen, Robert L. *Reluctant Reformers: Racism and Social Reform Movements in the United States*. Washington, D.C.: Howard University Press, 1983.

Bibliography

Allen, Theodore W. *The Invention of the White Race.* Vol. 1, *Racial Oppression and Social Control.* London: Verso, 1994.

————. *The Invention of the White Race.* Vol. 2, *The Origin of Racial Oppression in Anglo-America.* London: Verso, 1997.

America, Richard F., ed. *The Wealth of Races: The Present Value of Benefits from Past Injustices.* New York: Greenwood, 1990.

Anderson, James D. *The Education of Blacks in the South, 1860–1935.* Chapel Hill: University of North Carolina Press, 1988.

Anderson, Jervis. *A. Philip Randolph: A Biographical Portrait.* New York: Harcourt, 1973.

Aptheker, Herbert. *American Negro Slave Revolts.* New York: International Publishers, 1974; 1943.

————., ed. *A Documentary History of the Negro People in the United States 1933–1945.* Secaucus, NJ: Citadel, 1974.

Archdeacon, Thomas. *Becoming American: An Ethnic History.* New York: Free Press, 1983.

Auerbach, Frank L. *The Immigration and Nationality Act: A Summary of Its Principal Provisions.* New York: Common Council for American Unity, 1952.

Avins, Alfred, ed. *The Reconstruction Amendments' Debates: The Legislative History and Contemporary Debates in Congress on the 13th, 14th, and 15th Amendments.* Richmond: Virginia Commission on Constitutional Government, 1967.

Axtell, James. *The Invasion Within: The Contest of Cultures in Colonial North America.* New York: Oxford University Press, 1985.

Baldwin, James. *The Price of the Ticket: Collected Nonfiction, 1948–1985.* New York: St. Martin's, 1985.

Bartlett, David W. *The Life and Public Service of Hon. Abraham Lincoln.* Freeport, NY: Books for Libraries Press, 1969; 1860. .

Beifuss, Joan Turner. *At the River I Stand: Memphis, the 1968 Strike, and Martin Luther King.* Brooklyn: Carlson, 1989.

Bell, Derrick A., Jr. *And We Are Not Saved: The Elusive Quest for Racial Justice.* New York: Basic, 1987.

————. *Faces at the Bottom of the Well: The Permanence of Racism.* New York: Basic, 1992.

————. *Gospel Choirs: Psalms of Survival for an Alien Land Called Home.* New York: Basic, 1996.

————. *Race, Racism, and American Law.* 2nd ed. Boston: Little, Brown, 1980.

Bennett, Lerone, Jr. *Before the Mayflower: A History of Black America.* 5th ed. New York: Penguin, 1984; 1962.

————. *The Shaping of Black America.* New York: Penguin, 1993; 1975.

Benokraitis, Nijole V., and Joe R. Feagin. *Affirmative Action and Equal Opportunity: Action, Inaction, Reaction.* Boulder, CO: Westview Press, 1978.

Berlin, Ira. *Slaves without Masters: The Free Negro in the Antebellum South.* New York: Pantheon, 1974.

Berlin, Ira, and Ronald Hoffman, eds. *Slavery and Freedom in the Age of the American Revolution.* Charlottesville: University Press of Virginia, 1983.

Berlin, Ira, Barbara Jeanne Fields, Steven F. Miller, Joseph P. Reidy, and Leslie S. Rowland, eds. *Free at Last: A Documentary History of Slavery, Freedom, and the Civil War.* New York: Free Press, 1992.

Berman, William C. *The Politics of Civil Rights in the Truman Administration.* Columbus: Ohio State University Press, 1970.

Bernstein, Iver. *The New York City Draft Riots: Their Significance for American Society and Politics in the Age of the Civil War.* New York: Oxford University Press, 1990.

Billingsley, Andrew. *Mighty Like a River: The Black Church and Social Reform.* New York: Oxford University Press, 1999.

Bibliography

Billington, Ray Allen. *Westward Expansion: A History of the American Frontier*. 2nd ed. New York: MacMillan, 1960; 1949.

Bittker, Boris I. *The Case for Black Reparations*. New York: Random House, 1973.

Blau, Joseph, ed. *Social Theories of Jacksonian Democracy: Representative Writings of the Period 1825–1850*. New York: Hafner, 1947.

Bloch, Farrell. *Antidiscrimination Law and Minority Employment: Recruitment Practices and Regulatory Restraints*. Chicago: University of Chicago Press, 1994.

Boggs, James. *Racism and the Class Struggle: Further Pages from a Black Workers Notebook*. New York: Monthly Review, 1970.

Boswell, Thomas D., and James R. Curtis. *The Cuban-American Experience: Culture, Images, and Perspectives*. Totowa, NJ: Rowman and Allanheld, 1983.

Botkin, B. A., ed. *Lay My Burden Down: A Folk History of Slavery*. Chicago: University of Chicago Press, 1969; 1945.

Bowen, William G., and Derek Bok. *The Shape of the River: Long-Term Consequences of Considering Race in College and University Admissions*. Princeton, NJ: Princeton University Press, 1998.

Bowser, Benjamin P., and Raymond G. Hunt, eds. *Impacts of Racism on White Americans*. Ann Arbor, MI: Books on Demand, 1998; 1981.

Boyer, Richard O., and Herbert M. Morais. *Labor's Untold Story*. New York: UE, 1972; 1955.

Branch, Taylor. *Parting the Waters: America in the King Years 1954–63*. New York: Touchstone, 1988.

Brigham, Carl Campbell. *A Study of American Intelligence*. Princeton, NJ: Princeton University Press, 1923.

Brooks, Thomas R. *Toil and Trouble: A History of American Labor*. 2nd ed. New York: Delta, 1971; 1964.

Brown, Dee. *Bury My Heart at Wounded Knee*. New York: Holt, Reinhart and Winston, 1971.

Bukowczyk, John T. *And My Children Did Not Know Me: A History of Polish Americans*. Bloomington: Indiana University Press, 1987.

Burk, Robert Frederick. *The Eisenhower Administration and Black Civil Rights*. Knoxville: University of Tennessee Press, 1984.

Burton-Rose, Daniel, ed. *The Ceiling of America: An Inside Look at the U.S. Prison Industry*. Monroe, ME: Common Courage, 1998.

Caffentzis, George. *From Capitalist Crisis to Proletarian Slavery: An Introduction to Class Struggle in the U.S. 1973–1998*. Jamaica Plain, MA: Midnight Notes, 1998.

Calavita, Kitty. *U.S. Immigration Law and the Control of Labor 1820–1924*. London: Academic Press, 1984.

Campbell, Joseph, with Bill Moyers, ed., and Betty Sue Flowers, *The Power of Myth*. New York: Doubleday, 1988.

Carmichael, Stokely (Kwame Ture), and Charles V. Hamilton. *Black Power: The Politics of Liberation in America*. New York: Vintage, 1967.

Carnegie, Andrew. *The Gospel of Wealth and Other Timely Essays*. Edited by Edward C. Kirkland. Cambridge, MA: Belknap, 1962.

Carson, Clayborne. *In Struggle: SNCC and the Black Awakening of the 1960s*. Cambridge: Harvard University Press, 1981.

Carstensen, Vernon, ed. *The Public Lands: Studies in the History of the Public Domain* Madison: University of Wisconsin Press, 1963.

Carter, Dan T. *From George Wallace to Newt Gingrich: Race in the Conservative Counterrevolution 1963–1994*. Baton Rouge: Louisiana State University, 1996.

Bibliography

————. *The Politics of Rage: George Wallace, the Origins of the New Conservatism, and the Transformation of American Politics.* New York: Simon and Schuster, 1995.

Carter, Stephen L. *Reflections of an Affirmative Action Baby.* New York: Basic, 1991.

Catterall, Helen T., ed. *Judicial Cases Concerning American Slavery and the Negro.* Vol. 1. New York: Octagon, 1968; 1926.

Cecelski, David S., and Timothy B. Tyson, eds. *Democracy Betrayed: The Wilmington Race Riot of 1898 and Its Legacy.* Chapel Hill: University of North Carolina Press, 1998.

Chafe, William H. *Civilities and Civil Rights: Greensboro, North Carolina, and the Black Struggle for Freedom.* New York: Oxford University Press, 1980.

Chalmers, David M. *Hooded Americanism: The First Century of the Ku Klux Klan 1865–1965.* Garden City, NY: Doubleday, 1965.

Chan, Sucheng. *Asian Americans: An Interpretive History.* Boston: Twayne, 1991.

Chang, Robert S. *Disoriented: Asian Americans, Law, and the Nation-State.* New York: New York University Press, 1999.

Child, Lydia Maria. *Lydia Maria Child: Selected Letters, 1817–1880.* Edited by Milton Meltzer and Patricia G. Holland. Amherst: University of Massachusetts Press, 1982.

Churchill, Ward, and Jim Vander Wall. *Agents of Repression: The FBI's Secret Wars against the Black Panther Party and the American Indian Movement.* Boston: South End Press, 1990.

Clayton, Susan D., and Faye J. Crosby. *Justice, Gender, and Affirmative Action.* Ann Arbor: University of Michigan Press, 1992.

Clinton, Catherine. *The Plantation Mistress: Women's World in the Old South.* New York: Pantheon, 1982.

Cochran, Thomas C. *Frontiers of Change: Early Industrialism in America.* New York: Oxford University Press, 1981.

Conklin, Paul K. *The New Deal.* New York: Thomas Y. Crowell, 1969.

Coontz, Stephanie. *The Way We Never Were: American Families and the Nostalgia Trap.* New York: Basic Books, 1992.

Cose, Ellis. *The Rage of a Privileged Class.* New York: Harper, 1993.

Crawford, Vicki L., Jacqueline Anne Rouse, and Barbara Woods, eds. *Black Women in United States History.* Vol. 16 of *Women in the Civil Rights Movement: Trailblazers and Torchbearers, 1941–1965,* ed. Darlene Clark Hine. Brooklyn: Carlson, 1990.

Crenshaw, Kimberlé, Neil Gotanda, Gery Peller, and Kendall Thomas, eds. *Critical Race Theory: The Key Writings That Formed the Movement.* New York: New Press, 1995.

Cross, Harry, Genevieve Kenney, Jane Mell, and Wendy Zimmerman, eds. *Employer Hiring Practices: Differential Treatment of Hispanic and Anglo Job Seekers.* Washington, D.C.: Urban Institute Press, 1990.

Current, Richard Nelson. *Lincoln's Loyalists: Union Soldiers in the Confederacy.* Boston: Northeastern University Press, 1992.

Curry, George E., ed. *The Affirmative Action Debate.* Reading, MA: Addison-Wesley, 1996.

Curry, Leonard P. *The Free Black in Urban America 1800–1850: The Shadow of the Dream.* Chicago: University of Chicago Press, 1981.

Daniels, Lee A., ed. *The State of Black America 1998.* Washington, D.C.: National Urban League, 1998.

Delgado, Richard. *The Coming Race War? And Other Apocalyptic Tales of America after Affirmative Action and Welfare.* New York: New York University Press, 1996.

————. *When Equality Ends: Stories About Race and Resistance.* Boulder, CO: Westview Press, 1999.

D'Orso, Michael. *Like Judgement Day: The Ruin and Redemption of a Town Called Rosewood.* New York: Boulevard Books, 1996.

Bibliography

Douglass, Frederick. *The Life and Writings of Frederick Douglass*. Vol. 4, *Reconstruction and After*. Edited by Philip S. Foner. New York: International Publishers, 1955.

Drake, W. Avon, and Robert D. Holsworth. *Affirmative Action and the Stalled Quest for Black Progress*. Urbana: University of Illinois Press, 1996.

Dreyfuss, Joel, and Charles Lawrence III. *The Bakke Case: The Politics of Inequality*. New York: Harcourt Brace Jovanovich, 1979.

D'Souza, Dinesh. *The End of Racism: Principles for a Multiracial Society*. New York: Free Press, 1995.

Dubofsky, Melvyn. *We Shall Be All: A History of the Industrial Workers of the World*. Chicago: Quadrangle, 1969.

Du Bois, W. E. B. *Against Racism: Unpublished Essays, Papers, Addresses, 1887–1961 by W. E. B. Du Bois*. Edited by Herbert Aptheker. Amherst: University of Massachusetts Press, 1985.

———. *Black Reconstruction in America 1860–1880*. Cleveland: Meridian, 1968; 1935.

———. *John Brown: A Biography*. Armonk, NY: M. E. Sharpe, 1997; 1909.

———. *The Philadelphia Story: A Social Study*. Philadelphia: University of Pennsylvania Press, 1996; 1899.

———. *The Souls of Black Folk*. New York: Penguin, 1989; 1903.

———. *W. E. B. Du Bois: A Reader*. Edited by David Levering Lewis. New York: Henry Holt, 1995.

Dyson, Michael Eric. *I May Not Get There with You: The True Martin Luther King, Jr.* New York: Free Press, 2000.

Edley, Christopher, Jr. *Not All Black and White: Affirmative Action and American Values*. New York: Hill and Wang, 1996.

Edmonds, Helen G. *The Negro and Fusion Politics in North Carolina 1894–1901*. New York: Russell and Russell, 1973; 1951.

Egerton, Douglas R. *He Shall Go Out Free: The Lives of Denmark Vesey*. Madison, WI: Madison House, 1999.

Egerton, John. *Speak Now against the Day: The Generation before the Civil Rights Movement in the South*. New York: Knopf, 1994.

Ellis, Richard E. *The Union at Risk: Jacksonian Democracy, States' Rights, and the Nullification Crisis*. New York: Oxford University Press, 1987.

Enchautegui, María E. Michael Fix, Pamela Loprest, Sarah C. von der Lippe, and Douglas Wissoker. *Do Minority-Owned Businesses Get a Fair Share of Government Contracts?* Washington, D.C.: Urban Institute, 1997.

Fehrenbacher, Don E. *The Dred Scott Case: Its Significance in American Law and Politics*. New York: Oxford University Press, 1978.

Ferman, Louis A. *The Negro and Equal Employment Opportunities: A Review of Management Experiences in Twenty Companies*. New York: Frederick A. Praeger, 1968.

Filler, Louis. *Crusade against Slavery: Friends, Foes, and Reforms 1820–1860*. Algonac, MI: Reference, 1986.

Fink, Gary M., and Hugh Davis Graham, eds. *The Carter Presidency: Policy Choices in the Post-New Deal Era*. Lawrence: University Press of Kansas, 1998.

Fink, Leon. *Workingmen's Democracy: The Knights of Labor and American Politics*. Urbana: University of Illinois Press, 1983.

Fletcher, Arthur. *The Silent Sell-Out: Government Betrayal of Blacks to the Craft Unions*. New York: Third Press, 1974.

Foner, Eric. *Nothing But Freedom: Emancipation and Its Legacy*. Baton Rouge: Louisiana State University Press, 1983.

————., ed. *The New American History*. Philadelphia: Temple University Press, 1990.

Foner, Philip S., ed. *The Black Panthers Speak*. Philadelphia: J. P. Lippincott, 1970.

Foner, Philip S., and Robert James Branham, eds. *Lift Every Voice: African American Oratory, 1787–1900*. Tuscaloosa: University of Alabama Press, 1998.

Foner, Philip S., and Ronald L. Lewis, eds. *The Black Worker: A Documentary History from Colonial Times to the Present*. Vol. 1, *The Black Worker to 1869*. Philadelphia: Temple University Press, 1978.

————., eds. *The Black Worker: A Documentary History from Colonial Times to the Present*. Vol. 3, *The Black Worker during the Era of the Knights of Labor*. Philadelphia: Temple University Press, 1978.

————., eds. *The Black Worker: A Documentary History from Colonial Times to the Present*. Vol. 5, *The Black Worker from 1900 to 1919*. Philadelphia: Temple University Press, 1980.

————., eds. *The Black Worker: A Documentary History from Colonial Times to the Present*. Vol. 6, *The Era of Post-War Prosperity and the Great Depression, 1920–1936*. Philadelphia: Temple University Press, 1981.

————., eds. *The Black Worker: A Documentary History from Colonial Times to the Present*. Vol. 7, *The Black Worker from the Founding of the CIO to the AFL-CIO Merger, 1936–1955*. Philadelphia: Temple University Press, 1983.

Foner, Philip S., Ronald L. Lewis., and Robert Cvornyek, eds. *The Black Worker: A Documentary History from Colonial Times to the Present*. Vol. 8, *The Black Worker since the AFL-CIO Merger, 1955–1980*. Philadelphia: Temple University Press, 1984.

Formisano, Ronald P. *Boston against Busing: Race, Class, and Ethnicity in the 1960s and 1970s*. Chapel Hill: University of North Carolina Press, 1991.

Foster, James C., and Mary C. Segers. *Elusive Equality: Liberalism, Affirmative Action, and Social Change in America*. Port Washington, NY: Associated Faculty Press, 1983.

Fox-Genovese, Elizabeth. *Within the Plantation Household: Black and White Women of the Old South*. Chapel Hill: University of North Carolina Press.

Franklin, John Hope. *The Free Negro in North Carolina 1790–1860*. New York: W. W. Norton, 1971; 1943.

————. *The Militant South 1800–1861*. Cambridge, MA: Belknap, 1956.

Franklin, John Hope, and Alfred A. Moss Jr. *From Slavery to Freedom: A History of Negro Americans*. 6th ed. New York: McGraw-Hill, 1988; 1947.

Fraser, Steve, and Gary Gerstle, eds. *The Rise and Fall of the New Deal Order, 1930–1980*. Princeton, NJ: Princeton University Press, 1989.

Frazier, E. Franklin. *Black Bourgeoisie: The Rise of a New Middle Class in America*. London: Collier Books, 1969; 1957.

Frazier, E. Franklin, and C. Eric Lincoln. *The Black Church since Frazier*. New York: Schocken Books, 1974.

Freidel, Frank. *F.D.R. and the South*. Baton Rouge: Louisiana State University Press, 1965.

Friedman, Lawrence M. *American Law*. New York: W. W. Norton, 1984.

Gaines, Kevin K. *Uplifting the Race: Black Leadership, Politics, and Culture in the Twentieth Century*. Chapel Hill: University of North Carolina Press, 1996.

Garcia, Richard A., ed. *The Chicanos in America 1540–1974: A Chronology and Fact Book*. Dobbs Ferry, NY: Oceana 1977.

Garfinkel, Herbert. *When Negroes March: The March on Washington Movement in the Organizational Politics for FEPC*. New York: Atheneum, 1969; 1959.

Georgakas, Dan, and Marvin Surkin. *Detroit, I Do Mind Dying: A Study in Urban Revolution*. New York: St. Martin's Press, 1975.

Bibliography

Gilje, Paul A. *Rioting in America*. Bloomington: Indiana University Press, 1996.

Gillespie, Ed, and Bob Schellhas, eds. *Contract with America: The Bold Plan by Rep. Newt Gingrich, Rep. Dick Armey and the House Republicans to Change the Nation*. New York: Times Books, 1994.

Gitlin, Todd. *The Sixties: Years of Hope, Days of Rage*. New York: Bantam, 1987.

Gluck, Sherna Berger. *Rosie the Riveter Revisited: Women, the War, and Social Change*. Boston: Twayne, 1987.

Goldberg, Robert Alan. *Hooded Empire: The Ku Klux Klan in Colorado*. Urbana: University of Illinois Press, 1981.

Gompers, Samuel. *Seventy Years of Life and Labor: An Autobiography*. Vol. 2. New York: Dutton, 1925.

Gooding-Williams, Robert, ed. *Reading Rodney King/Reading Urban Uprising*. New York: Routledge, 1993.

Goodman, Mitchell, ed. *The Movement toward a New America: The Beginnings of a Long Revolution*. Philadelphia: Pilgrim Press, 1970.

Goodman, Paul. *Of One Blood: Abolitionism and the Origins of Racial Equality*. Berkeley: University of California Press, 1998.

Goodwyn, Lawrence C. *Democratic Promise: The Populist Moment in America*. Oxford: Oxford University Press, 1976.

Gottfried, Frances. *The Merit System and Municipal Civil Service: A Fostering of Social Inequality*. New York: Greenwood, 1988.

Graham, Hugh Davis. *The Civil Rights Era: Origins and Development of National Policy, 1960–1972*. New York: Oxford University Press, 1990.

Grant, Madison, ed. *The Passing of the Great Race, or the Racial Basis of European History*. New York: Charles Scribner's Sons, 1918.

Grant, Madison, and Charles Stewart Davison, eds. *The Alien in Our Midst, or "Selling Our Birthright for a Mess of Pottage."* New York: Galton, 1930.

Grant, Nancy L. *TVA and Black Americans: Planning for the Status Quo*. Philadelphia: Temple University Press, 1990.

Greenberg, Kenneth S., ed. *Confessions of Nat Turner and Related Documents*. Boston: Bedford, 1996.

Gronowicz, Anthony. *Race and Class Politics in New York City before the Civil War*. Boston: Northeastern University Press, 1998.

Grossman, James R. *Land of Hope: Chicago, Black Southerners, and the Great Migration*. Chicago: University of Chicago Press, 1989.

Gundaker, Grey, ed. *Keep Your Head to the Sky: Interpreting African American Home Ground*. Charlottesville: University of Virginia Press, 1998

Gutman, Herbert. *Work, Culture, and Society in Industrializing America*. New York: Knopf, 1976.

Gwaltney, John Langston. *Drylongso: A Self-Portrait of Black America*. New York: Random House, 1980.

Hacker, Andrew. *Two Nations: Black and White, Separate, Hostile, Unequal*. New York: Ballantine, 1995; 1992.

Hall, Jacquelyn Dowd. *Revolt against Chivalry: Jessie Daniel Ames and the Women's Campaign against Lynching*. Rev. ed. New York: Columbia University Press, 1993; 1979.

Hamilton, Alexander, James Madison, and John Jay. *The Federalist Papers*. New York: Mentor, 1961; 1787.

Hampton, Henry, and Sarah Flynn Fayer, eds. *Voices of Freedom: An Oral History of the Civil Rights Movement from the 1950's through the 1980's*. New York: Bantam, 1990.

Hanchett, Thomas W. *Sorting Out the New South City: Race, Class, and Urban Development in Charlotte, 1875–1975*. Chapel Hill: University of North Carolina Press, 1998.

Bibliography

Harlan, Louis R. *Booker T. Washington: The Making of a Black Leader 1856–1901*. London: Oxford University Press, 1972.

————. *Booker T. Washington: The Wizard of Tuskegee 1901–1915*. New York: Oxford University Press, 1986; 1983.

Harris, William H. *The Harder We Run: Black Workers since the Civil War*. New York: Oxford University Press, 1982.

Herrnstein, Richard J., and Charles Murray. *The Bell Curve: Intelligence and Class Structure in American Life*. New York: Free Press, 1994.

Hibbard, Benjamin Horace. *A History of the Public Land Policies*. Madison: University of Wisconsin Press, 1965; 1924.

Higginbotham, A. Leon, Jr. *In the Matter of Color: Race and the American Legal Process*. New York: Oxford University Press, 1978.

Higginson, Thomas Wentworth. *Army Life in a Black Regiment*. Lansing: Michigan State University Press, 1960; 1870.

Hill, Herbert. *Black Labor and the American Legal System: Race, Work, and the Law*. Madison: University of Wisconsin Press, 1985; 1977.

Hill, Herbert, and James E. Jones Jr., eds. *Race in America: The Struggle for Equality*. Madison: University of Wisconsin Press, 1993.

Hine, Darlene Clark, ed. *Black Women's History: Theory and Practice*. Vol. 1. Brooklyn: Carlson, 1990.

Hofstadter, Richard. *The American Political Tradition and the Men Who Made It*. New York: Knopf, 1959.

————. *Social Darwinism in American Thought, 1860–1915*. Philadelphia: University of Pennsylvania Press, 1944.

Holloway, Joseph E., ed. *Africanisms in American Culture*. Bloomington: Indiana University Press, 1991.

Holt, Thomas. *Black Over White: Negro Political Leadership in South Carolina during Reconstruction*. Urbana: University of Illinois Press, 1977.

The Holy Bible, King James Version. New York: American Bible Society, 1990; 1611.

Horne, Gerald. *Black and Red: W. E. B. Du Bois and the Afro-American Response to the Cold War, 1944–1963*. Albany: State University of New York Press, 1986.

————. *Fire This Time: The Watts Uprising and the 1960s*. Charlottesville: University Press of Virginia, 1995.

Hurt, Gaillard, ed. *The First Forty Years of Washington Society Portrayed by the Family Letters of Mrs. Samuel Harrison Smith. . . .* New York: n.p., 1906.

Hyman, Harold M. *American Singularity: The 1787 Northwest Ordinance, the 1862 Homestead and Morrill Acts, and the 1944 G.I. Bill*. Athens: University of Georgia Press, 1986.

Ignatiev, Noel. *How the Irish Became White*. New York: Routledge, 1995.

Ignatiev, Noel, and John Garvey, eds. *Race Traitor*. New York: Routledge, 1996.

Industrial Research Unit, Department of Industry, Wharton School of Finance and Commerce, University of Pennsylvania. *The Racial Policies of American Industry: Report*. Philadelphia: University of Pennsylvania Press, 1968.

Jackson, Kenneth T. *Crabgrass Frontier: The Suburbanization of the United States*. New York: Oxford University Press, 1985.

Jacobs, Harriet. *Incidents in the Life of a Slave Girl*, in *The Classic Slave Narratives*. Edited by Henry Louis Gates Jr. New York: Mentor, 1987.

Jacobson, Julius, ed. *The Negro and the American Labor Movement*. Garden City, NY: Anchor, 1968.

Jacobson, Matthew Frye. *Whiteness of a Different Color: European Immigrants and the Alchemy of Race*. Cambridge: Harvard University Press, 1998.

Bibliography

James, C. L. R., George Breitman, Edgar Keemer, and Fred Stanton, eds. *Fighting Racism in World War II.* New York: Monad, 1980.

Jaynes, Gerald David. *Branches without Roots: Genesis of the Black Working Class in the South, 1862–1882.* New York: Oxford University Press, 1986.

Jefferson, Thomas. *Notes on the State of Virginia.* Chapel Hill: University of North Carolina Press, 1954; 1785.

Jones, Charles E. *The Black Panther Party Reconsidered.* Baltimore: Black Classic Press, 1998.

Jones, Jacqueline. *Labor of Love, Labor of Sorrow: Black Women, Work and the Family, from Slavery to the Present.* New York: Vintage, 1986.

Jordan, Winthrop D. *White Over Black: American Attitudes toward the Negro, 1550–1812.* Baltimore: Penguin, 1969.

Kaplan, Sidney. *American Studies in Black and White: Selected Essays 1949–1989.* Edited by Allan D. Austin. Amherst: University Press of Massachusetts, 1991.

Kaplan, Sidney, and Emma Nogrady Kaplan, *The Black Presence in the Era of the American Revolution.* Rev. ed. Amherst: University of Massachusetts Press, 1991.

Kelley, Robin D. G. *Hammer and Hoe: Alabama Communists during the Great Depression.* Chapel Hill: University of North Carolina Press, 1990.

———. *Into the Fire: African Americans since 1970.* New York: Oxford University Press, 1996.

———. *Race Rebels: Culture, Politics, and the Black Working Class.* New York: Free Press, 1994.

Kennedy, Randall. *Race, Crime and the Law.* New York: Pantheon Books, 1997.

Kennedy, Stetson. *The Jim Crow Guide: The Way It Was.* Boca Raton: Florida Atlantic University Press, 1990; 1959.

Kessler-Harris, Alice. *Out to Work: A History of Wage-Earning Women in the United States.* New York: Oxford University Press, 1982.

Kincheloe, Joe L., Shirley R. Steinberg, Nelson M. Rodriguez, and Ronald E. Chennault, eds. *White Reign: Deploying Whiteness in America.* New York: St. Martin's Press, 1998.

King, Martin Luther, Jr. *A Testament of Hope: The Essential Writings of Martin Luther King, Jr.* Edited by James Melvin. Washington. San Francisco: Harper and Row, 1986.

———. *Where Do We Go From Here: Chaos or Community?* New York: Harper, 1967.

———. *Why We Can't Wait.* New York: Mentor, 1968; 1964.

Kolchin, Peter. *American Slavery 1619–1877.* New York: Hill and Wang, 1993.

Kolp, John Gilman. *Gentlemen and Freeholders: Electoral Politics in Colonial Virginia.* Baltimore: Johns Hopkins University Press, 1998.

Kothe, Charles A., ed. *A Tale of 22 Cities: Report on Title VII of the Civil Rights Act of 1964 Compiled from NAM Seminars.* New York: National Association of Manufacturers, 1965.

Kousser, J. Morgan. *Colorblind Injustice: Minority Voting Rights and the Undoing of the Second Reconstruction.* Chapel Hill: University of North Carolina Press, 1999.

———. *The Shaping of Southern Politics: Suffrage Restriction and the Establishment of the One-Party South, 1880–1910.* New Haven, CT: Yale University Press, 1974.

Kraditor, Aileen S. *Means and Ends in American Abolitionism: Garrison and His Critics on Strategy and Tactics, 1834–1850.* Chicago: Ivan R. Dee 1989; 1969.

Krickus, Richard. *Pursuing the American Dream: White Ethnics and the New Populism.* Bloomington: University of Indiana Press, 1976.

Laham, Nicholas. *The Reagan Presidency and the Politics of Race: In Pursuit of Colorblind Justice and Limited Government.* Westport, CT: Praeger, 1998.

Bibliography

Lawrence, Charles R., III, and Mari J. Matsuda, eds. *We Won't Go Back: Making the Case for Affirmative Action.* Boston: Houghton Mifflin, 1997.

Lawson, John. *A New Voyage to Carolina.* Edited by Hugh Talmage Lefler. Chapel Hill: University of North Carolina Press, 1967; 1709.

Lawson, Steven F. *Running for Freedom: Civil Rights and Black Politics in America since 1941.* New York: McGraw-Hill, 1991.

Lebsock, Suzanne. *The Free Women of Petersburg: Status and Culture in a Southern Town, 1784–1860.* New York: W. W. Norton, 1985.

Lemann, Nicholas. *The Promised Land: The Great Black Migration and How It Changed America.* New York: Knopf, 1991.

Lerner, Gerda, ed. *Black Women in White America: A Documentary History.* New York: Vintage, 1973.

Levine, Lawrence. *Black Culture and Black Consciousness: Afro-American Folk Thought from Slavery to Freedom.* New York: Oxford University Press, 1977.

Lewis, David Levering. *W. E. B. Du Bois: A Biography 1868–1919.* New York: Henry Holt, 1993.

——. *When Harlem Was in Vogue.* New York: Penguin, 1997; 1981.

Lewontin, R. C., Steven Rose, and Leon J. Kamin. *Not In Our Genes: Biology, Ideology, and Human Nature.* New York: Pantheon, 1984.

Lincoln, Abraham. *Abraham Lincoln: An Autobiography.* Edited by Nathaniel Wright Stephenson. Indianapolis: Bobbs-Merrill, 1926.

——. *Abraham Lincoln Complete Works.* Edited by John G. Nicolay and John Hay. Vol. 2. New York: Century, 1902.

Lincoln, C. Eric. *The Black Church in the African-American Experience.* Durham, NC: Duke University Press, 1990.

Lipsitz, George. *The Possessive Investment in Whiteness: How White People Profit from Identity Politics.* Philadelphia: Temple University Press, 1998.

Litwack, Leon F. *Trouble in Mind: Black Southerners in the Age of Jim Crow.* New York: Knopf, 1998.

Loewen, James W. *Lies My Teacher Told Me: Everything Your American History Textbook Got Wrong.* New York: Touchstone, 1995.

Lofgren, Charles A. *The Plessy Case: A Legal-Historical Interpretation.* New York: New York University Press, 1987.

Logan, Rayford W. *The Betrayal of the Negro: From Rutherford B. Hayes to Woodrow Wilson.* Enl. ed. New York: Collier, 1965; 1954.

——. *The Negro in American Life and Thought: The Nadir 1877–1901.* New York: Dial, 1954.

——., ed. *What the Negro Wants.* Chapel Hill: University of North Carolina Press, 1944.

López, Ian F. Haney. *White by Law: The Legal Construction of Race.* New York: New York University Press, 1996.

Lott, Eric. *Love and Theft: Blackface Minstrelsy and the American Working Class.* New York: Oxford University Press, 1993.

Madhubuti, Haki, ed. *Why L.A. Happened: Implications of the '92 Los Angeles Rebellion.* Chicago: Third World Press, 1993.

Malcolm X. *The Autobiography of Malcolm X.* Edited by Alex Haley. New York: Grove Press, 1965.

——. *Malcolm X Speaks.* Edited by George Breitman. New York: Grove Press, 1966.

Marable, Manning. *Beyond Black and White: Transforming African-American Politics.* London: Verso, 1995.

——. *Black American Politics: From Washington Marches to Jesse Jackson.* London: Verso, 1985.

——. *Race, Reform, and Rebellion: The Second Reconstruction in Black America, 1945–1982.* Jackson: University Press of Mississippi, 1984.

Bibliography

Marx, Karl, and Frederick Engels. *Selected Works in One Volume*. New York: International Publishers, 1968.

Masotti, Louis H., and Don R. Bowen. *Riots and Rebellion: Civil Violence in the Urban Community*. Beverly Hills, CA: Sage, 1968.

Massey, Douglas S., and Nancy A. Denton. *American Apartheid: Segregation and the Making of the Underclass*. Cambridge: Harvard University Press, 1993.

McClain, Charles J. *In Search of Equality: the Chinese Struggle against Discrimination in Nineteenth-Century America*. Berkeley: University of California Press, 1994.

McPherson, James M. *The Abolitionist Legacy: From Reconstruction to the NAACP*. Princeton, NJ: Princeton University Press, 1975.

————. *Abraham Lincoln and the Second American Revolution*. New York: Oxford University Press, 1990.

————. *Battle Cry of Freedom: The Civil War Era*. New York: Ballantine, 1989.

————. *For Cause and Comrades: Why Men Fought in the Civil War*. New York: Oxford University Press, 1997.

Meier, August, and Elliot Rudwick. *Black Detroit and the Rise of the UAW*. Oxford: Oxford University Press, 1981.

Meier, Matt S., and Feliciano Rivera. *The Chicanos: A History of Mexican-Americans*. New York: Hill and Wang, 1972.

Melville, Herman. *The Confidence Man: His Masquerade*. New York: Airmont, 1966; 1857.

Messer-Kruse, Timothy. *The Yankee International: Marxism and the American Reform Tradition, 1848–1876*. Chapel Hill: University of North Carolina Press, 1998.

Midnight Notes Collective, eds. *Midnight Oil: Work, Energy, War, 1973–1992*. Brooklyn: Autonomedia, 1992.

Mikusko, M. Brady. *Carriers in a Common Cause: A History of Letter Carriers and the NALC*. Washington, D.C.: National Association of Letter Carriers, 1989.

Mitchell, Reid. *Civil War Soldiers*. New York: Viking, 1988.

Montgomery, David. *The Fall of the House of Labor: The Workplace, the State, and American Labor Activism, 1865–1925*. Cambridge: Cambridge University Press, 1987.

————. *Workers' Control in America: Studies in the History of Work, Technology, and Labor Struggles*. Cambridge: Cambridge University Press, 1986; 1979.

Moreno, Paul D. *From Direct Action to Affirmative Action: Fair Employment Policy in America, 1933–1972*. Baton Rouge: Louisiana State University Press, 1997.

Morgan, Edmund S. *American Slavery, American Freedom: The Ordeal of Colonial Virginia*. New York: Norton, 1975.

Morris, Aldon D. *The Origins of the Civil Rights Movement: Black Communities Organizing for Change*. New York: Free Press, 1984.

Murray, Pauli. *The Autobiography of a Black Activist, Feminist, Lawyer, Priest, and Poet*. Knoxville: University of Tennessee Press, 1990.

————. *Proud Shoes: The Story of an American Family*. New York: Harper and Row, 1984; 1956.

————. *States' Laws on Race and Color*. Cincinnati: Women's Division of Christian Service, 1950.

Myrdal, Gunnar. *An American Dilemma: The Negro Problem and Modern Democracy*. New York: Harper, 1944.

Newman, Louise Michele. *White Women's Rights: The Racial Origins of Feminism in the United States*. New York: Oxford University Press, 1999.

Newton, James E., and Ronald L. Lewis, eds. *The Other Slaves: Mechanics, Artisans, and Craftsmen*. Boston: G. K. Hall, 1978.

Bibliography

Oates, Stephen B. *The Fires of Jubilee: Nat Turner's Fierce Rebellion*. New York: Mentor, 1975.

O'Brien, Gail Williams. *The Color of the Law: Race, Violence, and Justice in the Post-World War II South*. Chapel Hill: University of North Carolina Press, 1999.

O'Brien, Ruth. *Workers' Paradox: The Republican Origins of New Deal Labor Policy 1886–1935*. Chapel Hill: University of North Carolina Press, 1998.

Oliver, Melvin L., and Thomas M. Shapiro. *Black Wealth/White Wealth: A New Perspective on Racial Equality*. New York: Routledge, 1997.

Olson, Keith W. *The G.I. Bill, the Veterans, and the Colleges*. Lexington: University of Kentucky Press, 1974.

O'Reilly, Kenneth. *"Racial Matters": The FBI's Secret File on Black America, 1960–1972*. New York: Free Press, 1989.

Oubre, Claude F. *Forty Acres and a Mule: The Freedmen's Bureau and Black Land Ownership*. Baton Rouge: Louisiana State University Press, 1978.

Parker, Freddie L. *Running for Freedom: Slave Runaways in North Carolina 1775–1840*. New York: Garland, 1993.

Patterson, Orlando. *Rituals of Blood: Consequences of Slavery in Two American Centuries*. Washington, D.C.: Civitas Counterpoint, 1998.

Patterson, William L., ed. *We Charge Genocide: The Historic Petition to the United Nations for Relief from a Crime of the United States Government against the Negro People*. New York: International Publishers, 1970; 1951.

Paulsen, George E. *A Living Wage for the Forgotten Man: The Quest for Fair Labor Standards, 1933–1941*. Susquehanna, PA: Susquehanna University Press, 1996.

Peterson, Robert. *Only the Ball Was White*. Englewood Cliffs, NJ: Prentice-Hall, 1970.

Phillips, Wendell. *Speeches, Lectures, and Letters*. Vol. 2. 2nd Series. Boston: Lee and Shepard, 1891.

———. *Wendell Phillips On Civil Rights and Freedom*. Edited by Louis Filler. 2nd ed. Washington, D.C.: University Press of America, 1982; 1965.

Piven, Frances Fox, and Richard A. Cloward. *Regulating the Poor: The Functions of Public Welfare*. New York: Pantheon, 1971.

Porter, Bruce D. *The Miami Riots of 1980*. Lexington, MA: Lexington Books, 1984.

Prather, H. Leon, Sr. *We Have Taken a City: Wilmington Racial Massacre and Coup of 1898*. Rutherford, NJ: Farleigh Dickinson University Press, 1984.

Quadagno, Jill. *The Color of Welfare: How Racism Undermined the War on Poverty*. New York: Oxford University Press, 1994.

Quarles, Benjamin. *Black Abolitionists*. New York: Da Capo, 1969.

———. *The Negro in the American Revolution*. Chapel Hill: University of North Carolina Press, 1961.

Raines, Howell. *My Soul is Rested: Movement Days in the Deep South Remembered*. New York: G. P. Putnam's Sons, 1977.

Rakove, Jack N. *Original Meanings: Politics and Ideas in the Making of the Constitution*. New York: Vintage, 1997.

Reed, Adolph, Jr. *Stirrings in the Jug: Black Politics in the Post-Segregation Era*. Minneapolis: University of Minnesota Press, 1999.

Remini, Robert V. *The Jacksonian Era*. 2nd ed. Wheeling, IL: Harlan Davidson, 1997; 1989.

———., ed. *The Age of Jackson*. Columbia: University of South Carolina Press, 1972.

Rifkin, Jeremy. *The End of Work: The Decline of the Global Labor Force and the Dawn of the Post-Market Era*. New York: Jeremy P. Tarcher, 1995.

Bibliography

Robinson, Paulette J., and Billy J. Tidwell. *The State of Black America 1995.* New York: National Urban League, 1995.

Robinson, Randall. *The Debt: What America Owes to Blacks.* New York: Dutton, 2000.

Roebuck, Julian B., and Komanduri S. Murty. *Historically Black Colleges and Universities: Their Place in Higher Education.* Westport, CT: Praeger, 1993.

Roediger, David R. *Towards the Abolition of Whiteness: Essays on Race, Politics, and Working Class History.* London: Verso, 1994.

———. *The Wages of Whiteness: Race and the Making of the American Working Class.* London: Verso, 1991.

Rose, Willie Lee. *Rehearsal for Reconstruction: The Port Royal Experiment.* New York: Vintage, 1964.

Ross, Davis R. B. *Preparing for Ulysses: Politics and Veterans during World War II.* New York: Columbia University Press, 1969.

Rosswurm, Steve, ed. *The CIO's Left-Led Unions.* New Brunswick, NJ: Rutgers University Press, 1992.

Ruchames, Louis. *Race, Jobs and Politics: The Story of the FEPC.* New York: Columbia University Press, 1953.

Rudwick, Elliot. *Race Riot at East St. Louis, July 2 1917.* Carbondale: Southern Illinois University Press, 1964.

Sakolsky, Ron, and James Koehnline, eds. *Gone to Croatan: Origins of North American Dropout Culture.* Brooklyn: Autonomedia, 1993.

Sale, Kirkpatrick. *SDS.* New York: Vintage, 1974.

Salmon, Marylynn. *Women and the Law of Property in Early America.* Chapel Hill: University of North Carolina Press, 1986.

Saville, Julie. *The Work of Reconstruction: From Slave to Wage Laborer in South Carolina, 1860–1870.* Cambridge: Cambridge University Press, 1994.

Saxton, Alexander. *The Indispensable Enemy: Labor and the Anti-Chinese Movement in California.* Berkeley: University of California Press, 1971.

———. *The Rise and Fall of the White Republic: Class Politics and Mass Culture in Nineteenth-Century America.* London: Verso, 1996; 1990.

Sayre, Nora. *Previous Convictions: A Journey through the 1950s.* New Brunswick, NJ: Rutgers University Press, 1995.

Schlesinger, Arthur M., Jr. *The Age of Jackson.* Boston: Little, Brown, 1947.

Schwartz, Bernard. *Behind Bakke: Affirmative Action and the Supreme Court.* New York: New York University Press, 1988.

———., ed. *Statutory History of the United States: Civil Rights Part 1.* New York: Chelsea House, 1970.

———., ed. *Statutory History of the United States: Civil Rights Part 2.* New York: Chelsea House, 1970.

Sears, David O., and John B. McConahay. *The Politics of Violence: The New Urban Blacks and the Watts Riot.* Boston: Houghton Mifflin, 1973.

Sennett, Richard, and Jonathan Cobb. *The Hidden Injuries of Class.* New York: Vintage, 1973.

Shapiro, Herbert. *White Violence and Black Response: From Reconstruction to Montgomery.* Amherst: University of Massachusetts Press, 1988.

Shulman, Steven, and William Darity Jr. *The Question of Discrimination: Racial Inequality in the United States Labor Market.* Middletown, CT: Wesleyan University Press, 1989.

Sitkoff, Harvard. *A New Deal for Blacks: The Emergence of Civil Rights as a National Issue.* Vol. 1, *The Depression Decade.* New York: Oxford University Press, 1978.

———. *The Struggle for Black Equality 1954–1992.* Rev. ed. New York: Hill and Wang, 1993; 1981.

Skerry, Peter. *Mexican Americans: The Ambivalent Minority.* New York: Free Press, 1993.

Bibliography

Skrentny, John David. *The Ironies of Affirmative Action: Politics, Culture, and Justice in America*. Chicago: University of Chicago Press, 1996.

Smith, Abbot Emerson. *Colonists in Bondage: White Servitude and Convict Labor in America 1607–1776*. New York: W. W. Norton, 1971.

Smith, Edward Conrad, ed. *The Constitution of the United States With Case Summaries*. 11th ed. New York: Barnes and Noble, 1979; 1936.

Smith, Theophus H. *Conjuring Culture: Biblical Formations of Black America*. New York: Oxford University Press, 1994.

Smith, Warren B. *White Servitude in Colonial South Carolina*. Columbia: University of South Carolina Press, 1961.

Solomon, Mark. *The Cry Was Unity: Communists and African Americans, 1917–1936*. Jackson: University Press of Mississippi, 1998.

Spencer, Jon Michael. *The Rhythms of Black Folk: Race, Religion, and Pan-Africanism*. Trenton, NJ: Africa World Press, 1995.

Spero, Sterling D., and Abram L. Harris. *The Black Worker: The Negro and the Labor Movement*. New York: Atheneum, 1969; 1931.

Stampp, Kenneth M. *The Peculiar Institution: Slavery in the Ante-bellum South*. New York: Knopf, 1956.

Steinberg, Stephen. *Turning Back: The Retreat from Racial Justice in American Thought and Policy*. Boston: Beacon, 1995.

Sterling, Dorothy. *Ahead of Her Time: Abby Kelly and the Politics of Anti-Slavery*. New York: W. W. Norton, 1991.

Stouffer, Samuel A. *Communism, Conformity, and Civil Liberties: A Cross-Section of the Nation Speaks Its Mind*. New York: Doubleday, 1953.

Sullivan, Patricia. *Days of Hope: Race and Democracy in the New Deal Era*. Chapel Hill: University of North Carolina Press, 1996.

Sullivan, Leon H. *Build, Brother, Build*. Philadelphia: Macrae Smith, 1969.

Sumner, Charles. *Charles Sumner: His Complete Works*. Edited by George Frisbie Hoar. Vols. 14 and 15. Boston: Lee and Shepard, 1900; 1874.

Tatum, Georgia Lee. *Disloyalty in the Confederacy*. Chapel Hill: University of North Carolina Press, 1934.

Taylor, Benjamin J., and Fred Witney. *Labor Relations Law*. Englewood Cliffs, NJ: Prentice-Hall, 1971.

Terborg-Penn, Rosalyn. *African American Women in the Struggle for the Vote, 1850–1920*. Bloomington: University of Indiana Press, 1998.

Theoharis, Athan G., and John Stuart Cox. *The Boss: J. Edgar Hoover and the Great American Inquisition*. Philadelphia: Temple University Press, 1988.

Thieblot, Armand J., Jr. *Prevailing Wage Legislation: The Davis-Bacon Act, State "Little Davis-Bacon" Acts, the Walsh-Healey Act, and the Service Contract Act*. Philadelphia: University of Pennsylvania Press, 1986.

Thomas, John L., ed. *John C. Calhoun: A Profile*. New York: Hill and Wang, 1972.

Thompson, Robert Farris. *Flash of the Spirit: African and Afro-American Art and Philosophy*. New York: Vintage, 1984.

Tourgée, Albion W. *A Fool's Errand: By One of the Fools*. Cambridge, MA: Belknap, 1966; 1879.

Turner, Margery Austin, Michael Fix, and Raymond J. Struyk, eds. *Opportunities Denied, Opportunities Diminished: Racial Discrimination in Hiring*. Washington, D.C.: Urban Institute Press, 1991.

Bibliography

Tyson, Timothy B. *Radio Free Dixie: Robert F. Williams and the Roots of Black Power.* Chapel Hill: University of North Carolina Press, 1999.

Van Deburg, William L. *New Day in Babylon: The Black Power Movement and American Culture, 1965–1975.* Chicago: University of Chicago Press, 1992.

Wade, Wyn Craig. *The Fiery Cross: The Ku Klux Klan in America.* New York: Simon and Schuster, 1987.

Walker, David, and Henry Highland Garnet. *Walker's Appeal and Garnet's Address to the Slaves of the United States of America.* Nashville: James C. Winston, 1994; 1848.

Wang, Peter H. *Legislating Normalcy: The Immigration Act of 1924.* San Francisco: R and E Research, 1975.

Washington, Booker T. *Up from Slavery.* New York: Airmont, 1967; 1901.

Weaver, Robert C. *Negro Labor: A National Problem.* New York: Harcourt, 1946.

Weir, Margaret. *Politics and Jobs: The Boundaries of Employment Policy in the United States.* Princeton, NJ: Princeton University Press, 1992.

Weiss, Nancy J. *Farewell to the Party of Lincoln: Black Politics in the Age of FDR.* Princeton, NJ: Princeton University Press, 1983.

———. *The National Urban League, 1910–1940.* New York: Oxford University Press, 1974.

Weiss, Robert J. *"We Want Jobs": A History of Affirmative Action.* New York: Garland, 1997.

Wellman, David T. *Portraits of White Racism.* 2nd ed. Cambridge: Cambridge University Press, 1993; 1977.

Wells, Ida B. *Crusade for Justice: The Autobiography of Ida B. Wells.* Edited by Alfreda M. Duster. Chicago: University of Chicago Press, 1972.

West, Cornell. *Race Matters.* New York: Vintage, 1994.

Wexler, Sanford. *The Civil Rights Movement: An Eyewitness History.* New York: Facts on File, 1993.

Whalen, Charles W., Jr., and Barbara Whalen. *The Longest Debate: A Legislative History of the 1964 Civil Rights Act.* Cabin John, MD: Seven Locks Press, 1985.

Wildman, Stephanie M., ed. *Privilege Revealed: How Invisible Preference Undermines America.* New York: New York University Press, 1996.

Wilentz, Sean. *Chants Democratic: New York City and the Rise of the American Working Class, 1788–1850.* New York: Oxford University Press, 1984.

Wilhoit, Francis M. *The Politics of Massive Resistance.* New York: G. Baziller, 1973.

Wilkinson, J. Harvie, III. *From Brown to Bakke: The Supreme Court and School Integration: 1954–1978.* Oxford: Oxford University Press, 1979.

Williams, Eric. *Capitalism and Slavery.* New York: Russell and Russell, 1961; 1944.

Williamson, Chilton. *American Suffrage: From Property to Democracy 1760–1860.* Princeton, NJ: Princeton University Press, 1960.

Wood, Peter H. *Black Majority: Negroes in Colonial South Carolina from 1670 through the Stono Rebellion.* New York: W. W. Norton, 1975.

Woodward, C. Vann. *The Strange Career of Jim Crow.* 3rd rev. ed. New York: Oxford University Press, 1974; 1954.

Wright, Nathan, Jr. *Ready to Riot.* New York: Holt, 1968.

Zappa, Frank, with Peter Occhiogrosso. *The Real Frank Zappa Book.* New York: Poseidon, 1989.

Zieger, Robert H. *The CIO: 1935–1955.* Chapel Hill: University of North Carolina Press, 1995.

Zinn, Howard. *A People's History of the United States.* New York: Harper, 1990; 1980.

Zuczek, Richard. *State of Rebellion: Reconstruction in South Carolina.* Columbia: University of South Carolina Press, 1996.

GOVERNMENT DOCUMENTS, ARCHIVES, STATUTES, AND COURT CASES

Abstracts of the Statistics of Manufacturers According to the Returns of the Seventh Census. Vol. 13. New York: Norman Ross, 1990; 1850.

Agriculture of the United States in 1860: Compiled from the Original Returns of the Eighth Census. Vol. 17. New York: Norman Ross, 1990; 1864.

Alaska Native Claims Settlement Act. Statutes at Large 85 (1971).

Bertie County Slave Papers, 1744–1815. North Carolina Division of Archives and History. Raleigh.

Carter, Jimmy. *Public Papers of the Presidents of the United States.* Washington, D.C.: GPO, 1982.

Clark, Walter, ed. *The State Records of North Carolina.* Vol. 23. *Laws 1715–1776.* Goldsboro: Nash, 1904.

Congressional Record. 68th Cong., 1st sess., vol. 65.

Davis-Bacon Act. Statutes at Large 46 (1931).

Eisenhower, Dwight D. *Public Papers of the Presidents of the United States.* Washington, D.C.: GPO, 1958.

Equal Employment Opportunity Commission. *"Best" Equal Employment Opportunity Policies, Programs, and Practices in the Private Sector: Task Force Report.* Washington, D.C.: GPO, 1998.

Equal Employment Opportunity Commission documents at EEOC website, http://www.eeoc.gov. Internet.

Freedmen's Bureau Act of 1865. Statutes at Large 13 (1865).

Freedmen's Bureau Act of 1866. Statutes at Large 14 (1866).

Glass Ceiling Commission. *Good for Business: Making Full Use of the Nation's Human Capital. The Environmental Scan: A Fact-Finding Report of the Federal Glass Ceiling Commission.* Washington, D.C.: Department of Labor, 1995.

Government Organization and Employees. U.S. Code. Vol. 5. (1991).

Homestead Act of 1862. Statutes at Large 12 (1862).

Immigration Act of 1924. Statutes at Large 43 (1924).

Johnson, Lyndon B. *Public Papers of the Presidents of the United States.* Washington, D.C.: GPO, 1968.

Labor Management Relations Act. Statutes at Large 61 (1947).

Morrill Land Grant Act of 1862. Statutes at Large 12 (1862).

National Labor Relations Act of 1935. Statutes at Large 49 (1935).

National Labor Relations Board. *A Layman's Guide to Basic Law Under the National Labor Relations Act.* Washington, D.C.: GPO, 1971.

Northwest Ordinances of 1784, 1785, and 1787. Library of Congress. [Online documents.] Available at http://www.thomas.loc.gov. Internet.

Original Returns of the Eighth Census of the United States of America in 1860. New York: Norman Ross, 1990; 1864.

Population of the United States of America in 1860: Compiled from the Original Returns of the Eighth Census. Vol. 16. New York: Norman Ross, 1990; 1864.

Population Schedules of the Eighth Census of the United States. 1860 Slave Schedules. North Carolina. Microfilm, roll 925. Vol. 3, 265–74. Washington, D.C.: GSA, 1967.

Proceedings and Debates of the Convention of North Carolina Called to Amend the Constitution of the State, which Assembled at Raleigh June 4, 1835. Raleigh: Joseph Gales, 1836.

Reconstruction Acts of 1867. Statutes at Large 14 and 15 (1867).

Bibliography

Report of the National Advisory Commission on Civil Disorders. New York: Bantam, 1968.

Second Morrill Land Grant Act. Statutes at Large 26 (1890).

Servicemen's Readjustment Act of 1944. Statutes at Large 58 (1944).

Statistics of the United States in 1860: Compiled from the Original Returns of the Eighth Census. Vol. 19. New York: Norman Ross, 1990; 1866.

Title VII. Civil Rights Act of 1964. U.S. Code. Vol. 42, secs. 2000(e)–2000(e-17) (1999).

U.S. Bureau of the Census. Statistical Abstract of the United States: 1994. 114th ed. Washington, D.C.: GPO, 1994.

U.S. Bureau of the Census. Statistical Abstract of the United States: 1999. 119th ed. Washington, D.C.: GPO, 1999.

U.S. Commission on Civil Rights. Funding Federal Civil Rights Enforcement. Washington, D.C.: GPO, June 1995.

U.S. Congress. House. Committee on Post Office and Civil Service. Appointment and Promotion of Veterans of World War II. 81st Cong., 1st sess., 3 June 1946.

U.S. Congress. House. Representative Nathaniel G. Taylor of Tennessee speaking on the Bureau of Refugees, Freedmen, and Abandoned Lands bill, 39th Cong., 1st sess., Congressional Globe, Vol. 36, card 10, roll 4171, text-fiche.

U.S. Congress. House. Subcommittee on Civil Service of the Committee on Government Reform and Oversight. H.R. 240, Veterans' Employment Opportunities Act of 1997. 105th Cong., 1st sess., 26 February 1946.

U.S. Congress. Senate. Committee on Military Affairs. Superseniority Rights of Veterans: Hearing before a Subcommittee of the Committee on Military Affairs. 79th Cong., 2nd sess., 12 July 1946.

U.S. Congress. 61st Cong., 3rd sess., Reports of the Immigration Commission: A Dictionary of Races and Peoples. Washington, D.C.: GPO, 1911.

U.S. President's Committee on Civil Rights. To Secure These Rights: The Report of the President's Committee on Civil Rights. New York: Simon and Schuster, 1947.

U.S. Supreme Court decisions.

Adarand v. Peña, 115 U.S. 2097 (1995)

Brown v. Board of Education, 347 U.S. 483 (1954)

Brown v. Board of Education [II], 349 U.S. 294, (1955)

Civil Rights Cases, 109 U.S. 3 (1883)

DeFunis v. Odegaard, 416 U.S. 312 (1974)

Dred Scott v. Sandford, 60 U.S. 393 (1856)

Firefighters v. Stotts, 467 U.S. 561 (1984)

Fullilove v. Klutznick, 448 U.S. 448 (1980)

Griggs v. Duke Power, 401 U.S. 424 (1971)

Hodges v. U.S., 203 U.S. 1 (1906)

Hopwood v. Texas, (1996)

Hughes v. Superior Court of California, 339 U.S. 460 (1950)

Metro Broadcasting v. FCC, 497 U.S. 547 (1990)

Milliken v. Bradley, 433 U.S. 267 (1977)

Missouri v. Jenkins, 515 U.S. 70 (1995)

Mobile v. Bolden, 446 U.S. 55 (1980)

Morton v. Mancari, 417 U.S. 535 (1974)

New Negro Alliance v. Sanitary Grocery Co., 303 U.S. 552 (1938)

Oliphant v. Suquamish Tribe, 435 U.S. 191 (1978)

Piscataway Board of Education v. Taxman, 522 U.S. 1010 (1997)

Plessy v. Ferguson, 163 U.S. 527 (1896)

Raley v. State of Ohio, 360 U.S. 423 (1959)

Rice v. Cayetano, 98 U.S. 818 (2000)

Richmond v. J. A. Croson Co., 488 U.S. 469 (1989)

Rosebud Sioux Tribe v. Kneip, 430 U.S. 584 (1977)

Shaw v. Hunt, 517 U.S. 899 (1996)

Shaw v. Reno, 113 U.S. 2816 (1993)

Shelley v. Kraemer, 334 U.S. 1 (1948)

Slaughterhouse Cases, 83 U.S. 36 (1873)

Swann v. Mecklenburg, 402 U.S. 1 (1971)

U.S. v. Fordice, 505 U.S. 717 (1992)

U.S. v. Reese, 92 U.S. 214 (1875)

U.S. v. Cruikshank, 92 U.S. 542 (1875)

United Steelworkers v. Weber, 443 U.S. 193 (1979)

University of California Regents v. Bakke, 438 U.S. 265 (1978)

Wygant v. Jackson, 467 U.S. 267 (1986)

Veterans' Benefits Acts. *U.S. Code*. Vol. 38, secs. 3001–7100 (1958).

Veterans' Preference Act of 1944. *Statutes at Large* 58 (1944).

Veterans' Preference Acts. *U.S. Code*. vol. 5, secs. 3301–63, 3501–4 (1999)

Williams, Stephen K., ed. *Cases Argued and Decided in the Supreme Court of the United States*. Book 15, Lawyers' ed. Rochester: Lawyers Cooperative Publishing, 1926; 1884.

INTERNET WEBSITES

AFSCME Corrections United (ACU), at website of American Federation of State, County, and Municipal Employees (AFSCME). Available at http://www.afscme.org.

Alabama State Archives. Available at http://www.archives.state.al.us.

American Federation of Labor–Congress of Industrial Organizations (AFL-CIO). Available at http://www.aflcio.org.

Americans United for Affirmative Action (AUAA). Available at http://www.auaa.org.

Black Radical Congress (BRC). Available at http://www.blackradicalcongress.org.

National Coalition of Blacks for Reparations in America (N'COBRA). Available at http://www.ncobra.org.

National Organization for Women (NOW). Available at http://www.now.org.

U.S. Department of Labor. Available at http://www.dol.gov.

U.S. Immigration and Naturalization Service. Available at http://www.ins.doj.gov.

INTERVIEWS, CONVERSATIONS, LETTERS, AND ORAL HISTORIES

McSurely, Alan, attorney for University of North Carolina–Chapel Hill Housekeepers Association. Telephone interview by author, 11 November 1996.

Moore, Jacqueline, National Alliance of Postal and Federal Employees monthly magazine editor, Washington, D.C. Telephone conversation with author, 21 April 1997.

Morgan, Anna Hass. Telephone conversation with author, 11 September 1994.

Rubio, Alfred M. Interview by author, 19 October 1996.

Rubio, Carlos M. Electronic communication to author, 8 April 1999.

Rubio, Mary Kranos. Telephone conversation with author, 7 March 1999.

Smith, Marian L. Senior historian, United States Immigration and Naturalization Service, Washington, D.C. Telephone conversation with author, 6 December 1999; and electronic communication to author, 14 December 1999.

LECTURES, SPEECHES, AND CONFERENCES

Crenshaw, Kimberlé. Keynote speaker on Critical Race Theory. "Black Women's Book Fair." Duke University, Durham, NC, 25 March 1999.

Donahue, Tom. "The Black-Labor Alliance: Strengthening the Partnership for Economic Justice." A. Philip Randolph Institute Conference. Chicago, 30 June 1995. [Online document.] Available at http://www.aflcio.org/newsonline/publ/speech95/sp06302.htm. Internet.

Hill, Herbert. "Race, Affirmative Action and the Constitution." Rosenberg/Humphrey Lecture. City College of New York, 27 April 1988.

"Plessy vs. Ferguson-100 Years Later: A North Carolina Perspective." Conference at North Carolina Central University, 25 October 1996.

"Race, Law and Justice: The Rehnquist Court and the American Dilemma." Conference at American University (AU), Washington, D.C., 21 September 1995; *American University Law Review* 45, no. 3 (February 1996). [Online journal.] Available at http://www.wcl.american.edu/pub/journals/law rev/45-3.htm. Internet.

MANUSCRIPTS

Morgan, Anna Hass. Unpublished autobiography, 1990. In author's possession.

MICROFILM

All at Perkins Library, Duke University, except North Carolina newspapers at Wilson Library, University of North Carolina–Chapel Hill

Eighteenth-Century North Carolina Newspapers. Raleigh: North Carolina Department of Archives and History, 1961.

Inner City Voice. Detroit: n.p., 1968–69.

Meier, August, and John Bracey Jr., eds. *Papers of the NAACP, Part 1 Supplement, 1951–1955.* Reel 8. Frederick, MD: University Publications of America, 1987.

————., eds., *Papers of the NAACP, Part 9, Discrimination in the United States Armed Forces, 1918–1955, Series C, Veterans Affairs Committee, 1940–1970.* Reels 6, 7, 8, 12. Bethesda, MD: University Publications of America, 1989.

————., eds., *Papers of the NAACP 1940–1955. Part 21. NAACP Relations with the Modern Civil Rights Movement.* Reel 20. Bethesda, MD: University Publications of America, 1994.

————., eds. *Records of the SCLC.* 1954–1970. Baltimore: University Publications of America, 1995.

Messenger. 1917–1921. Vols. 1–10. New York: Negro Universities Press, 1969.

Mr. Muhammad Speaks. New York: n.p., 1960.

Muhammad Speaks. Chicago: Muhammad's Mosque No. 2, 1961–1975.

Pittsburgh Courier. Pittsburgh: Pittsburgh Courier Publishing, 1910–1950.

MUSEUM EXHIBITS

"Wade in the Water." American History Museum, Smithsonian Institution, Washington, D.C., October 1997. Bernice Johnson Reagon, curator.

REFERENCE BOOKS

The Concise Columbia Encyclopedia. 2nd ed. New York: Columbia University Press, 1989.

Current, Richard Nelson, ed. *Encyclopedia of the Confederacy.* New York: Simon and Schuster, 1993.

Neely, Mark E., Jr., ed. *The Abraham Lincoln Encyclopedia.* New York: McGraw-Hill, 1982.

Wilson, Charles Reagan, and William Ferris, eds. *Encyclopedia of Southern Culture.* Chapel Hill: University of North Carolina Press, 1988.

TELEVISION AND RADIO PROGRAMS, FILMS, AND SOUND RECORDINGS

At the River I Stand. Produced and directed by David Applebee, Allison Graham, and Steven John Ross. 1 hour. Memphis State University, Memphis, 1993.

Beastie Boys. *Licensed to Ill.* Def Jam, 1986. Compact Disc.

The Black Press in America. Produced and directed by Stanley Nelson. 1 hour. Half Nelson, San Francisco, 1998.

Eyes on the Prize. Produced and directed by Henry Hampton. 6 hours. Blackside, Alexandria, VA, 1986.

Hollywood Shuffle. Produced and directed by Robert Townsend. 82 min. Samuel Goldwyn, Los Angeles, 1987.

It's a Wonderful Life. Produced and directed by Frank Capra. 229 min. RKO Radio, Los Angeles, 1946.

"Lead Story" newscast. Black Entertainment Television, 17 November 1996.

Miracle on 34th Street. Produced by William Perlberg. Directed by George Seaton. 97 min. Twentieth Century–Fox, Los Angeles, 1947.

Seeger, Pete. *Pete Seeger's Greatest Hits.* Columbia, ca. 1970. LP.

Wade in the Water. Bernice Johnson Reagon, creator. African American gospel music history. National Public Radio, 1996.

THESES AND DISSERTATIONS

Burgess, Allen Edward. "Tar Heel Blacks and the New South Dream: The Coleman Manufacturing Company, 1896–1904." Ph.D. diss., Duke University, 1977.

Bibliography

Dunlap, Jody. "A Study of the Conflict between Seniority Rights and the Anti-Discrimination Goals of Title VII and Affirmative Action." Ph.D. diss., Pepperdine University, 1986.

Hinshaw, John. "Dialectic of Division: Race and Power among Western Pennsylvania Steelworkers, 1937–1975." Ph.D. diss., Carnegie-Mellon University, 1994.

Tomlins, Christopher Lawrence. *The State and the Unions: Federal Labor Relations Policy and the Organized Labor Movement in America, 1935–1955.* Ann Arbor, MI: University Microfilms, 1984.

Tucker, Ronnie Bernard. "Affirmative Action, the Supreme Court, and Political Power in the Old Confederacy: An Impact Assessment, 1964–1995." Ph.D. diss., Mississippi State University, 1998.

Weiss, Robert John. " 'We Want Jobs': The History of Affirmative Action." Ph.D. diss., New York University, 1985.

INDEX

317